THE GIFT OF WINE

Gloria Bley Miller

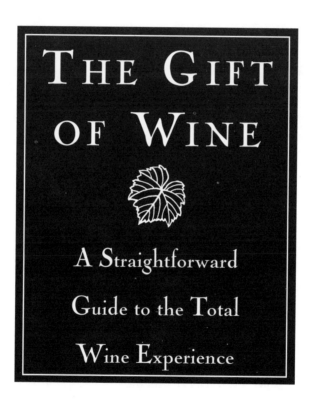

THE GIFT OF WINE

A Straightforward

Guide to the Total

Wine Experience

L&B

Lyons & Burford, Publishers

Printed in the United States of America

Illustrations by Hugh Harrison

Design by Kathy Kikkert

Typesetting and composition by CompuDesign

10 9 8 7 6 5 4 3 2 1

Library of Congress Cataloging-in-Publication Data

Miller, Gloria Bley
    The gift of wine: a straightforward guide to the total wine experience/Gloria Bley Miller.
        p.   cm.
    Includes index.
    ISBN   1-55821-444-5 (cloth)
    1. Wine and wine making.   I. Title.
TP548.M627   1996   *96-965*
641.2' 2–dc20   *CIP*

CONTENTS

For my father, who once made wine

About the Author

Gloria Bley Miller is a professional writer with a varied background in education and the fine arts. A native New Yorker, she attended schools in New Mexico, Philadelphia and New York and holds degrees from both Hunter College and the Bank Street College of Education.

Her previous book, *The Thousand Recipe Chinese Cookbook,* won the Tastemaker Award in the United States and a distinguished award from the German Gastronomic Society. (It was published in England and Holland as well as in Germany.) Praised for its clarity and lucidity, the volume was included in Craig Claiborne's Recommended Cookbook Library and selected by Williams-Sonoma as one of their 22 Classic Cookbooks. After selling nearly a quarter million copies in hardcover, it has gone through more than a dozen printings in paperback.

Ms. Miller lives in Greenwich Village with her husband, sculptor Richard McDermott Miller whose studio is in the SoHo district of lower Manhattan. She is a member of the Author's Guild.

FOREWORD

Nature has generously provided us with grapes, soil and climate, and the amazing process that transforms those grapes into wine. This is nature's gift. Man selects the grapes, encourages them to grow, then monitors their transformation into wine, completing the process.

For thousands of years, wine has been part of the human experience, a hallmark of civilization along with art, architecture, agriculture, and medicine. It has served as a focal point in religious services and in such social celebrations as birthdays, weddings and anniversaries. Wine has become a metaphor for the good life, a token of fellowship, an expression of romance. As the Old Testament sagely noted, "Wine maketh glad the heart of man."

Largely determining the character of a wine is the experience of its grapes. Following them on their journey from vineyard to bottle, we can chart their metamorphosis. In the pages ahead, we will make that journey. En route, we'll explore the essentials of wine making and define the basic types. We will look into the significance of vineyards, vintages, and vintners. Going behind the scenes, we'll visit the world's major wine regions—and the minor ones as well. Along the way, we'll decipher wine's seemingly unfathomable labels, consider the significance of estate-bottling, and clarify the all-important concept of appellations of origin.

Provided along with the basics on buying, storing and aging will be information on proper serving temperatures, on decanting and on when a wine should breathe or when it should not. Covered too will be the tasting of wines, how to hold a tasting, how to match wines with food, getting the most out of a restaurant wine list—and a great deal more.

In the following pages, just about every conceivable question related to wine will be considered. Yet through it all the mystery remains of the grape's miraculous transformation, the conversion of its rich, sweet juice into exhilarating wine. Perhaps that mystery is the greatest gift of all.

Gloria Bley Miller

WINE MAKING: NATURE'S ROLE

THE GRAPE

Wine making begins in the vineyard. It has been estimated that some 25 ½ million acres of the world's surface is occupied by vineyards. These differ considerably in the contours of their terrain and in their exposure to sunshine and rain, to heat and cold. Each vineyard affects the development of the grapes it grows and consequently of the wine it produces.

Wine making can be said to start in the spring when the sap rises in the vines, causing the buds to bulge and burst. This is the bud break. Downy shoots suddenly push out; tendrils and leaves appear. The foliage, trapping the sun's radiant energy by photosynthesis, draws carbon dioxide from the air, producing carbohydrates. These will fuel the vine's growth and nourish its developing berries.

In early summer when temperatures reach 65°F or so, the vine begins to flower. Delicate green blossoms appear, looking like miniature grape clusters. (Bordeaux vintners celebrate this blossoming near the end of June with a Fête des Fleurs, a "Feast of Flowers.") Some ten days after pollination, the delicate blossoms wither, revealing in the center of each a hard green berry. This is the grape set. By late summer, the clusters hang plump and heavy on the vine. Lovely colors develop: crimsons, purples and golds.

The once-opaque grape skins turn translucent and luminous.

More complicated than most fruits, the grape possesses some three hundred components including several sugars, a number of major acids and a quantity of minerals. Early in the grape's development, the acids predominate. Then, as the sun accelerates the production of the sugars—glucose and fructose—the grape fills with rich, sweet juice. The sugars, converted to alcohol by fermentation, will strengthen and stabilize the wine. (The alcohol will limit the survival of destructive organisms, such as mold. About 8 percent alcohol is needed to protect the wine, but most wines average 10 to 12 percent.) The acids—tannic, tartaric, lactic, malic and citric—endow the wine with a lively, attractive tartness. More significantly, they provide the structure that preserves the wine and lengthens its life in the bottle.

Before the fledgling vine can bear harvestable fruit, it must build a sturdy stalk to support the weight of its clusters, as well as a network of roots to extract nourishment from the soil. At least three years are required to produce suitable grapes for wine, and five or six before a vine can be fully productive. A premium plant

needs a decade or more to produce first-rate grapes. The older the plant, the more its roots proliferate, making for sweeter grapes and more intense wines. The older vines produce low yields, but grapes of a greater concentration. (Most vineyards replace their vines every twenty years or so. Rarely does the life span of a vine exceed thirty years.)

The grape grows only in temperate climates. It cannot survive tropical heat or arctic cold. It needs sunny days, long, cool nights, and enough—but not too much—rainfall. As one vintner said, "A long warm fall gives us plenty of time to ripen our crop and still harden our vines for winter dormancy." Yet the growing weather must not be too compatible. Bountiful vintages may produce good wines but never great ones: Abundant quantity and high grape quality rarely coincide.

Grapes can be grown successfully in the Northern Hemisphere between the 30th and 50th parallels, and in the Southern Hemisphere between the 20th and 40th. In the Northern Hemisphere, an imaginary line separates the growing regions into a cooler upper and a warmer lower zone. Characterizing the upper zone are four separate and distinct seasons: summers that are warm but not too hot, winters that are quite cold, and springs and autumns in which occasional frost occurs. Rain falls throughout the year. During the growing season the gradually accumulating heat slowly ripens the grapes, giving them time to concentrate their sugars and to develop their subtleties. The world's most distinguished grapes are cultivated in a band running along the 45th parallel that includes sections of France, Italy, Germany, Hungary and the United States. Grapes grown here yield complex, lively wines that are quite long- lived at their finest .

By contrast, in the Northern Hemisphere's warmer zone, essentially two seasons prevail. Hot, dry summers here blend almost imperceptibly into mild, moist winters. The grapes, ripening rapidly under the constant sun, grow fat and abundant. Their wines are robust and potent, but they lack for the most part finesse and longevity.

Wine making's predominant grape is the *Vitis vinifera,* also known as the European or Old World grape. Generally delicate with a thin, easily bruised skin adhering firmly to a fleshy pulp, the vinifera is susceptible to parasites, disease, and biting cold. Its best-known red varieties are the cabernet sauvignon and pinot noir. Its best-known whites are the chardonnay, riesling and sauvignon blanc. Vinifera wines at their finest are subtle and complex.

Hardier and more disease resistant is the *Vitis labrusca,* the New World grape. Indigenous to North America and generally grown east of the Rockies, it is sometimes called the slipskin because of the way its tough, occasionally inedible outer covering detaches easily from a slippery pulp. Labrusca wines are characterized by a grapy pungency which has been described as wild or "foxy." The red varieties include the concord, catawba and delaware. The whites include the niagara and diamond.

Some of the hybrids are vinifera mixtures, whereas others combine the style and subtlety of the vinifera with the sturdiness and disease-resistance of the labrusca. (The latter are generally grown in cooler regions where the more delicate viniferas might perish.) A number of hybrids are named for the geneticists who developed them. Red varieties include the ruby cabernet, chelois, baco noir, chancellor, maréchal foch, de chaunac and léon millot. White varieties include the müller-thurgau, seyval blanc and vidal blanc.

NOTE: Some grapes are meant exclusively for wine making. Details about them appear under "Grape Varieties." Other grapes are good for eating. Those serving both functions generally do not produce high-caliber wines.

THREATS TO THE VINE

In its transition from flower to fruit, the grape faces many obstacles. Excessive rain may prevent its pollination. High winds may strip away the blossoms, or intense heat can wither them. Inclement weather may stunt the berries. Drought can threaten them. In the spring and early summer, when the tender vine is particularly vulnerable, good weather is crucial. Rain suddenly becoming hail can batter the vines, breaking off their shoots and destroying their buds; later in the season, the hail can be ruinous, bruising the growing berries. A harsh spring frost can wreak havoc, wiping out an entire vineyard overnight. As one grower—noting the general anxiety—observed, "This is not a business for the faint-hearted."

Even in ideal weather no vineyard is trouble-free. Insects defoliate the vines; predatory molds and mildews attack them. Deer and rabbits nibble at the tender shoots. Birds peck at the juicy berries.

The most devastating threat of all has been a barely visible, aphidlike insect, *Phylloxera vastatrix*. Piercing the roots of the vine with its sharp proboscis, phylloxera feeds voraciously on the sap, preventing nutrients from reaching the grapes. First the clusters diminish, then the berries can no longer ripen. Finally, the aphid secretes a poison into the wound, killing the exhausted plant.

Phylloxera was introduced to Europe from the New World. It turned up in a London botanical garden in the 1860s. British viticulturalists seeking ways to curb oïdium, a common destructive fungus, had sent to America for hardier cuttings. (Grapes are generally cultivated from cuttings; the seeds do not pass the desired traits along as consistently.) Prolifically producing a dozen generations in a single year, the aphid spread like wildfire. No one knows exactly when it crossed over into France, but soon phylloxera was invading the finest vineyards in Burgundy and Bordeaux, attacking the soft, fat vinifera roots.

The desperate growers tried to fend off the onslaught but nothing seemed to work. The aphids, operating underground, clung tenaciously to the deepest roots. Spraying and burning had little

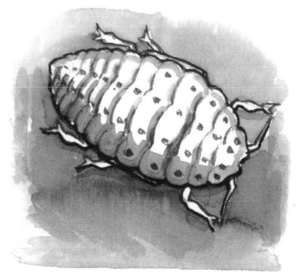

The Phylloxera vastatrix

effect, and flooding damaged the soil without drowning them all. Uprooting the plants proved futile; once the parasites were in the ground, they could not be eradicated.

As the wine makers stood helplessly by, their losses mounted to the billions. Seeking still-uncontaminated regions, some migrated from Bordeaux across the Pyrenees to Spain. Others retreated from the Rhône Valley to North Africa. The devastation continued, wiping out one wine region after another. The 1870s saw the invasion of Italy, Spain, Germany, Austria, Portugal, Greece, and Romania. By 1890, virtually every European wine-producing region had been destroyed.

The relentless aphid crossed oceans as well, invading Madeira, the Canary Islands, and Australia. Nor was California spared. In 1874, a Sonoma vineyard was found dying. In the Napa Valley, all but a few hundred acres were ruined. Sandy soil saved some parcels in Portugal and Austria where the aphid could not burrow deep enough to reach the roots. Spared too were random sites in Champagne, Australia, Spain and Cyprus.

Within three decades, phylloxera had virtually brought all of the world's wine making to a halt. Yet just when the vine seemed doomed, French botanists found a way to save it. They noted that the more fibrous roots of the tougher American vines healed quickly when pierced. Theorizing that coexistence might be possible between the parasites' and a host with greater resistance, the scientists grafted their vulnerable European vines onto the hardier wild American species, joining the vinifera scions to the sturdier and more resistant imported rootstocks. The scion, or budwood responsible for the leaf-bearing and fruit-bearing structures, determined the variety of the grape; the hardier, more resistant American rootstocks determined the character of the vine.

Arduous trial and error was required to create productive phylloxera-resistant vines and to find matches compatible with various soil and weather conditions in the affected vineyards. (France alone imported hundreds of thousands of rootstocks.) Slowly, painstakingly and at great cost, the gigantic task of replanting was accomplished. Then there was the three- to five-year period of waiting for the grafted plants to bear suitable grapes for wine. Eventually most of the world's vineyards—the great along with the commonplace—were returned to productivity.

NOTE: Some experts contended that the grafting process had diminished the wines, while others believed they were better than ever. The rarity of prephylloxera wines precludes any useful comparisons now.

Although most vintners believed the aphid was under control, all but a few continued to graft their vines. Then, in the mid-1980s, a more aggressive mutant turned up in the Napa Valley. Succumbing to the aphid were the nonresistant rootstocks that had been planted inadvertently. As yet no chemical or biological weapon has been found to dispel the intruder. The only effective method of eradication is to uproot the infested vines, replant them with more resistant ones, and then wait patiently for the replacements to mature.

A German wine maker inevitably confronted with insects, thunderstorms, hail, drought, early frost and harvest-time rains was asked why he tried to beat the odds. "It's an interesting life and I wouldn't trade it for anything in the world," he said. "There's hardly a profession left where an individual can produce a product by his own efforts."

THE SITE

The grape can adjust to a variety of terrains, but sloping land is best. Air circulation on the slopes is good, and brisk winds dry the grapes quickly after a rain, discouraging mold and mildew. The soil also drains well, keeping the roots from becoming waterlogged. (The vine does not like wet feet.) Most beneficial are midslope sites where warm air flows up. At the top, the vines are too exposed to the elements; at the bottom, cold air settles and pools form after a rain, waterlogging the roots.

South-facing slopes provide the best exposure. Burgundy's legendary Côte d'Or vineyards all face south. In Italy, the word *sori* preceding a vineyard name (as in Sori San Lorenzo) indicates a beneficial southern exposure. Slopes facing east are second best; they receive the morning sun. Least desirable are those facing north. With their limited sunshine, they retard the grape's blossoming and ripening.

The choicest locations were discovered by trial and error with a bit of common sense thrown in. In the ninth century, Charlemagne observed that snow melted first on a south-facing site in the Rheingau and ordered a vineyard planted there. That site, Schloss Johannisberg, remains active and productive to this day. In Germany's cool Mosel Valley, where the river executes a series of serpentine twists and turns, the siting of the vineyards shifts from bank to bank to capture as much warmth of the northern sun as possible.

Large bodies of water nearby are also beneficial. (The ancients said a vine should look at a river.) Water reflects the sun's rays onto the berries during the day, then retains the warmth at night, enhancing their ripening. Rivers, lakes and oceans extend the growing season by moderating land temperatures, dissipating the excessive heat in summer and mitigating the biting cold in winter. As one Long Island vintner noted, "The surrounding ocean waters moderate the winter temperatures, giving us a very late bud break in the spring so we don't have to worry about frost." Some of the best sites are also shielded by woodlands and mountains, which inhibit excessive rainfall and keep cold air away from the vines.

Scientific research has largely replaced trial and error in site selection. Viticulturalists now seek out microclimates—pockets of land, ranging from less than a hundred acres to about three square miles. (These are created by a combination of elevation, exposure, fog intrusion, humidity and so forth.) Cooling a too-warm California site, for instance, is a steady stream of air that flows in from San Francisco Bay through a gap in the mountains.

In recent years, urbanization and population growth have encroached on vineyard sties. Homes and grapes, it seems, prefer the same kind of land: both are partial to rivers that meander through an undulating terrain.

THE SOIL

The grape finds its nourishment in a wide variety of soils: shallow and deep, coarse and fine, fecund and barren. It might be assumed that the most desirable soils are well endowed and fertile. Yet in the majority of vineyards, they are so poor that they're practically unfit for other cultivated crops. The richer the soil, the poorer its wine. When nutritive substances lie close to the surface, the vines are not challenged; for their best growth, they require light, sandy, gravelly, stony or chalky soils in which most other crops would wither and die. Such unfriendly soils force the vines to send their roots down to greater mineral depths. The more profoundly the roots penetrate, the finer and more subtle the resulting wines.

Vineyard soils themselves are rarely homogeneous, consisting of various permutations of clay, sand, limestone, slate, gravel, and so on. In one Burgundy vineyard alone, there are six distinct types. It has often been noted that "soil speaks"—that one parcel may yield up a great wine while only a few feet away commonplace wines are produced.

In the Médoc region of France, a deep layer of rocks and pebbles—brought down by the Gironde River over the centuries—covers the mineral-rich earth. The soil, warming quickly and draining

well even in the wettest years, produces some of the world's most splendid wines. In Graves—whose name translates as "Gravel Bank"—a clay-and-limestone soil topped by sand and pebbles produces harmoniously balanced wines of great finesse. In the Southern Rhône, smooth-weathered stones carried down by the river absorb the sun's full impact during the day then slowly release the heat back at night, giving the wine a rich, almost roasted flavor. In the Mosel Valley, vintners set slabs of slate beneath their vines to capture as much beneficial warmth as possible from the thin northern sun. The slate, gradually disintegrating, also adds nutrients to the soil.

Volcanic soils give their wines a subtle aroma, an intriguing undertone and a slightly burned—but attractive—taste. They impart a gentle, bitter freshness to Orvieto wines and to those grown near Mount Etna. In Hungary, people once believed that gold originating deep in the earth was responsible for the excellence of Tokay wines. Investigating geologists found only volcanic rock.

Perhaps the most complex and extraordinary volcanic soil of all is found on the island of Madeira. The island was uninhabited and thickly wooded when the Portuguese discovered it in the fifteenth century. To clear the land for farming, they set its forests ablaze. Smoldering sporadically for years, the woods added potash to the accumulated centuries of leaf mold. The wines of Madeira are characterized by a refreshing acidity, a pungent nutlike taste and the potential for great longevity.

A chalky soil in southern Spain enables the sherry grapes to survive both torrid heat and virtually rainless summers. Hardening to a glasslike crust, the chalk beats back the fierce rays of the sun while sealing in the reserves of moisture below. The chalk also requires the vines to probe more deeply for their nourishment. And the soil's natural acidity offsets the grapes' high sugar levels. Sherry makers had observed that when their grapes were transported to the winery in open carts, roadside dust blown onto them added a stimulating tang to their wines. (The gypsum in the dust increased the wines' tartaric acid.) Andalusian wine makers initially duplicated this effect by sprinkling the dust directly on their grapes; eventually, they added the tartaric acid itself to their wines.

Chalky soil in the Champagne region of France gives its wine a crisp, dry flintiness, a delicate bouquet, and a tendency to sparkle. (Champagne's vast chalk deposit was formed when the primordial sea covered the land and the detritus of shellfish and other marine life gradually sank to the bottom.) This same deposit extends to the Chablis region, where a covering layer of loam adds a fine earthiness to the wine's characteristic austerity.

Clay soils are undesirably dense in themselves, but in combination with sand, are more permeable and quicker warming. Sand alone is low in nutrients and too porous to retain much water. Vines planted in sandy soil must be set down deep to reach a more sustaining subsoil. In Portugal's Colares region, for instance, the vines are planted in vertical trenches dug thirty feet down. As they grow toward ground level, the trenches are gradually filled in.

2

WINE MAKING: MAN'S ROLE

THE VINEYARD

"Wine," according to one well-known wine maker, "begins in the vineyard and always, always we must come back to the vineyard." Vineyards themselves range from tiny plots consisting of a few solitary vines to vast expanses stretching farther than the eye can see. Vines were once intermingled with trees, vegetables and grain. (The Italians call this *coltura promiscua,* indiscriminate cultivation.) Now the vines are planted more systematically, set out in neat, orderly rows separated by wide "avenues" that allow tractors and harvesters to pass through.

As the vine develops, buds form on the branches, becoming spurs (which are called canes when they mature). In the spring, when the average daily temperatures reach about 50°F, the vine begins to grow and to put out the shoots that will bear the current crop. (Unlike most plants, the vine bears its fruiting units on a single year's growth.) For its proper development, the vine must be trellised and pruned. According to legend, a donkey was the first pruner. While its master was occupied elsewhere, the untethered beast nibbled away greedily at the young shoots. The following year, the stripped-down plants yielded their best fruit and produced their most memorable wine.

Pruning cuts back the plant to guide its growth and control its yield. Young vines are suckered in spring—their nonessential shoots rubbed off by hand. Mature vines are not cut back until winter, when they are dormant. (Their sap has stopped flowing and their pruning cuts won't bleed.) This is when the canes that bore the previous year's growth are eliminated, since they won't produce fruit again.

Wielding a knife or a pair of shears, the pruner diligently clears away all counterproductive growth, removing the extraneous shoots and long trailing branches, keeping only enough fruiting

Pruning

wood to ensure a proper crop level. Should he retain too many buds, the shoots would be feeble and their canes unable to support the weight of the clusters. Should the plant blossom too freely, it would set its fruit poorly, producing low-sugar grapes that yield thinner, weaker wines. While lesser plants are usually pruned to be as productive as possible, superior vines are generally pruned to decrease their yield. Reducing the clusters produces a smaller crop with a greater intensity of fruit. Keeping the yield down concentrates the vine's vigor on fewer berries and heightens the quality of the resulting wine.

Trellising supports the vine and its clusters and distributes the bearing wood evenly to expose the berries more fully to sunlight and air. Grapevines in the wild attach themselves to neighboring trees. In Italy, some can still be seen clinging to poplars, pear trees and weeping willows. A trellis typically consists of two or more horizontal wires strung between wood or concrete posts, but trellis styles vary with climate and custom. In Spain's Galicia region, with its wet soil and elusive sunshine, the vines are trained on high wires for maximum exposure to warmth and air.

THE HARVEST

Wine making's most critical and hectic time is the harvest. The French call it *vendange,* the Italians *vendemmia,* the Germans *weinlese,* the Americans *the crush.* Determining its starting date are the grape variety, site, soil and previous six months of weather. In some places, an official decree or communal vote sets the date. In others, the individual growers decide for themselves.

Anticipation is always high as the time to gather the grapes approaches. In the weeks before the harvest, dry, sunny weather is essential. The French say, "August makes the grape and September the wine." An unexpected downpour can bloat the grapes and dilute their sugars, turning a triumphant crop into a disaster. Too much heat can lead to a grape surplus or a wine lake, or it can produce grapes overwhelmed by their sugars and yielding dull, flabby wines.

Knowing when to pick calls for a mixture of instinct, temperament, science and luck. One grower who brought in his crop before a heavy rain said, "I felt in my bones we had better pick. Others were not so fortunate." To determine the ripeness of their grapes, growers would crush a few between their fingers and could tell by the stickiness of the juice—which they call the *must* —when the berries were ready. Now they monitor the shifting ratio of grape sugars and acids with refractometers and hydrometers. The refractometer, a hand-held prism, indicates the density of the grape's sugar by the amount of light it bends or refracts. Needing only a few drops of juice for a reading, it can be used

Harvest

directly in the vineyard. The calibrated and more precise hydrometer floats correspondingly higher in the must as the density of the grape sugar increases.

A harvest may last days, weeks or months, depending on the size of the vineyard and on the number of pickers available. As the clusters begin to form in early summer, the grower takes a bunch count and, by applying a certain formula, can estimate the potential tonnage with surprising accuracy. To recruit pickers, he draws on family, friends and neighbors, or hires migrants or other itinerants. In the Champagne region, families plan their annual vacations to coincide with the grape harvest. In Burgundy, foreign workers pour in for the picking each year. In Portugal, musicians playing pipes and drums are sent into the hinterlands to attract pickers. In Andalusia, gypsies help to bring in the sherry crop.

The pickers do not pull the individual berries from their stems, but clip or snip the clusters with knives and shears. Often used is a hooked knife called a serpette, which goes back to ancient times; its curved blade acts as an extension of the hand. Catching the clusters from below, the pickers gently drop them into boxes or buckets. At intervals men, carrying back-baskets with a 100-pound capacity, collect the grapes. Or the pickers deposit them in gondolas, large containers set at the end of the rows.

NOTE: For premium Champagnes, specially trained workers spread the grape clusters on trays; then, in a careful, selective process known as *épluchage,* they discard the underripe, overripe and blemished berries.

Ideally, the grapes are gathered under a blazing sun. Moving systematically up and down the rows, the pickers crouch over the vines or crawl underneath to get at the berries. The work is particularly backbreaking if the vines are trellised high or low, or if the terrain slopes precipitously. Other occupational hazards are sore knees and scratched fingers. During a heat wave, the pickers must scramble to collect the fruit before it spoils. A sudden rainstorm can drench them to the skin, and plummeting temperatures can freeze their hands and feet.

On average, an individual picker can harvest about half a ton of grapes a day. Harvesting machines, widely used in large-scale wine making, can collect anywhere from twelve to twenty-four tons an hour. Lumbering high off the ground, they shake the clusters loose with rods and paddles, catch the grapes on a conveyor belt and deposit them in the gondolas. A vineyard that needs ten days of hand labor can be picked clean in a matter of hours.

Grapes are generally gathered at optimum ripeness, when their sugars are at the maximum and their acids are at the minimum. Some growers prefer to pick the fruit prematurely, however, whereas others delay the harvest. In warmer climates, earlier picking ensures a better acid balance in the grapes, making for tarter, lighter and more lively wines. The Portuguese pick their berries prematurely for vinho verdes, the French for Muscadets and the Californians for some Chardonnays.

Growers who prefer their grapes riper than usual cut away some clusters to expose the others more fully to the sun. This accounts for the richness, sweetness and generosity of Amarone wines in Italy. (These wines are also called Reciotos, from *recie*—ears—in the Veronese dialect, because the remaining clusters stand out on the vine like ears.)

Growers in the cooler, more volatile growing regions often seek an extra measure of sun by leaving their berries on the vine long after the normal harvest. To increase the sugars in the grapes and to concentrate their sweetness. White grapes lend themselves best to such late harvesting, particularly the rieslings, chenin blancs, gewürztraminers and chardonnays. In good years in Alsace, the berries—left on the vine to shrivel—become almost pure sugar, although their natural acids remain to balance them out. Reaching their ultimate ripeness, the grapes yield sweet, intensely flavored wines with highly distinctive personalities. A late-harvest wine in Alsace is called a *vendange tardive.*

A rare few late-harvested grapes are subject to a unique fungus that transforms them remarkably. The French call this fungus *pourriture noble,* the Germans *edelfäule.* In English, it is known as noble rot or noble mold. Its scientific name is *Botrytis cinerea.* Thriving in semisheltered environments near large bodies of water, the botrytis appears in late autumn, encouraged by mist and fog. (It needs alternating periods of humidity and warmth to flourish.)

Turning up perhaps twice in a decade and only in the finest vintages, the fungus attacks the grapes at random over a period of weeks. Assuming the form of an ash gray film, it pierces the berries with a series of microscopic holes, mottling and thinning their skins. The sun, able now to penetrate more readily, shrivels the berries, evaporating out 50 percent or more of their moisture. The remaining dense juice ferments out slowly but not quite fully, so that alcohol levels may remain as low as 7 percent. The acids, however, do not diminish, as in normal ripening, but remain to offset the sweet intensity of the wine and to preserve it as well. Noble rot wines are splendidly smooth, luscious and marvelously unctuous; they display a fullness of bouquet, a subtlety of aroma and a lingering freshness. Discernibly sweet yet never cloying, they may even seem dry on the palate.

NOTE: Noble rot enhances only white grapes, being ruinous to the pigments of the reds. In years when the fungus does not appear, the grapes yield their usual dry wines.

Vineyards in both Germany and France have been credited with the discovery of the botrytis. In any case, the harvest was inadvertently delayed one year, causing the grapes to shrivel and become progressively mottled and mold-covered. When they were finally vinified, their wine was a superb golden nectar, the best anyone had ever tasted. Sampling it, the proprietor of Château d'Yquem in Sauternes reportedly said, "Never again will I let my grapes be picked until they are completely rotten."

To gather grapes with the proper degree of rot, the pickers must make frequent forays into the vineyard, culling the affected berries methodically with long-bladed shears and separating them out one at a time when necessary. In Sauternes, the pickers go out six to twelve times between September and December. Lesser makers can afford only three or four sorties and as a result, their wines are lighter bodied and less complex.

NOTE: Noble rot wines are made more for prestige than for profit because of their labor-intensive requirements and their exceedingly high costs. Moreover, that late in the season, the makers run the risk of an unexpected rain bloating the berries or a sudden frost decimating them completely.

Among the naturally sweet and luscious botrytized late-harvest wines are those of Sauternes and Barsac in Bordeaux, the Auslese wines of Germany and the Tokays of Hungary. Botrytized wines are also produced in Austria, Switzerland, South Africa, Hungary, Australia and the United States. (When not indigenous, the mold is artificially introduced by spraying.) Such wines however can never match the honeyed flavor and character of the prime French and German examples.

The latest-harvested wine of all is Eiswein ("Ice Wine"), made from slow-to-ripen grapes that are left on the vine until they freeze; they are not harvested until late December or mid-January. Since the grapes don't all freeze to the proper degree at once, they must be gathered individually; the pickers, who collect only a handful at a time, cannot wear gloves even on the coldest days. The grapes themselves are crushed without thawing. Only the water in their juice freezes and is discarded, leaving behind a highly intensified must that slowly ferments out to become a rich, sweet, lovely wine. Although Ice Wines are as concentrated as other late-harvest wines, their taste is not as honeyed. Characterizing them are an intense fruitiness and a vibrant acidity. Eisweins are produced in the cooler regions of Germany, Alsace, Austria and the United States. When they are made in warmer regions, their grapes are kept in cold storage for several months before being crushed and fermented.

NOTE: The grapes best suited to Eisweins are German and Austrian rieslings, as well as Alsatian gewürztraminers and the vidal blancs grown in the Finger Lakes region of New York State.

THE SUGAR-ACID BALANCE

Crucial to a wine's taste and survival is a proper balance in its must of the grape sugars and acids. The must—the grape juice ready for fermentation—is a complex aqueous solution composed chiefly of water and grape sugar, but including other substances of vegetable and mineral origin. When the sugars in the must outpace the acids, the resulting wines will be cloyingly sweet and flabby. Low acid levels also mean the wines will be ready to drink sooner. On the other hand, when the acids overwhelm the sugars, the wines will be lighter at best, and overly tart and thin at worst, some even lacking enough alcohol to survive. (Wine descriptions appear in *The Vocabulary of Taste*.)

The sugars in the grapes are measured in degrees of *brix,* which is a way of calculating their density. (Each degree represents 1 gram of sugar per 100 grams of must.) Brix values help the growers determine the time to pick the grapes and enable them to estimate their yield of alcohol. Red grapes are considered in full possession of their character at 21 to 24 degrees brix. White grapes generally reach 20 to 23 degrees, but register considerably more when botrytized. The grapes for sparkling wines may be picked earlier—at about 18 degrees brix—since higher acids are most desirable for them.

Because every 2 percent of grape sugar converts out to about 1 percent of alcohol, multiplying the brix by 0.55 indicates the wine's potential alcohol. Grapes harvested at 20 degrees will yield wines with about 11 percent alcohol; 22 degrees, about 12 percent; and so on. (The Germans and Swiss use an Oechsle scale, which divides their readings by 8: Grapes with a 73 Oechsle will produce a wine with 9.6 percent alcohol.)

A wine's acids are measured in part by a pH rating that rises when their levels are down and falls when they are up. A pH of 4, for instance, indicates a high-sugar or alkaline wine, while a pH of 2.85 indicates a decidedly acid one.

Many factors can disrupt a wine's sugar-acid balance. A powerful sun can send the grapes' sugar level soaring while it burns out much of their acids. (Grapes subject to less sun yield better-balanced wines as a rule.) Insufficient sunshine or excessive cold can slow the ripening process and coarsen the grapes. In late summer, a heavy rain can dilute the grape sugars. Yet nature is always resilient. A bright sun emerging after a chilly rainy spring can raise the grape sugar levels, producing a respectable crop after all. And vines hit by a spring frost can experience a second budding.

The wine maker can intervene if necessary to ensure a more felicitous sugar-acid balance. In warmer regions, he can keep the grape sugars down and create a more stable acid level by trellising his vines higher, away from the reflected heat of the soil. He can cultivate hybrid varieties capable of retaining their acidity even in desert heat. Or he can gather his berries earlier in the season—or perhaps in the coolness of the night. He can also add unripe, acidy grapes to his exceedingly sweet ones before crushing. Or he can stabilize his inordinately high sugar wines by fortifying them with additional alcohol.

In cooler regions, the grower can increase the sugars in his grapes by trellising the vines closer to the ground and letting them be warmed by the reflected heat of the soil. Should the acids still outdistance the sugars, he can *chaptalize* his wines by adding cane or beet sugar during fermentation. (The practice is named for Jean Chaptal, the nineteenth-century French chemist who devised it.) The added sugar converts out to alcohol when the grapes' natural sugars do, strengthening but not sweetening the wine.

And certain natural processes modify the acidity of young wines, bringing them into better balance. One such process is *malolactic fermentation,* which is brought about by lactic bacteria. Widely distributed in nature, these occur commonly in grape musts. Slower-growing than yeasts, lactic bacteria consume nutrients not of interest to the yeasts. Beginning to build up toward the end of fermentation, they attack the wine's harsh malic acid, breaking it down into a softer lactic acid. This reduces the young wine's excessive acidity, smooths out its abrasiveness, increases its palatability and adds to its depth. Malolactic fermentation, for example, modifies the taste of Champagne from a green-apple tanginess to a buttery smoothness. It also softens the flavor of California Chardonnays and makes for rounder, fuller Chablis wines.

Another acid reducer is detartration. Accounting for a good part of the must's acidity is potassium bitartrate, which isn't very soluble in alcohol. In detartration, the tartrates in the newly formed wine slowly crystallize and precipitate out; some clinging to the sides of the container but most falling to the bottom as lees or sediment. Lowering the temperature can accelerate this detartration. Vintners once speeded up the process by throwing open their cellar doors in winter. Now they use cold stabilization, chilling the wine briefly—but sharply—to about 50°F.

Some vintners, seeking maximum sugars in their grapes, deliberately deprive their vines of water. This practice, known as dry farming, stresses the plant, reducing the number and size of the grapes and intensifying their sugars. Other wine makers (such as the producers of Malvasia and Moscato wines) concentrate the sugars after the harvest by suspending the grape clusters on racks in airy attics or by stringing them from the rafters to dry. The makers of sherries and Málagas heap their grapes on straw mats out of doors to raisin in the sun, evaporating out as much of their moisture as possible. In Switzerland and in the cooler sectors of France, when the weather permits, the berries are left out on straw mats until early winter. The resulting *vins de paille* ("straw wines") are luscious and quite high in alcohol.

CRUSHING AND PRESSING

After the harvest, the grapes are crushed and pressed. Crushing applies just enough pressure to break the skins while leaving intact the stems and seeds that contain harsh concentrations of tannins and off-tasting oils. Crushing releases about 40 percent of the juice, known as the free run. Pressing, on the other hand, exerts a greater force, extracting the remainder—known as the press run—but also bruising the stems and seeds. As a rule, the free run and the harsher press run are blended together for a better balance.

The simplest form of crushing is called bleeding the vat. It piles the clusters one atop the other so that their accumulated weight gently breaks the skins and lets the juice ooze out slowly. Bleeding the vat is associated with the finest rosés, rare Málaga wines and noble rot Hungarian Tokays.

The first instrument for crushing was the human foot, whose treading action could bring out the grape's soft jelly without disturbing either the tannic seeds or stems. The foot's warmth also stimulated the fermentation process. In Portugal and elsewhere, barefoot men climbed into great stone troughs, called *lagares,* filled with freshly gathered grapes. Often spurred on by musical accompaniment, the men linked arms while steadily and rhythmically stomping the grapes, liberating the pulp and releasing the juice. Treaders in Jerez wore hobnailed clogs, which broke the skins more quickly but left the seeds and stems intact.

Crushing is now accomplished in huge horizontal drums equipped with high-velocity paddles or blades. The paddles slap the berries from their stems and break the skins. The must itself flows into a holding tank below through perforations in the drum.

The earliest presses were great, weighty stones raised up by ropes and long levers. Slamming down ferociously, they virtually demolished the grapes. Later, a giant wooden screw with a heavy lid was set in the center of the lagar. Several men turned the screw to bring down the lid, pulverizing the crushed grapes and expelling their remaining juice.

Presses are now either the batch type or the continuous type. The first must be cleaned after each batch is processed. The second runs without interruption at higher speeds and recovers a maximum of juice. The simplest batch press is the basket press, an upright cylinder made of sturdy wooden slats with a solid-board plate attached to a screw at the center. Bringing the plate down expels the juice of the crushed grapes, which quickly gushes out through the slatted sides into a catch basin below. A mechanized version consists of a horizontal cylinder with a piston running its entire length. Plates at either end move slowly toward one another, pressing the grapes between them. A variant features a thick-walled rubber bag inflated by compressed air, which squeezes the berries and expels their juice.

The continuous press, consisting of a giant cylinder fitted with an auger, operates much like a meat grinder. Crushed grapes are fed in at one end, their solids expelled out from the other, while the juice flows out separately. The earliest continuous presses were crude and excessive in their friction, chewing up the grapes, browning the pulp and bruising the seeds. Their pressure can now be adjusted with greater precision.

Pressing fractionally releases the grape juice. The first pressing exerts the lightest pressure, affecting the center of the berry but not the seeds. The second pressing has some contact with the seeds, while the third, exerting the greatest force, releases the harshest juice, which includes more tannins and off-tasting oils. The third pressing is not used in wine making but is generally distilled into brandy or industrial alcohol.

Champagne was traditionally subjected to four pressings: *vin de cuvée, premiere taille, deuxième taille,* and *rebêche.* (The last was done on a smaller press.) In the past, makers of premium Champagnes vinified only their first pressings, selling off their seconds and thirds to lesser firms. Now such Champagnes may

The continuous press

include second pressings as well. The same is true of premium table wines: Their makers once used only the first pressings, but now often include the seconds in their blends as well.

Crushing and pressing leave behind a pulpy mass of skins, stalks and seeds. This solid residue, called the pomace, is not discarded. Its pigments are employed in the manufacture of inks and dyes. Its tannins tan leather. Its grapeseed oils are used in food processing and in the making of soaps and paints. Its residual alcohol is distilled into a coarse brandy called *grappa* in Italy, *marc* in France, *aguardiente* in Spain and *tresterschnapps* in Germany. Its pulp is dried as a fuel or pulverized into a mulch. The pomace also serves as a rich compost, which renews the depleted energies of the vineyard after the growing season.

FERMENTATION

Fermentation, which is at the heart of the wine-making process, can occur virtually by itself. The time it takes depends on the type of grape used, the wine being made, the ambient temperature and other considerations. Fermentation can occur within hours and continue for a few days or for several months. After the grapes are crushed, a slight movement can be seen in the juice—a bubbling around the edges. Then the juice becomes agitated: fretting, frothing, heaving and turning unpleasantly muddy. Gradually quieting down, the liquid becomes cleaner, clearer, more vinous and potent. The sweet, mild grape juice has become raw wine. Vintners once tipped their hats to their vats in deference to this unaccountable phenomenon.

The mystery was deciphered in the nineteenth century when Louis Pasteur, a French chemist, observed through the lens of his microscope strange single-celled creatures interacting with the sugar in the grape juice. Pasteur called the creatures *microbi vini.* We call them yeasts. (Their scientific name is *Saccharomyces cereviseae.*) Pasteur came to realize that their life processes were inextricably linked with the transformation of the grape juice into wine. Boiling or "pasteurizing" the juice destroyed the microbi vini. The liquid never became wine.

Like all living creatures, the yeasts—ever present in the atmosphere—need a source of nourishment. This is provided by the sugar in ripe grapes. Irresistibly drawn to the sweetness inside, the yeasts settle on the grapes by the millions, held fast to the skins by a whitish, waxlike bloom. When overripeness or crushing breaks the skins, the yeasts gain access to the sweet juice they crave.

Once inside, the microorganisms secrete an enzyme that triggers an intricate series of reactions. The sugar molecules are split in two; one half becoming ethyl alcohol, a colorless, odorless, highly volatile liquid, the other half a gas, carbon dioxide or CO_2. Rising quickly to escape, the gas pricks the surface of the liquid with tiny bubbles, creating the illusion of boiling. In fact, the term *fermentation* derives from the Latin *fermentare*, meaning "to boil."

Unlike most single-celled organisms, yeasts do not divide in two but sprout vegetatively: small buds form on the mother cells, then split off as daughter cells. Turbulently increasing more than fourfold in number, they greatly expand the volume of the liquid. These violent molecular changes also make the process hot and tumultuous. (Yeasts require heat as well as sugar to function.)

Needing air to multiply, the yeasts find it in open vats. But the buildup of carbon dioxide soon blankets the wine, excluding the outside air. No longer able to reproduce, the yeasts shift from their aerobic (oxygen-requiring) mode to an anaerobic (alcohol-producing) mode. Needing only a fraction of the grape sugar for their own use, they convert the remainder to alcohol and secrete it willingly back into the liquid where it accumulates. Fermentation is in effect a two-phase process: the yeasts multiply in the primary or respiratory phase and produce the alcohol in the secondary airless or fermentative phase.

NOTE: Yeast strains vary in their tolerance for alcohol. Some, after producing 12 percent alcohol by volume, can proceed no further. Other strains are not perceptibly slowed down until the alcohol level reaches 14 or 15 percent. In the end, the alcohol the yeasts themselves have produced becomes their undoing and they can no longer function.

Ideally, fermentation temperatures should rise slowly to balance out the sugars and acids and produce fresh, lively wines with a certain bite. Excessive heat accelerates fermentation, driving off the acids, destroying the wine's delicacy, rendering it dull, off-flavored and rather short lived. In warmer regions, must temperatures can rise more than a degree an hour, causing the liquid to boil over, damaging the yeasts and causing a "stuck" or halted fermentation. To cool such feverish musts, vintners once lowered their casks into the sea, hosed them down with cold water or surrounded them with blocks of ice. They also added cooler juice to their overheated liquids or used smaller vats with a higher ratio of heat-absorbing surface to wine. Aided now by stainless steel technology, refrigeration and cold stabilization, wine makers can control their overly rapid fermentations. By chilling the must sharply but briefly and thus preserving a greater degree of its acidity, they can produce crisper, fruitier wines with more flavor and fragrance than were possible before.

NOTE: Fermentation can take place in wooden or stainless steel containers. The best Burgundies are barrel-fermented in small oak casks. For white wines, stainless steel is usually preferred, because it enables them to retain their fresh, fruity character.

Left to their own devices, the yeasts will convert out virtually all the grape sugar, leaving the wine bone-dry. (They generally proceed until only 0.2 percent sugar remains.) Vintners wishing to make their wines sweeter than usual can interrupt the process before the yeasts have completed their task. They may stun the yeasts with sulfur dioxide, add more alcohol than they can possibly tolerate or filter them out entirely.

Or, to produce richer, more intense wines, the vintners can prolong the fermentation process itself. In Hungary, Tokay makers add rich botrytized berries to the must, measuring these grapes out in 7-gallon tubs called *puttonyos*. (Puttonyos are wooden hods once used in collecting the berries.) The more puttonyos in the mix, the finer and more luscious the wine. In the nineteenth century, Tokays were enriched with 7 to 9 puttonyos and reserved for royalty. Nowadays the maximum employed is 5 or 6. (The number appears on the label.) Lesser Tokays attempt to simulate the richness of the best examples through the use of grape concentrates.

After the turbulent expansion caused by the yeasts' multiplication, the wine cools down and contracts, creating a space or vacuum above the liquid known as the *ullage*. This vacuum acts as a magnet, drawing in outside air, which brings with it spoilage microorganisms attracted by the wine's residual sugars and other substances. The most treacherous of these microorganisms is the acetobacter, which by its own enzymatic action dissolves certain minerals in the wine and forms various acetates including acetic acid, otherwise known as vinegar. In minimal amounts, acetic acid enhances the wine's bouquet and flavor; when present in excess, however, it makes the wine undrinkable.

Once the vinegar makers take over, there is no turning back. An early sign of their invasion is a reduction in the wine's alcohol level. As more and more of the alcohol is converted to acetic acid, the smell and taste of vinegar become apparent. At first, the wine is unpalatable; then it is completely ruined. It has become *vin aigre* (sour wine).

The spoilage organisms, unlike the beneficial yeasts, need oxygen to survive. While carbon dioxide blanketed the wine, they were held in check, but once air enters the ullage, they can proliferate freely. Pasteur realized that an aerated wine was defenseless against these spoilers. The only way to repel them was to eliminate the ullage. He taught French wine makers to top off their wines—to refill their vats and tanks fully by adding more wine. That put an end to sour wine. In wine-loving France, Pasteur became a national hero.

Subsequently, several more sophisticated methods were developed. To preempt the ullage, a colorless and inert nitrogen gas—which did not interact chemically with the wine—was pumped into the casks and tanks. Or fiberglass lids were floated on the wine's surface, which automatically dropped down as natural evaporation lowered the wine's liquid level. More recently, German scientists have devised an elaborate air-excluding system to seal off the entire wine-making process and protect everything: grapes, wine, pumps, even the bottling equipment. The system is extremely costly however and beyond the financial reach of most wine makers.

THE COLOR OF WINE

Wine, richly diverse in color, ranges from pale straw to amber and from pink to ruby and on to garnet and beyond. Yet there are only two basic wine colors: red and white. (Rosés are a subcategory of red wines.)

Determining a wine's color in large part is the color of its grapes—specifically, the pigments in the grape skins. (The pulp and juice are usually colorless.) Some grape varieties are much richer in their pigments than others. During fermentation, the newly formed alcohol dissolves these pigments, making them an integral part of the wine. Also responsible for the color is the degree of contact between the pigmented skins and the must. The more extensive the contact, the darker the wine. When the skins are separated out early, the pigments do not get a chance to leach out, leaving the wine virtually colorless.

NOTE: Red grapes need a warm but not an overly warm autumn to set their pigments properly. In cooler regions they tend to be lighter in hue, and in the coolest regions to lack color. White grapes are generally golden in the warmer regions and paler in the cooler ones.

Red wines, depending on their desired style, are steeped on their color-laden skins from several days to two weeks. The skins provide more than color; they're also the source of tannins and other organic compounds that give the wine its body, texture, depth and intensity. The more contact between skins and must, the more multifaceted the wine becomes and the more complex its flavor and aroma.

The skins of white wines are usually separated out early on to keep the wines light-bodied and delicate. (White wines need only enough tannin to provide a little texture.) A few examples however are exposed to twelve- to twenty-four-hour skin contact to make them richer and more flavorful. These are closer in character to red wines but, when fermented too long on their skins, they may become overly rich and heavy.

NOTE: Although a white wine may appear to be milder than a red, it might in fact be stronger, since a wine's strength is based on its alcohol content, not on its color.

Rosé wines remain on their skins just long enough to achieve the desired shade of pinkness. Classic rosés, pressed from lightly pigmented Mediterranean grapes, combine the richness of a red wine with the lighter character of a white. Other rosés are made from the less-intense fruit of younger vines.

The best rosés are made by the *saignée* method (bleeding the vat), which crushes but does not press the grapes. Macerating them in their own juice for twelve to forty-eight hours lets the juice pick up some color from the skins. The still pale colored must is then drained off and fermented like a white wine.

The simplest and cheapest way to achieve the desired pinkness in a rosé is to blend together red and white wines. Inexpensive bulk rosés, often made this way, are invariably innocuous and bland. In France, the practice is banned for rosé table wines but permitted for sparkling rosés or pink Champagnes—which in the Champagne-making process can undergo unpredictable changes of hue, creating an inconsistency of color from bottle to bottle.

A blush wine is somewhere between a white wine and a rosé. It's usually pressed from heavily pigmented grapes such as the zinfandel. Although the grape skins are soon removed, a bit of their intense color inevitably leaches out, imparting a pinkish tinge or blush to the wine.

As a rule, red and purplish grapes yield red wines, while white, yellow and green grapes yield white ones. But a canny vintner can produce both a red wine and a white wine from a single batch of red grapes. For the white wine, he immediately separates out half the juice from the skins and ferments it separately, while processing the remainder as he would any red wine. Or he can, if he wishes, produce both a rosé and a red wine from the same batch of grapes. He can make an almost immediately drinkable rosé by tapping off the paler free-run juice from the red-wine vat, and then pressing the remaining skins and pulp for a darker, stronger red, which will take a year or two to mature.

Both red and white grapes can go into the making of a white wine. Champagne, for example, is pressed from pinot noir and chardonnay grapes, among others. (The wine was initially tawny-colored until its makers learned to exclude the grape skins.) Champagne's variations include a Blanc de Blancs ("White of Whites"), pressed exclusively from the chardonnay. Pale, delicate, and light-bodied, this lacks the balance of the more typical red-and-white Champagne blends. Blanc de Noirs ("White of Blacks") is pressed from the dark purple—almost blackish—pinot noir grapes, whose skins are removed early on. Slightly amber in color and somewhat fuller in body and flavor than traditional Champagnes, the

Blanc de Noirs is sometimes bottled on its own but more often is used in Champagne blending.

During fermentation, the red wine's skins and solids, buoyed up by the carbon dioxide, become so densely packed that they form a thick crust known as a *chapeau* or cap, which floats on the surface of the wine while great heat is generated below in the liquid. Were the cap allowed to harden and float unbroken on the surface, it would seal in the heat—damaging the yeasts, disrupting fermentation and ruining the wine. If the yeasts are to be fruitful and multiply, the cap must be moistened and dispersed. Breaking up the cap not only cools and aerates the liquid but also speeds up the extraction from the grape skins of the pigments, tannins and other beneficial substances.

To disperse the dense crust, men once sat on the rims of the vats stomping the caps with their bare feet. Feeling the temperature with their skin, they knew just how much punching down was required. Now mechanical pumps drain cooler juice from the bottom of the vat and spray it back over the top. Some wineries punch down the cap with a pneumatic device consisting of a large paddle running on a track above the fermenting wine; its slow, gentle manipulation enables the vintner to get the best from his berries. Once the production of CO_2 ceases and the cap is no longer buoyant, the solids go to the press, which breaks down the grape solids further, extracting the remaining juice and accelerating the release of the skin pigments, tannins and other useful substances.

White wines by and large are not fermented on their skins. Their grapes go directly to the press after crushing. Since their solids here have not yet been broken down, their pressing is more difficult here. Some white wines are sent to special dejuicers, whose tumbling action helps to recover more of their juice.

BLENDING

Blending, one of the most respected arts in wine making, can create a specific style of wine, ensure greater consistency in a wine, heighten its desirable qualities, compensate for its inadequacies or mask its flaws. Some of the world's greatest wines are blends; so are some of the most disreputable.

Blending enables the vintner to counteract the vagaries of the weather. He can balance out the qualities lacking in one vintage with those present in another—combining, for example, the acidy wine of a rainy summer with the heavier product of a hot, dry season. (While each wine is unattractive in itself, blending improves them both.) As one wine maker declared, "When nature doesn't come through, we blend."

Swift modern transportation has enabled the vintner to transcend the limitations of his locale. He can draw his components from widely scattered sources. He can bring his grapes, musts or wines together from the same or different vineyards, from better or lesser soils, from the same or different harvests.

The blender can create body and structure in an otherwise soft or indifferent wine by adding a more tannic one. He can use a tart wine to offset the cloying sweetness of another, or a more robust wine to strengthen a weaker product. He can modify a coarser wine by adding a more delicate one or speed up the drinkability of a young wine by adding a more mature one.

Relying on his nose, palate and memory of other wines, the blender creates his own harmonies. He may add one component for body, another for color, a third for dryness, a fourth for fragrance and so on. The more diverse his combination, the more complex the result. The greater the blender's artistry, the more splendid his wine will be.

Also influencing the character of the blend are local custom and the house style of the winery. In Bordeaux, the eminent estates separate their grapes according to variety, age of the vines, and better or lesser sectors of the vineyard. In the spring, they vinify and blend the various batches together. German wine makers vinify each day's pressings separately for their premium wines, blending them selectively at the end of the season. Makers of noble rot wines also ferment each day's harvest separately, later blending their best batches together.

Burgundy uses the pinot noir for its red wines and the chardonnay for its whites. Because of the historic fragmentation of its vineyards, Burgundy draws the grapes from a number of parcels. Bordeaux traditionally blends the cabernet sauvignon, merlot, malbec, cabernet franc and other grape varieties, using the tannic cabernet sauvignon to supply structure and elegance, and the others to soften the wine's austerity and to contribute their own nuances. (Although the châteaus follow a general formula, they may change the blend from year to year depending on the weather and on how the various grape varieties have fared.) California blends Rhône Valley grapes—the syrah, mourvèdre and grenache—to create rich, dark red wines. New York State blends three hybrids—the baco noir, chelois, and maréchal foch—to produce a full-bodied red wine. More than a dozen grape varieties have gone into the Châteauneuf-du-Pape wines of the Rhône Valley and as many as thirty grapes into port-wine blends.

The epitome of a great blended wine is Champagne, which was created in the seventeenth century when the vintners of Épernay would donate some of their wines to the church as tithes. Pressed from the pinot noir, chardonnay and other grape varieties, the wines differed greatly. Some were tart and dry, others soft and round.

Deciding to balance them out was Dom Pérignon, the cellarmaster at the Benedictine abbey of Hautvillers. The monk—who was blind—and possessed a finely tuned palate—combined the texture, headiness and fruit of the Pinot Noirs with the delicacy, lightness and finesse of the Chardonnays, judiciously rounding out the mix with the others. (Some 60 percent of these were red wines and 40 percent white.) Dom Pérignon's blend proved so superior that few Champagnes after his time remained *vins de cru* (wines of one location).

Champagne producers usually don't own any vineyards, but purchase their grapes locally. Grape prices are set according to a rating system based primarily on vineyard soils. The finest berries, rated 100 percent, go into the rarest blends. Top firms generally buy grapes rated in the 90s, while good smaller firms buy those in the high 70s to low 90s.

Each Champagne house takes special pride in the uniqueness of its blend. The blend, known as the *cuvée* (translating as batch or tubful), is assembled in the spring when the new wines have settled down sufficiently to be tasted. Selecting samples from the various batches, the blender combines them on a small scale; then, when his assemblage is approved, the proportions of the components are extrapolated to the proper scale for the actual production. A Champagne blend usually combines anywhere from ten to thirty wines representing a number of vintages. A Grand Cru cuvée can combine as many as forty to fifty wines, drawn from six to ten harvests. Lesser Champagnes combine fewer wines from fewer years.

NOTE: Many firms set aside wines from good years to upgrade their blends. These are known as *vins de reserve* or correctives. The better Champagne houses keep at least a three-year supply on hand; lesser firms may not employ any correctives at all.

Another classic blended wine is sherry, which is blended and aged simultaneously. The process occurs in a solera system, through which the wine gradually passes. A solera consists of anywhere from two dozen to several hundred casks stacked atop one another in equal rows. Solera derives from *suelo,* which means "foundation" and refers to the floor on which the casks sit. (The 150-gallon casks are known as *botas* or butts.)

The simplest solera consists of three equal rows of casks. The first row is filled with wine the first year, the next two rows in the two succeeding years. At the end of the third year, wine is withdrawn from the bottommost row, usually no more than a third at a time. The casks are immediately refilled with a like amount drawn from the row directly above. These are replenished in turn with wine from the topmost row. Refilling the topmost row is a new wine of a similar style and quality.

NOTE: The wines were initially siphoned with hoses, but are now transferred from cask to cask with mechanical pumps.

Each solera has its own style and grade of wine. A typical system begins with a *criadera* (nursery solera) and ends with a shipping solera. Before its admission to the solera proper, a young wine may pass through two or three criaderas. Only those of the properly developed style and quality are permitted to move ahead. As the wines pass slowly and gradually through the casks, they are continually blended and reblended. The older, more mellow wines "educate" the younger, transmitting to them their mature richness, subtlety and depth of character. The younger wines refresh their elders giving them vivacity and tone. As the younger wines move progressively through several levels of increasingly older wines, they gradually become smoother and more complex, rounder and mellower, yet they remain remarkably fresh.

The solera system of fractional blending ensures a uniformity of style and a consistency of wine quality year after year. It guarantees a sherry as close as possible in color, flavor and character to the wine that emerged a decade before. Sherries from top vineyards spend about nine years in the system. The more old wines that pass through, the better and more expensive the blend. In really old systems—which go back more than one hundred years—a few drops of the original wine may still be dispersed among the casks. A solera system can be perpetuated indefinitely.

NOTE: Madeira wines are matured in a similar manner, with some of their components averaging eighty to one hundred years of age. (Here, no more than 10 percent may be drawn off for sale annually.) Marsalas may also be blended in a solera.

AGING

The aging of a wine is its gradual oxidation, which takes place in wood and glass. To stand up to such slow aeration, the wine must have enough tannin to hold it together. (Tannin is an assortment of organic compounds found in the skins, stalks and seeds of the grapes.) Absorbed by the must during fermentation, it gives the wine structure or backbone, preserving it and lengthening its life. Determining the grapes' tannin level is their variety as well as their general growing conditions and weather they experience. (Good vintages produce the best tannins.) Red wines, fermented on their skins, possess the highest levels and need the most aging. White wines, rarely fermented on their skins, exhibit relatively little tannin and need virtually no aging.

For preliminary aging, a wooden cask is ideal. Although its construction is airtight, the porous staves let in limited quantities of outside air, which gradually and evenly interact with the organic constituents in the wine. The wooden cask offers its own extractable elements—its own tannins, vanillins and aromatic substances. As these are absorbed, the wine nearest the staves becomes denser and heavier. Falling away, it is replaced by lighter liquid from the center. This constant circulation within the cask aerates the wine

Wood-aging

evenly, encouraging its slow and steady development.

NOTE: New casks, with their fresh extractables, are best. Those vintners who can afford to do so change their casks each year. Others put some of their wines in new barrels and some in older ones. Still others age their less expensive products in casks that had been used originally for premium wines.

The porosity of the wooden staves also permits evaporation; about 5 percent of the volume of the liquid is lost every year. This concentrates and intensifies the wine, but also creates an ullage at the top of the cask. Were this air space to remain, the wine would be subjected to excessive oxidation, robbing it of its character and hastening its demise. To prevent this and to assure the wine's stability and soundness, the casks are topped off regularly.

For red wines, wood-aging tempers their tannic astringency, gradually softening their initial harshness and rawness, rounding out their character and making their complexity more apparent. White wines, which lack the preservative power of tannin, are susceptible to overoxidation in wood. Champagne, however, acquires a toasty flavor, a lovely bouquet and a more complex roundness from its brief stay in the cask. California chardonnays can also achieve a measure of roundness and complexity with wood-aging, but are often overshadowed by too much wood. (The wood flavors should be sufficiently subdued so as not to overwhelm the wine's natural qualities.) At one time, white wines were aged extensively in wood and absorbed too much of the cask's extractables, becoming heavy and assertive. (Some tasted more like wood than wine.)

The time a red wine spends in the cask varies from vintage to vintage. The more pronounced its tannins, the more aging it needs. Customs also change. Long wood-aging was once considered routine in Italy and in most of Spain, but now about twenty-four months is often deemed a sufficient time. Even the most prestigious châteaus in Bordeaux rarely cask-age their wines more than eighteen months.

The best wood for aging is white oak, which not only adds flavor and aroma to the wine but also contributes its own tannins and organic compounds. Particularly prized is French white oak from Limousin, which is characterized by a high porosity and a rich vanillin that introduces a soft, subtle quality to the wine. Other good French oaks come from Nevers, Vosges, Tronçais and Allier. Suitable oaks also come from Germany's Black Forest, from the former Yugoslavia, Mexico and the southeastern United States.

Redwood and chestnut were once also widely used. (Most other woods are either too resinous or insufficiently porous.) The towering redwoods, indigenous to California, permitted larger cooperage than oak. (*Cooperage* refers to any bulk wine container; the term derives from *cooper,* the maker or repairer of barrels.) Redwood's extractable elements are more limited than those of oak, however, and impart little wood character, preserving the wine's fruitiness at the expense of its complexity.

NOTE: In recent years, the material of choice for aging wine has often been stainless steel. Its vats and tanks are not limited in size, as are those made of wood; they're also easier to clean and maintain. Stainless steel containers have no extractable elements, however, so the vintners may age their wines in them briefly and then complete the process in wood.

In wine aging, there is not only the cost of the barrels to consider but the cost of maintaining their storage space. The vintner gets no return on his investment while his wine is slowly maturing. This has led to shortcuts such as suspending oak chips in mesh bags in the wine for days or weeks, or perhaps using oak concentrates to impart an oaky smell and taste.

A highly tannic red wine emerging from its cask may be too closed-in for immediate consumption—still quite rough, raw, and unyielding. Further aging is needed to subdue the still-unresolved tannins that mask its fruit and bouquet. This additional aging takes place in glass. The process of oxidation in the bottle can proceed more slowly, enabling the wine to improve immeasurably.

Enclosed in inert and neutral glass, the wine ages by breathing in a small amount of air. (This takes the form of a bubble inevitably introduced at the time of bottling.) As the wine expands and develops, it sheds its youthful awkwardness and smooths out its raw edges, forming new compounds and releasing its flavors. Among the new compounds are esters, highly volatile combinations of acids and alcohol, which—although minor in quantity—are major in enhancing flavor, aroma and bouquet. During its aging in glass, the wine acquires new and fascinating nuances, and develops depth and complexity. Becoming supple, smooth and fragrant, it achieves the splendid balance of maturity.

A key consideration in aging is the size of the container. The larger the bottle, the better. A higher ratio of liquid to air prevents excessive oxidation, allowing the wine to develop at a more leisurely pace. The magnum is the ideal size, holding much more wine in proportion to air than does a standard bottle. A half-bottle, on the other hand, ages a wine twice as fast as a standard bottle. For wood-aging, the reverse is true: the smaller the cask, the better, since the higher ratio of wood surface to liquid exposes more of the developing wine to the porous staves, allowing the liquid to breathe more evenly.

The practice of bottle-aging began in the eighteenth century. Before this, the glass bottles were squat with irregular apertures and could not be stoppered securely. Improved technology that made for more uniform apertures enabled the wines to be tightly corked. The sides of the bottles also became straighter so the bottles could be stacked horizontally for long-term storage and aging.

The bottling process itself can be traumatic; a wine needs time to adjust to its confinement in glass. Some wines may become bottle-sick at first, exhibiting harshness and a loss of flavor. When they're allowed to rest before shipment, such symptoms usually disappear. Finer wines are binned away for several months; lesser ones for a briefer period.

Sealing the bottles are corks that come from the outer bark of a unique oak tree grown in warm-climates. Portugal produces more than half the world's cork supply; other sources are Spain, Algeria and Morocco. The bark, stripped off and processed, is formed into small cylinders. (It takes some forty years for the oak tree to mature and about ten years for its stripped-off bark to regenerate.) Poor harvesting practices in recent years have reduced the available cork supply. Premium wines were once routinely fitted with 2 1/2-inch stoppers, but now 2-inch corks are more the norm.

Faced with a shortage of good corks and a proliferation of bad ones, the wine industry has reluctantly sought out alternative stoppers. Wines meant for early consumption are often sealed with metal or plastic caps or with stoppers that combine cork, wood and plastic. The metal twist-off and pry-off caps familiar on beer and soda bottles are now used for some quality wines as well. (Experiments have shown that these can preserve the wine well for years.) And because premium wines have always been associated with corks in the public mind, there has been some experimentation with resilient cellulose and plastic resin stoppers, which look like corks and can be extracted like corks. (They may affect the wine's aroma, however.)

The more tannic red wines lend themselves best to glass-aging, with the most complex among them not reaching their ultimate development for years. The softer, less structured reds and rosés with their lighter tannins need little time in either wood or glass. Extended aging would only evaporate out their freshness and cause their delightful charm to decline.

Most white wines are now reared in stainless steel and bottled quite young to retain their fresh, crisp qualities. Prolonged aging for them would produce disagreeable fuzzy tastes and off-flavors. But the more full bodied among them can benefit from time in glass; they can achieve a greater vinosity and complexity with little loss of their freshness. Included here are the finest Chablis, the best German Rieslings and the noble rot wines. As noble rot wines age, the luscious sweetness that initially obscured their flavor subsides, letting other delightful intricacies come through.

Aging also transforms a wine's color. White wines, initially greenish or straw-colored, head toward yellow and then darken, taking on an amber hue. When overaged, they turn brown. Good red wines start out with a youthful purple color that changes in time to a more profound garnet. (The French call the subtle russet of fine old red wines *pelure d'oignon,* or "onion skin.") As a red wine continues to age, its color progresses first toward orange, then toward brown. A brick color indicates the wine has passed its peak. When completely brown, the wine is most likely undrinkable. Both red and white wines *maderize* in time—acquiring the brownish hue of a Madeira, combined with a vapid odor and an acrid taste. White wines, less protected by tannin, tend to maderize more quickly.

A number of vintners maintain that the public has neither the time nor the inclination to wait for a wine to slowly mature. Their motive is most likely economic. A winery has to be in good financial shape to let its wines age quietly for extended periods. On the other hand, a speeded-up wine offers a quicker return on its investment and is less expensive to produce. Vintners can speed up a wine's development by:

1. Using earlier-ripening, less tannic grapes.
2. Including fewer grape varieties in the blend. Châteauneuf-du-Pape once combined more than a dozen varieties, but now uses five or less.
3. Removing the tannic stalks and stems before crushing (a practice the French call *égrappage*).
4. Separating out the tannic skins within days or hours of fermentation.
5. Using hot pressing, a method that briefly heats the skins and must to accelerate the extraction of color from the skins.
6. Filtering the wine, pasteurizing it or dosing it with sulfur dioxide.
7. Vatting the wine more briefly and relying more on stainless steel containers.

Red wines that are ready to drink in two to four years are called useful, accessible or transition wines. The French describe them as *promptment buvable* (soon ready to drink). Two-year-olds from Bordeaux suitable for immediate drinking have been dubbed supermarket wines, since that is where they are frequently sold. Foreshortened wines have also been referred to as restaurant wines, because they can be added to a wine list on delivery.

However, a speeded-up, abbreviated product can never compare with a slowly evolving wine. Lighter, paler and more one dimensional, it lacks the intensity and complexity of a traditionally made product, as well as a potential for continuing development. After experimenting with various acceleration methods, some Rhône Valley vintners decided it was better for their wines to age naturally. As one said, "For it to grow old through some artificial process is not good for the wine at all." Echoing this sentiment, an American wine maker declared, "The minute you take a shortcut in the process, that's as good as your wine is going to be." And in parts of France, Portugal and Italy, wine makers still toss the tannic stems and stalks into their vats along with the grapes. "Although this makes it more trouble," one Frenchman noted, "it gives the wine a richer body."

CLARIFICATION

During fermentation, the wine churns up a violent froth containing bits of pulp, seeds and skins. These constitute the sediment. When fermentation is over and the production of CO_2 stops, the heavier particles settle out of the liquid. The wine is then said to "fall bright." The muddy sediment sinking to the bottom is known as the gross lees. A volatile deposit, it can reexcite fermentation, decompose and encourage the proliferation of the vinegar makers. This muddy sediment threatens the wine's stability and cannot be permitted to remain. Once the gross lees have settled out, they must be separated from the liquid. Removing this unwanted deposit is known as clarification. It involves racking and fining. For lesser wines, filtering is used.

Racking transfers the clear wine to another container by way of pumps and hoses, leaving the muddy sediment behind. Red wines, fermented on their skins and generating the heaviest deposits, require the most racking. Since those with more body and tannin also need greater oxidation; racking enables them to pick up the necessary oxygen. White wines are generally racked early to preserve their fruit and delicacy. A few however are steeped for a while on their sediment to enrich them. Muscadet sur Lie, as its name implies, ripens on its lees, acquiring a yeastier flavor and a more pronounced aroma, and becoming a brisker, fruitier, more full bodied wine. Champagne ages quietly on its spent lees to achieve a greater fragrance, depth and finesse. California Chardonnays, often reared in stainless steel, compensate for that metal's neutrality by spending some time on their organic deposits.

Wines from warmer climates are generally racked as soon after fermentation as possible to prevent spoilage. Those from richer, riper vintages are racked earlier than those from poor years. (Leaving the more meager examples longer on their gross lees compensates somewhat for their shortcomings.)

NOTE: A wine may also be racked before and after blending and during wood-aging. As red wines cast off their soluble pigments along with their sediment, they lose some color. The more often they're racked during aging, the tawnier they become.

While the gross lees soon settle out, the finer, lighter particles remain suspended in the liquid, clouding or "blinding" the wine and creating a certain harshness. Fining induces these particles to settle out as well by dispersing a coagulating agent through the liquid, which creates a soluble, filmlike net. This net, drifting slowly downward through the wine over a period of days or months, captures most of the particles that have not settled out by themselves.

Coagulating agents have included egg whites, skimmed milk, gelatin, boiled rice, beef blood, isinglass, plaster of paris and casein. Most powerful and fastest acting is bentonite, a porous, expansive clay with phenomenal absorptive qualities. Bentonite however removes the finer deposits along with the sediment: the valuable tannins, fruit acids and mineral salts responsible for much of the wine's flavor, character and longevity. Bentonite is not used for quality products.

While aging in glass, the wine continues to precipitate out small quantities of its finer deposits. Provided the liquid itself remains clear, a teaspoon or two of sediment at the bottom of the bottle is a good sign, an indication that the wine has matured slowly. In a tannic red wine, the sediment may appear as a muddy deposit, as brownish flakes, or as a loose, murky film adhering to the bottle's interior. (The French call the latter a "chemise.") Although this deposit is harmless to drink, its texture can disconcert the palate. Decanting the wines at serving time will leave the sediment behind.

Vintage Ports, aged primarily in glass, throw a series of precipitations inside the bottle that cohere as a hard, clinging crust. The bottles must be handled with particular care to keep this interior crust intact. Dislodging it would befoul the wine. To prevent this, the topside of each bottle is marked with a splash of white paint and the painted side is kept uppermost whenever the bottle is moved.

NOTE: Vintage Ports are best left to fall bright on their own but some producers fine them for export, wishing to prevent the formation of a crust that might become dislodged in shipping.

White wines and rosés throw a negligible deposit. Their sediment, if any, appears at the bottom of the bottle as solitary crystals or it resembles a few pale grains of sand. Neutral in taste and hardly evident in texture, it is easily ignored.

Filtering, another form of clarification, speeds up the process mechanically by forcing the liquid through a series of porous layers or finely meshed screens. By removing the most infinitesimal particles, it ensures that the wine will not precipitate heavily during shipment and storage, thus extending its shelf life. Filtering produces bright and impeccably clear looking wines by stripping away the very compounds that would sustain the wine and help it to develop. Used mainly for lesser products, this process thins and impoverishes the wine.

THE ECONOMICS OF WINE

The producers of wine range from small family-owned vineyards to vast industrialized empires. In between are the boutique, estate, cooperative and middleman wineries.

The family-owned vineyards, seen primarily in Europe, average little more than an acre and generally produce just enough wine for the grower, his family and a few friends. Boutique wineries, associated mainly with California, are small-scale operations that specialize in highly individualized wines. Their annual output typically runs from five thousand to twelve thousand cases. (The smaller establishments sell their products on the premises or by mail order.)

Estate wineries concentrate on a few quality wines produced in lots of a few thousand gallons, and are associated principally with France and Germany. They generally produce twenty thousand to forty thousand cases annually, although some average considerably less. Cooperative wineries are composed of growers who pool their resources not only to produce wine but also to market and distribute it. Some cooperatives are modest in size; others are mammoth. Middleman wineries do not deal with the public at all, but sell their products in bulk to others who then blend, bottle and distribute the wines.

In recent years, a handful of giant corporations have absorbed many medium-sized wineries and bulk processors. Their production starts at about three hundred thousand cases annually. (One huge California establishment churns out some four million cases a year.) Much of their activity is mechanized and computerized. Machines gather the grapes and transfer them to gondolas. The grapes themselves often travel long distances to the winery. They may be sprayed with sulfites or blanketed with nitrogen gas to prevent their oxidation or premature fermentation en route. On reaching the winery, the grapes go to powerful crusher-destemmers; their must is inoculated with cultured yeasts. Workers sitting at computer keyboards continuously feed the must through pipelines. Fermentation takes place in huge stainless steel tanks, fitted with temperature controls. (Should the heat begin to climb dangerously, coolants flow or alarms sound.) The raw wine flowing out is constantly monitored.

High-speed centrifuges precipitate out the wine solids. Filtering further clarifies the liquid. Blending occurs in quality control laboratories, first in milliliters, then in gallons. Cellars are rare and aging times are brief. Fast-moving machines bottle, label and pack the wine. (One giant winery can fill and cork 3,000 bottles an hour.)

NOTE: Some wineries have no vineyards of their own but purchase all their grapes, either establishing informal ties with the growers or signing them to multiyear contracts. Other wineries lease the vineyards themselves on a long-term basis. Still others farm out the entire wine-making process.

Commercial wine making calls for considerable capital. Many growers must borrow just to cultivate their crops; they pay their debts by selling off their grapes, musts or raw wines. Various middlemen—négociants, shippers, brokers—lend the growers money or sell their products to the wineries for them.

Some shippers buy raw wines, then blend, bottle and age them themselves in their own cellars. Others buy already-bottled wine and simply affix their own labels. In Bordeaux and Burgundy, local shippers stake out much of the crop: monitoring the grapes;

sampling, judging and choosing those they will purchase; then marketing and distributing the final product. The middlemen themselves often need to operate with borrowed funds. To survive economically, they must juggle grape prices and market conditions. Most successful are those who persuade the growers to sell them their finest berries and so are able to contrive the best blends. (Some middlemen have ended up owning the vineyards themselves.) In Burgundy, with its small fragmented vineyards, the shipper's reputation usually carries as much weight as the wine itself. (One shipper there blends the wines of three hundred vintners and fourteen cooperatives.) Shippers, who are foreign, operate extensively in Italy, Spain and Madeira.

Tension is inevitable between the growers and the shippers. As one shipper asked rhetorically, "How many businesses are there that buy their raw materials for the entire year all in a four-week period?" Meanwhile the grower, parting with his grapes for relatively little, sees them disappear anonymously. "When I sold my grapes," one said, "they got blended into other people's wine and I didn't like that at all." Nor do the growers profit when wine prices rise or when their wines become expensive and rare.

A number of small growers have found it more satisfying both psychologically and financially to vinify, bottle and market their own wines. Some in Burgundy sell the bulk of their crop to shippers but hold back a percentage of the grapes for themselves. In Champagne, a number are working through cooperatives to produce their own sparkling wines.

Mechanization in wine making has now largely replaced human toil and primitive equipment. Research, experimentation and fast-changing technologies have made it possible to control virtually every aspect of the craft. The grower can plant higher yielding, more disease resistant vines. He can clone them to shorten their growing cycle. He can time his harvests scientifically and compensate for the vagaries of the weather. He can speed up the development of his wines and also accelerate their aging process.

A few traditional wine makers believe however that too much technology produces homogenized products. Relying on the slower age-old methods, they work to preserve the flavors provided by nature herself, seeking to create an environment in which the wine in effect can make itself. "Each time you touch a wine," one vintner says, "its quality decreases." Another states, "I call myself a noninterventionist. I let the fruit make the wine." A third adds, "I let the wine be what it is."

Concentrating on limited production and high quality, these wine makers don't use weed killers or chemical fertilizers, which they say destroy the soil's bacterial and microbial life. And they continue to handpick their grapes, noting that the harvesting machines bruise and spilt the softest berries while indiscriminately gathering the defective grapes along with the good ones. They point out that the machines pick up bits of foliage as well, giving the wines an odd leafy taste.

Traditionalists also rely more on natural yeasts to ferment their grapes spontaneously. Commercial cultured yeasts, they say, alter the wine. They note that the presence of wild yeasts is inevitable anyway, and that the harsh processing needed to remove them only diminishes the taste and character of the wine.

A current trend is to combine the patient, time-honored methods with the new scientific developments. One wine maker says, "I try to follow tradition with as much technology as possible." Another adds, "I believe in modern equipment and the latest machines but also in the old traditions." And a third declares, "If I have to use science, I use science, but my first preference goes to the art of wine making."

3

CHAMPAGNE AND OTHER SPARKLING WINES

Wine is classified in various ways: by its source—French, German, Italian, American, Swiss and so on; by its style—dry or sweet, light or full-bodied; by its function—dinner, cocktail (apéritif) or dessert; by its color; or by its CO_2 content. There are however only three basic types: still, sparkling and fortified. Still or table wines are produced by the processes previously described. Sparkling and fortified wines begin as still wines but they receive additional processing.

Champagne, originating in France, is the prototype of sparkling wines now made throughout the world. Some of these wines follow the unique vinification method developed by the French. Others do not. All reflect the specific climate and environment that produces them. The most distinctive feature they share is a lively effervescence that enhances them visually and gives them a delightful piquancy. The source of their exhilarating bubbles is the carbon dioxide they generate during fermentation. In still or table wines, the CO_2 escapes into the air and vanishes. Sparkling wines retain this charming effervescence.

Champagne captures its carbon dioxide in a remarkable way. During vinification, the cellar doors and windows of the winery are deliberately flung open at the end of November to admit the chill autumn air. This sends the yeasts into hibernation prematurely. The following spring, when the wine has settled down sufficiently to be tasted, it is blended, bottled and tightly sealed with a temporary cork. A metal clamp anchors that cork firmly in place.

The dormant yeasts, awakened by the warmth of spring, resume their normal activities inside the sealed bottle, splitting the sugar molecules in two, generating alcohol and carbon dioxide. The CO_2, trapped inside the bottle with no way to escape, is absorbed by the liquid, becoming part of the wine, but builds up considerable internal pressure—more than a hundred pounds per square inch. Uncorking the bottle eventually liberates the CO_2, which quickly reexpands and, in rising, forms the tiny bubbles that are the exhilarating fizz.

The great internal pressure at first caused the bottles to explode, hurling their shards throughout the cellars. People thought the wines were bewitched. Although thicker, more stress resistant bottles were eventually developed, many still continued to shatter. The culprit was finally identified as the natural sugar in the must. The more sugar, the more carbon dioxide generated, and the greater the pressure inside the bottle. Champagne vintners realized they could keep this pressure at safe levels by controlling the sugar levels in the wine. So they fermented out their wines completely dry, then, just before bottling, stirred in a precisely measured solution of cane sugar. This created the lively bubbles in the wine but not the unwanted explosiveness.

Sparkling wines came to prominence in the eighteenth century. Credited in large part with their development was Dom Pérignon, the blind cellarmaster at the Benedictine abbey of Hautvillers. Dom Pérignon was the first to introduce cold air into the cellars, the first to create the Champagne *cuvée* (or blend) and the first to bottle the still-fermenting wine. He also sealed the bottles with thick cork plugs that were able to withstand the fierce internal pressure of the volatile carbon dioxide.

In the classic *méthode champenoise*—the Champagne method —the wine never leaves its original bottle; the consumer buys it in the self-same bottle in which secondary fermentation has taken place. The steps in this intricate, labor-intensive process are: tierage, riddling, disgorging, adding the dosage and recorking.

Tierage stacks the bottles in deep underground vaults where the coolness and the quiet encourage the wine's gradual ripening. As it ages anywhere from one to six years on its yeasty deposit, enzymes break the yeast cells down in a process called autolysis. This liberates the various wine compounds while diminishing the acidity. Initially hard and even thin, the wine begins to fatten up, acquiring a depth of character and an extraordinary bouquet, developing a richness, lusciousness and finesse.

Champagne, like other wines, must be separated from its spent lees or sediment to ensure its stability. Conventional racking and fining would require opening the bottle and dissipating the bubbles. An ingenious technique known as riddling was devised instead to spirit out the unwanted sediment but not the fizz. Its inventor, Nicole Barbe-Clicquot, better known as Veuve Clicquot, was the widow of a nineteenth-century wine maker.

Riddling rotates the bottle systematically until its yeasty deposit has gradually shifted into the neck. The bottle is placed in a slotted A-shaped rack neck-forward, given a quick quarter-turn, rapped sharply and tilted slightly every day, then returned to its slot. Expert bottle turners, using both hands and working with astonishing speed, could twirl about thirty thousand bottles a day. More sophisticated racks have now increased the daily totals to some one hundred thousand bottles. After three months, the bottles stand neck-down in their slots with the sediment lodged compactly against their corks.

Disgorging then dips the bottle neck into a brine solution, which freezes the sediment into an icy lump. When the metal clamp holding the temporary cork is released, the bottle's internal pressure expels the cork. Flying out in one swift burst, it takes the clump of congealed sediment with it. The bottle meanwhile loses some of its wine, creating an ullage or small air space at the top. To protect the wine against excessive oxidation, this ullage must be eliminated. This is done by topping off the wine with a dosage syrup: a mixture of reserved wine, cane sugar and brandy. The dosage not only enhances the taste of the wine but also discourages any remaining viable yeasts from engaging in further fermentation.

Riddling

Once the dosage has been added, the bottle is swiftly resealed with a mushroom-shaped cork, which is anchored firmly in place with a wire hood or muzzle.

NOTE: To minimize any loss of fizz, the steps of disgorging, adding the dosage and recorking are carried out with dexterity and dispatch. They are also scheduled as close as possible to the wine's shipping date.

Since Champagne begins as a dry wine, the added dosage determines its final style. There are five classifications here. In ascending order of sweetness these are: brut, extra-sec, sec, demi-sec and doux. Never having been standardized, they vary from one Champagne maker to the next.

For *brut,* which translates as "unmodified" or "unrefined," the dosage ranges from no sugar at all to about 1.5 percent. (*Extra-brut* denotes a sugar level below 0.6 percent, while wines labeled *sans dosage, ultra brut, nature or naturel* usually have no added sugar at all.)

Extra-sec or *extra-dry,* often assumed to be the driest of Champagnes, can contain up to 2 percent sugar. *Sec,* despite translating as "dry," contains as much as 3.5 percent. *Demi-sec* has 4 to 6 percent, while *doux,* the sweetest of all, contains 6 to 10 percent sugar.

NOTE: Because of the current preference for dryness, demi-sec and doux Champagnes have virtually disappeared from the market.

Like the still wine from which it derives, Champagne develops best in large-sized bottles. The ideal size is the magnum, although the standard 750-milliliter bottle is physically easier to handle. Sparkling wines sold in tiny splits or in huge bottles are never directly fermented in them, but transferred there just before shipping.

Automation has modified the classic Champagne method in recent years. Mechanically operated or computerized riddling frames have replaced the dextrous bottle-turning workmen. Such devices can twirl as many as a thousand bottles at a time and work tirelessly around the clock. And assembly line machines are now freezing the sediment, extracting the temporary corks, adding the dosage and inserting the mushroom-shaped corks.

ALTERNATE SPARKLING METHODS

True Champagne, produced in the delimited Marne Valley region of France, accounts for less than 2 percent of the world's sparkling wines. The fully sparkling French wines made outside this zone are not called Champagnes but *vins mousseux. (Mousse* means bubbles.) Hundreds of other sparklers are made throughout the world, utilizing the Champagne method itself or faster, less expensive alternate techniques. These include the Charmat method, transfer method and direct carbonation.

The Charmat method, also known as the bulk method, autoclave method and *en cuvée close,* is responsible for most of the low-priced sparkling wines. Invented in 1910 by a French scientist, Eugene Charmat, the process ferments the wine in huge pressurized tanks rather than in individual bottles. After anywhere from six weeks to three months, the yeasts are filtered out and the wine is bottled.

The transfer method, somewhat closer to the méthode champenoise and more costly than the Charmat process, calls for secondary fermentation to occur in the bottle. But afterward the wine is transferred to a large, pressurized tank that preserves the effervescence while filtering out the yeasty sediment. It is then transferred to fresh bottles. Only a few wineries use this method.

The cheapest method is direct carbonation, which injects the wine quickly with carbon dioxide in the manner of soda pop.

Wines made by the classic Champagne method are more complex, significantly richer and more profoundly flavorful, with smaller, finer, more persistent bubbles. Those made by the alternate methods are generally simpler and less interesting, with quickly dissipating bubbles. Moreover, the latter undergo considerable oxidation as they are transferred from bottle to tank and from tank to bottle. This darkens their color, affects their taste and accelerates their aging process. Sulfur dioxide is usually added to counteract these undesirable effects.

The effervescence of a sparkling wine is measured in units called *atmospheres.* The atmospheres in Champagne range from 3 to 6; that is, the pressure inside the bottle is three to six times greater than that of the atmosphere outside. Wines with about half of Champagne's internal pressure are called *crémant* (creamy). Those with an internal pressure measuring 2 atmospheres or less are described as *pétillant;* theirs is a delicate fizziness.

NOTE: In addition, a faint spontaneous prickliness can be seen in wines that spend some time on their lees and in those bottled before malolactic fermentation has run its course. This short-lived fizziness is seen in the Muscadets of France, the vinho verdes of Portugal and the Lambruscos of Italy.

As it evolves in its closed container, a sparkling wine needs enough acidity to keep it from going flabby. White wines—inherently more acid than red wines—are best suited to the process. In the Champagne region, the wines derive their acidity from a chalky soil and a cool climate that ripens their grapes slowly. Wines which lend themselves beautifully to the *methode champenoise* are crisp, light and low in alcohol; they demonstrate both breed and delicacy.

OTHER SPARKLING WINES

Sparkling wines grown outside the delimited Champagne region reflect their own climates and locales. The other French sparkling wines are as varied as their base wines. Their largest source is the Loire Valley; more than half of the French sparklers come from the area around Saumur. The best examples, noted for their fine character and flavor, generally blend the chenin blanc and cabernet franc grapes. Vouvray, in the center of Touraine, is famous for its fruity, not-too-dry sparkling wines. Anjou to the west produces commendable sparkling rosés. The Côte de Blancs village of Cramant—just outside the Champagne zone—employs the same grape varieties and is noted for its Crémant de Cramant. St-Péray in the Rhône Valley yields a substantial golden sparkler, while the Clairette de Die produced to the south is made either sparkling or semisparkling. Savoie is celebrated for its sparkling Seysalls; Alsace produces a quite dry and delicate Crémant with a lovely bouquet. Limoux, a little town south of Carcassonne, produces a fine

Blanquette de Limoux a blend of the chenin blanc and local grape varieties.

In Italy, *spumante* literally means anything that bubbles. Fully sparkling wines here are the *spumantes,* those with a slight sparkle are the *frizzantes.* Best known is Asti Spumante, whose finest examples employ the Champagne method and are tart and dry. Most others are made by the Charmat process and tend to be on the sweet side. Spain's sparkling wines, called *vinos espumosos,* come from the Penedés region near Barcelona. Pressed entirely from indigenous grapes, these are typically full-flavored and fruity. When made by the Champagne method and aged on their yeasts at least nine months, they're called *cavas;* when made by the Charmat method, they're called *granvas.* Portugal is celebrated for its fresh, slightly sparkling vinho verdes, which are sometimes carbonated for export.

Germany's sparkling wines are called *schaumweins* or *sekts.* The finest, pressed from riesling grapes and following the classic Champagne method, are fruity, flowery and not too dry. Germany's lesser sparklers, made by the Charmat process, are often the overly acidy products of poor vintages, either chaptalized or bolstered with high-sugar wines. Most Soviet sparklers are made by the Charmat method and are produced in Georgia and the Ukraine. Some of the best originate in Odessa near the Black Sea.

The United States, employing the Champagne method and all of its alternates, relies on labrusca and hybrid grapes as well as on viniferas. New York State was an early leader in sparkling-wine production but California now dominates. (French Champagne firms, which own a number of California wineries, have brought over their own wine makers and enologists. Spanish firms are also producing sparkling wines in the state.) California often uses typical Champagne grapes, but harvests them while their sugars are still low and while their acids remain firm to offset the berries' natural richness. The sparkling wines here are typically more fruity than the French. In addition to appropriating the French terminology for dry, extra-dry, semidry and sweet, American wine makers indicate an absence of sweetness by labeling their wines "natural," "special reserve" or *"sehr trocken."*

NOTE: Sparkling wines made outside the Champagne zone

often have their grapes picked early to ensure lower sugars and firmer acids. Even when made by the classic method, they're usually bottled later, undergo secondary fermentation at warmer temperatures, spend less time on their yeasts and do not undergo the enriching autolysis process to the same degree. Such wines are usually fined and filtered as well.

Although red wines can also be made effervescent, they need slightly warmer fermentations and a greater degree of oxidation than do the whites. They also need a touch more sweetness to offset the slight bitterness created by the juxtaposition of their tannins with the carbon dioxide. Best known among the effervescent reds are the sparkling Burgundies. The finest of these, pressed from the pinot noir, follow the Champagne method and spend at least nine months on their yeasts. The French rosés made sparkling are known as pink Champagnes.

Italy's best red sparkler is a Nebbiolo Spumante, but more widely known is the somewhat sweet and spontaneously fizzy red Lambrusco. For export, the Lambruscos are generally made effervescent either by the Charmat method or by direct carbonation. Portugal is celebrated for its naturally effervescent rosés. These, however, are often carbonated for export.

4

FORTIFIED
WINES

Fortified wines are generally high-sugar wines strengthened by the addition of alcohol. The fortification process was "invented" by the British and other northern Europeans who added alcohol to the Mediterranean products they were importing, enabling those wines to survive the rigors of sea travel. Fortification not only stabilized the wines and prevented their spoilage in shipping, but greatly enhanced their character and extended their longevity as well. As the wine slowly assimilated the added alcohol—a high-proof spirit, usually brandy—it developed a more intense flavor, a vinous aroma and a mouth-comforting warmth. Neutral spirits may also be used, but since they are more readily absorbed and faster acting, the wines they strengthen are never as complex or as interesting.

Determining the dryness or sweetness of a fortified wine is the point at which the alcohol is added. Introduced at the start of fermentation, the alcohol inactivates the yeasts, leaving more residual sugar behind. Added midway, it balances out the sugars that have been converted with the sugars that have not. When the alcohol is added after fermentation has run its course, the wine remains bone-dry.

The best-known fortified wines are ports, sherries and Madeiras, along with vermouths and Marsalas. These vary considerably in their base wines as well as in their processing.

PORT

In the fifteenth century, Portuguese fishermen casting for cod off the coast of England bartered their red wines for the sturdy British woolen goods they coveted. Those red wines, produced under a strong sun in the Douro Valley, were full-bodied, fruity and generous. When war with France deprived the British of their customary clarets, enterprising English merchants purchased the Douro wine in bulk and fortified it for the turbulent journey across the Atlantic. They named the wine port for Oporto, the Portuguese town of its origin.

Fortification not only made port stout and bracing, it created an intensity of flavor, a delightful aroma and a sweetness that did not cloy. Serving as a perfect antidote to Britain's damp, chilly climate, port soon became a national drink. George Saintsbury, a nineteenth-century fancier of the wine, defined its appeal when he said, "It strengthens as it gladdens as no other wine can do."

Port wines range from off-dry to sweet. After fermenting for several days, the still-active must is racked into casks containing a predetermined amount of brandy (usually 1 part brandy to 4 parts wine). This halts fermentation, allowing the wine to retain some of its natural sugar. During the winter months, the wine settles down, precipitating out its heavier impurities. In the spring, when it falls bright, it is racked into fresh casks and sent downriver to the shippers' lodges at Vila Nova de Gaia. (Picturesque sailing boats once carried the wine downriver but trucks are now the main form of transport.) Arriving at the lodges, the wine is tasted, blended, aged and further fortified according to its desired type and style.

Although port wines vary considerably in sweetness, color and alcohol content, there are only two basic types: those aged primarily in wood—which constitute the majority—and those aged primarily in glass. Wood-aged ports are ready to drink when bottled; bottle-aged ports usually need additional time to mature. Since the bottle-aged wines undergo less oxidation, they're generally more subtle.

The basic wooded ports are ruby and tawny. Both are drawn from a number of harvests and blended to achieve a certain house style. Ruby, the simplest and least expensive, is made up of predominantly younger wines and spends three years or less in the cask. Retaining much of its bright red color, it exhibits a brash, grapelike freshness and a youthful aroma. Ruby ports range from dry to semisweet.

Tawny port spends anywhere from three years to several decades in the cask. As it sheds its pigments, the wine gradually evolves in color from a deep, youthful ruby to a tawny, golden brown. Slowly oxidizing in wood, tawny port becomes lighter, smoother and more delicate, with a lingering aftertaste. The wines aged longest in wood achieve an optimum balance of vivacity and flavor, becoming more complex and liqueurlike. Lesser tawnies are produced by blending ruby and white ports together.

NOTE: A rare variant is Colheita Port, drawn from a single vintage and generally not released until it has spent ten to thirty years in wood.

More complex styles include Vintage Port and its variants. Vintage Port, which accounts for less than 5 percent of the annual port output, is the most expensive and rarest of the wines. Known as the "Queen of Ports," it's pressed from the grapes of a single outstanding harvest. Although spending its first two years in wood, it is primarily bottle-aged. It is in glass that its tannins slowly disintegrate and form a heavy interior crust on which the wine ripens gently. Coarse at first with an astringency that masks its sweetness, the wine gradually gains in character and subtlety, attaining a firmness of structure, an intensity of color, a concentrated, fruity flavor and a highly complex bouquet. The finest Vintage Ports achieve lusciousness, balance, and breed. The wines need a minimum of ten to twenty years to mature; the greatest do not reveal their qualities for at least fifteen years. Some have improved over three or four decades and have survived more than a century.

NOTE: In Britain it was the custom to lay down some bottles of Vintage Port at the birth of a son. Some twenty years later when the lad had attained his majority, the wine had also matured and was ready to drink.

The more affordable variants of Vintage Port differ in their vintage requirements and in the time they spend in wood and glass. These are Late-Bottled Vintage Port (LBV), Vintage Character Port, Single Quinta Port and Crusted Port. LBV and Vintage Character

Ports are ruby ports that seek to capture the flavor and style of a true Vintage but bear only a passing resemblance to it. LBV is the wine of a single year. Although not of vintage quality, it is good enough to merit a separate bottling and spends at least four—and no more than six—years in the cask, where it precipitates out most of its sediment. It is ready to drink when bottled.

Vintage Character Port is a blend of LBVs. Throwing a crust in the cask during wood-aging, the wine becomes ripe and flavorful. Ready to drink when bottled, it has been called the "Vintage Port for the Impatient." There is also Port of the Vintage, a single-vintage wine aged in wood and usually lighter and tawnier than either an LBV or a Vintage Character Port.

Single Quinta Port is a wine aged primarily in glass. Grown in a high-quality vineyard and drawn from one or a number of harvests, it forms a crust in the bottle as does the Vintage Port. Crusted Port is drawn from several vineyards and from several vintages, making it in effect a ruby port treated like a Vintage Port. After spending a few years in wood, it is aged about four years in glass and forms a heavy crust during its time in the bottle.

Other Douro wines are Porto Seco and White Port. Porto Seco, as its name implies, is fermented out completely dry before fortification. White Port, pressed from white grapes and matured in wood, is amber-colored and usually reserved for blending. The wine may be vinified bone-dry or made medium-sweet. The Scandinavians and other northern Europeans serve the light, dry version as a chilled apéritif.

SHERRY

The English discovered sherry while purchasing salt at the Spanish ports of Cádiz and Sanlúcar de Barrameda. After fortification, the wine proved so suited to the British climate and temperament that, like port, it also became a national drink.

Sherry's vinification is unique. The wine is deliberately oxidized, set out-of-doors in loosely stoppered casks and never topped off at all. It is then further exposed to air in the solera system, where it is siphoned from cask to cask. Such excessive aeration would ruin any other wine, but sherry is protected by *flor* (flower), a unique and remarkable yeast. Indigenous to southern Spain and multiplying vigorously in the warmth of Andalusia, flor forms a deep, soft, creamy crust, which floats on the surface of the wine like a water lily. Acting as a barrier against both overoxidation and spoilage organisms, the yeast not only keeps the wine from turning vinegar, but also makes possible its slow and gradual aeration, giving sherry a delightful, nutlike flavor and aroma and a gently bitter "rancio" taste. The flor is also largely responsible for the lovely bouquet of the wine.

Sherries are ruggedly individualistic. Some are affected by flor, others hardly at all. In December, after fermenting out most of their grape sugar, the wines are ready for their first classification (flor or nonflor). Those most affected by flor become the *finos;* those with scant flor or none at all become the *olorosos.* Because of the yeast's unpredictability, the wines are continually classified and reclassified. Sampling them periodically, the blender chalks their appropriate symbol on the head of each cask. (Since the casks in the solera are not always stacked in strict chronological order, this means of identifying them is essential.)

The fino category is subdivided into three subgroups: manzanilla, fino and amontillado. The manzanillas, the crispest and lightest sherries, are grown in the vicinity of Sanlúcar de Barrameda, a fishing village on the Atlantic coast. Exposed to the bracing sea air, they are fresh, dry and almost salty in taste; sometimes they are so pale in color as to be almost clear. The fino sherries, also light, dry and delicate, range in color from white to pale gold and on to amber. They are distinguished by a crisp, clean taste, a light but pungent nutty aroma and a refreshing, somewhat sharp finish, which has been described as the "tongue-on-stone."

NOTE: When a cask of manzanilla is brought inland, the wine becomes less dry and austere. Conversely, when a Jerez fino is transferred to Sanlúcar de Barrameda where it's exposed to the crisp sea breezes, it acquires a distinctly manzanilla taste and aroma.

Amontillados are mature finos whose flor has mysteriously disappeared. Medium in body, topaz in color and ranging from very dry to medium-dry, these wines are characterized by an intense vinosity coupled with a robust, nutty flavor. Becoming more concentrated, darker, firmer and more pungently aromatic with age, they acquire a rich, penetrating bouquet that suggests ripe tropical fruit, smoked almonds and roasted walnuts.

NOTE: A number of commonplace sherries have appropriated the *amontillado* name but possess none of the charms of the authentic version.

The olorosos, possessing less flor than finos, lack an effective shield against the wine's characteristic oxidation and so undergo a greater interaction with the air. Picking up more color and flavor from their casks as well, they become coarser, darker, more full bodied and quite fragrant. In fact, they're the most aromatic of the sherries. (*Oloroso* translates as agreeable odor.) The oldest, finest examples are concentrated, dark and pungent, with richly satisfying flavors.

NOTE: Whereas some olorosos are vinified completely dry, others are sweetened with an intense liqueurlike wine made by adding brandy to the juice of raisined pedro ximénez (or PX) grapes. Lesser olorosos are sweetened with a *mosto apogado,* the boiled-down concentrate of lesser grapes.

Oloroso sherries range from dry to off-dry and often seem sweeter than they actually are because of their heightened levels of glycerine, which create an opulent effect. Olorosos range in color from honeylike to a rich, dark chestnut or mahogany. Some acquire an amberlike hue with the addition of *vino de color,* a thick concentrated, reddish black syrup produced by slowly boiling down the juice of raisined PX grapes.

The oloroso group is subdivided into amoroso, brown and cream sherries. *Amoroso* is medium-dry and relatively light bodied. Brown sherry is rich, walnut-colored and lusciously sweet, with a full-bodied nuttiness. Cream sherry is golden brown, highly concentrated, full-bodied and vinous—almost viscous in texture, with a raisinlike or prunelike taste. The best cream sherries are sweetened judiciously.

Other variants are Palo Cortado, Pale Dry Sherry, Pale Cream Sherry, Golden Sherry and Solera Sherry. Palo Cortado, somewhere between an amontillado and an oloroso, combines the bouquet of the former with the fuller flavor of the latter. Although drier and leaner than the olorosos, Palo Cortado nevertheless possesses a full-bodied style and an aged nose. Pale Dry Sherry a blend of fairly undistinguished wines, is not completely dry despite its name. Pale Cream Sherry, lighter in color than Cream Sherry, is not very sweet, whereas Golden Sherry is decidedly so. Solera Sherry—misleadingly named, since all true sherries pass through a solera system—is dark, heavy and usually quite sweet.

MADEIRA

Madeira was a rough, rather ordinary fortified wine serving as an item of sea trade in the eighteenth century. When an unsold shipment was returned from the East Indies, the wine proved surprisingly splendid. Transformed by its long months of travel in the hold of the sailing ship, it had improved dramatically. The rocking and pitching on the high seas had accelerated its oxidation, and the tropical heat had caramelized its residual sugar. The wine acquired a deep golden color, a wonderful softness, a smooth texture and an attractively bittersweet taste.

The Madeira vintners began sending their wines to sea so that these too could experience the enveloping heat and the rolling motion and pitching of the ships. (The casks often acted as ballast for transoceanic shipping.) Soon, sailing vessels from England and the United States were making unscheduled stops at Madeira to pick up casks of the wine, stowing them away in their holds to ripen.

Eventually, the Madeira vintners learned to re-create the seagoing conditions on land. They baked the new wine in specially heated chambers called *estufades,* gradually increasing the temperatures to about 110°F then slowly letting them drop back to normal. This enabled the wines to achieve the desirable smoky quality and attractive caramel-like flavor they had acquired at sea.

The Madeira wines differ in their variety of grapes and their degree of ripeness, as well as in their vinification methods. Ranging in color from pale straw to an almost blackish brown, they are either fermented quite dry or allowed to retain a degree of natural sweetness. There are four types of Madeira: Sercial, Verdelho, Malmsey and Bual. Malmsey and Bual come from the lower costal vineyards where the grapes are gathered in early September. Sercial and Verdelho come from a high volcanic plateau in the cooler north where the grapes mature somewhat later and are also late-harvested to concentrate their sweetness.

Sercial, the leanest and lightest-colored wine, is crisp and dry. It displays at its finest an extraordinary fragrance and bouquet. *Verdelho,* medium-dry and a bit darker, is softer, more fruity and quite fragrant, with a faintly honeyed sweetness. A variant known as *Rainwater* is a blend of fairly light Verdelhos, developed by a Savannah, Georgia, wine importer in the nineteenth century. Pale in color, it is vinified both dry and medium-sweet. Bual and Malmsey are the sweetest Madeiras. *Bual* (*Boal* in Portuguese) is a shade darker, sweeter and more full bodied than Verdelho, combining a fragrant, lovely bouquet with a fresh, clean, bittersweet aftertaste. *Malmsey,* the sweetest, richest and darkest of all, is luscious and velvety with a great fragrant bouquet. This wine is generously spirited and long-lived.

VERMOUTH

Vermouth is a flavored as well as a fortified wine. The custom of flavoring wines goes back to ancient times, when flowers, leaves, roots, bark, herbs and spices were added to improve the palatability of the unaged, coarse and rough wines then made. The Sumerians, Egyptians and Greeks all flavored their wines to make them more drinkable. The Romans modified them with honey and flavored them with spices and with roasted date pits.

Herb-infused wines have long been associated with the healing arts. In the fourth century B.C., Hippocrates administered such a wine; in the Middle Ages, apothecaries dispensed a similarly prepared "hippocras." In the seventeenth century, flavored wines were taken as antidotes against the plague. And in the alpine regions of France and Italy, where herbs and aromatics grow in profusion, farm women still add them to wine to create various home remedies.

Vermouth gets its name from one of its principal flavorings, wormwood—*wermut* in German—a woody herb with slightly aromatic blossoms, which imparts a characteristically wry taste and a slightly bitter tang. Other flavoring agents include minty hyssop, bitter orange, angostura, cardamon, nutmeg, vanilla beans, cloves, allspice, cinnamon, cinchona bark, quinine bark, sweet marjoram, rosemary, sage, savory, thyme, hops, saffron, angelica, gentian root, cassia wood, linden tea, wild strawberries and rhubarb.

A typical vermouth formula calls for about fifteen flavorings, although as many as fifty have been employed. Characterizing the best examples is a well-balanced flavor rather than the predominance of any one ingredient. Most formulas are privately held; some are so closely guarded that they're handed down as proprietary secrets only within the family.

The base wines for vermouths—either white or red—are generally undistinguished since vermouth's character derives mainly from its botanicals and aromatics. The flavorings are introduced by either maceration or infusion. Maceration slowly steeps the flavorings in a small amount of wine to produce a concentrate, which is then added to the base wine. Infusion adds the flavorings directly to the wine. After these ingredients have flavored several batches, they are replaced with fresh ones. (Lesser vermouths steep their aromatics in a high-proof alcohol to speed up the flavor-extracting process.)

NOTE: Quality vermouths are aged two to four years; lesser vermouths aren't aged at all, but are filtered or pasteurized.

The wines are vinified both dry and sweet. The lighter-bodied dry vermouths contain 2 to 4 percent sugar; the sweet, as much as 14 to 16 percent. Dry vermouths are generally quite pale, but their pallor is not necessarily a sign of quality. (Charcoal filtering often lightens the wines.) France is generally associated with the dry vermouths and Italy with the sweet, although each country produces them both. The French use rather dry acidic wines, such as thin Heraults from the Midi and lesser Sauternes. (They enhance and round out their best examples with *mistelle,* a sweet concentrate that combines brandy and unfermented grape juice.) The Italians use muscat wines and produce somewhat rounder, more direct vermouths. The Italian versions are available in four styles: *secco* (dry white), *bianco* (sweet white), *rosso* (semisweet red) and *rosé* (semidry rosé).

Vermouths are now produced all over the world: in Spain, Portugal, South Africa, Australia, South America and the United States. They range widely in both their base wines and in their flavorings.

MARSALA

Marsala acquired its name from Mash-el-Allah—Arabic for "Haven of God"—the Sicilian port from which the wine was first shipped. (Sicily had long been under Arab domination.)

Marsala began as a potent but generally undistinguished wine produced under a hot Mediterranean sun. When a Liverpool merchant added brandy to prevent its spoilage in shipping, the wine acquired a rich full flavor and a sherrylike texture. The British, looking for fortified alternatives to the more expensive ports and sherries, began to import Marsala in quantity. In the process, they refined and modernized its production. By the mid-nineteenth century, Marsala had become another British favorite.

Straw-colored at first, the wine often acquires a deep brown color. It may be vinified relatively dry or sweetened with a grape concentrate. Traditionally, Marsala is fortified with *sifone* or *mistella,* a mixture of distilled wine alcohol and the must of nearly overripe grapes aged in wood for several months.

Marsala is made in several styles: *fini, superiori, and vergini.* The fines and superiores are sweetened with *mosto cotto,* a syrup of boiled-down grape must. *Fini* Marsala, containing 5 percent sugar, is aged in wood for at least a year. (It is used mainly in cooking.) *Superiori,* which may contain as much as 10 percent sugar, is aged for two years and serves as a dessert wine. (A special superiori, Vino da Meditazione, full-bodied, semisweet and silky, includes in its blend reserve wines dating back to the last century.) *Vergini,* the highest quality, is an entirely unsweetened wine brought up to 18 percent alcohol by fortification and aged for at least five years. Its excellence is due in part to its passage through a solera system. (It is also known as *soleras* and *vino perpetuo.*) *Stravecchio* or *riserva vergini* is wine that has been aged in a solera for a decade.

5

HISTORY AND
GEOGRAPHY

INTRODUCTION

Historians have traced the grape to a site in Asia Minor between the Black and Caspian Seas. They have dated the origins of wine making to sometime between 6000 and 4000 B.C.

Both the Old and New Testaments frequently allude to wine. In Judaism, wine is used to consecrate the sabbath. In Christianity, it sanctifies the Eucharist. (Although the Koran, the bible of Islam, permits grape cultivation, it forbids the drinking of wine.)

The Persians, Hebrews, Egyptians, Greeks, Etruscans and Romans all established their own vineyards. A Sumerian epic tells of an enchanted place whose wine made the drinker immortal. Grape seeds and wine jars have been found in Egyptian tombs dating back to 3000 B.C. or so. (The wine was apparently intended for the pharaohs' refreshment in the afterlife.) The Greeks spread wine making along with their culture throughout the Mediterranean region in the fourth century B.C., bringing the practice to Sicily, Italy, the Iberian peninsula and southern Gaul.

Subsequently the Roman legions, invading as far north as the Rhine and eastward along the Danube, planted vineyards wherever they went. Wine sustained the morale of the troops and comforted officials far from home. Virgil noted that the wines of Greece and Rome were as innumerable as the grains of sand in the sea.

Demonstrating that the grape could flourish in a wide range of soils and climates, the Romans established the foundations of some of the world's greatest wine regions. By the second century A.D., the broad outlines of French and German viticulture were already evident.

During the Middle Ages, wine making was largely an ecclesiastic activity. "Wherever a monk may go, a vine is sure to grow," was the saying then. Through decades of trial and error, the monks became greatly skilled at grape cultivation and wine making; in Burgundy and Germany, the church developed some of the world's finest vineyards.

The returning crusaders planted vines brought back from the Middle East as souvenirs, introducing a number of new grape varieties to Europe. During the Renaissance, wine was the symbol of the power of the princes. In the seventeenth and eighteenth centuries, kings and nobles gave their royal approval to the wines of Champagne and Burgundy, raising them to great prominence. In the eighteenth and nineteenth centuries, Europeans of considerable wealth acquired their own vineyards. The rise of great banking and industrial fortunes early in the nineteenth century enabled their owners to invest in the famous Bordeaux châteaus. Less fortunate citizens, seeking a better life, migrated to North and South America, South Africa, Australia and New Zealand, bringing their wine-making skills along with their meager possessions to these new lands.

Wine is now a vital element in the economy of many nations. The largest producers are Italy, France, Russia, Spain, Argentina and Chile. (Italy and France alone account for about half of the world's wine production.) Other prolific countries are the United States and Portugal. Wine making also plays a significant role in the economies of Germany, Switzerland, Hungary, the former Yugoslavia, Romania, Greece, Bulgaria and Israel. It is practiced as well in South Africa, Australia, New Zealand, Syria, Turkey, Algeria, Morocco, Egypt, Mexico, Russia, Brazil and Uruguay.

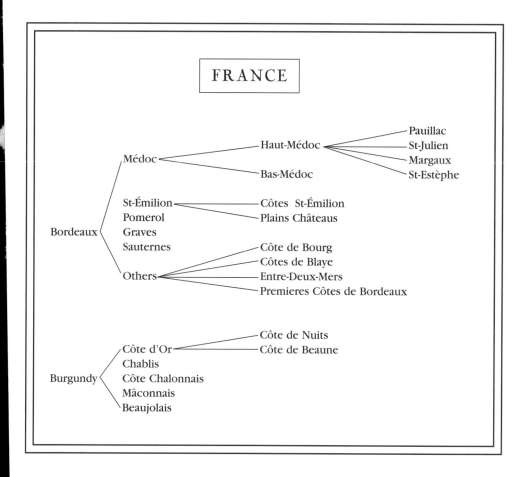

FRANCE

France produces some of the world's most magnificent wines, along with countless commonplace ones. The Romans, on their arrival, found southern Gaul already engaged in viticulture. (The Phoenicians had planted muscat vines near what is now Marseilles; grape growing subsequently moved north through the Rhône Valley into Alsace.) The Romans disseminated the grape further, planting vines in Burgundy, the Loire Valley and Champagne. As admiration for the wines of Gaul grew, those of Rome began to lose favor. In A.D. 92 the Roman emperor Domitian issued an edict called for uprooting all vineyards north of the Alps. That edict was only partially heeded.

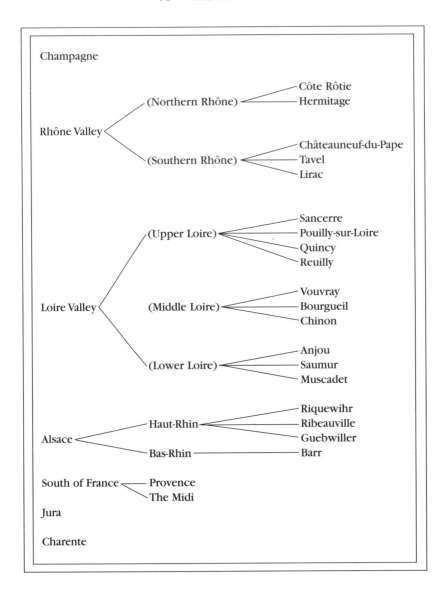

Champagne

Rhône Valley
- (Northern Rhône)
  - Côte Rôtie
  - Hermitage
- (Southern Rhône)
  - Châteauneuf-du-Pape
  - Tavel
  - Lirac

Loire Valley
- (Upper Loire)
  - Sancerre
  - Pouilly-sur-Loire
  - Quincy
  - Reuilly
- (Middle Loire)
  - Vouvray
  - Bourgueil
  - Chinon
- (Lower Loire)
  - Anjou
  - Saumur
  - Muscadet

Alsace
- Haut-Rhin
  - Riquewihr
  - Ribeauville
  - Guebwiller
- Bas-Rhin
  - Barr

South of France
- Provence
- The Midi

Jura

Charente

French wine growing now covers more than three million acres, stretching from the sunny south, where it began, to the cooler regions northeast of Paris. (In the south, the country is warmed by Mediterranean breezes; in the north, it is chilled by austere winds from the Atlantic Ocean.) French wine growing encompasses seven major regions: Bordeaux, Burgundy, Champagne, Alsace, the Rhône Valley, the Loire Valley and the South of France.

BORDEAUX

Bordeaux in southwestern France, with more than two hundred thousand vineyard acres under cultivation, is the country's largest and most important wine region. Its earliest champions were the Romans. Julius Caesar himself admired its wines and the poet Ausonius once owned a vineyard here.

Bordeaux takes its name from its port city, located on the banks of the Gironde River. (The Gironde, a broad estuary formed by the confluence of the Garonne and Dordogne Rivers, flows in a north-westerly direction to the Bay of Biscay and out into the Atlantic Ocean.) Although the city itself is located fifty miles inland, the Gironde River has made it into a major port, giving the citizens of Bordeaux easy access to the outside world and helping the region's wines to become widely known.

However, it was the English and not the French, who were largely responsible for the fame of the Bordeaux wines. In 1152, when Eleanor, daughter of the French Duke of Aquitaine, married Henry Plantagenet of England, her dowry included the province of Gascony, which encompassed all of Bordeaux. Two years later, when Henry ascended to the throne of England, Gascony became a possession of the British Crown. The English, producing virtually no wines of their own, were enchanted by the red wines of Bordeaux, admiring their bright ruby color and sumptuous bouquet. They called them *clarets*. (*Clairet* is French for clear.) By the fourteenth century, nearly half the Bordeaux wines were shipped to England, duty free.

When the French reclaimed their territory in 1453, some Britons stayed on as wine merchants and exporters. The French, however, tightly circumscribed their activities. The English were not allowed to live inside the city walls nor to establish their offices there. Permitted to enter only between the hours of sunrise and sunset, they set up outposts on the Quai des Chartrons, a three-mile stretch along the Garonne River. Through their energy and enterprise, the British amassed considerable wealth and power. Through intermarriage, they acquired land of their own. By the nineteenth century, a number of Bordeaux vineyards were carrying such Anglo-Saxon names as Lynch-Bages, Talbot and Langoa Barton.

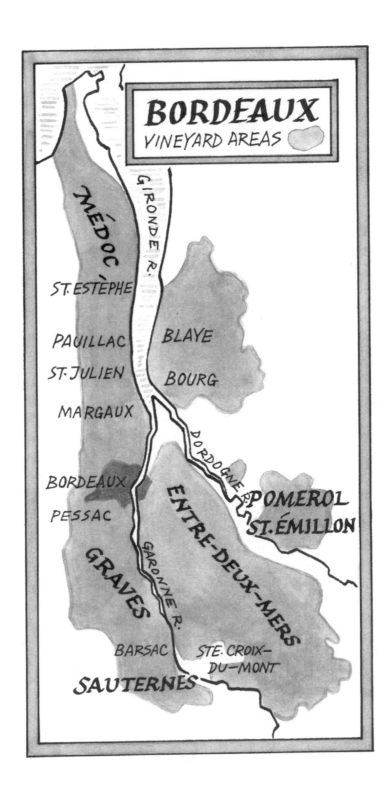

The Bordelais adopted the English law of inheritance, which was to influence their grape growing and wine making. French law divided a father's property among all his children, but English law passed the estate on to the eldest child, leaving the large vineyards relatively intact. Many are still extensive, averaging one hundred to two hundred acres and giving wine making a greater continuity and consistency here than elsewhere in the country.

Bordeaux wines cover a wide gamut, ranging from the acclaimed offerings of the great estates to uncomplicated and even inconsequential products. The region's northern sector specializes largely in red wines, the southern in white wines, while the central sector produces both. The red wines blend the austere cabernet sauvignon with the merlot, cabernet franc, malbec and petit verdot. Uncompromisingly rough when young, these wines at their finest possess the ability to age magnificently. While retaining a basic austerity, they acquire at maturity a rich plummy depth of flavor, a black currant bouquet and a lingering aftertaste. The white wines—pressed from the sauvignon blanc, sémillon, and muscadelle—are also full-bodied and flavorful. They range from the steely whites of Graves to the luscious noble rots of Sauternes.

The most significant of Bordeaux's thirty-five wine districts are the Médoc, St-Émilion, Pomerol, Graves and Sauternes.

The Médoc

The Médoc, a large peninsula on the west bank of the Gironde, extends some fifty miles north of the city of Bordeaux almost to the point where the river flows into the Atlantic. Well over half of the best French vineyards are located here. Its southern sector is the Haut-Médoc, a long strip of gently rolling land. Produced here are some of the world's most elegant and complex wines, characterized by great charm and finesse, by rich fruit and fragrance. The smaller northern sector, the Bas-Médoc—whose terrain is flatter—produces wines with less concentration and of lesser interest. (References to Médoc wines are usually to the wines of the Haut-Médoc.)

Of the twenty-eight wine-producing townships or communes in the Médoc, the largest and most prestigious is Pauillac, located some thirty miles north of the city of Bordeaux. Pauillac is notable for the subtlety, intensity and elegance of its red wines. Its top estates, sited on alluvial slopes above the Gironde estuary, are the world-famous Châteaus Lafite-Rothschild, Latour and Mouton-Rothschild. Their wines, unsurpassed in magnificence and refinement, combine a great generosity with an underlying intensity and the assured potential of great age. Traditionally, Mouton wines are the most robust and Latours the softest, while the Lafites demonstrate a fine balance between powerful tannins and excellent fruit. Other major Pauillac estates are the Châteaus Pichon-Lalande, Pichon-Baron, Clerc-Milon, Lynch-Bages and Pontet-Canet.

The communes following Pauillac in their concentration of high-quality vineyards are St-Estèphe to the north, St-Julien directly to the south, and Margaux farther south.

St-Èstephe, the northernmost, brings forth on its claylike soil the sturdiest and most robust reds of the Médoc. Harder and less yielding than the Pauillacs, they are rough-edged and tannic at the start but at maturity they acquire a superb concentration and richness of flavor. They are also quite long lived.

Margaux, the southernmost of the top Médoc communes, features the thinnest soil and the highest proportion of rough gravel. Its red wines, remarkable for their delicacy and elegance, are at their finest silky, yet intensely powerful. They display a lovely ethereal quality and a haunting violetlike bouquet. Margaux also produces an exquisite white wine in small quantities.

St-Julien, the smallest of the key Médoc communes, yields some of the district's most approachable wines; they are never harsh or tannic. Fuller than the Margaux and faster-maturing than the Pauillacs, these are medium-bodied and well knit, generous in their fruit, and ready to drink at a fairly young age. St-Julien's best-known vineyard is Château Ducru-Beaucaillou, whose name translates as "Beautiful Pebbles," a reference to its generally gravelly soil.

Other significant Médoc communes are Moulis, Cantenac and Listrac. Moulis, located between Margaux and St-Julien, produces dependable, well-balanced red wines, firm at first but possessing the ability to age well. The outstanding Moulis vineyard is Château Chasse-Spleen, translating roughly as "Chasing the Blues Away." Cantenac adjoins Margaux. Its wines, which share some of the same delicacy and grace, are often labeled "Cantenac-Margaux." Listrac, north of Moulis, long associated with ordinary wines, is now the site of Château Clarke, an estate created by Baron Edmond de Rothschild and his son Benjamin, who transformed the arid and unprepossessing acreage here into a notable vineyard.

St-Émilion

The most productive of the top Bordeaux districts, St-Émilion, is located on the right bank of the Dordogne some twenty-five miles east of the city of Bordeaux. Its soil, almost the reverse of the Médoc's, is a heavy, generally gravelly stretch of sand covered by clay and chalky limestone. Its predominant grape is the softer merlot, not the austere cabernet sauvignon of the Médoc.

St-Émilion's wines, generally a blend of the merlot, cabernet franc and bouschet, are the heartiest of the great red Bordeaux. Sturdy, supple and generous, rounder and more approachable than the Médocs, they display a great depth of color along with a spicy fullness. Nicely balancing their roundness is a degree of flintiness.

The relatively small vineyards here, clustered around the ancient town of St-Émilion, are divided into an inner group called Côtes St-Émilion and an outer group called the Plains Châteaus. Côtes St-Émilion is situated on the mostly chalky slopes of a rocky plateau adjacent to the town. The preeminent estate here is Château Ausone, named for Ausonius, the fourth-century Roman poet who once owned the property. Other notable inner-group estates are the Châteaus Canon, La Magdelaine, La Gaffelière, Pavie, Clos Fourtet, Bel-Air and Beauséjour. The outer Plains Châteaus are located on a gravelly plain below the town. Other notable estates here are the Chateaus Figeac, La Tour-du-Pin, Croque-Michotte, Corbin, and Dominique–St-Émilion.

Five small villages nearby and a portion of a sixth are legally permitted to append St-Émilion's name to their own although their wines share neither St-Émilion's exposure nor the quality of its wines. These five villages are St-Georges–St-Émilion, Montagne–St-Émilion, Sables–St-Émilion, Puisseguin–St-Émilion, Lussac–St-Émilion and Parsac–St-Émilion.

Pomerol

The tiny commune of Pomerol, the smallest fine-wine district in Bordeaux, consists of only some two thousand acres and is tucked in as an appendage of St-Émilion. Long considered a satellite of St-Émilion, Pomerol declared its autonomy early in the twentieth century to become an official wine district of its own.

The predominant grape variety here, as in St-Émilion, is the merlot, grown on somewhat sandier soil and producing some of the Médoc's most accessible wines. Although similar in structure, taste and bouquet, these at their finest are richer, more robust, rounder and more plummy wines. The French say they have more *gras* (fatness) than the other Médocs. Pomerol's wines also display a lustrous dark ruby color, a violet bouquet and a remarkable trufflelike scent. The leading estate here is Château Pétrus.

Three nearby communes of interest are Fronsac to the west and Lalande-de-Pomerol and Néac to the north. Fronsac, on the banks of the Dordogne, is known for its robust, deep-colored reds, which display a great softness of body and fruit. Its notable properties are Côtes de Fronsac and Canon-Fronsac; the latter is best known for its Château Canon wine. Lalande-de-Pomerol, which is separated from Pomerol by a small stream, shares the same sandy soil but not quite the same exposure. Its somewhat lighter red wines lack the concentration and consistent quality of their more esteemed neighbors. Neac's wines are generally ordinary but on occasion they bear a passing resemblance to those of Pomerol.

Graves

Directly south of the Médoc is Graves, named for its characteristically gravellike soil. Because of its more southerly location, the grapes here ripen earlier than those of the Médoc. Their wines, however, are so similar in breed and finesse that they're often mistaken for the Médocs. Velvety and quite dry, they are remarkable for their dark, brilliant color, their subtlety of character and their long life.

The most outstanding commune in Graves is Pessac, home of the world-famous Château Haut-Brion. Of almost comparable importance is Château La Mission–Haut-Brion, an estate located just across the road and under the same ownership. To the south-west is Château Pape-Clément, known for its high-quality red wines, which are generally somewhat lighter in color.

Graves also produces many fine white wines, ranging from fairly dry to medium-sweet. The best of these display a richness and depth combined with a long, lingering aftertaste. Enhancing them further is a faint yet distinctive metallic edge. The most celebrated white-wine estates in Graves are the Châteaus Carbonnieux and Olivier.

NOTE: Many notable Graves vineyards produce both red and white wines. Château Haut-Brion, best known for its reds, devotes about a tenth of its output to whites. Château Carbonnieux, best known for its whites, yields good red wines as well. Other red-and-white vineyards are located in Martillac, a commune to the south.

S a u t e r n e s

Sauternes, located on the west bank of the Garonne River about twenty miles south of the city of Bordeaux, is the southernmost of the major Bordeaux districts. Specializing in white wines, it grows sémillon, sauvignon blanc and muscadelle grapes. Sauternes is named for one of its five top communes; the others are Barsac, Pommes, Preignac and Fargues. An area of gently rolling hills and misty low-lands, the district covers about forty square miles.

Sauternes is particularly celebrated for its noble rot wines, the quintessential example coming from Château d'Yquem, an estate situated on one of its highest hills. A wine of luscious splendor, described as "pure gold by the glass," Château d'Yquem exhibits an astonishing fullness of body and depth of vinosity. A lovely subtle perfume balances out its opulent richness. Another outstanding botrytized wine comes from Château Rieussec in the commune of Fragues.

Directly north of Sauternes is the larger commune of Barsac, growing the same grape varieties and employing the same vinifi-cation methods. Barsac's wines tend to be a shade drier, somewhat more austere and a bit less concentrated.

NOTE: In years when the grapes don't achieve their botrytized ripeness and yield drier, more ordinary wines, Château d'Yquem labels them "Y" and Château Rieussec labels them "R."

Other Bordeaux Districts

Located directly across the Gironde from the Médoc are two other red-wine districts: Côte de Bourg and the larger Côtes de Blaye to the north. Growing mainly the cabernet franc on their fertile high-clay soils, these districts produce light-colored, fruity, unpretentious and quick-maturing wines. Côtes de Blaye also produces some white wines.

Across the Garonne from Graves and Sauternes are a number of primarily white wine districts. One is Entre-Deux-Mers (whose name translates as "Between Two Seas"). A large triangular wedge formed by the confluence of the Garonne and Dordogne Rivers, Entre-Deux-Mers grows sémillon and sauvignon blanc grapes. Its naturally sweet wine, somewhat similar to a simple Sauternes, is now often vinified dry to suit current tastes.

Across the river from Sauternes and Barsac are the Premières Côtes de Bordeaux, St-Croix-du-Mont, Loupiac, Cadillac and Cérons. Their sweet, pleasant white wines are generally not very full bodied or intense. The Premières Côtes de Bordeaux is a narrow ridge of limestone cliffs, forming the east bank of the Garonne and extending for about thirty miles. Its southern sector produces decidedly sweet small-scale whites; its northern sector, quickly developing reds. Loupiac and Cadillac are also red-and-white-wine producers. The tiny Cérons district north of Barsac is noted for its sweet white dessert wines, which range in body from light to medium. Those of St-Croix-du-Mont are extremely sweet and high in alcohol.

The Bordeaux Classifications

Most influential in establishing the current prices for Bordeaux wines is a classification system that was casually introduced in 1855. That year, at a universal exposition in Paris designed to showcase French products, the Bordeaux Chamber of Commerce, in its wish to promote the region's wines, decided to draw up a list of its leading vineyards. The Chamber established a committee made up mainly of wine brokers to do so. After some bitter infighting, the committee's members reached a consensus, basing their selections largely on the relative values of the vineyard soils and on the prices the wines had been fetching in recent years.

The 1855 list, known as the Classement des Grand Crus de la Gironde (Classification of the Gironde's Great Growths), included a number of red-wine vineyards in the Médoc and a number of white-wine vineyards in Sauternes. The wines themselves were called *crus classés* (classified growths).

Of the more than three thousand red-wine properties in Bordeaux, only sixty-one were selected. These were divided into five categories: Premier Cru Classé (First Classified Growth), and Deuxième, Troisième, Quatrième and Cinquième Crus (Second, Third, Fourth and Fifth Classified Growths). Of the four estates awarded Premier Crus, three were in the Médoc: Châteaus Lafite-Rothschild, Latour and Margaux; the fourth, Haut-Brion, was in Graves. Fifteen of the remaining red-wine vineyards were classified as Second Growths, fourteen as Thirds, ten as Fourths and eighteen as Fifths.

Established, too, were four lower red-wine classifications: Cru Exceptionnel, Cru Bourgeois Supérieure, Cru Bourgeois (CB) and Artisans et Paysans. Proprietors assigned the latter rank—and not pleased to find themselves in the lowest classification—appropriated the next-higher one, rendering their own category obsolete.

The 1855 listing of white wines included twenty-two Sauternes vineyards divided into three categories: Premier Grand Cru (First Great Growth), Premier Cru (First Growth), and Deuxième Cru (Second Growth). Awarded the highest rank was the estimable Château d'Yquem. The Premier Cru was given to nine others and the Deuxième Cru to another twelve.

In 1932, another classification established new categories for nearly four hundred fifty of the Médoc, red-wine estates that had been excluded from the original listing. They were: Bourgeois Supérieure de Haut-Médoc, Bourgeois de Haut-Médoc, and Bas-Médoc. Proprietors assigned the Bas-Médoc classification—and displeased with its lower connotation—featured only "Médoc" on their labels, rendering their own category obsolete. Subsequently, a hundred other excluded Médoc vineyards formed their own syndicate, giving a Cru Exceptionnel to eighteen of its members and a Cru Bourgeois (CB) to sixty others.

St-Émilion and Pomerol vintners, rankled by their complete exclusion from the 1855 listing, decided to establish their own classifications. In St-Émilion they gave themselves so many Premier Crus that their beleaguered Chamber of Commerce turned to the government for help. In 1955, four official categories were created here, the first two being the most significant: Premier Grand Cru Classé (First Classified Great Growth), awarded to twelve vine-yards, and Deuxième Grand Cru Classé (Second Classified Great Growth), awarded to seventy others. Transcending both was Hors Classé (In a Class by Itself), the equivalent of a Médoc First Growth. It was awarded to St-Émilion's two preeminent estates: the Châteaus Ausone and Cheval Blanc.

Pomerol, not to be outdone, established three classifications of its own: Premier Grand Cru, Premier Cru and Deuxième Cru. The top rank went to ten vineyards. Pomerol's most esteemed estate, Château Pétrus, was declared Hors Classé. In 1959, Graves established its own classifications for thirteen of its wines, giving Château Haut-Brion the same Premier Cru it had received in the original 1855 listing and elevating its neighboring estate, Château La Mission–Haut-Brion, to the same prestigious rank. Named the leading white-wine estate of Graves was Château Carbonnieux.

The 1855 classifications have become an almost immutable force in the pricing of Bordeaux wines and have wielded consid-erable influence over the international wine trade as well. Still commanding the highest sums are the elite Cru Classés. Yet experts agree that the Bordeaux classifications are in need of a serious overhaul. They say that the rigid sequential structure invariably implies the inferiority of the lower-ranked wines. In professional tastings, however, so-called lesser wines have scored consistently higher than some of the top-ranking examples. A second growth may now outshine a first and a fifth be the equivalent of a second, while a Cru Bourgeois may rival its classified neighbors.

Critics point out that of the original sixty-one vineyards, only thirty or forty still export their wines in significant quantities. They note that although St-Julien contains more classified châteaus than any other Bordeaux commune, it does not have a single Premier

Cru vineyard. Moreover, certain châteaus have moved from their original sites or have incorporated additional parcels of land. Nor have the inevitable changes of ownership been taken into account. Some estates have deteriorated in the hands of indifferent or absentee owners, while others have been much improved. Some vineyards have introduced new grape varieties and modified their viticultural and vinification practices. In 1951, Château Prieuré-Cantenac consisted of some thirty-two acres of run-down vines; it now encompasses about one hundred seventy thriving acres. Some years ago, when the Japanese took over Château Lagrange in St-Julien, they not only restored its vineyards and cellars but modified its wine blend as well.

Some vineyard names have also been changed. Prieuré-Cantenac is now Prieuré-Lichine. Château Longueville au Baron de Pichon-Longueville has been shortened to Pichon Baron and Pichon-Longueville Comtesse de Lalande abbreviated to Pichon Lalande. Château Mouton d'Armailhacq had been renamed Mouton-Baronne in memory of the wife of owner Baron Phillipe de Rothschild. After his death in 1988, his daughter changed the name back to Armailhac, dropping the *Mouton* prefix and the final *q.*

The owners of the high-ranking estates have blocked most attempts to update the 1855 listings, fearing that a drastic overhaul might demote their properties or exclude them from the list entirely. In the 1950s, the owners of classified châteaus established a committee to work on a revision, but its proposals created such furor that the effort was quickly abandoned.

So fixed have these classifications become that only one major change has been made in more than a century. In 1973, after fifty years of active campaigning, Philippe de Rothschild finally succeeded in advancing Château Mouton-Rothschild from Second to First Growth status. (The Minister of Agriculture issued a special decree to that effect.) The château's motto had been: *Premier ne puis. Second ne daigne. Mouton suis.* (I cannot be first. I do not wish to be second. I am Mouton.) After the elevation, its motto became: *Premier je suis. Second je fus. Mouton ne change.* (I am first. I was second. Mouton never changes.)

Today, three of the four most prestigious vineyards are owned by foreign interests or international families. Château Haut-Brion is the property of an American banking firm. Latour, having been run by a British food and beverage conglomerate for thirty years, has been returned to French ownership. Lafite has been acquired by another branch of the Rothschild family.

In the 1960s and 1970s, the French government, seeking to deter further foreign acquisitions, declared that its important vineyard estates were national treasures. In 1974, when the prestigious Château Margaux came on the market, the government turned down the bid of an American firm to purchase the estate, permitting the Greek-born owner of a French grocery chain to acquire the property instead.

In the 1980s, the French government shifted its position, declaring that long-term investments by foreign interests could contribute to the dynamism of the French wine industry. Important properties have since been acquired by Japanese, American, Danish, Swiss and German interests. However, the winds seem to be shifting again. French banks and insurance companies are now competing to purchase a number of Bordeaux's leading wine estates.

BURGUNDY

Burgundy, in the east-central part of the country, is the second major wine region of France. Less than a sixth the size of Bordeaux, it extends about one hundred eighty miles south from Chablis to Lyon. The weather here is generally volatile; only one vintage in every three or four can be considered good.

Burgundy's vineyards are a patchwork of divided ownership whose fragmentation goes back to the French Revolution. The big estates owned by the church and the nobility were then parceled out to the people. The French law of inheritance, which divides a father's property among all his children, split the land into even tinier parcels through successive generations. Now, many vineyards average less than twenty-five acres, with some consisting of only a few rows of vines. (Shippers have long dominated Burgundy's wine industry.)

Despite sharing certain fundamental characteristics of site and soil, the Burgundian wines vary substantially in style. The region's

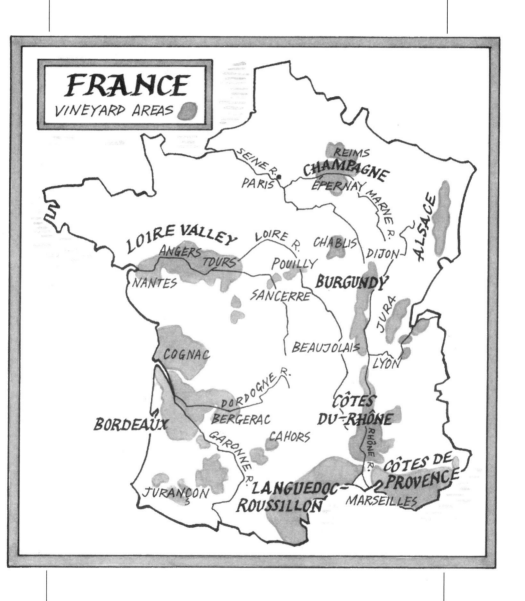

hundreds of small producers in the region differ not only in their individual approaches to pruning, harvesting and vinification, but also in their wine-making experience and skills. Even in the most famous vineyards, wine quality can vary widely from owner to owner.

Burgundy's wines are red, white and rosé, still and sparkling. The reds, pressed primarily from the pinot noir, account for about 75 percent of the output. Less austere than those of Bordeaux and generous and full-bodied at their finest, they are characterized by an intensity of flavor, a velvety texture, a remarkably perfumed bouquet and an unmistakable rich earthy quality, known as *goût de terroir* (taste of the soil). The white wines, pressed primarily from the chardonnay, combine a rich fruitiness and a definite dryness at their finest; they possess an intensity of flavor and a somewhat spare elegance as well. The other white-grape varieties here are the pinot blanc and the aligoté.

There are five major wine districts in Burgundy: Côte d'Or, Côte Chalonnais, Mâconnais, Beaujolais, and Chablis.

Côte d'Or

The Côte d'Or in central Burgundy, the region's most important wine district, covers some twenty-two thousand acres. A narrow limestone shelf, never much more than a mile wide, it begins at Dijon and extends about forty miles southwest, ending at Santenay. The name Côte d'Or, which translates as "Golden Slope," comes from the burnished appearance the vineyards take on in autumn when their foliage blazes with color. The best Côte d'Or vineyards, sited eight hundred to a thousand feet above sea level, on a sunny southern slope sheltered from the wind and the rain sweeping in from the west. (Wines grown on the district's northern slope carry the lesser "Haute Côte de Nuits" label.)

The Côte d'Or is just about evenly divided in two. In the north is the Côte de Nuits, extending from Dijon to Beaune; in the south is the Côte de Beaune, extending from Aloxe-Corton to Santenay.

Côte de Nuits

The Côte de Nuits, beginning near the town of Fixin and ending about twelve miles south near Prémeaux, is named for its principal city, Nuits-St-George. Grown here on a limestone, silica and clay soil are Burgundy's greatest red wines. Deep-colored and velvety textured, rich, fruity and delightfully tart, they combine a big mouth-filling flavor with a subtle, haunting bouquet.

The main townships or communes of the Côte de Nuits are Gevrey-Chambertin, Chambolle-Musigny, Vosne-Romanée and Nuits-St-Georges, which are followed by Échézaux, Flagey-Échézaux, Morey-St-Denis, Vougeot and Fixin.

The uncontested leader among Gevrey-Chambertin's nine small vineyards is le Chambertin, whose red wine is renowned for its magnificent character and power. Napoleon himself was partial to it and Alexander Dumas said of the wine, "Nothing makes the future seem so rosy as contemplating it through a glass of Chambertin." Hilaire Belloc, recalling a youthful idyll, wrote, "I forget the name of the place; I forget the name of the girl but the wine ... was Chambertin."

The nearby Chambertin-Clos de Bèze vineyard is also known for the splendor of its wine. And across a narrow road is Charmes-Chambertin, whose admirable red wine exhibits only a touch less body and distinction. To the south are the estimable Mazoyères-Chambertin and Latricières-Chambertin vineyards, sharing much the same soil and exposure as le Chambertin. They too yield rich, full-bodied and distinguished red wines. Other significant Gevrey-Chambertin vineyards are Mazis-Chambertin and the smaller Chapelle-Chambertin, whose wines are also notable for their strength and finesse.

To the south is the commune of Morey-St-Denis, encompassing three outstanding vineyards: Clos de la Roche, Clos de Tart and Clos St-Denis. Distinguishing their sturdy, full-bodied wines is an underlying firmness. South of Morey-St-Denis is the commune of Chambolle-Musigny, whose wines are considered the most charming and fragrant of the Côte d'Or reds. Lighter than the Chambertins, they display at their finest delicacy, refinement and breed. The outstanding vineyards here are les Musigny (whose ten owners share twenty-five acres) and the adjoining les Amoureuses to the east, along with les Charmes to the north and les Bonnes Mares still farther north and west. The commune of Chambolle-

Musigny also produces a small amount of white wine.

Directly to the south is the commune of Vougeot, the site of Clos de Vougeot, the Côte d'Or's largest and most famous vineyard. Consisting of some forty acres, it is owned by more than a hundred proprietors, including a number of syndicates. (At the last count there were 107 small plots owned by 82 different wine makers.) Clos de Vougeot owes much of its fame to the Confrèrie des Chevaliers du Tastevin (Order of the Knights of the Tasting Cup), a celebrated eating and drinking society. It was founded in the 1930s by local wine merchants who had been battered by a generally depressed economy and a series of poor vintages, and who were desperate to improve their lot.

The Confrèrie's headquarters is housed in a magnificent structure built in the twelfth century by Cistercian monks, which stands in the midst of the Clos de Vougeot vineyard. Held here are a series of ceremonial dinners whose ostensible purpose is to induct new Confrèrie members. Hundreds of guests in formal dress attend. The merchants, presiding over the ceremonies, wear sumptuous robes of crimson velour. During the elaborate rites, the initiates solemnly swear to empty their glasses whenever full, and to fill them whenever empty. They vow that no wine other than a Burgundy shall cross their lips except under conditions of extreme duress. Then they sip some of the Clos de Vougeot wine. The presiding officer, with equal solemnity, taps each inductee three times on the shoulder with a vine staff, then slips over his head a red and yellow ribbon to which a tastevin, the symbol of the Confrèrie, is attached. The *tastevin* is a small, shallow silver tasting cup faceted with a row of indents around the bottom that reflect the light. The cup is used in the dim cellars of Burgundy to judge the wine's color and clarity as well as its taste.

The elaborate ceremonies at Clos de Vougeot and their related public relations efforts proved so successful that the Confrérie now operates chapters in a number of countries. (About 90 percent of the Clos de Vougeot wine is sold abroad.) Other groups, impressed with the Confrèrie's success, have set up their own promotional activities, emphasizing pomp and circumstance and featuring festive rites, medieval robes, and so on. Such groups include the Compagnons de Beaujolais and the Confrèrie des Vignerons de

Saint Vincent et Macon in Burgundy; and the Commanderie du Bontemps de Médoc et Graves, the Jurade de St-Émilion and the Chevaliers des Lascombes de Margaux in Bordeaux. Sauternes and Barsac have their own commanderies. Wine merchants in the Rhône Valley have established a Commanderie des Côtes du Rhône of their own, and in Alsace, they've set up the Confrérie de St-Etienne. The idea has spread to New York's Hudson Valley, where a local winery sponsors a Société de Vignerons, whose members help to bring in the harvest and buy most of the wine.

South of Vougeot is Vosne-Romanée, a commune much celebrated for its incomparable red wines. Preeminent among its forty-six vineyards is the prestigious Domaine de La Romanée-Conti or D.R.C., named for the Prince of Conti, who successfully outbid Madame Pompadour for the property in the eighteenth century. (That lady, once the favorite of Louis XV, had apparently lost her legendary charms and was unable to persuade the king that the estate should be hers.)

Considered the greatest red-wine vineyard in Burgundy, the Domaine de La Romanée-Conti is little more than four acres of stony red soil consisting of fragmented limestone with a high level of iron oxide. Its wine, perfectly balanced at its finest, demonstrates a velvety texture, a great depth of flavor and an extraordinary bouquet. Since annual production here is less than seven hundred cases, Romanée-Conti is sold only by the bottle, not by the case.

Just a few feet uphill and to the west is the tiny two-acre la Romanée, celebrated for its satiny, intensely perfumed wines. Nearby, the thirteen-acre Romanée-St-Vivant and the fifteen-acre La Tâche yield finely scented wines, characterized by a great depth of flavor and a long, lingering aftertaste. At the southernmost end of the Vosne-Romanée commune is Aux Malconsorts, whose wine displays outstanding finesse, scent and breed as well. At the northern end is le Richebourg, bounded by La Romanée-Conti and la Romanée. Richebourg's more deeply colored wines are generally sturdier and fuller in body than those of its more aristocratic neighbors.

The vineyards of les Échézaux and les Grands-Échézaux to the north, although not actually within the communal borders of Vosne-Romanée, yield wines close enough in character to be grouped with the Vosne-Romanées. Light-colored, light-bodied and displaying considerable finesse, the wines are more remarkable for their subtlety than for their strength.

The last major commune is Nuits-St-Georges, located at the southern end of the Côte de Nuits. The three leading vineyards here are les St-Georges, les Cailles and les Vaucrains. Their well-balanced reds are soft and generous with a pleasant, slightly earthy flavor. Prèmeaux, the southernmost commune, also produces agreeable red wines.

At the opposite or northernmost end of the Côte de Nuits is Fixin, whose outstanding vineyard is Clos de la Perrière. Another vineyard of note here is Clos du Chapitre to the east. Also located at the northern end is the little town of Marsannay-la-Côte, simply called Marsannay, produces a delightful rosé pressed from pinot noir grapes.

Côte de Beaune

The southern sector of the Côte d'Or is the Côte de Beaune, extending southward from Aloxe-Corton to Santenay. More prolific than the Côte de Nuits, the Côte de Beaune produces about twice as much wine. It too specializes in red wines, although producing excellent whites as well. The red wines, pressed from the pinot noir, are less robust and lighter in color than their Côte de Nuits counterparts. The whites, pressed primarily from the chardonnay, are characterized by a richness, floweriness and a long, lingering bouquet.

The most important commune of the Côte de Beaune is Aloxe-Corton, best known for its red wines although its whites are also highly regarded. The commune's leading vineyard, le Corton, produces a rich dark red, considered one of the district's finest wines. To the east is les Bressandes, a vineyard sharing a similar soil and exposure and yielding full-flavored and scented red wines. To the south and west is the eighty-five-acre Corton-Charlemagne, renowned for its scented Chardonnays, which at their finest display depth, complexity and a superb, unforgettable bouquet.

Tucked up on the side of the mountain behind the commune of Aloxe-Corton is the tiny village of Pernand-Vergelesses, primarily a red-wine producer. (White wines constitute about 10 percent of its output.) The red-wine labels here read "Corton," the white-wine, "Corton-Charlemagne." To the south and west is another red-and-white-wine producer, Savigny-les-Beaune, which produces predominantly red wines.

Farther south is Beaune, Burgundy's ancient capital and the home of most of the region's shippers. Like its neighbors, Beaune specializes in red wines while producing white wines as well. The city is perhaps best known for *les Trois Glorieuses,* an annual three-day harvest festival, which culminates in a famous wine auction held on the third Sunday in November and attended by dealers and wine enthusiasts from all over the world. The auction's significance extends far beyond the precincts of Beaune: the wines offered provide a good indication of the size and character of the Burgundy crop; and the prices the auction establishes indicate the market not only for Burgundy wines, but also for French wines in general each year.

Originally organized in the fifteenth century to benefit an almshouse, the auction generates enough income to support the Hospices de Beaune, a local hospital that treats the sick and aged of the city without charge. The Hospices founders and patrons over the years have bequeathed vineyard properties to the establishment, as well as providing financial aid. These donated parcels, scattered among more than forty sites—and sometimes totaling no more than a quarter-acre each—represent nearly one hundred fifty acres of choice vineyard land.

NOTE: As has been the case with other successful promotions, the philanthropic auction idea has been adopted by a number of communities. Beaujolais holds an annual auction for its Hospices de Beaujeu and Nuits-St-Georges for its Hospices de Nuits.

South of Beaune is the commune of Pommard, which produces some of Burgundy's most popular red wines. Fruity and not too deeply colored, the're celebrated for their scent and finesse, as well as for the unusual and gracious softness they demonstrate at an early age. Les Épenots and les Rugiens are Pommard's leading vineyards.

To the south, on a hilly slope is the commune of Volnay, which produces both red and white wines. It is best known for its reds, which display breed, bouquet and an intensity of flavor at their finest. The softest and most delicate of the fine red Burgundies, these—although light-colored and light-bodied—are nevertheless round and velvety wines. Volnay's most acclaimed vineyard is les Caillerets; others of note are les Champans and les Chevrets. The white wines here carry neither a commune nor a vineyard designation but are labeled "Meursault," the name of a commune to the south that specializes in white wines.

Southwest of Pommard is the commune of Monthelie, known for its lightly scented red wines, which are similar to the Pommards. Also to the south is Auxey-Duresses, a commune that produces red and white wines, with the reds predominating. Still farther south is Blagny, a hamlet producing red and white wines; it is best known for its fine whites.

South of Volnay is Meursault, known as the "Home of the Great White Burgundies." (Its output is 90 percent white.) Meursault's dry and tangy yet full-bodied wines display a remarkable softness, roundness and scent, offering at their finest a luxuriously rich taste a sumptuous texture and a lingering hazelnut bouquet. The most notable vineyard here is les Perrières, whose central sector, Clos des Perrières, is particularly admired.

At the southern edge of Meursault are the adjacent communes of Puligny-Montrachet and Chassagne-Montrachet. Although producing almost twice as much red wine as white, they are best known for their flavorful whites. While resembling the Meursaults in breed and class, these wines are not nearly as soft or round. Rather they demonstrate a certain firmness along with a flowery richness.

Burgundy's most celebrated white wine comes from the legendary twenty-acre le Montrachet vineyard, which is shared by more than a dozen owners. (Their parcels range from about a tenth of an acre to some five acres.) The estate is situated half in Puligny, where it's called le Montrachet, and half in Chassagne, where it's called just plain Montrachet. Its wine, pale gold with a hint of green, and dry but not excessively so, has been described as the "quintessential Chardonnay." Generous and smooth-tasting, it combines great depth and complexity with an underlying softness and succulence. In certain vintages it attains an extraordinarily subtle flavor and a tremendous bouquet. Alexander Dumas said of le Montrachet, "I drink it only with head bared and on bended knee." About three thousand cases are produced annually.

Two nearby vineyards are Chevalier-Montrachet, located on a slight slope to the west, and Bâtard-Montrachet to its east and on the slope below. They too yield pale gold, eminently dry wines that display an extraordinary wealth of flavor and bouquet at their finest.

Other notable white-wine vineyards on the Côte de Beaune are Bienvenue-Bâtard-Montrachet and Criots-Bâtard-Montrachet, situated respectively in the communes of Puligny and Chassagne. At the southern end of Chassagne is Morgeot, a ten-acre vineyard noted for its unusually deep colored, long-lived red wines. Also known principally for its red wines is Santenay, the southernmost of the important Côte de Beaune communes. Its rather full bodied reds register high levels of tannin but are nevertheless quite soft and light.

Côte Chalonnais

The Côte Chalonnais, located at the southern end of the Côte d'Or, is a natural continuation of the Côte de Beaune. It takes its name from the town of Chalon-sur-Saône, which faces the Saône River. Although the Côte Chalonnais produces light, crisp, inexpensive white wines, both still and sparkling, it is associated mainly with excellent red; some pressed exclusively from the pinot noir, others a blend of the pinot noir and the gamay. Closely related to the red wines of Beaune but usually lighter in body and shorter-lived, they display a considerable perfume and charm.

The major communes of the Côte Chalonnaise are Mercurey, Rully, Givry and Montagny. Mercurey to the south produces both red and white wines. The reds, dark-colored, fruity and fragrant, with an earthy component, are the most structured of the region but nevertheless quick-maturing. The whites are quite light in character. Rully specializes in clean, fresh-tasting whites, some made sparkling. These demonstrate at their finest a surprising intensity of bouquet and flavor. The red wines here are labeled "Mercuryes." Rully also produces sparkling Burgundies. Givry, farther south, is associated primarily with red wines. Montagny, the southernmost commune, is known for its fresh, light and very dry white wines.

Mâconnais

The Mâconnais is named for Mâcon, its capital city and one of the centers of the Burgundy wine trade. Situated south of Chalon-sur-Saône, the region is subject to a somewhat mild climate. Many of its vineyards are sited on rolling, often rocky hills that face the Saône River.

Although growing both red and white wines, the Mâconnais is the traditional source of millions of gallons of Burgundy's moderately priced whites. Pressed from the chardonnay, sometimes blended with the aligoté, these are fresh, fruity, engaging and well-defined wines, with a touch of acidity. The region's red wines, pressed from the pinot noir and gamay, are straightforward, pleasantly fruity and quite soft on the palate.

The best-known Mâconnais white wine is Pouilly-Fuissé, produced in the town of that name and in four small villages nearby: Solutré, Fuissé, Chaintré and Vergisson. Crisp, dry and fruity, it is much like the other Mâconnais whites, perhaps because of its strange-sounding name it has become popular in the United States. The French call it the "American wine." A similar, less expensive wine is St-Véran, produced in six hillside villages to the south. Two other significant communes nearby are Pouilly-Loché and Pouilly-Vinzelles; they too produce fresh, fragrant, moderately dry white wines.

Notable Mâconnais wine towns are Vire and Lugny, whose labels usually append the Mâcon name with a hyphen to their own. Vire's leading vineyard, Clos du Chapitre, produces an excellent bone-dry, fragrant, fruity and quite delicate white wine. Lugny's white wines are also engaging.

Produced too in the Mâconnais are a number of anonymous blends, which appear under such names as Mâcon Blanc, Pinot Chardonnay de Mâcon, Mâcon-Villages, and Aligoté. The Aligotés, named for their grape variety, were initially inferior acidy wines, but a number have been upgraded lately.

Beaujolais

Beaujolais, just below Mâcon at the southern tip of Burgundy, takes its name from the little town of Beaujeu. A strip of land on the west bank of the Saône, it is about forty miles long and five to ten miles wide. Beaujolais is red-wine country. Its principal grape is the gamay rather than the ubiquitous pinot noir that characterizes the rest of Burgundy.

One of the country's most prolific regions, Beaujolais offers almost as many wine styles as there are producers; its wines run the gamut from rich and full-flavored to thin and acidic. The premier examples, sharing some of the firmness, depth and power of the better Burgundies, come from the northern sector, where the hills are rolling and the soil is largely granitic. These wines are beautifully colored, well balanced and relatively long lived. Characterizing them are a warmth and a rich intensity.

The major northern wine communes are Moulin-à-Vent, Morgon, Chénas, Juliénas, Fleurie, Chiroubles, St-Amour, Brouilly, Côte de Brouilly and Régnié. Moulin-à-Vent's wines are the biggest and most full bodied. Strong and solid when young, they open up beautifully with age, demonstrating considerable breed and a good depth of character. Morgon's similarly robust but earlier maturing wines exhibit a raspberrylike fruitiness. The Chénas wines are soft, smooth and comparatively full flavored, while those of Juliénas are characteristically firm and generous. (Juliénas is named for Julius Caesar, whose legions once marched through its hills.)

The other notable northern communes—Fleurie, Chiroubles, Brouilly, Côte de Brouilly, Régnié and St-Amour—are known for their more aromatic and delicate but shorter-lived wines. Those of Fleurie are fruity and gentle, combining body and breed with lightness, grace and a wildflower bouquet. Similarly scented and charming is the wine of Chiroubles. Brouilly and Côte de Brouilly yield the most youthful wines. Although quite full bodied, they are endowed with a wonderful fruity softness. Régnié's wines are light and berrylike. The St-Amour commune is located farthest north. Its fruity, supple wine is particularly prized for its bouquet.

NOTE: Beaujolais also produces an occasional rosé and some Chardonnays. The white wines, known as Beaujolais Blancs, come from the region's northern reaches that adjoin the Mâconnais.

The most typical reds however come from thirty communes in Bas Beaujolais, the southernmost sector, whose soil is mostly clay combined with limestone. Light-colored, soft, supple and fruity, the greatest attraction of these wines is their disarming freshness and a general lack of complexity. After spending the winter and early spring in wood, they are bottled and shipped out.

Ready to drink about five months after the harvest, these constitute about two-thirds of the Bas Beaujolais production. The rest are the Beaujolais Nouveaus (new wines). Harvested in September and ready for sale six weeks later, they are essentially half-finished wines, purplish in color, with a strong grapy flavor. Their greatest charm is the tingling freshness and yeasty aroma of their very recent fermentation.

The early release of the Beaujolais Nouveaus began when local vintners brought casks of their new wines to the town square in mid-November for the villagers to sample. Subsequently, the wines were dispensed from their casks in local cafés and eventually made available in heavy-bottomed 40-centiliter bottles called *pots*. The Nouveaus proved a boon to their makers, who could sell them in November and pay off many of their debts before Christmas.

The novelty of the Nouveaus' quick drinkability prompted a number of Lyon and Paris bistros and restaurants to offer the wines to their patrons. This led to the promotional idea of organizing an annual "race" to see which establishment would receive its shipment first. The idea was to create a sense of anticipation and excitement about the Nouveaus. To generate as much publicity as possible, the race was extended to England and to the United States and Japan.

The official release date is now set for one minute after midnight on the third Thursday in November. (The date had originally been scheduled a week earlier, but the logistics of getting the wine to restaurants and retail shops in time proved too daunting.) At the moment of release, trucks and helicopters speed their shipments to every point in France and to channel ports and airports. A number of promotional bottles are shipped to the United States by air for arrival the next day. (They are known as the "Air Nouveau.") The bulk of the wines however travel by sea, with the first shipment generally arriving in early December.

These incomplete vulnerable wines, shipped great distances, must often be toughened up to survive. Sugar may be added to boost their alcohol levels, or sulfur dioxide introduced to discourage refermentation in the bottle. Some vintners speed up the wine's already abbreviated development with carbonic maceration, which blankets the uncrushed grapes with CO_2. This releases their color, fragrance and fruity flavor more quickly. Also known as whole berry fermentation, the process may preserve freshness, but it makes the wine less stable. Filtering or pasteurization is often required to compensate.

The successful marketing of the Nouveaus has prompted vintners both inside and outside France to produce their own accelerated wines. These may rely on earlier-maturing grapes or on berries picked from younger vines. The quickly developing wines are named for their grape varieties (Muscadet Nouveau, Gamay Nouveau) and for their locales (Bordeaux Nouveau, Côtes du Rhônes Nouveau). The Italians call them *nuovos* or *novellos*.

Chablis

Chablis, one of the country's most northerly wine regions, is usually considered part of Burgundy although it's not contiguous with it. (Situated forty miles northwest of the Côte d'Or, it is actually closer to the Champagne region.) Great vagaries of weather severely limit wine production here. Sudden frosts and devastating hail frequently buffet the vineyards.

The Chablis name applies both to a little village set in the hills and to the large crescent-shaped area surrounding it, which encompasses twenty communes. The region's best wines are produced in the seven communes that share a single chalky, south-facing slope on the Serein River. Their combined area is about two hundred acres. These top communes are le Clos, Vaudésir, Preuses, Grenouilles, Bougros, Valmur and Blanchot.

Pressed from the chardonnay grapes, Chablis wines are more austere than their counterparts in southern Burgundy. Pale straw with a hint of green, they are magnificently crisp and dry at their finest. A steely taste in combination with a luscious nectarlike quality gives them a uniquely subtle style and endows them with great finesse. They have been likened to springwater in sunlight. Lesser examples are produced on the outskirts of the town of Chablis and at the region's outer borders.

The Burgundy Classifications

Because of the historic fragmentation of its vineyards, Burgundy's wines are classified differently than the other wines of France; they're ranked more by vineyard quality than by geographic distribution. The vineyards themselves are classified according to variations in the soil, terrain, exposure, etc., of their *climats* or individual parcels.

Burgundy's wines were first classified in 1861 when the Comité d'Agriculture de l'Arrondissement de Beaune (Agricultural Committee of Beaune) set up rankings for the red wines of the Côte d'Or. These were Tête de Cuvée (Top Growth), followed by the Premier, Deuxième and Troisième Crus (First, Second and Third Growths). Subsequently, the rankings were simplified to Grand Cru (Great Growth) and Premier Cru (First Growth). The Côte d'Or's leading Grand Cru vineyard is the Domaine de La Romanée-Conti, followed by les Bonnes Mares, le Chambertin, Chambertin Clos de Bèze, les Grands Échézaux, le Musigny, le Richebourg and la Tâche. Among the white-wine vineyards, le Montrachet is deemed in a class by itself.

In 1938, four other classifications were created for the wines of Chablis. Based on vineyard locations and on alcohol levels, these were Grand Cru, Premier Cru, Chablis and Petit Chablis. The Grand Crus, demonstrating the highest levels of alcohol, come from the seven top communes on the north bank of the Serein (le Clos, Vaudésir, Preuses, Grenouilles, Bougros, Valmur and Blanchots.) The Premier Crus come from the town of Chablis and from a number of nearby villages. Chablis alone covers the wines grown on the outskirts of the town of Chablis and in the communes where the soil is less chalky and the exposure to sun is more limited. Petit Chablis covers the rather acid wines drawn from the region's outermost boundaries.

The classification system for Beaujolais wines is quite different. Here a Grand Cru covers a whole commune rather than a *climat* or an individual parcel. Awarded Grand Cru status have been the nine top northern-sector communes: Moulin-à-Vent, Morgon, Chénas, Juliénas, Fleurie, Chiroubles, Brouilly, Côte de Brouilly and St-Amour. In 1988, a tenth Grand Cru was added and awarded to Régnié.

While the Burgundy classifications demonstrate little of the rigidity of Bordeaux's 1855 listing, they nevertheless have their critics, who contend that the ongoing fragmentation of the properties has made it virtually impossible to rank the individual vineyard plots with any degree of precision. The critics also note that the problem is compounded because the individual proprietors who share ownership in a given vineyard will markedly differ in their approaches to grape growing and wine making. This lack of consistency, they say, makes it difficult to create a system with equal standards for all of the Burgundy wines.

RHÔNE VALLEY

South of Beaujolais is the Rhône Valley or the Côtes du Rhône, an extensive strip of hillsides encompassing some one hundred thousand acres of vines. Here, running from north to south, is the Rhône River, which rises in the Swiss Alps, passes through Geneva, then travels almost due west to France where it's joined at Lyon by the Saône River, one of its major tributaries. Turning abruptly south, the river then flows toward Marseilles and finally into the Mediterranean Sea.

Experiencing a long growing season, the Rhône Valley produces vast quantities of red and white wines. The reds, among the fullest-bodied and fullest-flavored in France, are aromatic and heady at their finest and often suffused with the scent of peppers and blackberries. Many are noted for their longevity. The majority of reds however are fruity and uncomplicated, somewhat like a typical Beaujolais although a bit drier. The Rhône whites are also big-bodied and flavorful; some are crisp and clean, others are broadly flowery with a marked spiciness. At their finest they combine a rich nutty character and a refreshing dryness. A number are unusually powerful, demonstrating high levels of alcohol. Some are relatively long lasting for a white wine.

The Rhône Valley cultivates some twenty grape varieties, many of them indigenous. Predominant among the red grapes are the syrah and grenache, followed by the cinsault, carignan, mourvèdre, picpoule, terret noir and picardan. The significant white grapes are the marsanne, roussanne, clairette and viognier.

Dividing the valley into northern and southern sectors is the 45th parallel just north of the city of Valence. The Northern Rhône, geographically closer to Burgundy, experiences a generally more temperate climate and yields the more elegant wines. The Southern Rhône, closer to the Mediterranean Sea, is subject to a hotter, drier climate and produces bigger, warmer wines.

The Northern Rhône

In the Northern Rhône, where the vineyards cling to the riverbank, the key districts are Côte Rôtie, Condrieu, Hermitage, Crozes-Hermitage, St-Joseph, Cornas and St-Péray. Northernmost is the Côte Rôtie (translating as roasted hillside), a steep slope on the west bank of the river that gets its name from the fierce sun beating down on the vines in summer. Two sectors, each named for the color of its soil, make up the Côte Rôtie: Côte Brune, or dark slope, in the north and Côte Blonde, or fair slope, in the south. Côte Brune's dark soil, soaking up the sun and retaining the heat, enables the grapes to mature more gradually. Côte Blonde's fair soil deflects the sun's rays back onto the grapes, accelerating their ripening. The wines of the two sectors are usually blended together for a better balance.

About four-fifths of the Côte Rôtie's wines are red. Pressed from the syrah grape, they are richly colored, robust, potent and velvety at their finest, often exuding the flavor of very ripe raspberries. The white wines are pressed mainly from the viognier grape, and a number of these are also splendid.

NOTE: Since the entire output of the Côte Rôtie totals only twenty thousand or so cases a year, most of these wines are available mainly in the luxury restaurants of the district.

Directly to the south is Condrieu, known for its white wines. Pressed from viognier grapes, they range from fairly dry to moderately sweet, depending on the character of their vintage and on their vinification style. Characterizing some examples is the mingled aroma of muscats and violets. Condrieu produces the Rhône's most esteemed white wine, Château Grillet. Grown in a tiny four-acre vineyard, it is fermented slowly and not bottled for two years. Big, elegant, fruity and redolent of spices, the wine is high in alcohol, yet light and ethereal.

Farther south and across the river is Hermitage Hill, a steep, spectacularly terraced slope about half a mile wide and less than two miles long, whose soil is a flinty bedrock covered with a thin layer of chalk. The hill acquired its name in the twelfth century when a returning crusader, kneeling wearily at a roadside shrine, decided to live out his life there as a hermit. Planting vines brought back from his pilgrimage to the Middle East, he established the hill's first vineyard.

Most Hermitage wines are red. Among the region's most deeply colored, they are fruity, substantial and vigorous with an almost overwhelming spicy scent. Forthright in flavor when young, they develop a degree of subtlety with age. The Hermitage white wines are full-bodied and dry, with a broad flavor. They display a definite aromatic character at their finest, sometimes surpassing the red wines in intensity.

North of Hermitage Hill are eleven communes known collectively as Crozes-Hermitage. These produce light soft red wines meant for early consumption, along with generally commonplace white wines. Across the river is St-Joseph, which produces gentle reds, generally accessible at an early age, together with sturdy white wines and light fruity rosés.

To the south of St-Joseph is the smaller commune of Cornas, whose red wines are sturdy and agreeable. The best, grown on steep hillsides, are dark and powerful; exhibiting a berrylike fragrance and a somewhat earthy quality. Farther south is the small commune of St-Péray, which specializes in white wines, a number of them made effervescent. To the east is the township of Die, also known for its sparkling wines, particularly its Clairette de Die, a rather sweet wine with a pronounced muscat flavor.

The Southern Rhône

The Southern Rhône, situated between the cities of Orange and Avignon, is subject to a hot, dry climate, although mistral winds help to temper its scorching sun. The vineyards here are spread out twenty to thirty miles on either side of the river. Largely constituting its coarse alluvial soil are stones and pebbles washed down over the centuries from the Alps. Smoothed out by the flowing river, the stones reflect the strong rays of the sun onto the vines during the day, then radiate its heat back at night. The grapes, developing inordinately high levels of sugar, yield big warm wines, rich in fruit and considerable in body.

The Southern Rhône's leading districts are Châteauneuf-du-Pape, Côtes du Ventoux, Beaumes-de-Venise, Tavel and Lirac. Châteauneuf acquired is name in the fourteenth century when the French popes who dominated the Holy See transferred the papacy to Avignon. On the east bank of the river they built an enclave that included a huge summer palace. (*Châteauneuf-du-Pape* translates as the Pope's New Castle.) Bordeaux-born Pope Clement V encouraged the development of local viticulture here; estate-bottled wines still carry a papal coat of arms on their labels.

There are now more than three hundred vineyards in Châteauneuf, covering some eight thousand acres. They yield primarily red wines, characterized at their finest by a deep, almost purplish color, a rich heartiness and a great vinosity. The wines, produced in a number of styles, vary according to the grapes used in their blends. The grape varieties are the grenache, syrah, mourvèdre and cinsault, along with the muscardin, vaccarese, cournoise, picpoule, terret noir and picardan. By law, vintners are permitted to include as many as thirteen varieties in their wines, but they generally limit themselves to six or seven. Some employ only four grape varieties.

Châteauneuf's white wines were first made when the popes found the reds too heavy for morning mass. Pressed from the bourbolene, clairette and roussanne, the whites are still known as the *vins de messe*. Full-bodied and intensely perfumed with a clean finish, at their finest they also age well.

North of Châteauneuf near the city of Orange is the Côtes du Ventoux, named for the six-thousand-foot-high Mount Ventoux, whose active winds cool the vineyards. The Ventoux wines, red, white and rosé, are rough and uncomplicated as a rule, although a number are capable of some subtlety and smoothness. Located on the lower slopes of Mount Ventoux are the communes of Gigondas and Rasteau, which produce solid high-alcohol red wines. Those of Gigondas are big, astonishingly dark, rich and concentrated at their finest, displaying a spicy, almost peppery flavor. They are also quite long lived. The Rasteau wines, grown farther north, also tend to be big and intense and sometimes taste of plums and spices. Rasteau is known as well for its sweet amber-colored Muscat wine, which resembles a White Port.

South of Gigondas is Beaumes-de-Venise, which produces lush, peppery red wines and full-flavored but relatively dry whites. Beaumes-de-Venise is best known however for its late-harvest Muscat, a deep golden, mouth-filling, lusciously sweet and extravagantly perfumed wine with nuances that suggest apricots, honey and orange blossoms.

Farther south and across the Rhône river are the sun-baked communes of Tavel and Lirac, celebrated for their full-bodied rosés, which range from pale orange to a deep, dark pink. Among the leading rosé wines of France, these include many of the same grape varieties as the Châteauneufs, although the grenache predominantes here. Tavel's rosés, grown on a rocky, arid and shallow soil, are sturdy, warm and vivacious, yet clean and austerely crisp. Exhibiting a tendency toward sharpness, they have been described as having "the taste of a rock warmed by the sun." The rosés of Lirac to the north are somewhat softer. Nearby Chusclan specializes in pleasant warm rosés too.

NOTE: Both Tavel and Lirac also produce other red wines, as well as white wines.

CHAMPAGNE

Champagne, France's northernmost wine-growing region situated some ninety miles northeast of Paris, is a largely flat plain, punctuated by a series of bunched-up hills. (*Champagne* literally means open field.) Running through its center from east to west is the Marne River.

Despite cold winds in winter and scorching heat in summer, grapes have long flourished in the region's chalky soil. Viticulture was already thriving here when Caesar's legions arrived; the Romans soon set up vineyards of their own. When Emperor Domitian issued his infamous edict in A.D. 92, most of the vines were uprooted and not replanted until two centuries later.

Champagne consists of three principal areas: Montagne de Reims, Vallée de la Marne and Côte des Blancs. Most important is the Montagne de Reims, south of the city of Reims. (Reims is one of the region's major wine centers; the other is Épernay, a town on the Marne River.) Montagne de Reims, planted primarily with pinot noir grapes, yields rich, full wines notable for their body and power. Farther south is the Vallée de la Marne, also growing the pinot noir but producing softer and rounder wines. Southernmost is the Côte des Blancs, a white-wine district that grows the chardonnay grape. Characterizing its wines are a lightness, delicacy and finesse. The wines of all three districts are usually blended together.

Champagne is celebrated for its sparkling wines, which range in color from pale gold to deep pink, and in style from light and sprightly to smooth, elegant and complex. The region also produces red and white table wines, initially called Vins Nature de la Champagne but now called Coteaux Champenois. Best known among these is Bouzy Rouge, a red wine named for its village in Montagne de Reims and pressed from pinot noir grapes. The Vallée de la Marne also produces a noneffervescent white that displays a Champagne nose and a flintiness reminiscent of a fine Chablis. Saran Nature, another still white wine, is made from the second pressing of the chardonnay and other grapes.

LOIRE VALLEY

The Loire River, the longest waterway in France, originates in the Massif Central southwest of Lyon and travels some six hundred miles north and west, finally reaching the Atlantic Ocean. The valley itself is a vast expanse encompassing half a million acres in vines. The Loire region is known primarily for its great variety of white wines, ranging from light, delicate and short-lived to big, succulent and long-lasting. Yet all share a certain family feeling characterized by a sprightly freshness, a lively fruitiness, a distinctly graceful charm and a more-or-less floral bouquet. A hint of smokiness or flintiness is often evident in their aftertaste.

Although the Loire Valley consists of twenty separate viticultural areas, it is perhaps best understood when divided into upper, middle and lower sectors, based in part on their geography and in part on their predominant grapes.

The Upper Loire

The Upper Loire, at the eastern end of the valley, features the sauvignon blanc grape; its best-known wines come from Pouilly-sur-Loire and Sancerre. Pouilly-sur-Loire, on the east bank of the river, is the source of Pouilly-Fumé, also known as Blanc Fumé de Pouilly. (*Fumé,* the local name for the sauvignon blanc, translates as smoky, and refers to the pale mist associated with noble rot that drifts over the vineyards at harvesttime.) Pouilly-Fumé wines range from sharp and acidic to rich, full-bodied, full-flavored and soft. In great vintages, they can acquire a fine botrytized sweetness.

NOTE: Pouilly-Fumé is often confused with the similar-sounding and better-known Pouilly-Fuissé, which comes from the Mâconnais region and is pressed from the chardonnay grape.

Sancerre, to the north and on the river's west bank, is a district of slightly rolling hills and chalky soil, with some four thousand acres in vines. Encompassed here are fourteen wine-producing communes whose leaders are Chavignol, Bué, Champtin, Crezancy, Amigny, Reigny and Verdigny.

Straw-colored or greenish yellow, the Sauvignon Blancs are responsible for the praiseworthy reputation of Sancerre's wines. Long the favorites of the bistros and brasseries of Paris, these are generally fresh, sprightly and bone-dry wines. Some of the best among them are austere, clean and sharp, with a crispness suggesting a steely or flinty edge, while others are somewhat fuller bodied. Many of the wines exhibit a lightly vegetal or herbaceous quality and are redolent of new-mown grass. A blander late-harvest version is also made. Produced as well in Sancerre are sturdy red wines and good rosés.

In the hamlets of Quincy and Reuilly thirty miles to the southwest, the Sauvignon Blanc wines are similarly fresh, dry and slightly vegetal, but they are also somewhat softer and more delicate. Some exhibit an underlying flintiness, while others are pleasantly tangy or spicy.

The Middle Loire

The Middle Loire, the region's largest sector, is also known as Coteaux de Touraine or simply Touraine. (The name derives from an ancient province surrounding the city of Tours.) Grown here on limestone slopes are red and white wines, with the whites being best known. Responsible for about half of them is the chenin blanc grape, known locally as the pineau de la loire. Its wines—charming, soft and not entirely dry—combine a fresh, fruity scent with an elusive flintiness. Other white grapes grown in the sector are the sauvignon blanc, pinot gris and arbois.

The most notable Middle Loire wines come from Vouvray. Situated on the north bank of the river near the city of Tours, Vouvray encompasses eight communes within its borders. Its white wines at their finest are fresh, fruity, soft and scented; they also display a delicate quincelike aroma. Depending on the character of their vintage, they may be vinified *sec* (dry), *demi-sec* (partially dry), or *molleux* (naturally sweet). When the weather permits, the wines acquire a great concentrated sweetness, offset by a fine acidity. Some of the Vouvrays wines are naturally sparkling; others have their effervescence added.

Across from Vouvray on the south bank of the river is the smaller Montlouis district, which shares a similar soil and also grows the chenin blanc. The wines of Montlouis are slightly softer and somewhat sweeter, sometimes resembling a simple Sauternes. (A number are now vinified dry to suit current tastes.)

The red grapes of the Middle Loire are the predominant cabernet franc and the grenache and gamay, along with the cabernet sauvignon, malbec and meunier. The cabernet franc's fresh fruity, light-colored wine can display the brisk, dry, slightly tannic character of a light Bordeaux or resemble a typical Beaujolais. The most outstanding examples come from Bourgueil and Chinon, two villages that face each other across the river, Bourgueil on the north bank and Chinon on the south. Bourgueil's best wine is characterized by a bouquet of wild raspberries, while a violetlike perfume typifies Chinon's best. St. Nicholas de Bourgueil to the northwest also produces a noteworthy Cabernet Franc wine.

The Lower Loire

The Lower Loire is at the western end of the valley, closest to the Atlantic Ocean. Its key districts are Anjou, Saumur, Pays Nantais and Gros Plant du Pays.

Most versatile is Anjou, which produces some of the most charming white wines in France. Fresh, fruity and scented, these are vinified both sweet and dry. Anjou is particularly celebrated for its rich yet delicate, late-harvest Chenin Blancs; some of the most luxurious come from the slopes of Quarts de Chaume. This Coteaux du Layon vineyard benefits from a peerless southern exposure and is known for its noble rot wines. Combining breed and splendid texture, they are comparable to the elegant late-harvest wines of Germany and Sauternes. Nearby, the Bonnezeaux vineyards produce similarly luxurious wines. Others from the Coteaux du Layon range from the fairly crisp and dry to the very sweet. The latter include late-harvest wines with fruitlike and naturally honeyed flavors suggesting quinces and nectarines.

Anjou produces excellent red wines and rosés as well. One of the best reds, a tender, fragrant Cabernet Franc, is grown in the tiny village of Champigny to the south. (The wine is similar to—but a bit lighter than—the Chinons grown upstream.) The rosés of Anjou, among the best in the Loire, are pressed exclusively from the cabernet franc grape. (Most other Loire rosés are pressed from the gamay.)

Saumur, on the river's south bank, produces almost equal quantities of red and white wines. Best known are the big, heady, long-lived Chenin Blancs, which display an agreeable trace of sweetness. Some of these are made sparkling. Saumur also produces large quantities of rosé wines, including the pleasantly fresh Cabernet Rosé de Saumur, which is generally sweeter than most French rosés.

Savennières, on the north side of the river not far from the city of Angers, is a tiny area known for its fragrant and excellent Chenin Blancs. These range from the delectably dry, tart and elegant to the late-harvested and sweet. The dry wines are similar to, but generally drier than, the Vouvrays; the sweet wines at their finest are evocative of honey and flowers. Savennières's most distinguished vineyards are La Roche-aux-Moines and the Clos de la Coulée de Serrant. The latter, a twenty-one-acre estate, has been making wine for some six hundred years.

Closer to the mouth of the river is the flat, windswept coast of lower Brittany, known as the Pays Nantais (The Area around Nantes). A prolific district, it produced mainly red wines until early in the eighteenth century when a disastrous freeze one year wiped out most of the grapes. According to legend, only the white muscadet grape survived. Known locally as the *melon de bourgogne* because of its Burgundian origins, it became the principal grape of the district.

Muscadet wines vary from light to heavy, and from dry and steely to medium-sweet. Chill air gusting in from the Atlantic keeps the vineyard temperatures down and the grape acids generally up. Microscopic salt crystals blown onto the grapes from the sea impart to the wines a slightly briny aftertaste. Some Muscadets are made *sur lie*—that is, steeped on their sediment for several months to give them an extra measure of flavor and intensity. Others are bottled early to retain their slight natural effervescence. (A number are carbonated for export.) At their finest, the wines are pale, fruity, light-bodied, crisp, clean and tangy.

NOTE: Initially considered unimportant wines, the Muscadets were consumed mainly by the district's poor. Fashionable now, they are produced in great quantities for domestic use and for export.

Three types of wine are produced in the Pays Nantais: Muscadet, Muscadet de Coteaux de la Loire and Muscadet de Sèvres-et-Maine. (The latter's name comes from two rivers that flow into the Loire near Nantes.) Basic Muscadet is produced in the westernmost reaches of the valley, nearer the mouth of the river. Muscadet de Coteaux de la Loire is produced upstream, northeast of Nantes. The best wines come from Sèvres-et-Maine, situated about twenty-five miles east of the point at which the Loire empties into the Atlantic.

The Lower Loire's largest wine-producing district is Gros Plant du Pays, which is located nearest the mouth of the river. Made in great quantities here are white wines pressed from the folle blanche. They are fairly dry and somewhat coarse and a bit short on fruit.

NOTE: Haut-Poitou, situated between Nantes and Saumur and considered part of the Greater Loire, produces both red and white wines. The whites, pressed from the sauvignon blanc and chardonnay, are crisp, solid and pleasant. The reds, pressed from the gamay, are nicely agreeable.

ALSACE

Alsace, a small region in northeastern France, extends from Strasbourg—its principal city—to the Swiss border. (Strasbourg antedates Julius Caesar; the Romans called this crossroads settlement Strateburgum or City of Roads.) The vineyards of Alsace, scattered through the gently rolling foothills of the Vosges Mountains, are shielded from the harshness of the northern weather by three- to four-thousand-foot peaks. Also acting as a buffer for the vineyards is Germany's Black Forest, located just across the Rhine.

Tucked in between the Vosges Mountains and the river, Alsace is geographically part of the Rhine Basin and has been closely linked with Germany. Until 1648, the region was ruled by Teutonic princes. Then, under the Treaty of Westphalia, France acquired the territory. The Germans retook it in 1870, retaining control until World War I. France then recovered the territory. During World War II, German troops seized it again. Alsace was not finally integrated into France until after the war, in 1945.

To keep Alsatian wines from competing with their own, the Germans had dispersed the region's vineyard holdings, permitting only the most minor grapes—primarily the chasselas—to be cultivated and turning the region into a source of cheap high-alcohol wines. (These wines were used in such commonplace German blends as Liebfraumilch.) On retrieving their territory during World War I, the Alsatians replaced these with more noble ones, but during World War II, the reoccupying Germans again uprooted the vines and replaced them with lesser varieties. Not until the 1950s was Alsace able to restore its wines to the quality levels attained nearly a century before.

Alsace is divided into the Haut-Rhin (Upper Rhine) and Bas-Rhin (Lower Rhine). Haut-Rhin, a twenty-five-mile stretch of land between the towns of Hippolyte and Guebwiller, encompasses the region's central and southern sectors, and produces the best wines. Other famous Haut-Rhin towns are Turckheim, Colmar, Éguisheim, Rouffach and Winzerheim. The Bas-Rhin, to the north, whose leading commune is Barr, produces generally less substantial wines.

The Alsatian vineyard holdings are small, averaging only an acre or two; a number of the growers cultivate their grapes as a sideline to other crops. Some hold full-time jobs in factories or mills, tending their vines in the evenings and on weekends. Other growers belong to cooperatives. Most sell their grapes to the big producers and shippers who dominate the wine trade here. (The Alsatian wineries depend heavily on such purchased grapes.)

In many ways Alsace remains more closely linked to the German traditions than to the French. Its wines, primarily white, are a combination of the Gallic and the Teutonic, however. Although slightly more alcoholic than the German, they exhibit some of the same lightness and grace. Yet they're more like the French in that virtually every bit of their grape sugar is fermented out. Bone-dry and delicate with an engaging charm, they represent a remarkable balance between fragrance and fruit. Although their noble rot wines are characteristically unctuous, they demonstrate only a hint of sweetness, despite their rich fruit and expansive bouquet.

Alsatian wines are named for their grapes rather than for their locales. Most outstanding is the Riesling, a clean, crisp wine with a naturally high acidity. Combining richness and depth with delicacy and aroma, the Rieslings at their finest are endowed with elegance, complexity and finesse. More characteristic of the region however is the Gewürztraminer, a fragrant, heady wine that combines a mouth-filling richness of fruit with distinctly herbal and pungent undertones. Riquewihr in Haut-Rhin is noted for its Rieslings and Gewürztraminers. Ribeauville to the north is also known for its fine Rieslings, while Guebwiller to the south produces somewhat richer and distinctly softer ones.

Other Alsatian grape varieties are the sylvaner, pinot blanc, pinot gris, muscat, chasselas and knipperlé. The sylvaner—which was the region's primary grape until the gewürztraminer superceded it—is responsible for soft, flowery, light-bodied wines with a delicate flavor. (Barr in Bas-Rhin is noted for its refreshing Sylvaners.) The pinot blanc yields fresh, light, fragrant, but generally undistinguished wines. The pinot gris, known locally as the tokay d'alsace, yields austerely dry wines with good body and very round flavors. The wines of the muscat grape are slightly drier here than elsewhere. Best known is the Muscat d'Alsace, which displays a fresh intense grapiness and aroma. It's usually served as an apéritif. A late-harvested muscat yields a wine of immense depth and power whose great natural sweetness is balanced out by its high acidity. The region's peasant grapes—the chasselas and knipperle—usually go into miscellaneous blends. The Alsatian red grapes— the pinot noir and meunier—yield some good rosés, but their red wines are generally light-colored and undistinguished. Barr in Bas-Rhin is noted for its commendable pinot noir rosés.

THE SOUTH OF FRANCE

The South of France, which borders the Mediterranean, includes Provence, also known as Côtes-de-Provence, and the Midi. Provence extends from the mouth of the Rhône river east to the Italian border, and the Midi stretches west toward the Pyrenees and Spain. The South of France grows a great variety of red, white and rosé wines. Also grown here are highly pigmented grapes called *tinturiers,* which are used to darken and enhance the paler wines of the north.

Provence, whose vineyards are sited between the foothills of the Alps and the Mediterranean, encompasses Marseille, Toulon, Nice and Aix-en-Provence. Its white wines produced here are crisp and citric with plenty of body; its red wines are rich, dark and somewhat herbal in flavor. Of particular distinction are the rosés of Provence, pressed from the grenache and such other varieties as the cinsault, syrah, mourvèdre and cabernet sauvignon. The best Provençal rosés, grown between Aix and St-Raphael, are fresh, light-colored and fruity wines, with a delightful bouquet. Other good examples come from Bandol, some twenty-five miles southeast of Marseille, which is also noted for its sturdy red wines and pleasant whites. The Bandol reds are pressed from the carignan and grenache, the whites from the clairette and ugni blanc. Palette near

Aix produces sturdy red and white wines, whereas Toulon specializes in reds. The most famous Provençal wine is the crisp white, delightfully dry Cassis, named for its village some twenty miles east of Marseille. Cassis serves as the base wine for the popular Kir apéritif.

To the west is the Midi, a wide and prolific sweep of land that has been an immense vineyard since Roman times. The Midi, with its hot climate, produces about 40 percent of the entire wine output of France. Once better known for its wine quantity than for its wine quality, the region has been gradually upgraded. In the 1960s, the French government prodded the growers to replant their vineyards and to replace their commonplace vines with those yielding fewer but more respected grapes. Grown now are the cabernet sauvignon, merlot, chardonnay and sauvignon blanc. And the vintners, by using modern vinification methods, are producing wines that demonstrate good fruit and bouquet. These include clean, fresh whites and spicy, rustic reds.

The Midi is made up of two ancient provinces, Languedoc and Roussillon. Languedoc's largest producers are Hérault, Aude and Gard. Hérault is known for its white wines, including sweet Muscats—grown in Lunel and Frontignan—and for its full-bodied Clairette du Languedoc, pressed from partially raisined grapes. Hérault also produces the thin whites on which the country's best vermouths are based. Aude turns out red, white and rosé wines.

Limoux, located near the ancient fortress town of Carcasonne, is known chiefly for its sparkling Blanquette de Limoux. Corbieres, southeast of Carcassonne, produces Fitou, a blend of grenache and carignan grapes and one of the region's best reds. Minervois, pressed from the same grape varieties and produced east of Carcassone, is a big, heavy red wine with a ripe, earthy character. Gard, south of Nîmes, is noted for its fine Camargue rosé and for its soft, dry Clairette de Bellgrade.

Roussillon, a hilly district around the city of Perpignan near the Spanish border, is principally known for its fortified dessert wines. Also produced here is the acclaimed Banyuls red, a wine pressed from late-gathered grenache grapes and reminiscent of a tawny port.

OTHER FRENCH REGIONS

In the Charente, a broad area north of Bordeaux, thin white wines are produced. Although uninteresting in themselves, they are distilled into the splendid spirit known as Cognac. In northeastern France near the Swiss border and Lake Geneva is Haut-Savoie, which produces light-bodied, very dry white wines, often made sparkling. (Of particular interest are the wines of Crépy.) Another effervescent wine producer is Seysell, set in the alpine reaches of the southeast; its vin mousseux is considered one of the country's best. The Jura near the Swiss border is celebrated for its late-harvest *vin jaune,* or yellow wine, which is fermented under a veil of flor for six years. Dark and rich but austerely dry, it demonstrates legendary keeping qualities; some vin jaunes have remained drinkable for seven decades. Bugey, situated in the foothills of the Alps, halfway between Haut-Savoie and Beaujolais, is noted for its good red wines—pressed from gamay, pinot noir and poulsard grapes, among others—and for its white Chardonnay and rosé wines.

Ardèche, a sparsely settled region on the west bank of the Rhône River not far from Beaujolais, is known for its red and white wines grown on chalky soil. Its Gamay red displays the freshness and uncomplicated grapiness of a typical Beaujolais, although it is sometimes a bit lighter. Its Chardonnay is fuller and richer than most of the Mâcon whites produced nearby, yet exhibits a good acid balance.

Southwestern France, commonly known as Gascony, produces red and white wines. Its dark-colored reds are concentrated in flavor and usually hard when young. Its whites are primarily dry but occasionally sweet. Wine-growing districts here include Bergerac and the Côtes du Duras. Bergerac, in the Dordogne Valley almost sixty miles east of Bordeaux, produces wines similar enough to be grouped with those of Bordeaux. These include fruity, well-balanced reds (blends of the cabernet sauvignon, cabernet franc and merlot) and whites that are somewhat drier than a typical Sauternes. (They're a blend of the sémillon and the muscadelle.) The Côtes du Duras, situated between Bergerac and Entre-Deux-Mers, also grows the same red varieties as Bordeaux and produces solid young wines. Madiran, another Gascony wine, combines the cabernet sauvignon and cabernet franc with the tannat, a local grape. It's so hard in its youth that, according to law, the wine must be aged for at least twenty months in wood before bottling.

Gascony's sweet wines come from Jurançon and Monbazillac.

Jurançon's vineyards, situated in the foothills of the Pyrenees near the Spanish border, were once known for their late-harvest wines redolent of quinces, nectarines and plums. Now large quantities of undistinguished white wines are mainly produced here. The white wine of Monbazillac, grown on rolling hills, bears a passing resemblance to the wines of Sauternes.

One of the oldest French viticultural regions is Cahors, situated some one hundred and twenty miles east of Bordeaux on the banks of the Lot River, which flows into the Garonne. Cahors is famous for its robust, tannic and inky *vin noir* (black wine). Pressed initially from the malbec, vin noir needed about a dozen years of aging; at maturity it exhibited a rich concentration of fruit and a great fullness of flavor. Made now in a more rapidly maturing style by the inclusion of the merlot and other grape varieties, the wine is lighter-colored and softer-textured. A number of Cahors vintners however are trying to bring back the earlier, richer, more slowly evolving versions of the wine.

In the Mediterranean Sea off the coast of Italy, the French island of Corsica has been engaged in viticulture since the ancient Greeks planted the first vines here. Corsica did not emerge as a notable producer however until the 1960s. At that time, Algeria had declared its independence from France and its new Muslim-led government virtually put an end to the country's wine production. The Algerian wine makers, forced to leave, transferred their operations to Corsica. Acknowledging its proximity to Italy, the island grows many Italian grape varieties but generally follows the Midi's style of vinification. Corsica's best-known wine is the full-bodied, high-alcohol red Patrimonio. Also grown on the island is a Beaujolais-like red wine, as well as some good rosés.

Although "France" has become synonymous with the most esteemed wines in the world, the country devotes more than four-fifths of its production to *vins ordinaire* or commonplace blends, and imports many additional wines as well. The imports come from Italy, Greece, Spain, Madeira, Tunis and Morocco, whose warm-climate wines are blended with high-acid, low-alcohol French wines for domestic consumption.

France exports most of its best products to western Europe, the United States and Japan. (Foreign sales attract higher prices.) A number of top vineyards in Bordeaux export anywhere from 50 to 80 percent of their output, while the proportion for some of Burgundy's vineyards is even higher. The French themselves have traditionally shown little interest in drinking their own best wines, but the emergence of a sizable middle class in recent years has created a larger domestic market for the country's finest wines.

NOTE: The French have also extended their wine-making operations beyond their own borders, investing in vineyards and wineries in Portugal, Chile and California.

ITALY

Italy, described as "one vast vineyard," grows grapes from virtually one end of the country to the other, from its Alpine valleys in the north to its sunny shores in the south. Italy is one of the leaders in the world's wine production. Encouraging the abundant and prolific yields here is a felicitous combination of soil and climate.

Long casual about its wine making, the country has been associated with flavorful but rough and often overoxidized wines; but seeking recognition as a serious producer, Italy has recently upgraded its vineyards and invested more heavily in its wineries. Moving into premium production, it has become the source of a number of elegant wines—while it continues to turn out great quantities of commonplace jug wines.

Of the hundreds of grapes cultivated, the nebbiolo is preeminent among the reds, followed by the barbera, freisa, grignolino, lambrusco, dolcetto, sangiovese and bonarda. In recent years French grapes have been introduced, particularly the cabernet sauvignon, merlot and pinot noir. Most widely planted among the white varieties are the trebbiano verdicchio, pinot bianco, malvasia, cortese, tocai and schiava, followed by the pinot grigio, chardonnay, sauvignon blanc, gewürztraminer and riesling.

Italy literally makes thousands of wines: red, white and rosé; still, sparkling and fortified. Most outstanding are the reds; robust, vinous and vigorous at their finest, with rich sustaining qualities. The whites, once characterized by a heavy, oxidized style, are now made fresher, leaner, livelier and more charming by modern vinification methods.

ITALY*
(AND SOME OF ITS WINES)

THE PIEDMONT
  Barolo
  Barbaresco
  Gattinara
  Barbera
  Ghemme
  Dolcetto
  Freisa
  Brachetto
  Cortese di Gavi
  Gavi dei Gavi
  Asti Spumante
LOMBARDY
  Valtellina: Sassella,
    Inferno and
    Grumello
  Oltrepo Pavese
  Lake Garda:
    Chiaretto,
    Lugana
ALTO ADIGE
  Terlano
  Santa Maddalena
  Kuechelberger
  Lagrein
FRIULI-VENEZIA-GIULIA
  Tocai Friulano
  Picolit
VENETO
  Bardolino
  Valpolicella
  Soave
  Recioto
  Torcolato
EMILIA-ROMAGNA
  Lambrusco
  Sangiovese di
    Romagna
  Gutturnio
  Albana di
    Romagna
LIGURIA
  Cinqueterre
  Dolceaqua
TUSCANY
  Chianti

Brunello di
  Montalcino
Rosso di
  Montalcino
Vino Nobile de
  Montepulciano
Vernaccia di San
  Gimignano
Galestro
Vin Santo
MARCHE
  Verdicchio
  Rosso Piceno
  Rosso Conero
UMBRIA
  Orvieto
  Rubesco
  Torgiano
LATIUM
  Frascati
  Velletri
  Albano
  Marino
  Grottaferrata
  San Giorgio
  Est! Est! Est!
CAMPANIA
  Lacrima Christi
  Taurasi
  Falerno
  Gragnano
APULIA
  Torre Quarto
  San Severo
CALABRIA
  Greco di Bianco
  Cirò
SICILY
  Corvo
  Faro
  Etna
  Malvasia delle
    Lipari
  Marsala
  Moscato di
    Siracusa

* The wines listed are but a small sampling of the country's prodigious output.

These now range from light, fruity and crisp to rich and full-bodied. A number are made both sweet and dry; the dry whites generally are intended for export.

Significant among Italy's twenty major wine-producing provinces are the Piedmont, Lombardy, Alto Adige, Friuli-Venezia-Giulia, Veneto, Emilia-Romagna and Liguria in the north; Tuscany, Marche, Umbria and Latium in the central sector; and Campania, Apulia and Calabria in the south, along with the island of Sicily. The premier Italian provinces are the Piedmont and Tuscany. The most prolific are Veneto, Apulia, Emilia-Romagna and Sicily.

THE PIEDMONT (PIEMONTE)

The Piedmont (Piemonte) is a small, somewhat austere province in northwestern Italy bordered by the Alps and the Appennine Mountains. Its capital city is Turin. Flowing through the region are the Po and Tanaro Rivers, with the prime vineyards sited on the banks of the Tanaro in the low but steep foothills of the Alps around Alba. (*Piedmont* translates as Foot of the Mountain.)

The Piedmont is celebrated for a host of outstanding red wines, pressed primarily from the nebbiolo grape. Other varieties include the barbera, freisa, dolcetto and grignolino. In recent years, the French cabernet sauvignon and merlot have been introduced. The Piedmont's premier red wines are Barolo, Barbaresco, Gattinara and Barbera; the first three are pressed exclusively from the nebbiolo, while the fourth is named for its own grape variety.

Barolo, sometimes referred to as the "King of Italian wines," is named for its village of origin southeast of Turin. Grown on the chalky soil of steeply terraced vineyards here, it is a deep ruby wine, robust and brawny, yet nevertheless displaying a certain austerity. Serving as a counterpoint to its hearty pungency is a rich, memorable bouquet suggesting roses and faded violets. Barolo is a slow-maturing, long-lived wine that acquires its delicious subtleties with age. Similar in style but earlier-maturing is Barbaresco, known as "Barolo's younger brother." Grown along the lower mountain slopes near the Tanaro River, Barbaresco is a lighter, rounder and slightly drier wine.

Less structured than Barolo but nevertheless slow-maturing

and long-lived is the rich, robust Gattinara, grown in the Novarra Hills near Milan. This wine at its finest exhibits a fruity aroma and an attractive aftertaste that suggests bittersweet almonds. Barbera, grown around the town of Asti, is a deep-colored, full-bodied wine, high in alcohol, with a sturdy softness. Some Barberas are vigorous in flavor and aroma, while others display a lighter, fruitier style.

Other Piedmont reds include Ghemme, Dolcetto, Freisa and Brachetto. Ghemme from the Novarra Hills is a powerful, full-bodied wine capable of considerable aging. Dolcetto, named for its grape, ranges from light and delicately dry to strongly flavored, depending on the character of the vintage and the style of vinification employed. There are in fact seven Dolcettos, each named for its own commune. Best known is the Dolcetto d'Alba, fresh-flavored and velvety, dry and yet fruity. Dolcettos from Aqui and Ovada are somewhat more astringent.

Freisa is also named for its grape variety. Vinified dry and semisweet, it is sometimes made sparkling. A particularly notable example is Freisa di Chieri, grown near Turin, a light, dry, fragrant wine with a raspberrylike aroma. Brachetto, also named for its grape and grown east of Barbaresco, is vinified sweet and dry too and is sometimes made sparkling.

The Piedmont is a region of intense white-wine production as well. Its leading white grape, the cortese, is responsible for the region's best-known Cortese di Gavi. (This white wine is named for the ancient village of Gavi, where the grapes grow close enough to the Italian Riviera to benefit from its balmy Mediterranean breezes.) Cortese di Gavi is a charming, crisp, aromatic and somewhat flinty wine, demonstrating a fine balance between fresh fruit and acidity. More rare is Gavi dei Gavi, which displays unusual richness and body for a white wine. The Piedmont is also the source of the best Asti Spumantes, while its lesser white wines serve as the base for the better Italian vermouths.

NOTE: Bearing a certain resemblance to the Piemontese wines are the red and white wines of Valle d'Aosta, an autonomous French-speaking district near Mont Blanc and the Swiss border. The alpine vineyards here rise more than two thousand feet above sea level.

VALLE D'AOSTA

TRENTINO-ALTO ADIGE

FRIULI-VENEZIA-GIULIA

LOMBARDY

VENETO

PIEDMONT

LIGURIA

EMILIA-ROMAGNA

TUSCANY

MARCHES

UMBRIA

LATIUM

ABRUZZI

MOLISE

SARDINIA

CAMPANIA

APULIA

ITALY

BASILICATA

CALABRIA

SICILY

LOMBARDY

Lombardy, extending from Lake Maggiore east to Lake Garda, encompasses three widely separate and disparate wine districts: Valtellina, Oltrepo Pavese and the southwestern shore of Lago di Garda (Lake Garda). Milan is its capital city. The Etruscans and Romans planted their vines in the region.

An alpine region of rugged mountains and quiet lakes, Valtellina is not far from the Swiss border. Some of its vineyards are sited twenty-five hundred feet above sea level on south-facing terraced land that slopes down to the Adda River and is sheltered from the harsh winds blowing south from Switzerland. Pressed almost entirely from the nebbiolo grape, Valtellina's red wines are deep-colored, sturdy, and rather dry. Unattractively hard in youth, they develop a real delicacy and a pronounced bouquet with age. Best are the wines of Sassella, Inferno and Grumello, grown in three hill-side areas centered around the town of Sondrio. Sassella is a bright ruby red with a delicate, fruity bouquet. Inferno, named for the summer heat of its wind-sheltered vineyards, is somewhat lighter in body. Grumello shares the qualities of the other two but to a lesser degree. Nearby Valgella produces a similarly sturdy and slow-maturing wine.

Valtellina is also celebrated for its rich, rare Sfursat or Sforzato, a concentrated, full-bodied and long-lived wine. Made from selected nebbiolo grapes that are left to dry in airy lofts for about two weeks, Sfursat can attain an unusually high level of alcohol for a table wine—about 14 percent or so.

Oltrepo Pavese, extending south and west of Lake Garda, is a hilly area near the city of Pavia. Its wines are often named for their principal grape. The barbera leads the reds, while the whites are pressed from the pinot bianco, cortese and riesling, among others.

Grown on Lake Garda's western shore is the gentle Chiaretto rosé, combining a delicate nose with a light, attractive bitterness in its aftertaste. From the southern edge of Lake Garda comes the white Lugano, a wine named for its tiny village. Pressed from the trebbiano grape, it is agreeably light, dry and delicately flavored.

ALTO ADIGE

Italy's northernmost producer is Alto Adige, a three-thousand-square-mile stretch of the Tyrol whose vineyards are sited in the Dolomites, the foothills of the Alps. The provincial capital here is Bolzano. Once part of the Austrian Empire and known as the Sud Tyrol, it became an autonomous region of the Italian Republic in 1919. Alto Adige is now bicultural and bilingual; its official documents and wine labels are printed in both Italian and German. The region's northern sector tends to be more German in its outlook, while the southern sector, is more Italian in its language and culture. (The larger political district is known as Trentino–Alto Adige.)

The grapes growing along the banks of the Adda River here include a number of white varieties associated with Germany and Austria—the riesling, sylvaner, gewürztraminer and müller-thurgau—along with the pinot grigio, pinot bianco, sauvignon blanc, chardonnay and muscat. Alto Adige's wines, among the country's finest whites, are dry, aromatic and fruity, with a rich softness. (A notable example is Terlano, named for its village, located not far from the Austrian border.) Some of the Alto Adige wines are made sparkling; others are exported in bulk to Germany, Austria and Switzerland for use in blending with their own wines.

Alto Adige also grows a number of red grapes associated with Italy and France. These include the pinot noir (called the blauburgunder or blue burgundian), the merlot and cabernet franc, along with local varieties such as the friuli, lagrein and schiava. The red wines here are generally light in color, low in tannin and early-maturing; a number display an attractive nutlike bitterness in their aftertaste.

The Lago di Caldaro district, called the Kaltersee in German, is noted for its fine reds. A prime example is the light, fruity, and delicate Santa Maddalena, grown on a mountain above Bolzano (Bozen in German). Northwest of Bolzano, the resort town of Merano produces Kuechelberger, another light fragrant red wine. Also noteworthy is Lagrein, a light- to medium-bodied red, named for its grape and displaying a faint touch of bitter almonds in its aftertaste. Produced in Alto Adige as well are light, fragrant, and often intensely fruity rosé wines.

FRIUILI-VENEZIA-GIULIA

Wedged between the Alps and the Adriatic in northeastern Italy is Friuli-Venezia-Giulia, one of Europe's oldest wine regions. It is bordered by Austria to the north and Slovenia to the east. The capital city here is Trieste.

Friuli produces large quantities of light, refreshing and generally quite dry red wines, pressed from cabernet sauvignon, cabernet franc and merlot grapes. The region is best known for its dry delicate whites, however, pressed from the pinot bianco, pinot grigio, chardonnay, tocai, malvasia and ribolla, among other varieties. The Pinot Gris wines are smooth, round and mouth-filling; the Chardonnays, clean and fresh-tasting. One of the most popular and appealing whites is Tocai Friulano: a fruity but subtle wine, with moderate acidity and a long finish. Friuli is particularly celebrated for its sweet golden Picolit, a legendary dessert wine.

VENETO

Veneto, one of Italy's largest and most varied wine regions, is in the northeast, stretching from Lake Garda to the Adriatic Sea. Its capital city is Venice.

Premium-wine production here centers around the Adige River, which rises in the Alps near Austria, then travels south and east. After a turbulent descent, the river flows serenely through the city of Verona before emptying into the Adriatic below Venice. Veneto's wines are fruity, light-bodied, soft-textured and relatively low in alcohol. Best known among the reds are Bardolino and Valpolicella, while Soave leads the white wines.

Bardolino, a fresh young wine pressed from local grapes, is named for a pretty hill town on the eastern slopes of Lake Garda. Known as the "Italian Beaujolais," Bardolino displays a charming fruity flavor, a faintly sweet character and a refreshing sharpness. Hardly darker than a rosé, it is sometimes described as one. Veneto also makes a true Chiaretto rosé.

Valpolicella, also pressed from local grapes, is produced in the foothills of the Alps near Verona. A smooth, supple wine with a pleasant fruity flavor, a delicate bouquet and a gently bitter after-taste, it is more deeply colored and fuller in body than a Bardolino, although still quite light in alcohol. Similar light red wines are produced in the nearby Valpantena district, named for a valley north of Verona. The best of these are labeled "Valpolicella-Valpantena."

Veneto also produces the robust, powerful and thickly textured Recioto della Valpolicella, made from selected grapes that are set aside to raisin for several months and then are slowly vinified. Intense, lush and complex, with tremendous depth, the wine exudes an aroma of violets and honeysuckle and displays a long lingering, raspberrylike finish. Yet austerely dry, the Recioto at its finest is a synthesis of astringency and richness. (Those aged for about three years are known as Amarones.)

Veneto's white wines are pale, dry and fragrant; some are made sparkling. The primary white wine is Soave, pressed from the garganega grape blended with the trebbiano or riesling. Medium-bodied and soft-textured, Soave is light and clean on the palate, fairly dry and zesty without being acid. Balancing out its fruitiness and imparting a fresh, piquant quality is a grassy or reedy undertone. The best Soaves come from the foothills of the Alps; those grown on the more prolific plain below are of a lesser quality. Adjoining the Soave district is Gambellara, which cultivates the same grape varieties and yields a similar but a generally lighter wine.

From north of Venice comes a dessert wine called Torcolato. (*torcolato* means twisted.) Its grapes, local varieties, are late-harvested and left on their branches, which are then braided into giant corkscrewlike strands about twelve feet long; these are hung indoors to dry for about three months. After the grapes are pressed, the wine is aged for a year in small oaken casks, and for an additional half-year in glass. The resulting wine is a sweet, rich, vinous and opulently mellow wine. Another rich dessert wine here is Prosecco, named for its grape. (A dry version is made as well.)

EMILIA-ROMAGNA

South of Veneto is Emilia-Romagna, bounded by the Appennines on the south and the Po River on the north. Its capital city is Bologna.

An extremely prolific region, Emilia-Romagna grows most of its grapes on a flat, fertile plain in the Po River Valley, although some are cultivated on the Appennine slopes above. The grape varieties include the red sangiovese di roma, lambrusco and barbera, as well as the white trebbiano, albana, sauvignon blanc and malvasia.

Emilia-Romagna produces vast quantities of red and white wines. Best known is the red Lambrusco, grown west of Bologna. Named for its grape, Lambrusco is a light-colored, very fruity wine, somewhat on the sweet side and often naturally effervescent. Other notable reds here are the dry Sangiovese di Romagna, produced near the Adriatic port city of San Marino and the light red Gutturnio, produced in the hills south of Piacenza. Of particular interest among the white wines is the excellent and semisweet Albana di Romagna, produced near San Marino and named for its grape.

LIGURIA

Liguria is a remote and rugged arc of land on the Italian Riviera, curving along the crescent of the Gulf of Genoa from Monte Carlo to just beyond Portofino. Running the entire length of the arc are steep, craggy cliffs. Strong retaining walls at the water's edge protect the terraced vineyards. The geographic and economic center of the region is Genoa.

Liguria produces both red and white wines. Most celebrated is its white Cinqueterre, whose name, translating as "Five Lands," refers to the five wine-producing villages that border the gulf between Chiavari and La Spezia. Known since medieval times, Cinqueterre—pressed from raisined grapes—is golden and luscious with an intensely aromatic bouquet. Now, however, the wine more often is vinified crisply dry. Liguria's best-known red wine is the light dry, ruby-colored Dolceaqua, produced near the town of San Remo.

TUSCANY

Tuscany in central Italy is a rugged landscape of undulating hills and wooded valleys. Its capital city is Florence. The region's dominant grapes are the red sangiovese and its clone, the sangioveto. Tuscany is famous for its great red wines: Chianti, Brunello di Montalcino and Vino Nobile de Montepulciano.

The world-famous Chianti district—bounded by Florence, Arezzo and Siena—includes seven separate wine-producing areas, covers some one hundred seventy-five thousand acres and encompasses about seven thousand vineyards. (A number of vineyards have been passed down within the same family for as many as ten generations. One Florentine citizen represents the twenty-sixth generation of his family in the wine trade.) At the center of the district is the Chianti Classico zone, officially delimited in 1716, a one-hundred-square-mile area deemed superior in its soil and climate. The Chianti Classico wines—dark, tannic, rich and concentrated—display an attractive astringency that makes them lively on the palate. At their finest they combine both great character and a certain delicacy. An enchanting violetlike bouquet and a long, lingering aftertaste characterizes them as well.

As a group, however, Chianti wines can vary considerably. Some are light and fresh while others are dark and heavy. Some are thin, some fat; some soft and others rough. Some are full-bodied and intensely flavored, others are light and uncomplicated. Some are soon ready to drink, others need further aging. Many are light grapy and unpretentious at best, or harsh and acidic at worst. The lesser examples may be bolstered by the addition of *il governo,* a richly sugared concentrate boiled down from dried grapes. Causing the new wines to referment, *il governo* increases their alcohol, body and vinosity. It not only perceptibly sweetens the wines, but introduces a fresh "burnt" flavor.

Chiantis have traditionally blended together red and white grapes . (The wines were initially called "vermiglios" because of their bright scarlet color.) The classic blend, devised in the late nineteenth century, combines the red sangiovese, canaiolo and other varieties with the white trebbiano and malvasia. The official formula calls for 70 to 90 percent red grapes and 10 to 30 percent white. By law, only those Tuscan red wines that meet these requirements can be called Chiantis.

In the 1960s, the Tuscan vintners—seeking to produce darker, richer wines—began placing a greater emphasis on the red grapes and reducing the proportion of the whites or omitting them alto-gether. They also began to use such atypical grapes as the cabernet sauvignon, cabernet franc and merlot. The resulting wines could not by law be called Chiantis. Instead they were given such names as Solaia, Sassicaia, Carmagnano, Ornellaia, Pomino, Tiscvil and Tiganello.

Produced beyond the southernmost reaches of the Chianti zone is Tuscany's most complex wine, Brunello di Montalcino. (It's named both for the sangiovese grape—known locally as the brunello—and for the hill town of Montalcino.) Darker, richer and more powerful than the Classico Chiantes, Brunello di Montalcino was created in the nineteenth century when a particular san-giovese clone was isolated. Big, warm and deeply concentrated, the wine at its finest displays a velvety texture combined with rich fruit flavors and aromas. A subtle dryness balances out its intense richness. In good vintages, a Brunello needs decades of develop-ment.

NOTE: The growing demand for Brunello has resulted in the expansion of its vineyard acreage—initially limited to a total of fifty acres. In some cases, it has also led to vinifying the wines for earli-er maturation.

Tuscany also produces Rosso di Montalcino called "Brunello's younger brother." Pressed from the same grape varieties as the Brunello but from the fruit of younger vines, and aged more briefly in wood, it is a more accessible wine, ready to drink much earlier. Produced some thirty miles south of Siena and named for a lovely hill town there is Vino Nobile de Montepulciano, pressed from the same grape varieties as traditional Chiantis. An outstanding full-fla-vored, medium-bodied red wine, it is delightfully dry with a good bouquet.

Tuscany is also associated with generally fresh and agreeable white wines. Best known is the pale gold Vernaccia di San Gimignano, produced in the heart of Chianti country and named for its many-towered medieval city south of Florence. Medium in body, the wine displays a delicate but penetrating bouquet at its finest, accompanied by a somewhat dry finish. Galestro, one of the region's modest little white wines, is pale, dry, and crisp; it sometimes displays a slight natural effervescence. And particularly celebrated is Tuscany's vin santo, a lusciously rich dessert wine.

MARCHE

Marche in central Italy, extending from the Appennines to the Atlantic, was a medieval borderland (a *marca*) between the north and south. Its capital city is Ancona. Marche is famous for its white Verdicchio, named for a local grape that is blended with the trebbiano and the malvasia. Light and fruity, with a delicate bouquet enhanced by a crisp, dry undertone, Verdicchio is also pleasantly bitter in its aftertaste.

Among the red wines of Marche are Rosso Piceno and Rosso Conero. Rosso Piceno, pressed primarily from the sangiovese, is a soft, slightly dry wine with a pleasant bouquet. Rosso Conero, pressed mainly from the montepulciano, is a robust and agreeably dry wine.

UMBRIA

Umbria is a small landlocked region west of Marche. Its capital city is Perugia. Umbria grows both red and white wines but is generally noted for its whites. Best known is Orvieto, named for a famous cathedral town perched on a mountainlike outcropping of rock. A fruity white, Orvieto is vinified both as a semidry and a dry wine. The semidry version is delicate and fragrantly sweet with no hint of cloying; the dry is fresh and crisp with a flowery bouquet and a slight, attractive bitterness in its undertone.

Best known among the Umbrian red wines is Rubesco, pressed from sangiovese and canaiolo grapes. Deep ruby in color and excellent in body and bouquet, Rubesco takes well to aging, becoming soft, round, generous and velvety smooth at its finest. Another noteworthy Umbrian red is Torgiano, named for its town of origin. A number of the region's other reds reflect the current trend of including French grapes in their blends. Some are half-cabernet sauvignon and half-pinot noir in their composition.

LATIUM

Latium, Lazio, south of Umbria, lies between the Appennines and the Tyrrhenian Sea. Its capital city is Rome. Latium is known for its fruity white wines, pressed from trebbiano and malvasia grapes. They range from the crisp and dry to the semisweet and on to the decidedly sweet. Particularly noteworthy are the Castelli Romani (Roman Castle) wines, grown in a number of hill villages southeast of Rome. These include Frascati, Velletri, Albano, Marino, Grottaferrata and San Giorgio.

Frascati's fresh and fragrant wine, famous since the Renaissance, displays a good degree of fruit combined with a touch of acidity and a slight attractive bitterness in its aftertaste. (An almost neutral version is made for export.) Velletri, produced nearby, is somewhat lighter bodied and lighter flavored. The modest white Albano grown in six communes in the fertile uplands of the Colli Albani (Alban Hills) is vinified both semidry and dry.

From the slopes of Lake Bolsena north of Rome comes Est! Est! Est!, a white wine that acquired its curious name in the twelfth century. According to legend, a wine-loving bishop on his way to Rome was in the habit of sending his manservant ahead to scout out the best possible inns to stay the night. Whenever the manservant found a likely place, he would chalk the word *est* on the door, short for *vinum bonum est* (the wine is good). In the little village of Montefiascone, the wine proved so splendid that the manservant enthusiastically scrawled "Est! Est! Est!" on the door of the inn. Apparently the bishop agreed. He never resumed his journey, but lived out his days in Montefiascone happily savoring the pleasures of the local wine.

NOTE: Est! Est! Est! was initially a light-bodied, semisweet wine pressed exclusively from muscat grapes. It is now a trebbiano and malvasia blend and vinified somewhat drier.

CAMPANIA

Campania lies on a fertile plain south of Rome. Hovering above is the volcanic Mount Vesuvius. The region's capital is Naples. Campania produces both red and white wines. Of special interest is the white Lacrima Christi (Tears of Christ), a fairly dry, somewhat aromatic wine pressed from the greco della torre grape, grown on the south-facing slopes of Vesuvius. (A richer, sweeter version is made from raisined grapes.)

NOTE: Although a number of Italian wines have appropriated the colorful Lacrima Christi name, only the authentic versions carry the phrase "del Vesuvio" on their labels.

Among Campania's red wines are Taurasi, Falerno and Gragnano. Taurasi, which traces its lineage back to the Greeks, is pressed from the aglianico grape, sometimes blended with the barbera or sangiovese. Robust and full of complex fruit, it has been called the "Barolo of southern Italy." Falerno is a singularly fragrant, medium-bodied wine that is often vinified semidry, while Gragnano is a soft, light and fruity red.

Offshore from Campania are the islands of Capri and Ischia, facing each other across the Bay of Naples. Capri produces white wines, a number of them clean and dry, while others are somewhat sweetish. Ischia is known for its good red and white wines and—perhaps wishing to associate itself with Capri's reputation for fantasy and romance—has often borrowed the Capri name for its wines, as have other wines from the nearby mainland.

APULIA

Apulia, Puglia, located in the heel of Italy's geographic boot, is a prolific province and the country's largest wine producer. Its regional capital is Bari. A rugged land with a rich, claylike soil, Apulia is best known for its strong, hearty, uncomplicated red and white wines. Of special interest is its red Torre Quarto from the Castel del Monte district, a wine with a good bouquet. Also noteworthy are the sturdy reds and rosés of San Severo.

As a rule though, Apulia's wines lend themselves best to blending; the medium- to full-bodied reds usually act as body builders for the thinner wines of the north, while the whites serve as base wines for Italian vermouths. However, modern vinification methods have enabled Apulia to improve its red wines and to produce clean, fresh-tasting white wines as well.

CALABRIA

Another prolific province is Calabria, located in the toe of the Italian boot and characterized by rough terrain and a hot, dry climate. The capital city here is Reggio. Calabria's generally coarse wines are best suited to blending; its heavy reds are shipped in bulk to northern Italy and France to strengthen their thinner wines, and its full-bodied whites serving as base wines for Italian vermouths. But produced here as well are medium-bodied, dry red wines and sturdy, flowery whites. Of particular interest is the white Greco di Bianco, along with the red, white, and rosé wines of Ciro.

NOTE: Basilicata, a region north of Calabria, is known for its dry, intense, and bold red wines, and particularly for its Aglianico del Vulture.

SICILY

Lying offshore from Calabria and almost within sight of North Africa is the island of Sicily, whose capital city is Palermo. Seven centuries before the birth of Christ, the Greeks and Carthaginians were planting their muscat vines here.

Sicily's volcanic soil and warm climate yield wines that are full in body and high in alcohol. Best known are the red and white Corvos grown south of Palermo, near the little town of Casteldaccia. The red Corvos, soft, fine and velvety, yet almost austerely dry, display an abundance of fruit, a mouth-filling flavor and a berrylike bouquet. The somewhat more ordinary whites have been made clean and crisp by modern vinification.

From the northeastern sector of Sicily near Messina comes the ruby-colored Faro, which exhibits qualities unusual in a warm-climate wine: these are a lightness of body, a dryness of flavor and a delicate nose. From eastern Sicily come the Etna wines, named for the great volcano towering over the city of Catania. The red Etnas are full-bodied and not too alcoholic; their good acidity makes them pleasantly dry. The white Etnas are straw-colored and intensely aromatic.

Sicily is particularly known for its luscious, sweet, aromatic dessert wines, pressed from raisined grapes. Especially celebrated are those from the small Lipari Islands lying off Sicily's northern coast. A wine of particular interest is the deep-colored Malvasia di Lipari, which at its finest possesses a ripe velvety taste and a rich aroma suggesting ripe apricots; it's somewhat reminiscent of a good Sauternes. From the torrid expanses of Sicily's west coast come the world-famous Marsalas, generally dark and sweet with a raisiny flavor. Among the rich, heady Muscat wines of the south-eastern sector is the fine Moscato di Siracusa.

NOTE: Sicily ships many of its wines out in bulk, often sending its reds to Germany to strengthen that country's paler red wines. Sicily's white wines usually remain at home to serve as a base for Italian vermouths or to be distilled into brandy.

SARDINIA

Some one hundred and twenty-five miles away from the Italian mainland is the island of Sardinia, lying just below Corsica in the Tyrrhenian Sea. Its regional capital is Cagliari. On its mountainous terrain, Sardinia grows many of the same grape varieties as the mainland. The island is best known for is white wines, vinified both dry and sweet. Of particular note is its Vernaccia di Oristano, a rather dry aromatic, high-alcohol wine that serves as an apéritif. (A sweeter version is made as well.) Sardinia also produces sweet Muscat wines and savory red wines, made both dry and sweet.

NOTE: Other Italian wine regions of note include Abruzzi or Abruzzo and Molise. Abruzzi in central Italy is known for its lusty red wines (including the Montepulciano d'Abruzzo), and for its complex dry whites (including the Trebbiano d'Abruzzo). Molise on the Adriatic coast produces clean dry whites, along with sturdy red and rosé wines.

SPAIN

Spain, like Italy, is a largely mountainous country, but it's somewhat more arid. Currently it has more than four million vineyard acres under cultivation. Although devoting more of its acreage to grape growing than either Italy or France, Spain produces relatively less wine because of its general aridity.

The Phoenicians planted vines here. The Romans, on their arrival, found viticulture already thriving, and soon Iberia was supplying wine to Imperial Rome. When the Roman emperor, Domitian, sought to suppress competitive wine growing in A.D. 92, Iberia was singled out as one of his prime targets, but it was not easily subdued.

SPAIN

RIOJA	MÁLAGA
CATALONIA	LA MANCHA
Penedés	Valdepeñes
Alella	THE LEVANT
Tarragona	Valencia
Priorato	Alicante
ANDALUSIA	CASTILLA-LEON
CÓRDOBA	Ribera del Duero
GALICIA	

After weathering this crisis, Spanish wine making had remained essentially unchanged for centuries. The vintners would toss the tannic stalks and stems into their vats and age their wines in a leisurely fashion. In recent years, Spain, seeking to expand beyond its largely domestic market, has been exporting its wines in earnest. It has in the process updated its vineyards and modernized its wineries. A number are now capable of immense production.

Spanish wines reflect the generous warmth of their climate. Red wines predominate. They range from the simple and uncomplicated to the more formal, subtle and sophisticated. White wines run the gamut from light and aromatic to full-bodied and floral. The country makes good rosé wines as well.

Cultivated among the red grapes are the native tempranillo, parellada, garnacha (grenache), graciano, cariñena, mazuela and xarello, along with the French cabernet sauvignon and cabernet franc. White grapes include the indigenous viura, verdejo and albariño, along with the French chardonnay.

There are seventeen wine-producing regions in Spain; the major ones are Rioja and Catalonia in the north and Andalusia in the south. Other wine regions of note are La Mancha, the Levant, Castilla-Leon and Galicia.

RIOJA

Rioja, the premier table-wine region, lies along the banks of the Ebro River in north-central Spain. The Ebro is joined near Pamplona by a smaller tributary, the Rio Oja, whose name in shortened form has become the name of the region.

Rioja is a small, largely treeless area surrounded by chalky white cliffs. Many of its terraced vineyards, sited more than fifteen hundred feet above sea level, are sheltered by the Pyrenees from the cold winds of the north. Encouraging the slow and gradual ripening of its grapes is a long spring season with abundant rainfall, giving way to a relatively gentle summer, followed by a warm, prolonged autumn.

The Romans made wine in the region in the first century. Six centuries later the Moors conquered the territory and—observing the teachings of the Koran—forbade wine making. In the Middle Ages, Benedictine monks restored its production. In the nineteenth century when phylloxera devastated France, many of Bordeaux's vintners fled over the Pyrenees to Rioja, greatly influencing the style of the region's wine making and helping to establish its noteworthy reputation.

NOTE: Because Rioja is essentially a landlocked region, its wines were little known to the outside world at first. Those that were exported had been used primarily in blending. However extensive road building after World War II provided greater access to Rioja and its wines.

About three-fourths of Rioja's wines are red. The main grapes employed are the tempranillo and garnacha (grenache), followed by the mazuela and graciano. The wines themselves range from the darker, fuller-bodied Tintos, which display a strong tannic backbone and intense berrylike flavors, to the lighter-colored, lighter-bodied and velvety Claretes. Classic Riojas reflect the

French influence. Matured extensively in wood, they exhibit the body and much of the elegance of a good French Bordeaux combined with a deeper, more assertive Spanish bouquet. Under the more recent influence of American importers, less tannic, more moderately oaked and earlier-maturing red wines are now being produced. Lacking the solid structure of their classic prototypes, they are softer, more supple and more accessible wines.

Traditionally, the region's white wines, like the reds, were fermented and aged in wood and considered drinkable only when quite oxidized and tasting heavily of oak. Vinified in stainless steel now and bottled young, they are lighter, fresher and ready to drink in about six months. Most are vinified dry, but a number are made semisweet. The white grape varieties include the viura, malvasia and calgrano.

Rioja encompasses three subregions: Rioja Alta, Rioja Alavesa and Rioja Baja. Rioja Alta, to the west, is subject to a moist, cool climate and grows its grapes about twelve hundred feet above sea level. Its vineyards are clustered around the city of Haro, the principal center of the region's wine trade. Produced in Rioja Alta are some of Spain's best table wines; characterized by good acidity and a great potential for aging. The finest among them demonstrate both distinction and elegance.

Rioja Alavesa, located at the tip of the Basque province of Alba, shares the terrain, climate and soil of Rioja Alta, but its sheltering mountains keep the vineyards warmer and drier. The wines here are richer, fruitier and softer, and as a rule show less capacity for aging. Rioja Baja is the region's vast lower sector. Subject to a hotter climate, it yields somewhat heavier and coarser wines. Usually, the products of all three sectors are blended together for better balance. (The house styles of the individual producers determine the relative proportion of each sector's wine in the blend.)

NOTE: Another important Spanish wine producer is Navarra, just east of Rioja. (It is also the site of Pamplona and the running of the bulls.) Situated in north-central Spain and extending from the Pyrenees to the Ebro River basin, Navarra is noted for its red and rosé wines, many of them pressed from such Bordeaux grapes as the merlot, cabernet sauvignon and cabernet franc, as well as from native Spanish varieties.

GALICIA

CASTILLA-LEÓN

RIOJA

CATALONIA

DUERO R.

EBRO R.

RUEDA

ALELLA
PENEDÉS
TARRAGONA

PORTUGAL

MADRID

LA MANCHA

VALENCIA

VALDEPEÑAS

ALICANTE

GUADALQUIVIR R.

ANDALUSIA
MONTILLA-MORILES

JEREZ
SANLÚCAR DE
BARRAMEDA

MÁLAGA

SPAIN
VINEYARD AREAS

CATALONIA

Catalonia, east of Rioja, lies adjacent to the Mediterranean coast. Its principal wine districts are Penedés, Alella, Tarragona and Priorato.

Penedés is about twenty-five miles west of Barcelona. A wedge-shaped area of chalky hills sloping down to the sea, it was a center of wine production under the Romans but fell into disuse under the Moors and did not reemerge as a substantial wine producer until late in the nineteenth century.

Penedés (Penedés in the Catalan language) is celebrated for its surprisingly light dry white wines, grown in the mountains along the coast. Relatively high in acidity and low in alcohol, they are particularly well suited to the production of sparkling wine.

Traditional white grapes grown here are the parellada, maccabeo, viura and cariñena, but cultivated as well now are the muscat, riesling, gewürztraminer, sauvignon blanc and chardonnay. Penedés red wines are robust, lush and velvety at their finest, displaying a rich texture and a fruity aroma. Their blends include such traditional Spanish grapes as the tempranillo and garnacha along with the French cabernet sauvignon, cabernet franc, pinot noir and carignan.

The Alella district north of Barcelona is one of the smallest wine producers in Spain. It grows grapes on its granite slopes, and four-fifths of its wines are white. Among the country's best whites, Alella's wines are usually vinified semisweet.

Southwest of Barcelona is Tarragona, once a wine supplier to Imperial Rome. Produced here are red, white and rosé wines. Best known among the reds is the sweet full-bodied Tarragona; the whites include sweet Muscatels. A number of the wines are fortified. (France employs them in its apéritif blends.) To the north is Priorato, a small area specializing in strong dry reds, characterized by a lush blackberrylike fruitiness.

ANDALUSIA

Andalusia in southern Spain is the home of the world-famous sherries. Many invaders marched through the region: Phoenicians,

Greeks, Carthaginians, Romans, Visigoths, Vandals and Moors. The main town of Jerez some three thousand years ago was a Phoenician outpost called Zera. The Greeks modified its name to Shera; the Romans to Serit. The Moors, crossing over from North Africa, called it Sherez later to become Jerez (pronounced *hair-ETH)*. During the five centuries of Moorish occupation, grape cultivation continued here, but most of the berries were consumed as raisins. (Some were vinified however and their wine was sold to the infidels.) The Moors were ousted in the thirteenth century. By the fifteenth, Jerez had become a fortress on the Christian-Moslem border and had appended the phrase *de la Frontera* (of the Frontier) to its name.

The sherry zone is bordered on two sides by the Rio Guadalquivir and the Rio Guadelete, and on the third side by the Atlantic Ocean. It is known as the "Golden Triangle." Located within a twenty-mile radius are the towns of Jerez de la Frontera, Puerto de Santa Maria and Sanlúcar de Barrameda.

Low, hilly and treeless, the Jerez district experiences cool winters, rainy springs and fiercely hot summers whose temperatures often rise to 100 degrees. Gentle breezes and dry winds blowing in across the sea from North Africa mitigate the intense heat. Produced here are low-acid white wines, ideal for sherry making. The grape varieties cultivated include the palomino, pedro ximénez (PX) and, to a lesser extent, the moscatel. The palomino is responsible for the delicate fino wines and the pedro ximénez is employed in the fuller-bodied olorosos.

Three distinct kinds of soil characterize the Jerez district: albariza, barros and arenas. Albarisa—whose name derives from *albero,* meaning white—is lime-rich and chalky, yielding rich wines that demonstrate the greatest finesse. The denser, more clay-like *barros* produces heavier wines, whereas the sandier, more prolific *arenas* yields somewhat thinner ones. For better balance, the wines of all three soils are generally blended together.

Northwest of Jerez and about one hundred miles inland is the province of Córdoba, encompassing the vineyards of Montilla and los Moriles. Cultivated here are PX grapes. The Montilla-Moriles wines are grown on arid chalky soil too, but are subject to cooler upland conditions. They bear a strong resemblance to the sherries

and are often confused with them although they're usually characterized by less bouquet and breed than first-rate sherries. They display at their finest exceedingly delicate flavors and aromas.
Because their alcohol levels naturally reach as high as 16 percent,
these wines receive little or no fortification.

About one hundred miles east of Jerez on the southern coast
of Spain is Málaga, celebrated for the fortified wines that bear its
name. Pressed from PX and muscat grapes, these wines are rich,
raisiny and intense.

LA MANCHA

La Mancha in central Spain south of Madrid is the country's largest
wine producer, accounting for about half of its wine output. A vast
province with more than a million acres in vines, it is subject to a
hot, dry climate comparable to that of the French Midi or
California's Central Valley.

La Mancha is best known for its red wines, many of them light,
fruity and refreshing, and not much darker than a dark rosé. (They
have been called the Beaujolais of Spain, while the region's more
tannic reds are usually marketed as Spanish Burgundies.) Of La
Mancha's five wine-producing villages, Valdepeñas (whose name
translates as Valley of Stones), is the most important. It is located in
rolling upland country near Andalusia. The red wines of La
Mancha's other villages tend to be more ordinary. Also produced in
the region are white wines, somes now vinified crisp and dry to
suit the current preference.

THE LEVANT

The Levant, situated on the east coast and subject to a hot dry climate, is another vast wine-growing area. The region's deep, heavy,
high-alcohol reds, produced in great quantities, are usually exported
for blending, while its medium-bodied whites generally serve as bar
wines. The Levant's best-known wines come from Valencia, famous
for its orange groves. Another noteworthy producer is Alicante, located farther south and known for its full-bodied red wines, its light
rosés and its rather bland whites, along with some sweet Moscatels.

CASTILLA-LEON

Castilla-Leon is in northern Spain. Running through it is the Duero River, which becomes the Douro when it flows almost due west into Portugal. Grapes have been grown on the banks of the river and wines made here since Roman times. Castilla-Leon includes the newly demarcated Ribera del Duero district near Valladolid, the source of dark red wines that are well-structured, fruit-filled and succulent at their finest. Legendary among them is the rare and expensive Vega Sicilia, a blend of local grapes—primarily the tempranillo—and such classic French varieties as the cabernet sauvignon, merlot and malbec. Vega Sicilia is made only in exceptional years and aged extensively in oak, sometimes for more than a decade. Intensely rich and densely textured, the wine demonstrates a great subtlety of flavor and aroma. Another noteworthy red, Pesquera del Duero, also grown near Valladolid, is made almost entirely from the local tinto del pais grape and extensively aged in wood. Dark and brawny, rich and concentrated in its fruit, Pesquera exhibits at its finest the intensity and elegance of a high-caliber St-Émilion or a Pomerol.

GALICIA

Galicia in northwestern Spain is the country's coolest and wettest province. Produced here are red, white and rosé wines. The whites, pressed from the albariño, are similar to the Portuguese vinho verdes grown across the border. Smooth-textured, somewhat acid and vinified either bone-dry or near-dry, these exhibit at their finest an applelike crispness and a rich fragrance. The red wines include Vino de Riverso and Ribeiro del Avia; the former is pleasant and fruity with a pronounced flavor, the latter is big and rough. Galicia produces good rosé wines as well.

CANARY ISLANDS

The Canary Islands, which lie in the Atlantic Ocean off the northwest coast of Africa, were much celebrated in Shakespeare's day for their extraordinary Malvasia wines grown on the islands' volcanic soil. In the nineteenth century, phylloxera wiped out the wine industry here and it never quite recovered. Although the Canaries still produce some wine, little of it is exported.

PORTUGAL

Portugal, which shares the Iberian Peninsula with Spain, experiences virtually the same soil and climate but relies more on hand labor in its wine making. (Many of the wines are still fermented in the same stone lagars in which the grapes are crushed.) Portugal is best known for its fortified ports, its rosés and its slightly sparkling vinho verdes. Less familiar are its noteworthy red and white table wines. The reds, which range from fruity and light to bold and deep-bodied, display at their finest subtlety, complexity and distinction. The whites, substantial and aromatic, are now made clean and crisp by modern vinification methods.

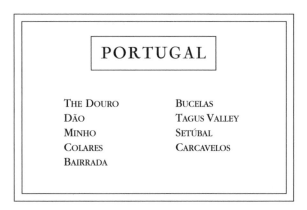

PORTUGAL

THE DOURO	BUCELAS
DÃO	TAGUS VALLEY
MINHO	SETÚBAL
COLARES	CARCAVELOS
BAIRRADA	

Most of the country's wine growing is concentrated in the northern and western sectors. Portugal's main wine regions are the Douro, Dão and Minho.

THE DOURO

The rugged Douro Valley in the northeast, beginning near the mouth of the Rio Douro (River of Gold), is the source of the world-famous port wines. The region was officially delimited in 1756. The Douro River, a great waterway, rises in the mountains north of Madrid (where it's called the Duero), then runs for some seventy miles in a westerly direction before turning abruptly south at the Portuguese border. After plunging more than a thousand feet in a series of gorges and rapids, the river again turns westward and flows swiftly to the Atlantic Ocean.

Port wines are grown in the Alto Douro (Upper Douro), a bleak mountainous, almost inaccessible area extending for some thirty miles on either side of the river. Lining its steep banks are terraced vineyards that cling precipitously to the slopes. (Many of these vineyards were created by blasting the rugged rocks with dynamite.) Winters are severely cold here, frequently with heavy frost, while summer temperatures often exceed 100 degrees. The rainfall is sufficient but not excessive. A long growing season, with the sun blazing down from April through October, enables the grapes to ripen intensely.

Douro wines range from youthful rubies and tawnies to splendid and elegant Vintage Ports. Their grapes include the indigenous touriga, tinta, bastardo and alvarelhão. (Anywhere from seven to several dozen varieties go into the port-wine blends.)

The Douro's traditional wine centers are Oporto, the hillside city for which the wine was named, and Vila Nova de Gaia downriver, where the young wines are taken in the spring for blending and aging. (Until 1987, it was illegal to bottle or ship port wines from anywhere in the country but the lodges of Vila Nova de Gaia.)

The Douro is also the home of another prestigious red wine, the full-bodied, long-lived and richly flavored Barca Velha developed in the 1950s. Its predominant grape is the tempranillo. Barca Velha is made only in exceptional vintages. Another noteworthy Douro red wine is Ferreirnha, grown at the region's northern edge. The Douro produces somewhat fruity rosé wines as well.

Dão

Some fifty miles southeast of Oporto is Dão, a small mountainous region characterized by a hard granitic soil. Dão is well known for its red table wines, which range from the robust, intense and full-flavored to the soft, fruity and easy-to-drink. Some Dao wines exhibit a berryish taste, a slightly puckerish quality, and a long, tart, pleasing finish reminiscent of a Bordeaux. Other Dão wines display the spicy aromas and flavors associated with the Rhône Valley. The finest examples, pressed from the same grape varieties as port, are noted for their longevity. The Dão region also produces firmly structured and not-too-dry white wines and rosés.

OTHER PORTUGUESE DISTRICTS

Minho in the northwest is known for its naturally effervescent white wines, particularly its vinho verdes, pressed from the alvarinho grape. Other Portuguese districts of note are Colares, Bucelas, the Tagus Valley, Setúbal and Bairrada. Colares, on the Atlantic coast west of Lisbon, yields dark tannic wines. Unappealingly harsh when young, they acquire a soft, flowerlike bouquet with age. (Salt air blowing in from the ocean adds a certain piquancy.)

NOTE: The vines of Colares, among the very few ungrafted in the world, have been able to resist phylloxera because they are planted so deep in sandy soil that the destructive aphid cannot reach their roots.

The hill country of Bucelas north of Lisbon, is noted for its white wines. Some are dry, fresh and lively, while others are quite sweet. The Tagus Valley, northeast of Lisbon, is known for its deep-colored reds, which demonstrate soft smooth flavors with age. Immediately south of Lisbon is the peninsula of Setúbal, celebrated for its sweet Moscatel de Setúbal. This white wine, fermented on grape skins, acquires a honeylike taste, an almost overwhelmingly rich bouquet and a definite potential for aging. Also south of Lisbon is Carcavelos, whose high-alcohol, almond-flavored wine serves as an apéritif. Bairrada in the west-central part of the country near Coimbra has been called the "Bordeaux of Portugal" because its red wines are noted for their ageability and finesse.

GERMANY

Germany is Europe's most northerly wine-growing country, with a latitude roughly that of Newfoundland. Despite a relatively harsh climate, the temperatures during its short growing season are mild enough to ripen the grapes properly. The Romans cultivated vines here in the first century. By the third, the Mosel Valley represented the northern frontier of the Roman Empire. In the ninth century, Charlemagne was setting up his vineyards. By the tenth, Germany was exporting its wines to Britain.

About 85 percent of the German wines are white; the best of them are among the world's finest. Rich, flavorful and ripely scented, they achieve a remarkable balance between high fruit acidity and a natural sweetness. They also tend to be low in alcohol—generally between 8 and 11 percent.

German grape varieties include the riesling, müller-thurgau, sylvaner, rulander, gewürztraminer, gutedal, kleinberger and kerner. The riesling is responsible for the most elegant wines. Relatively light in alcohol and possessing less body as a rule, these can more brilliantly and distinctly reveal their subtle nuances of flavor and aroma. However, the more widely distributed wines are Liebfraumilch, Moselblumchen, Zeller Schwartze Katz and Niersteiner Domtal. They are usually characterized by a blandness and an often cloying sweetness. Germany's few red wines, pressed from spätburgunder (late-ripening Burgundy) and dornfelder grapes, are relatively low in tannin and generally soft and thin. They are often bolstered by more robust high-alcohol wines imported from warm-climate countries.

The wine regions of Germany are the Rhineland and its subdivisions, and the Mosel-Saar-Ruwer, Franconia and Baden, followed by Nahe, Hessiche Bergstrasse and Württemberg. Of greatest viticultural importance are the Rhineland and the Mosel-Saar-Ruwer.

RHINELAND

The Rhineland encompasses the valleys of the Rhine River and its tributaries. The country's most valuable wine region, it consists of the Rheingau—the preeminent district—the Rheinpfalz or Pfalz and Rheinhessen, as well as Mittelrhein, Ahr and Assmannhausen.

The Rheingau

The prestigious Rheingau is situated on the north shore of the Rhine River. That river, after following a long, impetuous course down from Switzerland, is deflected by the Taunus Mountains

GERMANY

RHINELAND	NAHE
Rheingau	FRANCONIA
Rheinpfalz or	BADEN
Pfalz	HESSICHE
Rheinhessen	Bergstrasse
Mittelrhein	WÜRTTEMBERG
Ahr	
MOSEL-SAAR-RUWER	

when it reaches Mainz, causing it to turn briefly westward. The Rheingau region is located on this straight and narrow stretch of land running from east to west. (It begins near Hochheim and ends just west of Rüdesheim.) Only some twenty miles long and two to five miles wide, the Rheingau encompasses many of the country's greatest vineyards. These, sited on steeply terraced slopes, enjoy an incomparable southern exposure, while the Taunus Mountains shield them from the harsh cold winds of the north. Because the grapes often grow a thousand or more feet above sea level here, some vineyard names end in -berg meaning "mountain," as in Steinberg and Ruppertsberg.

Four-fifths of the Rheingau's wines are Rieslings. Austere but mouth-filling, these are generous, well-rounded, firm and complex wines. Offsetting their fruity, flowery flavors is a definite crispness. They exhibit at their finest extraordinary grace and breed, amazing vitality and great stamina. With a fine acid balance, even the richest among them possess the potential for aging.

The great wine villages of the Rheingau include Rauenthal, Eltville, Erbach, Hattenheim, Hallgarten, Oestrich, Winkel and Geisenheim; some are sited on the banks of the Rhine River, others are set farther back in the hills. Erbach is celebrated for its scented fruity wines, especially those grown in the Marcobrunn vineyard. Hattenheim's wines are distinguished by grace and elegance; Oestrich's heavier soil yields wines that are fuller in body. Rauenthal's finely scented wines demonstrate a certain spiciness. Those of

AHR

KOBLENZ

MOSEL R.

RHEINGAV

FRANKFURT

MOSEL-SAAR
RUWER

BINGEN

FRANCONIA

RHEINHESSEN

NAHR

RHEINPFALZ

WÜRTTEMBURG

GERMANY
VINEYARD AREAS

RHINE R.

NECKAR R.

BADEN

FREIBURG

Hallgarten are often the most pronounced in flavor, while Eltville's wines are consistently charming.

One of the Rheingau's leading wine estates is Schloss Johannisberg, sited on a high slope above the river's north bank. Its wines are particularly prized for their concentration and scent. This vineyard was established by Charlemagne, who observed that snow in the spring melted here sooner than elsewhere. In the nineteenth century, the Congress of Vienna ceded Schloss Johannisberg to the Austrian emperor, who in turn deeded it to Prince von Metternich. The von Metternich family still retains a degree of ownership in the property.

Another estimable estate here is Schloss Vollrads, nestled in the nearby hills above Winkel. This vineyard has been in the hands of the same family for six centuries. Its wine displays at its finest a great fruity character and an impeccable balance. The notable Steinberg vineyard, situated directly behind the village of Hattenheim, was established in the twelfth century by a monastic Cistercian order and secularized some seven centuries later. It is now the property of the German Staatsweingut, or State Domain. (Kloster Eberbach, the original monastery adjacent to the vineyard, has been converted into a wine museum.) Steinberg's typically fruity and powerful Rieslings demonstrate a great deal of breeding.

On reaching Rüdesheim, the most westerly village of consequence, the Rhine River abruptly shifts from its straight east-to-west course and resumes its generally northerly direction. Located to the east where the Rhine is joined by the Main, one of its tributaries, is the village of Hochheim. Although technically Hochheim's wines are produced outside the boundaries of the Rheingau, they are so similar in style and character that they're generally grouped with the Rheingaus. Their most notable vineyards are Kirchenstuck and Domdechaney.

NOTE: Hochheim's wines have long been popular with the British, who shortened their name to *hock;* this subsequently became the generic name for all German white wines.

At the western end of the Rheingau, between Rüdesheim and Lorch, is Assmannhausen, an eighty-five-acre tract growing spätburgunder grapes and responsible for Germany's best-known red wines. These are velvety and fiery in some vintages and not very powerful in others. Produced in Assmannhausen as well are note-worthy late-harvest rosé wines.

Rheinpfalz or the Pfalz

The Rhineland's next important subdivision is the Pfalz, located south of the Rheingau. It's also known as the "Rhenish Palatinate," having been named for one of Rome's seven hills. The vastest wine-producing region in the country, the Pfalz is a fertile plain about 50 miles long and 2¹/₂ to 4 miles wide. Situated on the river's left bank, it lies along the lower slopes of the Haardt Mountains—a continuation of the French Vosges—which shield its vineyards. Spring here arrives early, and a strong sun during the growing season makes the Pfalz one of Germany's warmest and driest areas.

The aristocratic riesling is grown on its better soils but müller-thurgau and sylvaner grapes predominate, followed by the rulander, tokayer, traminer and muscat. The Pfalz wines range from mild and thirst-quenching to big, heavy and robust; they display at their finest breed and bouquet coupled with a definite but unobtrusive sweetness. Lesser wines here tend to taste heavily of the soil.

The Pfalz is divided into Ober, Mittel, and Unter Haardt (Upper, Middle, and Lower Haardt) sectors. The Upper and Lower Haardt are areas of large production. Their heavier soil yields generally undistinguished wines, many of them not bottled at all but served from the cask as carafe wines or consigned to commonplace blends. The Middle Haardt, the most favored sector, shares the climate but not the soil of the other two. (The soil in its best vineyards is a sandy, schistous basalt.) The most notable Middle Haardt estates are Diedesheim, Forst, Ruppertsberg and Wachenheim.

Rheinhessen

Located north of the Pfalz on the west bank of the Rhine is Rheinhessen, also known as Rhenish Hessia. Running parallel to the Rheingau across the river, Rheinhessen begins near the city of Worms, continues north as far as Mainz, then extends west to Bingen. A plateau with a few wooded areas, it is sheltered from harsh weather by a series of hills. Because its characteristically heavy soil contains dark reddish sandstone, some of its vineyards have been named Rotenberg (Red Mountain) and Scharlachberg (Scarlet Mountain).

Rheinhessen is Germany's largest wine producer. Only about a fourth the size of the Pfalz, it devotes almost as much acreage to grape growing. Its subdistricts are Nierstein, Wonnegau and Bingen. Most important is Nierstein, whose sunny vineyards yield full, fruity, fragrant wines. Nierstein's leading wine towns are Nackenheim, Oppenheim and Dienheim. To the north is the village of Ingelheim—the site of Charlemagne's palace—specializing in white wines but known for its reds as well.

In Rheinhessen, the riesling grape yields full-bodied, vigorous and fragrant wines characterized by great fruit. (As a rule these do not age as gracefully as their more austere counterparts in the Rheingau.) The bulk of Rheinhessen's wines however are pressed from sylvaner and müller-thurgau grapes. Soft and moderately dry, they often lack real character. Those grown in heavier soils acquire an earthiness and a sweetish quality; they are generally consigned to commonplace blends.

Rheinhessen's most widely exported product is Liebfraumilch. Pressed originally from the riesling grape and produced in a monastic vineyard on the outskirts of the city of Worms, it was a mild, fragrant and delicate wine with a light earthy taste that reflected its alluvial soil. Over the years, however, Liebfraumilch has become a haphazardly blended and somewhat sweet wine pressed primarily from the sylvaner. More representative of the region are the wines produced by three vineyards located at the original monastery site: Liebfrauenstift, Liebfrauenstift Klostergarten and Liebfrauenstift Kirchenstueck. Another commonplace and widely exported Rheinhessen wine is Niersteiner Domtal. (This is not a Niersteiner wine at all, but a miscellaneous blend drawn from various vineyards that may or may not be located in the region.)

Other Rhine Districts

The Mittelrhein is an eighty-four-mile stretch of gentle slopes and slatey, claylike soil north of the Rheingau. (It's traversed by the

Rhine River, which, after passing through the Rheingau, resumes its northward course.) The Mittelrhein wines are full-bodied, vigorous and hearty, more pronounced in their fruit and acidity than those of the Rheingau.

Farther north and across the river is the Ahr, named for its own river, which joins the Rhine north of Koblenz. Germany's largest continuous red-wine region, the Ahr cultivates spätburgunder and portugieser grapes. Their generally light wines—more pink than red—are for the most part consumed locally. The Ahr also produces steely white wines, pressed from riesling and müller-thurgau grapes.

MOSEL-SAAR-RUWER

The Mosel-Saar-Ruwer region, north and west of the Rheingau, consists of three interconnecting river valleys: the Mosel and its tributaries, the Saar and the Ruwer. The region cultivates some three hundred thousand acres in vines.

The Mosel Valley

The Mosel River, rising in the Vosges Mountains of France (where it's called the Moselle), sweeps northward toward Lorraine, then skirts Luxembourg to enter Germany at Trier. Before joining the Rhine River at Koblenz, it meanders capriciously in a northeasterly direction for nearly a hundred miles. Following a twisting serpentine course, the river executes a bizarre series of hairpin turns, which encompass a number of microclimates. The vineyards are sited wherever the exposure is favorable—some on the left bank, some on the right. The vines themselves are cultivated on the incredibly steep terraced slopes lining the river.

More than half of the Mosel wines are pressed from the riesling. (Other grape varieties are the müller-thurgau, kerner and bacchus.) The wines, generally airier and more delicate than others in Germany, are characterized more by bouquet than by body. At their finest, they display a great but unobtrusive sweetness combined with a tart, refreshing bite. Mosel wines have been described as a "mingling of honey and steel: honey in the scent and steel in the finish." The slate-strewn soil of the region is in part responsible for their delightful freshness and unique flowery scent.

The Mosel Valley is divided into upper, middle and lower sectors. Yielding generally undistinguished wines are the Upper Mosel at the southern end of the valley and the Lower Mosel, where the river runs a straighter course. Of greatest importance is the Middle Mosel, where the river is most serpentine. Notable wine towns here are Piesport and Bernkastel, followed by Wehlen, Zeltingen, Graach and Trittenheim.

Piesport's south-facing vineyards, sited on 120 acres of steep, rocky terrain, rise some five hundred feet above the river. Its wine, wonderfully light, delicate, and subtle, has been called the "Queen of the Mosel." Preeminent among the vineyards here is Piesporter Goldtröpfchen, whose name translates as Golden Droplets. Bernkastel, another notable wine town, is across the river and dominated by the Doktorberg (Doctor Hill). Its most celebrated vineyard, Bernkasteler Doktor, acquired its name in the fourteenth century when—according to legend—the Prince-Bishop of Trier was stricken by a mortal illness. When all other treatments had failed, the prelate drank the Doktorberg wine and was miraculously cured.

Light, engaging wines are also produced in Trittenheim, south of Piesport. Those of Wehlen north of Piesport are prized for their delicacy. In Ürzig, north of Wehlen, the brick red soil yields interesting, spicy wines that are among the region's longest-lived. Zeltingen, farther north and across the river, produces some of the fullest-bodied of the fine Mosels. The village of Erden, north of Zeltingen, is famous for its Treppchen vineyard, whose name translates as Little Staircase. (Steps cut into its stony slope provide better access to the steeply terraced vineyard.) South of Zeltingen is the tiny but well-known village of Graach, noted for its fine Himmelreich and Josephshofer wines.

Saar

The Saar River also rises in France and, flowing in a generally northerly direction, joins the Mosel a few miles west of Trier. While some parts of the Saar Valley are warm and well protected, others are vulnerable to the harsh northern winds. Frost is not uncommon in May, and hailstorms are always a possibility in summer.

The prime vineyards here are sited on steeply slanted slopes; their soil is slatelike and crumbly. Their riesling grapes, higher in acidity than those of the Mosel, yield generally more austere wines. At their finest, these wines display an especially firm, elegant character and a great depth of flavor. They have been likened to a "steel fist in a velvet glove."

The Saar's largest and most important wine town is Wiltingen, located southwest of Trier. Cultivated here on a few south-facing and incredibly steep hills are some 330 acres of vines. Wiltingen's most notable vineyard is Scharzhofberg, which yields complex and finely scented Riesling wines. (Occupying some seventy acres or so, it is shared by a number of owners.) The Rieslings of the adjoining town of Oberemmel are somewhat similar. To the west is Kanzem, whose wines also closely resemble those of Wiltingen but tend to be a bit fuller in body.

Other Saar communes of note are Ockfen and Ayl, which are situated on opposite banks of the river. Ockfen is known for its great Bockstein vineyard, much celebrated for its scented, well-balanced Rieslings. Ayl's eminent vineyards are Herrenberg and Scheidterberg. Also noteworthy in the Saar Valley is the Vogelsang vineyard, situated in the village of Serrig.

R u w e r

A few miles downstream from Trier is the much smaller Ruwer region. (It's only about six miles long.) Ruwer's typically light dry wines are closer in character to those of the Saar than to those of the Mosel. Gently subtle with a bit of spice, they combine at their finest a considerable bouquet, a delicate floweriness and a certain elegance.

A number of famous vineyards line the Ruwer River's slaty banks, most notably Maximin Grunhaus in Mertesdorf, and Karthauserhofberg in Eitelsbach. Maximin Grunhaus—which was the property of the St. Maximin monastery in the tenth century— is now owned by the family that acquired it nine centuries later. Karthauserhofberg, once operated by Carthusian monks, is now a much subdivided vineyard.

NAHE

Nahe, another of the smaller regions in Germany, lies west and north of Rheinhessen. Its river, running in a generally northeastern direction for about eighty miles, joins the Rhine after passing through Bad Kreuznach. The open and undulating Nahe Valley, located between the cities of Bingen and Bingerbruch, encompasses some eight thousand acres of vines.

Its climate is mild, dry and generally sunny, with an early spring and a long autumn. The soil on its often steep hillsides is diverse, consisting of slate, gravel, fertile loam, igneous rock and sandstone. Grown here are riesling, sylvaner and rulander grapes. Nahe wines—somewhere in character between those of the Mosel and the Rhine—range from the markedly flowery, fragrant and delicate to the full-bodied and powerful.

The Nahe is divided into upper, middle and lower sectors, with the Middle Nahe chiefly responsible for the region's fine reputation. Its most famous vineyards are Kreuznach and Schloss Bockelheim. The Kreuznach wines—fresh, clean-tasting and well balanced—display a soft fruity charm, whereas those of Schloss Bockelheim tend to be somewhat lighter. Other noteworthy Nahe towns are Roxheim, Niederhausen and Norheim. Roxheim's wines are clean, fresh and fruity; those of Niederhausen are more full flavored, while the Norheim wines range in quality from fine to fair.

In the Upper Nahe, where the soil consists of slate and igneous rock, fresh. lively Rieslings and other good white wines are produced. In the Lower Nahe, where the river assumes a predominantly northern course and the vineyards are confined to the left bank, the wines are somewhat fuller bodied.

FRANCONIA

Franconia, east of Rheinhessen, is situated in the upper valley of the Main River. As that river winds its way through the Franconian hills in an erratic series of turns, bends and loops, it creates a discontinuous region characterized by both desirable microclimates and by patches of land that are not at all suitable for the grape. Spring is generally short here and frost always a possibility, even in mid-May. The summers are, however, long and dry.

On its generally heavy soil, Franconia grows sylvaner, müller-thurgau and riesling grapes. Their sturdy, full-bodied wines, lower in acidity than the other Rhine wines, are dry and well balanced at their finest and exhibit an earthy firmness. They also possess an unsuspected alcoholic strength and great keeping powers.

Franconia's principal town and main wine center is Würzburg. (Other villages of note are Randersacker and Escherndorf.) Würzburg is celebrated for its prestigious Stein vineyard, whose chalky slope is called the Steinmantle. The Steinweins, largely riesling in their composition and among Germany's longest-lived, bear a greater resemblance to the drier wines of France than to the sweeter Rhine and Mosel wines. (The Steinweins are bottled in distinctively shaped *bocksbeutels,* or goat pouches, which are rounded glass flasks with flat sides.

NOTE: Although other Franken and German wines have borrowed the *Steinwein* name and have been bottled in bocksbeutels, the authentic wines come only from the prestigious Stein vineyard.

BADEN

Baden is Germany's most southerly wine region. Situated in the foothills of the Alps and subject to a rather dry climate, it yields primarily white wines, ranging from the gentle, low-acid and low-alcohol to the full-bodied and robust. These are pressed from rulander, sylvaner, gutedal (chasselas), riesling and gewürztraminer grapes. About a fourth of Baden's wines are red. Pressed primarily from the spätburgunder, they range from velvety to fiery.

Baden's prize district is the Kaiserstuhl (King's Throne), a small cluster of low volcanic hills rising from a plain northwest of Freiburg. The Kaiserstuhl became a viticultural area in the nineteenth century when a German army surgeon visiting Italy observed vines flourishing on the slopes of Mount Vesuvius and thought a vineyard might thrive on Baden's volcanic soil as well. Because of its warm climate and great productive capacity, the Kaiserstuhl was called the "Kitchen of Bacchus," named for the Roman god of wine. The best wines here are white and pressed from rulander grapes, grown on the southern slopes.

The Markgräfler subregion is located between Freiburg and Basel near the Swiss border. Its principal grape, the gutedal—known locally as the markgrafler—yields a pleasant but short-lived white wine. Ortenau, situated across the Rhine from Strasbourg in Alsace, cultivates the gewürztraminer, as its French counterpart does, and the Ortenau wines sometimes achieve an Alsatian charm. Nearby is Breisgau, growing a noteworthy *weissherbst* (rosé wine). Bodensee, on the north shore of Lake Constance close to the French border, is noted for its light red Seewein (Lake Wine), pressed from the spätburgunder grape.

HESSICHE BERGSTRASSE

Hessiche Bergstrasse is a thirty-three-mile stretch of vineyards across from Rheinhessen on the east bank of the Rhine, running between Heidelberg and Darmstadt. Its climate is one of Germany's mildest, and its soil is extremely fertile. Hessiche Bergstrasse's wines have long been grouped with those of Baden. Although quite heady, they're generally drier than the Rhine wines and display less bouquet, but they're enlivened by a refreshing acidity. Most of the wines are consumed locally.

WÜRTTEMBERG

Württemberg, in the Neckar Valley east of Baden, is primarily a red-wine area. (Its principal city is Stuttgart.) Württemberg grows spätburgunder and portugieser grapes, among others, producing fruity hearty wines that exhibit an attractive and earthy aftertaste. Also produced here is a light red Schillerwein, which blends together red and white grapes. Its white wines, pressed from riesling, sylvaner, müller-thurgau and traminer grapes, are also somewhat robust in character. Most of Württemberg's wines are consumed locally.

NOTE: Germany also imports a number of warm-climate products from Europe and elsewhere to strengthen its paler red wines and to fill out its sparkling-wine blends. German producers have been involved with wine making outside their own borders as well. In the eighteenth and nineteenth centuries, they set up their own Champagne-producing establishments in France. The successful dynasties they created then continue to function to this day.

THE UNITED STATES

The United States, which spans three thousand miles from the Atlantic Ocean to the Pacific, produces wine in more than forty of its fifty states. Its commercial wine production, however, is concentrated mainly on the East and West coasts; California alone accounts for about 90 percent of the country's output. Other major western states are Washington and Oregon. The leader in the East is New York, followed by Virginia, Florida, Pennsylvania, Arkansas, New Jersey and Ohio. Among the other wine-producing states are Idaho, Connecticut, Michigan, Illinois, Missouri, Arizona and Texas.

NOTE: West of the Rocky Mountains, vinifera grapes are cultivated, whereas in the East, labruscas predominate; they're supplemented by hybrids. An increasing emphasis on growing vinifera grapes has recently been evident in the East.

NEW YORK AND THE NORTHEAST

In the eleventh century, the Vikings landed near what is now Massachusetts and found wild grapes growing there in abundance. They named the locale "Vinland the Good." Some five centuries later, English colonists domesticated the indigenous grapes but found their wines quite unlike those they had known at home. Characterizing them was an unfamiliar pungency, a certain "foxy" flavor.

Attempting to reproduce the more familiar Old World wines, the colonists began importing vinifera cuttings from France, Germany and Italy. They also recruited vintners from Europe. Yet all their efforts failed. The northeastern growing season was too brief for the tender viniferas and the fluctuations in climate too extreme: intense heat marked the summers, while winter temperatures could plummet to minus 17°F. And ever present were mold, mildew and other forms of vine disease.

In the nineteenth century, when phylloxera decimated the vineyards of Europe, attention was shifted there to the hardier, more resistant American vines. (Transplanted rootstocks were to save the European viniferas from extinction.) As a result, American vintners began to single out and cultivate the premium labruscas. Although the definite foxy character of their wines persisted, the Americans found they could subdue some of the excessive pungency.

Nevertheless, attempts continued to produce more "European-tasting" wines despite the accepted wisdom that only indigenous grapes and sturdy hybrids could withstand the harsh northeastern winters. Some wine makers, believing the viniferas could survive with proper care, began to grow these grapes again in the 1950s, employing more advanced methods of cultivation and grafting. Since the 1970s, more and more growers have been planting viniferas, although they continue to cultivate native grape varieties and hybrids as well.

With its generally short growing season, the northeastern United States is better suited to the cultivation of white grapes. Among the viniferas grown are the riesling, chardonnay, sauvignon blanc, gewürztraminer, aligoté and muscat. Although red grapes experience more difficulty, the pinot noir, merlot and cabernet sauvignon are also grown here. Native American grapes include the white diamond, dutchess, aurora, diana, elvira and ives, and the red concord and catawba and delaware. Joining them are such hybrids as the white seyval blanc, seibel, cayuga, vidal blanc and ravat, and the red alden, baco noir, bath, beta, buffalo, chelois, clinton, de chaunac, léon millot, maréchal foch, schuyler, van buren and yates.

New York State

New York is the Northeast's major wine-producing state. Its naturally high acid white wines have proved particularly suited to sparkling-wine production. (At the time of the Civil War, New York accounted for about half of the American sparklers produced.) In the early 1900s, the emphasis was on growing indigenous high-sugar concord grapes and on fortifying the resulting wines, making them sweet, rich and syrupy. An increasing interest in cultivating viniferas has led to a wide variety of table wines—red, white and rosé—in addition to those that are fortified or made sparkling.

New York's main viticultural regions are the Finger Lakes, Lake Erie, the Hudson Valley and Long Island.

The Finger Lakes

New York's premier wine producer is the Finger Lakes region, situated between Rochester and Syracuse. A compact, eighty-square-mile area of rolling countryside, it encompasses mostly small farm wineries. (The lakes themselves are long, narrow bodies of water that moderate the chill of the northern climate.) Of greatest importance is Lake Keuka near Hammondsport, where the first vines were cultivated in 1812. By 1860, Keuka's wines, particularly its sparkling wines, were widely known. (The other Finger Lakes of note are Canandaigua, Seneca and Cayuga.)

The Hudson Valley

One of the oldest wine areas in the country is the Hudson Valley, located north of New York City. In 1677, French Huguenot refugees planted vines here near New Paltz. And before the Civil War, a Croton Point winery was selling its products in New York City. In recent years, the valley has seen a considerable expansion of its vineyard acreage, mostly in the lower sector. A number of wineries are now active in Ulster, Dutchess and Orange Counties.

Lake Erie

Westernmost is the Lake Erie region in Chautauqua County. It begins at Buffalo, stretches along the southern border of Lake Erie, and continues over the Pennsylvania line into northern Ohio. The region, accounting for about 50 percent of New York's vineyard acreage, produces red and white wines. Most of these are consumed locally.

Long Island

Although wine was made on Long Island as early as the seventeenth century, production on a commercial scale was not launched until the 1970s. (It began with an experimental vineyard in what had been a potato field.) Wine is now produced on the eastern end of Long Island, which is divided into North and South Forks. Of the more than a dozen vineyards operating, most are concentrated on the North Fork, between Mattituck and Southold. This area, located between a bay and a sound, enjoys a moderate maritime climate that creates a longer growing season than is experienced by most of New York's other wine districts.

Long Island grows vinifera grapes. White varieties include the chardonnay, gewürztraminer, johannisberg riesling, fumé blanc, chenin blanc and pinot blanc. (The Chardonnay wines at their finest display a rare crispness and delicacy here.) Long Island has also proved suitable for red-grape cultivation. The merlot, a consistent performer, has emerged as the leading red varietal, yielding a medium-bodied wine with lively flavors and aromas. The cabernet franc also produces appealing wines and the cabernet sauvignon has shown substantial gains.

NOTE: Since Long Island growers do not always produce enough grapes to meet their own wine-making needs, they sometimes purchase additional berries, primarily from California and Oregon.

THE PROHIBITION ERA

In 1919, American wine making was brought to a standstill by the Eighteenth Amendment to the U.S. Constitution. Better known as Prohibition, the amendment banned the sale of all alcoholic beverages. Although essentially aimed at hard liquor, it forced nearly all of the country's wineries to shut down. A handful survived by producing sacramental wines and medicinal spirits. (The spirits, euphemistically described as "tonic medicines," required a doctor's prescription and were dispensed by pharmacies.)

Although described as a "noble experiment" by some, Prohibition worsened the problem it was intended to solve. It ushered in an era of political corruption and organized crime. Illegal sales, known as bootlegging, flourished, and dealers often resorted to violence to obtain and sell the illicit beverages. After a decade and a half of lawlessness, the amendment was finally repealed in 1933 and the right to regulate the sale of alcoholic beverages was returned to the states.

During Prohibition, many fine vineyards had been neglected or uprooted, with their grapes largely replaced by fruit trees, corn or other crops. The few vintners who remained were cultivating table grapes or selling grape juice. The labels on the bottles of grape juice warned that adding yeast could result in fermentation, but many purchasers saw this as a recipe, not an admonition.

When repeal finally came, most of the wineries had fallen into disrepair, their equipment rusted away or sold for scrap. Skilled wine makers had drifted off into other occupations. Cooperage and storage facilities were inadequate. There was no system for marketing or distributing wine. In short, the industry needed to be totally reconstructed. Yet just as the growers were beginning to replant and the wine makers to retool, the Depression of the 1930s struck, followed by World War II. American wine making did not come into its own until three decades later.

CALIFORNIA

California is a vast state stretching more than seven hundred miles from north to south and two hundred miles from east to west at its widest. Found within its borders is an astonishing diversity of topography, soil and climate. The weather in the cooler north, along the shores of San Francisco Bay, is somewhat reminiscent of the northern Rhône. Yielded here are high-sugar, low-acid grapes whose wines are sweeter, richer and heavier than their French counterparts in Bordeaux and Burgundy. Earlier harvesting and other modifications have improved their sugar-acid balance. In the Central Valley are torrid conditions resembling those of the Mediterranean Basin. And Southern California, too, is relatively hot.

California's first vines were planted in the seventeenth century by Spanish missionaries who had moved north from Mexico and needed wine to celebrate mass. (Importing wine from the mother country was a slow, uncertain process.) A Jesuit priest, Juan Ungarte, set up a vineyard in Baja California. By 1769, Padre Junípero Serra, a Franciscan monk, had established the first American settlement, the Mission San Diego, and planted vines around its tile-roofed adobe buildings. The vines flourished; their grapes were called mission grapes.

Under Padre Serra's direction, the Franciscans gradually moved north to the state's cooler valleys, setting up a chain of twenty-one missions in the five hundred miles between what are now the cities of San Diego and Sonoma. (Each mission was located a day's journey by horseback from the next.) Linking them together was the Camino Real, the "King's Highway." Many important California cities were to develop around these missions: Santa Barbara, Santa Clara, San Luis Obispo, San Gabriel, San Miguel and San Francisco.

Eventually, the missions were secularized and subsequently shut down. Private citizens began to take over the abandoned vineyards and to set up vineyards of their own. (The Franciscans had inadvertently stimulated local interest in wine when they bartered their excess sacramental wine for necessary supplies.) The first major secular pioneer was Bordeaux-born Jean-Louis Vignes, who planted more than a hundred acres of imported French vines in the pueblo of Los Angeles.

Vignes should have been named the Father of California Viticulture, but that title went to Agoston Haraszthy, a flamboyant Hungarian entrepreneur with an engaging manner and a knack for impressing others. Haraszthy, who claimed to be an aristocrat and later took to calling himself Colonel, set up his first vineyard near San Diego in 1852, then gradually moved north as the Franciscans before him had done. By 1857, he had established one of the state's largest wineries in Sonoma.

Haraszthy proved a first-class wine promoter, convincing the newly formed California legislature that the state could produce some of the world's finest wines and persuading the governor to send a commission abroad to study wine making, with himself at its head. The commission visited France, Italy, Germany, Spain and Russia, and acquired some two hundred thousand cuttings, representing nearly five hundred vinifera varieties. Haraszthy planted some of these in his own vineyard, handing out the others to his fellow growers on a random basis. (His disorganized method of distribution was to create viticultural confusion in the state for many years to come.)

Earlier, the nineteenth-century Gold Rush had given California's fledgling wine industry a boost. The prospectors, thirsty for wine, stimulated the expansion of vineyards to the foothills of the Sierra Madre Mountains, virtually next door to the mines. Further impetus came at the turn of the century with the arrival of immigrants from Italy who brought with them their wine-drinking and wine-making traditions. (A number of major California wineries trace their origins back to this time.)

Prohibition devastated western viniculture as it had the eastern. Fine California vineyards were converted to fruit orchards or cattle pastures. Only six or seven wineries escaped dismantling; they were producing sacramental wines and medicinal spirits. Yet the demand for California wine grapes continued, coming mainly from European immigrants who were settling in the East. Accustomed to taking wine with their meals, they were making it at home. (Then, as now, the U.S. government permitted each one-adult household to make 100 gallons a year for personal consumption.) The immigrants were buying thin-skinned viniferas from California, but the grapes—shipped across the country by rail—did not hold up very well. Sturdier, more durable varieties had to be substituted. Their wines however were more sugary and heavier-bodied, requiring fortification to preserve them.

Characterizing the early western wine industry were huge vineyards growing lesser grapes and giant wineries producing sweet wines in bulk, generally for fortification. With the repeal of Prohibition, California began to rebuild. Its wine makers became experimenters and innovators. Less bound by tradition than their European counterparts and stimulated by developments in enology, agricultural research and industrial techniques, they made respectable the application of technology to wine growing and wine making.

Influencing them at first were studies undertaken by scientists at the University of California at Davis, who had analyzed the state's viticultural characteristics and divided California into a number of climate zones based on the weather during the growing season and on the degree-days of heat observed. The Californians, believing that soil and viticulture were secondary to weather, championed the idea of climate as the main quality factor in wine making. The Europeans, on the other hand, have stressed the primacy of the soil. Recently, California has focused more on soil and plant culture, too. Adapting various grape varieties to local growing conditions, California has been producing higher-quality wines.

California now grows more than one hundred twenty-five viniferas commercially, most of them meant for wine. (The others are employed as table grapes or raisins.) Leading the red grapes are the cabernet sauvignon, zinfandel, pinot noir and merlot. Other red varieties include the gamay beaujolais, grenache, petite sirah, barbera, charbono, grignolino, carignane and ruby cabernet. Leading the white grapes are the chenin blanc, chardonnay and johannisberg riesling. Other white varieties include the sauvignon blanc, pinot blanc, traminer, sémillon, gray riesling, sylvaner, colombard, folle blanche, emerald riesling, green hungarian, muscat, málaga, aligoté, gewürztraminer, müller-thurgau, palomino, pedro ximénez (PX) and thompson seedless. There has also been an emphasis in recent years on cultivating such Rhône grapes as the syrah, cinsault and mourvèdre, and on growing Italian grapes—especially the sangiovese, a Tuscan favorite.

California now produces a wide array of red, white and rosé wines—still, sparkling and fortified. The best examples come from the more northerly regions, where the morning fog and sea breezes mitigate the heat of the day. Most of the wines, however, come from the state's hotter and drier central and southern sectors.

California encompasses some two hundred and thirty wine regions. Wine growing begins at the Mexican border and extends north to Mendocino, but is perhaps best understood when divided into the North Coast, Central Coast, Central Valley and Southern California regions.

North Coast

The North Coast, which fans out beyond the upper reaches of San Francisco Bay, encompasses Napa, Mendocino and Sonoma Counties, although its actual boundaries have never been officially drawn up. Because of its various microclimates, the North Coast experiences widely different growing conditions. At its northern end, it's warm enough to grow robust zinfandel grapes; at its southern end it's cooled by the bay's fog and breezes, making it better suited to the white chardonnay and riesling and the red cabernet sauvignon and pinot noir.

The prime wine area here, sometimes called the "American Médoc," is Napa Valley, set between the Mayacamas and Howell mountain ranges. About thirty miles long and five miles at its

widest, Napa stretches north from the Carneros district at the northern tip of San Francisco Bay to Calistoga. While the city of Napa itself is situated east of the Mayacamas range, its vineyards and wineries are located farther north—near Yountville, Oakville, Rutherford, St. Helena and Calistoga.

NOTE: Napa's main subregions are Rutherford and Stag's Leap. Carneros, which is also considered a subregion, straddles the southern ends of both Napa and the adjacent Sonoma County.

Napa Valley is celebrated for its well-balanced, plummy and slow-maturing red wines, pressed mainly from the cabernet sauvignon grape cultivated in the cool uplands. Some of the best examples come from Rutherford, specifically from Rutherford Bench, a three-mile stretch whose topsoil sits on a gravel bed deposited by an old stream. (*Bench* indicates the low slopes of a ridge.) The majority of the cabernets, however, are grown on the valley floor below. Napa is notable as well for its outstanding sparkling wines.

Sonoma, directly to the west and running virtually parallel to Napa—is separated from it by the Mayacamas range—is also known as the "Valley of the Moon." A large, sprawling district, almost seventy-five miles long and about fifteen miles at its widest, Sonoma produces about twice as much wine as Napa. Bordering the Pacific, it's subject to morning fog but also to a warmer afternoon sun. Sonoma yields generally softer wines than Napa.

Its subregions are Dry Creek, Alexander Valley and Russian River. Russian River is best known for its chardonnay grapes, and Dry Creek for its zinfandels, while the versatile Alexander Valley grows the cabernet sauvignon, chardonnay, riesling, gewürztraminer and chenin blanc. (Carneros, a cool, foggy district straddling Napa and Sonoma Counties, grows chardonnay and pinot noir grapes.)

NOTE: In recent years, the Napa and Sonoma vineyards have attracted the interest of French, Spanish, British and Japanese investors, who have made substantial purchases of these properties. Much of Napa's wine making is now under corporate ownership and largely high-tech in character, although a few small traditional vintners continue to operate here.

Mendocino, directly above Sonoma, and the most northerly of the North Coast counties, is a heavily forested coastal area. (Its grape cultivation is limited to the inland valleys.) Spring here is warmer than in Napa but the summers are somewhat cooler. The Russian River rises in the eastern half of the district; whereas the western half—the site of Anderson Valley—is more subject to fog and frost and has proven ideal for sparkling-wine production. Most of the Mendocino vineyards are centered around the town of Ukiah. The primary red grapes grown are the cabernet sauvignon and zinfandel. (The latter produces the best wines.) The primary white grapes are the chardonnay, colombard and sauvignon vert. Mendocino produces great quantities of red and white wines, including a large share of the state's jug wines.

Other North Coast districts include Lake and Amador Counties. Lake County, a landlocked area east of Mendocino and Sonoma, is known for its rounded red wines. Amador, some one hundred miles east of Napa, specializes in full, rich zinfandels, although it grows cabernet sauvignon and chardonnay grapes as well. Also considered part of the North Coast are El Dorado, Calaveras and Nevada Counties.

Central Coast

In the 1960s, population growth and accelerating real estate prices forced many North Coast wine makers to relocate to previously undeveloped land south and east of San Francisco Bay. These new areas, involving thousands of acres, are sometimes considered part of the North Coast but can more properly be classified as Central Coast, although the boundaries here, too, are also vaguely defined. The Central Coast has been variously described as extending from Monterey to Santa Barbara, or from south of San Jose to Santa Ynez, or as beginning just below San Francisco and stretching all the way south to Los Angeles. The district does, however, encompass Monterey, Santa Cruz and Alameda Counties, along with Santa Barbara, San Luis Obispo and the Sierra foothills.

Its hot, dry climate was once considered suitable only for growing alfalfa and for grazing cattle, but cool breezes blown in from the Pacific temper the heat of the sun while the fog reduces its intensity. Scientists, armed with sophisticated soil and weather data, have found a number of suitable microclimates. Grown here now are the red cabernet sauvignon and pinot noir and the white chardonnay and sauvignon blanc, among other varieties. There has also been a recent emphasis on growing such Rhône Valley grapes as the grenache, syrah, mourvèdre and cinsault.

Some of the best Central Coast vineyards are situated between San Francisco and Monterey. Monterey, the most extensive wine-growing county, features granite slopes, sandy soil and hot springs, and experiences a long growing season. Its most successful grapes are the white johannisberg riesling, chardonnay and gewürztraminer. Monterey also grows the sauvignon blanc, chenin blanc and riesling. Red grape varieties have proven more difficult here. Wines pressed from the cabernet sauvignon have often exhibited vegetal flavors and odors that suggest cabbage or green peppers; improved by modifications in their trellising arrangements however, they are leaner and sharper now. The pinot noir grape, grown in the chalky soil of the Gavilan Mountains high above the Salinas Valley has achieved a degree of success in Monterey.

Alameda County, on the eastern shore of San Francisco Bay, includes Livermore Valley, where grape growing began more than a century ago. (A Frenchman, finding the sea breezes salubrious here, planted cuttings he had brought from his native land.) Livermore's generally gravelly soil is similar to that of Graves and its white wines are among California's best. Grown are the sauvignon blanc, sémillon and chardonnay, along with the pinot blanc, ugni blanc and gray riesling. Alameda also produces soft and generally early maturing red wines.

Stretching south to San Luis Obispo and Santa Barbara is a subregion known as the South Central Coast. It encompasses San Benito County, whose limestone soil resembles that of Burgundy's Côte d'Or and is hospitable to the pinot noir. (Most of the vineyards here date from the early 1980s.) Nearby areas of note are the Templeton district, the Santa Ynez and Santa Maria Valleys in Santa Barbara County, and the Edna Valley in San Luis Obispo County; the latter is particularly known for its Chardonnays. Also in the vicinity is York Mountain, with elevations of 1,600 to 1,800 feet. The area, only seven miles from the Pacific, is subject to a maritime climate of fog and rain.

Central Valley

California's Central Valley, a vast region lying between the Sierra Madres and the Coast Ranges, extends from San Joaquin in the north to Bakersfield in the south. A hot, fertile, intensively cultivated and highly industrialized region, it accounts for more than half of the state's wine output.

Summers in the Central Valley are cloudless with temperatures hovering at more than 100°F for days at a time. The humidity is negligible since mountains block any rainfall. The soil, baking in the blazing heat, forms a hard clay surface that must be periodically broken up and constantly irrigated. Grapes grow abundantly here, yielding high-sugar, low-acid wines. The region had long been known for its heady, fortified, port- and sherry-style wines but having adopted modern vinification methods in the 1960s and 1970s, now produces table and sparkling wines as well. (These outnumber the fortified by a wide margin.) Cold stabilization has helped some of the table wines achieve a lighter, fresher style, but most are consigned to wine coolers and other inexpensive blends.

The leading red grape in the Central Valley is the carignane (spelled with an *e*), followed by the zinfandel, barbera, grenache, petite sirah, alicante bouschet and mission. The white grapes include the french colombard, thompson seedless, palomino, muscat and chardonnay. Also grown are hybrids such as the ruby cabernet and carnelian. These are designed to retain as much acidity as possible under the dry growing conditions and intense heat. And the search goes on for new varieties that can withstand the region's torrid climate and still produce distinctive wines.

Southern California

Southern California, which lies between Los Angeles and San Diego, is also a relatively arid region, requiring extensive irrigation. Its climate is too hot and its soil too rich for growing quality grapes. Many of the same varieties are cultivated here as in the Central Valley, but with a greater emphasis on grapes of Italian origin. Produced are big, pronounced wines, best suited to fortification. They are made primarily as port- and sherry-style wines.

Southern California's finest growing district is Temecula in Riverside County. It is particularly known for its good sparkling wines.

THE PACIFIC NORTHWEST

In the 1970s, the increasing cost of California real estate also spurred the expansion of viticulture to the Pacific Northwest. Vintners discovered that the region's northern light and volcanic soil made it a fine place to raise wine grapes. Although subject to mercurial weather, the Pacific Northwest enjoys enough sunshine to encourage their slow ripening. (The rainfall, although heavy, is generally restricted to the winter months, when the vines lie dormant.) First to garner attention here were the Riesling and Chardonnay wines. Acclaim has also been consistent for the Pinot Noirs of western Oregon and the Merlots and Cabernet Sauvignons of Washington State.

Oregon

In the nineteenth century, Oregon was producing folk wines pressed from various fruits and berries. Despite the assumption that grapes could not prosper in its volatile climate, newly arrived European immigrants began to cultivate them. Encouraged by a felicitous combination of soil and weather, the grapes thrived. Shielding the fog-shrouded vineyards from cold air blowing down from Canada were the Cascade Mountains to the east and the Coast Ranges to the west.

Oregon now cultivates a number of grape varieties with great success; the wines they yield are generally soft, fruity and accessible. Among the red grapes, the temperamental pinot noir does particularly well, producing, some say, a world-class wine. Since 1980, its acreage has been increased tenfold and California vintners have been purchasing the grapes for their own wines. (In addition, a number of wine makers from Burgundy have set up shop in the state.) Other thriving varieties are the cabernet sauvignon, merlot and zinfandel. Among the whites are the chardonnay, riesling, sauvignon blanc, pinot gris and gewürztraminer.

The state's major growing areas are the Willamette and Hood River Valleys. Most of the vineyards are located in the west, in Willamette, a strip of land about one hundred forty miles long and forty miles wide, nestled between two mountain ranges and running from Portland to Eugene. Willamette enjoys a long growing season. The Hood Valley, near Portland, is subject to slightly warmer and more consistent weather. Oregon's other recently developed viticultural areas are in the warmer Umpqua district and in Roseburg, located farther south.

Washington State

Washington State is the country's second largest wine producer after California. Its climate is moderate. Long warm days help to ripen the grapes, while cool nights preserve their fragile acidity. Most of the vineyards are concentrated east of the Cascade Mountains in three valleys: Yakima, Columbia and Walla Walla. (Yakima accounts for about 85 percent of the wine production.)

Although Washington State has grown grapes for decades, serious wine making did not begin until the 1970s. Successfully grown now are a number of premium French and German grapes. The state's reputation rests largely on its white wines, characterized by a buoyant fruitiness and a distinctive acidity. The best examples are pressed from riesling and johannisberg riesling grapes. Typically quite heady, these wines often reach alcohol levels higher than 13 percent. Other white grape varieties are the sémillon, sauvignon blanc, chardonnay, gewürztraminer, chenin blanc, müller-thurgau and muscat canelli. Washington State's best red wines are characterized by a fine structure and balance. The merlot is a popular grape there whereas cabernet sauvignon yields a wine more restrained in its fruit and bouquet than its counterpart in California. The concord grape, which accounts for about half of the state's grape production, is used primarily for juice and jellies.

OTHER AMERICAN STATES

American wine makers away from the East and West Coasts are

generally part-timers who earn their livelihoods at other pursuits. Most of the wines they produce are consumed locally.

In Virginia, the earliest attempts at wine making were hampered by disease and insects. German settlers revived grape growing here in the eighteenth century, but the first commercial winery was not established until 1970. Virginia is known primarily for its white wines, pressed from riesling, chardonnay, gewürztraminer and seyval blanc grapes. In Ohio, Nicholas Longworth planted vines in the hills overlooking Cincinnati. German settlers also established vineyards in the state, cultivating their vines on the banks of the Ohio River. Large-scale plantings were subsequently made on the Lake Erie islands and on the south shore of Lake Erie. A notable wine producer before the Civil War, Ohio was the source of America's first commercial sparkling wine, an effervescent Catawba. Currently, more than two dozen wineries are in operation in the state.

In Texas, Franciscan missionaries were making sacramental wines in the El Paso Valley in the midseventeenth century. The state now grows a wide variety of grapes: the red merlot, ruby cabernet, barbera, zinfandel, grenache and petite sirah; the white johannisberg riesling, sauvignon blanc, chenin blanc, sémillon and emerald riesling. Blending the sauvignon blanc and sémillon here makes for a fresh-flavored white wine with a fruity bouquet.

Idaho experiences a climate similar to that of Oregon, but located some four hundred fifty miles inland from the Pacific, it is not subject to as much rainfall. Idaho grows the johannisberg riesling and the chardonnay but purchases half its wine grapes from nearby Washington State.

Wine making in New Mexico dates back to the seventeenth century. On a thirty-five-hundred-foot-high plateau here, the growing conditions are ideal for the grape—the days are warm and the nights cool. Varieties grown include a number of French-American hybrids. New Mexico produces sparkling wines as well as still ones.

In southeastern New England, Connecticut, Rhode Island and Massachusetts are making Chardonnay wines. Most of their wineries are located close to Long Island Sound. When the wine makers don't grow enough chardonnays to meet their own needs, they buy them from vineyards in the Finger Lakes region or on Long

Island. In Connecticut, the state legislature, wishing to encourage the wine industry, passed a law in 1978 permitting winery owners to sell their products directly to the public on their own premises.

Hawaii has been cultivating grapes on its volcanic slopes. It has most recently experimented with the carnelian, a hybrid developed especially for California's torrid Central Valley.

NOTE: In addition to its own great domestic output, the United States imports wines from all over the world, purchasing more premium wines from France than any other single country. America accounts for some 20 percent of all French wine exports.

OTHER COUNTRIES

ALGERIA

Algeria made wine in Roman times, but produced little between the eighth and nineteenth centuries, while under Arab rule. In the nineteenth century, France annexed the country and restored its viniculture. When phylloxera decimated the European vineyards, Algeria became an important source of wine. By the end of World War II, nearly a third of the labor force was engaged in the wine industry. But after winning its independence from France, in 1962, Algeria reasserted its Moslem traditions and uprooted most of the vineyards.

Grapes here were grown on a coastal Mediterranean plain that rises to a high plateau. Produced were red and white wines, the reds being the most noteworthy. The French had planted such commonplace varieties as the carignan, alicante bouschet and clairette blanc, which yielded generally rough hearty wines, more notable for their strength than for their finesse. They were used to strengthen the French vin ordinaires and apéritifs and to bolster the lesser Bordeaux and Burgundies.

Subsequently Algeria cultivated better grape varieties. Its more outstanding wines came from the western sector, near Oran, and from the uplands around the cities of Mascara and Tlemcen. The Coteaux de Mascara was famous for its deep-colored, full-bodied reds, while Tlemcen produced good whites as well as rich reds. Médéa, south of Algiers, was also known for its red and white wines.

NOTE: Other North African wine-producing countries are
Morocco and Tunisia, whose high-alcohol, low-acid wines are best
suited to blending. Adopting modern vinification methods, these
countries have begun to produce soft, pleasant reds; dry, fruity
rosés; and refreshing white wines.

ARGENTINA

Argentina is South America's largest wine producer. In the sixteenth century, Jesuit missionaries planted vines here. (The conquistadores had brought those vines from Spain.) Many of the early
colonists had come from Andalusia, bringing their wine-growing
traditions with them. In the nineteenth century, a great wave of
Italian immigration was to transform the country's viniculture from
a casual pastime into a full-fledged industry.

Argentinian wine growing now extends some seven hundred
miles, stretching south from the Cafayate region of Salta province
to Mendoza and beyond. There are three distinct wine regions: the
Northwest, including the province of Salta; the Central West,
encompassing Mendoza province and San Juan; and the Southern
Region, including the valleys of the Rio Colorado and the Rio
Negro. Mendoza, the premier province and main growing area,
accounts for more than 90 percent of the vineyard acreage.
Located some six hundred miles west of Buenos Aires, it is known
for its huge vineyards (some are located fifty-two hundred feet
above sea level) and for its large wineries.

The vineyards themselves are sited in the foothills of the Andes,
where the days are warm but mountain breezes cool the air.
Although the land is arid (the mountains block the rainfall) a
remarkable series of dams and reservoirs has been constructed to
irrigate the vineyards. These channel melted snow down from the
mountains on a fixed schedule during the growing season.

Argentina initially grew criolla and pedro ximénez grapes, but
a French specialist, who was commissioned to bring in fine vines
in 1853, imported the red cabernet sauvignon, malbec, merlot and
pinot noir and the white sauvignon blanc and sémillon, among others. The most widely planted varieties now are the red barbera and
the white chardonnay and riesling.

NOTE: Since phylloxera never reached South America, most Argentinian vines are cultivated on their own rootstocks.

The country produces red, white and rosé wines. The vintners, not overly concerned with quality, once stressed high production and concentrated on turning out inexpensive high-alcohol wines. These were designated for the country's own huge domestic market and for export in bulk to France, Spain and Scandinavia. (Argentina also sells great quantities of grape concentrates to Japan.) The introduction of stainless steel technology and cold stabilization has enabled the country to improve its wines now, particularly the wines designated for export.

AUSTRALIA

In Australia, the first attempt to grow grapes failed: vines that had been imported from South Africa and planted near Sydney proved incompatible with the soil and climate. In the nineteenth century, however, an expedition was sent to Europe to acquire better vines. It returned with about twenty thousand cuttings from the leading French and German vineyards, representing hundreds of grape varieties. These became the foundation of modern Australian viticulture. The predominant red variety now grown is the red hermitage (syrah); others are the cabernet sauvignon, pinot noir and shiraz. Among the white varieties are the chardonnay, sémillon, riesling, fumé blanc (sauvignon blanc), marsanne and muscat.

Experiencing generally warm, dry, sunny conditions during its growing season, Australia produces high-sugar, low-acid wines. The earliest examples were often fortified. (The country was initially known for its fine port and sherry-style wines.) In the 1960s, technological advances and the development of cooler growing sites made possible lighter, drier, more subtle wines. Produced now are a wide range of red, white, and rosé wines, along with sweet Muscats and botrytized Sémillons.

Australia's Cabernet Sauvignons, rich-flavored, smooth-textured and easy to drink, are similar to those of California. The Australians—unhampered by any long wine-making traditions and free to be innovative—are especially known for their Shiraz wines and their Shiraz-Cabernet blends. At their finest, these combine the richness of a Rhône wine with the elegance of a Bordeaux.

Australia's main wine-producing regions extend in a twenty-five-hundred-mile arc across the southern half of the country. They are South Australia, New South Wales, Victoria and West Australia. South Australia, which includes Adelaide and its environs, is responsible for about two-thirds of the country's wines. Its prime districts are Barossa Valley, Coonawarra, McLaren Vale and Clare.

Although the Barossa Valley, situated about thirty-five miles north of Adelaide, is subject to a hot climate, it sites its vineyards in the hills some fifteen hundred feet above sea level. In the nineteenth century, Silesian immigrants settled here and made German-style wines; their descendants continue to produce riesling wines remarkable for their acidity and delicacy. The other white wines are blends, combining the richness of the chardonnay with the fruitiness of the sauvignon blanc. Barossa is the home as well of great red vineyards and is known for its Hermitage and Cabernet-Shiraz wines, which exhibit a fine fruity character and considerable tannin.

The small, cool Coonawarra district is considered one of the country's best. Its late-ripening red grapes include the cabernet sauvignon, malbec, merlot and shiraz, among others; its Cabernet Sauvignon wines are much celebrated. Coonawarra's white grapes include the riesling, chardonnay and gewürztraminer. South of Adelaide is McLaren Vale, cooled by gentle sea breezes and specializing in chardonnays while producing good red wines as well.

One of the country's oldest wine producers is New South Wales, which encompasses Hunter Valley, the site of the big wineries. Best known for its white wines, Hunter Valley grows the sémillon (called the Hunter Valley riesling) and the riesling itself (called the Rhine riesling), along with the chardonnay and traminer. It also produces excellent reds, pressed from the shiraz grape, and highly esteemed rosé.

Australia's southernmost region is Victoria, whose principal city is Melbourne. Produced here are red and white wines. Some outstanding reds are grown on the lime-rich soil of the Yarra Valley. Notable too for its excellent reds is the small Goulburn Valley. Northeast of Melbourne is Rutherglen, known for its red and white wines and especially for its sweet Muscats. Grown here are the red cabernet sauvignon, pinot noir and shiraz, and the white chardonnay and sauvignon blanc. The newly developed Margaret River district near Perth in West Australia specializes in Cabernet Sauvignon wines.

AUSTRIA

Austria's one hundred thousand or so acres of vines are concentrated in the eastern third of the country, where the climate is sunny and ideal for grape growing. The generally small vineyard plots here range from twelve to fifty acres. About four-fifths of the wines are white. Similar to their German counterparts, they are fruity with a flowery fragrance and a good bouquet but—because of their warmer growing conditions—are a bit lower in acidity and somewhat higher in alcohol.

Austria's predominant grape is the indigenous veltliner, whose marvelously fresh, fruity white wines display a spicy, almost peppery flavor. Other white grapes, deriving mainly from German and Alsatian sources, include the müller-thurgau, sylvaner, gewürztraminer, chasselas, rheinriesling, wälschriesling, weissburgunder, muskat-ottonel, rotgipfler and furmint.

The Austrian red wines tend to be light-bodied and short-lived. (They are sometimes bolstered with imports from Italy and the former Yugoslavia.) The country's primary red grape is the pinot noir, also known as the spätburgunder or the blaufränkisch or blauerburgunder. Other red varieties are the blauer portugieser and St.Laurent.

The country's key wine regions are Vienna, Lower Austria, Burgenland and Styria. In Vienna and its environs, wine growing was once extensive but urbanization has preempted most of the vineyard land. (Little more than fifteen hundred acres remain within the city limits, and they are preserved and protected by law.) Nearby wine villages include Grinzing in Vienna's suburbs, Sievering, Nussberg and Kahlemberg.

Lower Austria, which extends north along the Danube from Krems to the border of the Czech Republic, produces Gumpoldskirchen, the country's best-known white wine. A blend of the gruner veltliner and rotigipfler gotherrt with the riesling, gewürztraminer and other varieties, Gumpoldskirchen ranges from the light, dry and charmingly scented to the fruity and full-bodied. Lower Austria's main white-wine area is Wachau in the Danube

Valley Wachau's most important wine town is Krems, located on a steep hillside. Krems is celebrated for its fresh, fragrant, gently rounded wines pressed from riesling, gruner veltliner and sylvaner grapes. Other notable wine towns here are Durnstein to the west and Loiben to the south.

In the southeast is Burgenland, surrounding the Neusiedler See—one of Europe's largest lakes. Burgenland, subject to a moist, sunny climate with warm autumns, is largely a red-wine area best known for its dry, dark, heady Vöslauer wines. It also produces high-quality white wines, including deep golden Ausleses, Beerenausleses and Trockenbeerenausleses—which aren't as sweet as their German counterparts. Situated on the gentle western slopes of the Neusiedler See is the village of Rust, famous for its Ruster Ausbruch, a sweet, almost syrupy wine pressed from late-harvested furmint and muscat grapes. Styria, across the border from Slovenia, produces good red and white wines.

Some Austrian wines are not bottled at all but dispensed directly from the cask in special taverns known as *heuriges*. (*Heurige*, a dialect word meaning this year, refers to the new wine of the season.) At first the wines had to be new, but now they can be sold throughout the year. The heurige taverns, located primarily around Vienna, originated in the eighteenth century when Emperor Joseph II permitted vintners to sell their wines directly to the public from their own premises. Typically the taverns feature modest interiors with whitewashed walls and plain tables. The wines themselves are served in *viertels* (fourths), thick glass mugs with a quarter-liter capacity. Accompanying them is a buffet of cold cuts, ham, sausage, pork, chicken, fresh vegetables and good bread.

BULGARIA

Wine growing in Bulgaria goes back two thousand years, to the time when the country was known as Thrace. Subsequent Turkish domination and Moslem rule banned the making of wine. (The Islamic influence prevailed until the nineteenth century.) After World War II, the country was socialized and huge vineyards were set out on flat blocks of land for machine cultivation. Wine making was also industrialized.

Most of Bulgaria's vineyards are located on a central plain east of Sofia. In the northeast is the coastal region of the Black Sea, known for its white wines pressed from the local misket grape along with the chardonnay and aligoté. Produced in the southern and western sectors are red wines, which range from light and dry to sweet and heavy. The south is also noted for its sweet, heavy Muscats. Of special interest are the red wines of Sukhindol, located north of the Balkans. These are pressed from the cabernet sauvignon and merlot, among other grapes.

NOTE: Bulgaria has thrown open its markets to western investors and entrepreneurs. Now one of the world's leading exporters, it ships out most of the wine it produces.

CANADA

Canada concentrates about 90 percent of its wine growing in southern Ontario on the Niagara Peninsula, a neck of land that separates Lake Erie and Lake Ontario. The lakes, which moderate the northern climate, make grape growing possible. Canada's wine industry, although active since the midnineteenth century, has only recently upgraded its production and recruited expert wine makers from Germany and Austria. Of the more than two dozen wineries now in operation, most have been established since 1979.

Ontario's growing conditions are much like those of the nearby Finger Lakes in New York State. Traditionally, labrusca grapes have been cultivated, but in recent years French-American hybrids and vinifera grapes have been grown as well. The viniferas include the chardonnay, riesling, pinot noir, cabernet sauvignon, cabernet franc and merlot. In addition to its red, white and rosé wines, Canada produces a winter-harvested Ice Wine, that is made in two versions: the more expensive employs the riesling grape, the less expensive the vidal, a hybrid. Wine is also made in British Columbia's Okanogan Valley, which grows viniferas imported from the Mosel region of Germany. And British Columbia is known as well for its good sparkling wines.

NOTE: Canada domestically consumes most of the wine it produces.

CHILE

Chile, situated across the Andes Mountains from Argentina, is a narrow strip of coastal land about twenty-eight hundred miles long and two hundred miles wide at its widest. The Spanish missionaries accompanying the Conquistadores planted the first vines here. Early in the nineteenth century, German immigrants colonized the southern farmlands and introduced their own styles and methods of vinification. At the end of the nineteenth century, the country sought to reorganize and expand its wine industry. It recruited French experts as advisers. Ever since, Chile has largely followed the French method of wine making.

The grapes grown reflect this French influence. The red varieties include the cabernet sauvignon, merlot, malbec and pinot noir, along with the cabernet franc and petit verdot. The whites include the sauvignon blanc, riesling, sémillon and chardonnay, along with the pinot blanc, pinot gris, gewürztraminer and sylvaner. Because the Andes Mountains and vast stretches of sandy soil protected the vines against phylloxera, these are among the few purebred descendants of vines dating back to the prephylloxera era.

Much of Chile's early production was in jug wines. Often overripe and heavy with a decidedly baked character, they were either sold locally or exported to the country's Latin American neighbors. Using modern fermentation methods now and aging them in small French oak casks, the Chileans have made their wines more attractive and supple.

Grape growing is divided into six regions here. Of greatest importance is the Maipo Valley, south of Santiago, a region that experiences intense sunshine during the day and a chill at night; its growing season ends with minimal rainfall. Maipo's soil is largely volcanic and alluvial. Produced here are red, white and rosé wines. Particularly outstanding is a powerful and concentrated Cabernet Sauvignon with plenty of character, a wine that at its finest is well balanced and elegant. Other Chilean reds display modest fruit and soft tannins. Doing especially well among the white wines are the Chardonnay and Sauvignon Blanc. Sparkling wines are also produced, as are such generics as Sauterne, Chablis, Rhin (Rhine) wine and Borgana (Burgundy).

In recent years, French, American and Spanish investors have updated and modernized Chile's wine industry and expanded its wine growing to the cooler regions south of the traditional zones. These foreign investments—along with government tax breaks designed to encourage entrepreneurship—have made Chile one of South America's leading wine producers and a major exporter of wine, particularly to the United States.

NOTE: In the past, the larger wineries were responsible for the exports, but many smaller establishments that have been making wine for more than a hundred years are now intent on gaining a share of this lucrative market. They had previously served mainly as suppliers to the larger enterprises.

CHINA

Although grapes are believed to be indigenous to China, wine making here has been a largely a foreign affair. (Wine has never been a part of the Chinese diet.) Catholic monks made wine in Beijing for the observance of mass in the nineteenth century. In the twentieth, French missionaries set up a winery in the city. Wine was subsequently produced commercially to supply the foreign community in China and for export to the Chinese overseas.

China's early wines were cloyingly sweet and unappealing. In the 1970s, increased contact with the West and a burgeoning tourist trade stimulated an interest in creating wines with a more "European" flavor. So the government signed contracts with various specialists from France, England and Austria: the Chinese were to supply the land, grapes and labor, while the foreigners were to provide the wine-making technology, equipment and skills. China is currently producing wines east of Beijing, near Tianjin and in Shandong province along the northeastern coast. Available in shops catering to the tourists is a light, dry, fruity white wine with a delicate bouquet, somewhat reminiscent of a Chenin Blanc. Some of the country's best wines are now produced in Shazikou, a coastal city in the east, 25 miles from Quindao. These wines are grown in a vineyard began in the 1980s by a Briton who transplanted chardonnay and riesling cuttings from Europe. Characteriz-ing the region are a lime-rich soil and slopes favored by a southern exposure.

NOTE: The Chinese themselves prefer a high-alcohol beverage called Shaoxing (Yellow Wine), which technically is not a wine at all since it isn't a grape product. Made with rice, wheat, water and yeast, it is similar in character to a sherry. Shaoxing ranges in color from pale apricot to dark amber and in taste from semidry to very sweet.

CYPRUS

The island of Cyprus in the eastern Mediterranean is said to have made wine centuries before the birth of Christ. Cyprus grows its grapes at elevations of nearly three thousand feet in the mountains of its southern sector.

The country makes a variety of red and white wines, with the red wines predominating. Especially esteemed is its red Commandaria, which dates back at least to the twelfth century. (The Crusaders are said to have introduced the original vines.) Initially sweet, liquorous, pungent and heady, Commandaria is now generally vinified lighter and drier. Cyprus also produces sparkling wines and quantities of sweet and semisweet fortified wines, including flor-style sherries. Most are turned out by four modern wineries. There are also several mountain monasteries producing wine in limited quantities.

NOTE: Because its vines were never exposed to phylloxera, Cyprus cultivates only indigenous grapes to avoid any possible contamination.

CZECH REPUBLIC

The Moravian region of the Czech Republic, as well as Slovakia, produce red and white wines; the whites are best. They reflect the influence of nearby Germany and Austria. Their main grapes are the German riesling—rizling or risling rinksi (Rhine riesling)—and the Austrian veltlinski (grüner veltliner); other white varieties are the traminer and sylvaner, the müller-thurgau and sauvignon blanc. Red grapes include the blauburgunder and portugieser.

Many Czechoslovakian wines are served in special restaurants called *vinarnas,* where they are offered by the glass as well as by the bottle. Accompanying them are simple foods, similar to those served in the heurige taverns of Austria.

GREAT BRITAIN

The British have long been growing grapes. In the Middle Ages, monasteries maintained vineyards here and the Norman invasion brought in French abbots accustomed to drinking good wines. When Henry Plantagenet married Eleanor of Aquitaine in the twelfth century, the English literally acquired all of Bordeaux as well as the Charente and the Loire. Becoming a world power with easy access to the great wines of Europe, England lost interest in producing its own wines and abandoned most of its vineyards. Although wine growing was to continue on a small scale, powdery mildew and downy mildew, which struck in the nineteenth century, killed off the vines that remained.

The 1930s saw a resurgence of grape cultivation, which gained some momentum after World War II. In 1946, Britain opened its first modern viticultural research station in Surrey. In the 1970s, small-scale wine making resumed with the introduction of modern viticultural practices and carefully selected clones, particularly in the south of England and Wales. White grapes fare best in Britain's short growing season. These have included such early-ripening varieties as the müller-thurgau and seyval blanc, whose light fruity wines sometimes demonstrate a touch of earthiness. Few observers, however, expect British wine making to become more than a marginal activity.

While the British have produced no significant wines of their own, they have been tremendously influential in the wine world. They more or less invented the practice of drinking fine wines and were the first to write about and romanticize the subject. Wine has long been considered a gentleman's calling in England.

The British had been acquiring French wines since Roman times. During the reign of Henry Plantagenet, England became a land of Bordeaux connoisseurs and the largest consumer of premier clarets. When war and import taxes cut off the French supply, the British turned to the wines of Spain and Portugal, helping in the process to "invent" fortified ports and sherries. These wines provided an appealing antidote to the country's chill climate. (It has wryly been noted that since the nineteenth century, the British have used port as a substitute for central heating.)

Sensing sherry's commercial possibilities, English wine merchants settled in Jerez in the fifteenth century, married into local wine-producing families and invested their time, labor and capital in the wine's production, ensuring its distribution in the world's major markets. The British called sherry *sack,* which derives either from *sacar,* meaning "to export," or *sec,* translating as "dry." (Shakespeare's Falstaff expressed his fondness for sherry by declaring that the first principle he would teach his sons would be to "foreswear thin potations . . . [and] addict themselves to sack.") Because England imports about 60 percent of all sherry produced, the wine is often considered more British than Spanish.

The British, who set up shipping houses in Portugal's Douro Valley some three hundred years ago, also went on to dominate the port-wine trade. The names of many English families are still linked to port, although conglomerates began buying up the British firms after World War II. Similarly, the British have been influential in the Madeira-wine trade. (Of the handful of families controlling the island's large wine interests, a number are Anglo-Madeiran.) The British have played a significant role as well in encouraging the development of fortified Marsalas in Italy, and have demonstrated great enthusiasm and support for Rhine and Mosel wines, which they call *hocks.*

NOTE: Despite their association with fine wines, the British also import great quantities of commonplace red and white wines in bulk from Italy, Spain, Germany and the South of France. These wines are known as *plonk,* thought to be a corruption of *vin blanc.*

GREECE

Greece has grown grapes for some three thousand years. Among the varieties cultivated are the indigenous red xinomavro (a deep purple grape), the pinkish rhoditis, the white assyrtiko and the muscat. Also grown is the red cabernet sauvignon of France.

Countless vineyards dot the Greek mainland and the nearby islands. The greatest concentration is on the Peloponnesus, the large peninsula in the south that is separated from the mainland by the

Gulf of Corinth. Its climate is Mediterranean; its soil is largely volcanic. The Peloponnesian peninsula is famous for its dark red Mavrodaphne (*mavro* translates as black), a full-bodied, richly flavored, sweet and aromatic wine with a velvety taste and an almost burnt aftertaste. Mavrodaphne is quite potent, ranging in alcohol from 15 to 20 percent. From the mountain vineyards in the eastern Peloponnese comes the full-bodied, deep-colored red wine of Nemea. Produced around Athens, where the vineyards are cooled by mountain breezes, are rather subdued red and white table wines.

NOTE: Macedonia, to the north of Greece, is celebrated for its Mavro of Naoussa, a dry dark red wine pressed from the xinomavro grape.

The Greek islands produce various wines. From Crete comes a fruity white vin de pays; from Corfu, a stout, sturdy red Robolo. Sámos is famous for its late-harvest Muscat, a sweet golden brown wine; a dry version is made as well. Santorini grows good white wines, some slightly acid, whereas others are semisweet.

Most widely exported are the Greek *retsinas,* or resinated wines, which are characterized by the unmistakable pitchlike taste of pine needles. Produced mainly in the Attica region north of Athens, the wines may be red, white or rosé. The practice of resinating wines goes back to ancient times when the Greeks fermented, stored and shipped their wines in *amphorae,* two-handled, porous clay vessels that tapered to a point at the bottom. To reduce the wine's oxidation and evaporation in the porous amphorae, vintners coated the interiors with a pine-sap resin whose pungency permeated the wine. People became accustomed to, and expected, this pronounced flavor in their wines. (Modern wine makers re-create the taste by adding the resinated flavoring during fermentation.) The wines themselves are usually quite light in alcohol, averaging no more than 9 percent.

In recent years, the Greeks have applied high-tech methods to their wine making and sought out the advice of French and English enologists. Produced now are a variety of wines ranging from crisp whites to robust and claretlike reds. (These are made mainly by a handful of family-owned enterprises.) Consuming most of its wine domestically, Greece exports only about 15 percent or so.

NOTE: Cooperatives usually supply the bulk market, shipping their

182 • THE GIFT OF WINE

wines to France, Switzerland and other northern European countries, which blend the Greek wines with their own thinner, paler ones.

HUNGARY

Thousands of years ago, Magyar tribes pushing out of Central Asia found grapes growing wild in the foothills of the Carpathians. The Roman legions went on to introduce other grape varieties. By the time of the Crusades, Hungarian wines were quite well known and in the Middle Ages, vast quantities of them were exported to Poland and Russia.

Hungary's major wine district is on the Duna, a great plain that extends over much of the country's middle sector. Most of the wines are sturdy whites, pressed from furmint and olaszrizling grapes, among others. Characterizing them generally are an intense grapiness and a certain headiness or fieriness. Some display a touch of sweetness. Distinctive red wines are produced here as well, pressed from the indigenous and widely planted kadarka grape, along with the merlot, pinot noir and other varieties.

Hungary's most celebrated wine comes from Tokay, a 150-square-mile district in the northeast. Encompassing twenty-eight hill towns, Tokay takes its name from one of these villages. Some twelve thousand acres in vineyards are located here along the low-lying slopes of the Carpathians. A sunny climate and a largely volcanic soil have made Tokay an ideal place for grape growing. The main variety it cultivated is the furmint.

Tokay wines range from dry and ordinary to sweet, rich and celebrated. In their ascending order of sweetness, the basic types are Furmint, Szamorodni, Aszu and Essenz or Eszencia. Furmint is the driest of all. Szamorodni, made dry and semidry, when full in body is similar to a light sherry. Some examples display a fresh flavor and bouquet, while others are rather harsh and heavy. Although the Szamorodnis are unfortified, their alcohol level is rarely less than 13 percent.

Tokay Aszu, made only in the best vintages, combines noble rot berries with normal grapes. (The proportion of botrytized grapes is indicated as puttonyos on the labels.) Dark gold or amber, sweet and luscious but never cloying, the Aszus are similar to the rich botrytized wines of France and Germany although somewhat spicier. Their highly perfumed bouquet is reminiscent of a fragrant green tea, a lingering hint of dryness offset their intensely honeyed richness. Louis XV of France called Aszu the "wine of kings and the king of wines." Before World War II, the finest Aszus were aged at least ten years in wood; they are now vinified to age for about six years.

Ranked among the world's finest unfortified dessert wines is Tokay Essenz or Eszencia. Pressed exclusively from noble rot grapes culled from special vineyards, it is made entirely from their free-run juice, which is left to ferment for years. Because its natural sugars are so concentrated, the alcohol level is low. Extremely rare, the legendary Eszencia is more of a liqueur than a wine. It is renowned for its concentrated honeylike flavor, its splendid bouquet and its great longevity. (Some examples have survived for two centuries.)

NOTE: Eszencia was never sold on the open market, but reserved for the imperial court. Since World War II, the little produced has been used primarily to sweeten Aszu wines. (The wine now sold under the Essenz, or Eszencia, label is at best a diluted, unaged version of the original.)

Other Hungarian white wines come from the north shore of Lake Balaton, Central Europe's largest freshwater lake. These are often highly potent, fiercely dry, flowery and scented. Among them is Kéknyelü, pressed from furmint and olaszrizling grapes. Similar wines pressed from the same grape varieties are produced farther north in Somlo. Also grown on the north shore of Lake Balaton in the Badacsony hills is Szürkebarát, a medium-dry white wine with an earthy undertone. Another white wine is the semidry and mellow Hárslevelü.

Hungary's principal red wine is Kadarka, coming from the central Duna. Better known however is Egri Bikavér, whose name translates as "Bull's Blood." Grown in the Eger Valley, a hilly district of volcanic soil in the northeast, Egri Bikavér is stout, sturdy, rich-colored and full-bodied at its finest. Fiery dry and velvety smooth wine, it is celebrated for a richness of flavor and aroma, a touch of spice in the taste and a fine bitterness in the aftertaste. Egri Bikavérs can differ widely, however. (Lesser examples may even include components from Algeria, Morocco or Bulgaria.) Another Hungarian red wine is Nagyburgunder, pressed from the pinot noir and grown in Villany, a small region along the Austrian border.

NOTE: Hungary, which heavily subsidizes its wine exports, sells about 40 percent of its production on the world market.

ISRAEL

Wine is said to have been produced in what is now Israel as early as 3000 B.C. During the centuries of Saracen and Turkish domination, wine making largely disappeared, not to reemerge in earnest until the early 1900s. European vines were then imported and the first modern winery built south of Tel Aviv under the sponsorship of Baron Edmund de Rothschild of the French wine family. Another branch of the family built a second winery near Haifa. Three-fourths of Israel's wine growing is still concentrated close to the Mediterranean Sea on a hot coastal plain whose climate is semi-arid. Other Israeli vineyards are scattered around Jerusalem, near Beersheba and in the Golan Heights.

The commonplace vines planted in the nineteenth century proved to be prolific bearers, but their heavy, undistinguished wines were somewhat on the sweet side and best suited to fortification. Aided by modern viticultural methods and irrigation, Israel is now cultivating premium vines including the red cabernet sauvignon and the white riesling. Other varieties grown are the white colombard, sauvignon blanc, sémillon and chenin blanc. The country now produces a wide range of red, white and rosé wines: still, sparkling and fortified. The red wines outnumber the whites.

A relatively new growing area, the Golan Heights cultivates its vines on volcanic soil eight hundred to eighteen hundred feet above sea level, where they are sheltered from the hot lowland winds and enjoy a more plentiful rainfall. The Golan's main grape is the sauvignon blanc, which yields a crisp, dry, elegant wine with a clear fruity character. The cabernet sauvignon also does well here.

JAPAN

Most of the Japanese vineyards are located in Yamanashi province west of Tokyo. Because the land available for cultivation in the country is limited and the demand for table grapes is great, only about a sixth of the crop is devoted to wine.

Late in the nineteenth century, the Japanese, seeking to upgrade their wines, traveled to Bordeaux to study its vinicultural methods. Grown now along with native koshu grapes and Chinese grape varieties are those imported from Europe and America. They include such viniferas as the cabernet sauvignon and sémillon, and such labruscas as the concord and delaware. Japan also buys large quantities of frozen grapes and grape juice concentrates from France, Germany, Italy, Algeria, Argentina and others countries. It produces a wide range of red, white and rosé wines and also imports more than a million gallons of wine annually for blending and bottling.

Since the 1970s, Japanese interests have been purchasing vineyard properties and wineries around the world (in California, France, Australia, Brazil, and Mexico). The Japanese have also acquired an interest in the French shipping firm that holds the distribution rights to Burgundy's most prestigious wine, the estimable Romanée-Conti.

MADEIRA

Madeira, a small island in the Atlantic Ocean, lies some three hundred fifty miles west of Morocco and occupies the same latitude as Casablanca. Only about thirty-five miles long and twelve miles at its widest, the island rises so abruptly from the sea that there are no natural beaches. Running through its center is a long-extinguished volcanic range. Madeira's rugged terrain is marked by many ravines and deep valleys.

When discovered by the Portuguese in the fifteenth century, the island was uninhabited and covered with deep woods. The colonists called it Madeira (Island of Trees). To farm the land, they burned off the forests, further enriching the soil. Along with other crops, they planted grapevines imported from Portugal, Spain, Crete and Germany. The grapes thrived in the mild climate, where year-round temperatures range from the 60s to the 70s. Rain is plentiful here in the spring when it's most needed.

Madeira is best known for its fortified wines, which date back to the eighteenth century when the island served as a victualing station for the clipper ships sailing around the Cape of Good Hope. The ships, taking on supplies at the port city of Funchal, also took aboard casks of the local wine, which had been fortified for the voyage. Rocking and rolling about in the holds of the sailing ships as they traveled through tropical seas, the wines acquired a wonderful smoothness of texture and a bittersweet taste. (The vintners subsequently duplicated these features by baking their wines in special estufa ovens.)

Madeira's grape varieties include sercial, bual, verdelho and malmsey. In the nineteenth century, oïdium, a mildew disease, wiped out virtually all of the island's vines. Twenty years later, phylloxera struck. Although some of the premium vines were replanted, many were replaced by cheaper ones. Now grown are such lesser varieties as the tinta negra mole, whose wine is shipped in bulk to France for use in cooking.

MEXICO

Mexico is believed to have produced the New World's first wine in the sixteenth century. Two centuries later, Spanish missionaries brought grape growing and wine making to Baja California.

Much of the Mexican climate is too hot for the cultivation of quality grapes. (The country's early sweet, heavy wines were usually distilled into brandy.) Aided now by the selection of better grape varieties, by cold stabilization and other modern vinification methods, Mexico is producing much-improved wines.

The country has also expanded grape growing to its largely mountainous north-central sector—to the states of Durango, Chihuahua and Coahuila—where cooler weather prevails. Mexico's best red wines, pressed in part from the cabernet sauvignon, are somewhat claretlike in character. Among its best whites are fruity blends of the chenin blanc and the ugni blanc.

NOTE: Mexico domestically consumes most of the wine it produces.

NEW ZEALAND

Early in the nineteenth century, European colonists established the first vineyard at Hawke Bay in eastern New Zealand, planting cuttings they had imported from France, Spain and Central Europe. Under cultivation now are some three thousand acres, most of them in the cooler areas not far from the sea. The country's principal wine districts—in addition to Hawke Bay—are Gisborne to the north and Auckland to the northwest.

Nearly four-fifths of the New Zealand wines were at first fortified. (Port- and sherry-style wines still predominate.) In the last few years, vintners—aided by stainless steel technology—have also been producing table wines.

Because of its generally cool climate, the country is better suited to white-wine production than to the red. The white wines, pressed from such classic viniferas as the chardonnay, sauvignon blanc, riesling and müller-thurgau, are generally lighter in body and somewhat more acid than their counterparts in Australia. Fresh, sometimes intensely flavored and relatively low in alcohol, they demonstrate a certain austerity and reserve at their finest.

ROMANIA

The best Romanian wines come from the foothills of the Carpathian Mountain range, which curves through the country. The growing season here is warm and sunny with sufficient rainfall, followed by a long, dry, mild autumn.

Romania is primarily a red-wine country; it grows the cabernet sauvignon, pinot noir and merlot as well as several indigenous varieties. Its white grapes include the riesling, chardonnay, furmint, pinot gris, sylvaner, aligoté, traminer and muscat. The country produces a number of table wines, including sweet Muscats, along with sparkling and fortified wines.

An important red-wine producer is the Dealul-Mare region in the southeast, which shares the same latitude as Bordeaux. The largest region however is Focşani, located east of the Carpathians. Grown on its sandy soil are both red and white wines. From the cool mountain plateaus of Transylvania come white wines, pressed from the sauvignon blanc and indigenous grape varieties. From the temperate coastal province of Moldavia in the northeast comes one of the country's best whites, Cotnari, a fine scented dessert wine with a great depth of flavor; it is somewhat reminiscent of the sweeter Hungarian Tokays.

NOTE: Romania is the world's eighth-largest wine producer but exports very little of its output.

RUSSIAN FEDERATION

Despite a northerly location, the Soviets have produced wine since ancient times. Grown in addition to their native grape varieties are the red cabernet sauvignon, merlot and malbec, and the white aligoté, riesling, sylvaner, pinot gris and muscat, along with various hybrids.

The largest viticultural region is in the south on the Crimean Peninsula, which borders the Black Sea. Produced in its arid subtropical climate are high-sugar wines. Since the late nineteenth century, the region has specialized in dessert and fortified wines, including flor sherries, made more or less sweet. Produced as well now are red and white table wines and sparkling wines. The latter are made near Odessa. Wine growing is also seen in other sectors of the Ukraine, in Georgia, Armenia and Moldova.

During the 1950s the wine industry here underwent an enormous expansion. Grapes were cultivated in huge collective farms and the wines processed in giant wineries. One of the world's top producers, the country not only consumes most of its own wines domestically but imports millions of gallons more from Eastern Europe, particularly from Hungary.

SOUTH AFRICA

In the seventeenth century, French Huguenots established South Africa's first vineyard in the Franschhoek Valley some forty miles east of Cape Town. (They planted cuttings they had brought from Europe.) The country's other viticultural pioneers were the Dutch, who set up a trading post at the Cape of Good Hope to supply food and wine to the ships sailing to and from the East Indies. By the eighteenth and early nineteenth centuries, South Africa's wines were among the best known in the world. Particularly notable was Constantia, a legendary sweet Muscat. (Louis XVI's cellar was said to contain more Constantia than claret.)

The center of the South African wine industry is now Stellenbosch in the mountains thirty-five miles east of Cape Town, not far from the site of the original vineyards. Other significant areas are Paarl and Hermanus. The grape varieties grown include the white chardonnay, steen (chenin blanc), riesling, clairette blanc, gewürztraminer, sauvignon blanc, sémillon, palomino and muscat; and the red cabernet sauvignon and shiraz (syrah), along with the cinsault, merlot, grenache, gamay, cabernet franc, hermitage and pinotage. Most of the grapes are cultivated on small farms whose growers sell their crops to producers rather than vinifying the wine themselves.

NOTE: According to informal estimates, about 40 percent of the annual crop goes into the production of commercial alcohol. Many of the growers plant high-yielding grapes, knowing that much of their crop will be used for this purpose.

Growing high-sugar grapes, South Africa had traditionally specialized in port- and sherry-style wines. Its mostly inexpensive table wines were shipped out in bulk. Modern viticultural and vinicultural methods have made possible the production of quality table and sparkling wines. The country's reputation is now based on its dry red wines, which range from those exhibiting a pronounced rusticity to those that are quite elegant. Among the best is a Burgundy-style Pinot Noir. Produced as well are a variety of white wines, ranging from crisp and dry to semisweet and sweet, and including a number of late-harvest wines.

SWITZERLAND

Switzerland produces wine primarily in its western and southern sectors. Most of its vineyards are tiny. Their sites range from warm valleys to colder mountain areas that sometimes grow their grapes four thousand feet above sea level. (The latter cling to south-facing Alpine slopes whose lofty peaks shield them from the northern weather.) Many of the best vineyards are sited along the banks of the Rhône River, which flows down from the Alps to Lake Geneva, then continues on its way to France.

Four-fifths of the Swiss wines are white. Their grape varieties include the riesling, pinot gris, chasselas, sylvaner, müller-thurgau, marsanne, chardonnay, gutedel, rauschling, muscat and petite arvine. Accounting for the finest wines, which are crisply dry, sprightly and fruity, is the riesling grape. More widely cultivated, however, and yielding sturdier lower-acid wines is the productive chasselas. Switzerland's red grapes are the pinot noir, gamay and merlot; the pinot noir produces lighter, fruitier wines here than it does in Burgundy over the border.

NOTE: Swiss grape names often vary from region to region: the chasselas is also known as the dorin or fendant; the sylvaner as the johannisberg; the marsanne as the ermitage; the pinot gris as the malvoisie. The pinot noir is variously called the blauburgunder, spätburgunder, clevener and schwartze klevner.

Switzerland produces wine in nineteen of its twenty-three cantons. About three-fourths of its output comes from Valais and Vaud. Other cantons of significance are Ticino and Neuchâtel.

Valais, the country's oldest and largest wine district, is in the upper Rhône Valley not far from the Italian border. Enjoying a stable climate with plenty of sunshine, it is one of the country's warmest and driest districts. Valais produces both red and white wines. Of particular interest is the white Fendant. Pressed from the chasselas, it is an impeccably light dry wine from Sion, the capital and principal wine center of the district. Other Valais white wines include the Johannisberg, Ermitage and various Muscat blends. The leading red wine here is Dole, a blend of gamay and pinot noir grapes. Fruity and generally dark in color, Dole ranges in body from light to full. (When pressed exclusively from the pinot noir, it's known as Petit Dole.) Valais also produces good rosé wines.

The canton of Vaud on the north shore of Lake Geneva is made up of La Côte, west of Lausanne, which produces especially light white wines and Lavaux to the east, which produces somewhat fuller ones. Vaud is divided into five districts; its wines are generally known by the names of their villages in those districts. Most celebrated is the Dézaley wine, whose village is on the outskirts of Lausanne. Pressed from the chasselas, which is grown in steeply terraced vineyards, Dézaley is fine, fruity and gently dry. Another fine white comes from St-Saphorin near Montreux. To the southeast are the wine towns of Aigle and Yvorne, whose white wines are fairly full bodied, yet somewhat flinty.

North of Vaud and less than twenty miles from the French border is Neuchâtel, a canton also known as Suisse Romande. Neuchâtel, situated on the shores of the lake from which it takes its name, grows red and white wines on its chalky soil. Among them is Cortaillod, pressed from the pinot noir and named for its village. A fruity, agreeable and quite a pale wine, virtually a rosé, Cortaillod is often labeled "Oeil de Perdrix" ("Eye of the Partridge") because of its pinkish color. Neuchâtel's white wines, pressed from the chasselas, are light, dry and fragrant. Some are naturally pétillant, while others have their effervescence added.

NOTE: Switzerland's most northerly wines are produced near Zürich, not far from the German border. The whites are pressed from the müller-thurgau and rauschling, the reds from the schwartze klevner (pinot noir).

Ticino in southern Switzerland is situated on the slopes of the Italian Alps near Lakes Lugano and Maggiore. A warm, sunny region, it is best known for its Merlot di Ticino, a robust fruity red wine with an attractive bouquet. Ticino's more ordinary reds are generally not bottled but served directly from the cask.

NOTE: The Swiss consume almost all the wines they produce domestically and import another 60 percent, which are mainly red wines from Burgundy, Bordeaux and Italy.

TURKEY

Historians believe that the Hittites first made wine in Anatolia, now Turkey, around 4000 B.C. Currently half the country's wine output comes from state-run wineries, the remainder from smaller producers. Turkey's red and white wines, little known outside the country, are generally light and agreeable. Included among them is a crisp, bone-dry Muscat.

(FORMER) YUGOSLAVIA

Yugoslavia has been said to have its feet in the Balkans and its head in the Alps. In its southern Mediterranean sector, the grapes ripen earlier, producing sturdy full-flavored wines. In its northern sector, where the climate is typically Central European, the later-ripening berries yield generally lighter and more aromatic wines.

The grape varieties grown in addition to the indigenous prokupac, malic and plavic, include the white riesling, sylvaner, sauvignon blanc and traminer, along with the sémillon, muscat, malvasia and pinot blanc, and the red merlot and cabernet sauvignon, along with the pinot noir and gamay.

Yugoslavia's principal wine regions are the hilly landscape of Slovenia in the north, the rugged Dalmatian coast of Bosnia-Herzegovina in the east and mountainous Serbia farther inland. Slovenia, bordering Italy and Austria and growing grapes associated with both countries, is responsible for the best wines, which are white. Dalmatia, on the shores of the Adriatic, produces a variety of red, white and rosé wines, including deep-colored, full-bodied and high-alcohol reds. From the Neretva Valley northwest of Dubrovnik come a strong full red Blatina and a dry fruit-scented white Zilavka. Serbia and Macedonia are known for their fruity and rather emphatic red wines and their good rosés. A distinctive Yugoslavian specialty is Prošek, a sweet and potent golden brown wine.

6

IDENTIFYING WINES

Different countries identify their wines in different ways; relying to some extent on the shapes of the bottles and to a greater extent on the labels affixed to them. The information that these labels do—or do not—provide offers revealing insights into the character and temperament of the countries issuing them.

BOTTLE SHAPES

The shape of the wine bottle can reveal the type and origin of its contents. The basic styles are Bordeaux and Burgundy bottles and German flutes. The Bordeaux bottle features straight sides and clearly defined shoulders with a concave indentation at the base called a kick, punt or pushup. (It is designed to hold back the sediment during pouring.) The somewhat stouter Burgundy bottle has shoulders that slope gently. The German flute also has sloping shoulders but a longer and more graceful neck.

The Italians call the Bordeaux bottles *bordoleses* and use them for their classic Chiantis; the Spaniards generally use them for their lighter Riojas and sherries. The French use the Burgundy-style bottles as well for their Champagnes, Rhône and Loire wines; the Italians use them for their Barolos and the Americans for their Pinot Noirs. The Alsatians and Austrians bottle their white wines in German-style flutes, whereas the Italians use these for their Soaves.

NOTE: A number of variants are seen in these basic bottle

BORDEAUX BURGUNDY GERMAN CHAMPAGNE

shapes. The Burgundy bottle flares out at the bottom for Spanish sparkling wines. The Bordeaux bottle features a slightly bulbous neck for port wines.

Other bottle styles include the bocksbeutel, clavelin, amphora, fiasco, and carafe. The bocksbeutel, a rounded, pouchlike flask with flat sides, is used in Franconia for German wines and in Portugal for rosé wines. The clavelin, a squat bottle with squared-off shoulders, is associated with the vin jaunes of the Jura. The amphora, a slender vaselike bottle tapered at the bottom like its ancient Greek forebears, is employed for Italian Verdicchios and French rosés from Provence.

The fiasco, a round-bottomed flask covered with woven straw or plastic, is associated with lesser Chianti wines. Its style originated with Tuscan farm workers who—taking wine with their lunch in the fields—wrapped their bottles with straw to prevent breakage (The covering also protected their wine from the midday sun.) A squatter, more truncated variant is the pulcianella, used for Orvieto wines. And seen in California is the carafe, a wide-necked bottle sealed with a thin metal lid.

The glass of the bottle is usually colored to keep out harmful rays of light. It's tinted green for Bordeaux, Burgundy, Champagne, Alsatian, Austrian and Mosel wines, and brown for Rhien wines. Clear glass is sometimes used to show off the fresh, bright hues of the white wines and rosés, meant for immediate consumption.

Replacing the bottle on occasion is the wine box (also known as the "bag-in-the-box"). A sturdy cardboard container holding a plastic bag filled with wine, it includes a built-in spigot to serve as the dispenser. When wine is withdrawn, the bag correspondingly collapses to eliminate the air space that is created. Not only less expensive to produce than a bottle, the wine box also takes up less space and eliminates breakage problems. (Meant for soon-to-be-consumed wines, the container should be stored in the refrigerator once it has been opened.)

READING THE LABELS

Wines were first identified by the writing on their stone jars. The jars, discovered in Egyptian tombs, bore the name of their owner, the grower and the date. The Greeks stamped the wine's place of origin on their pottery amphorae. Paper labels arrived in the eighteenth century with the mass production of bottles. They could provide more detailed information on the wine and eventually included its style or quality, its alcohol content and the amount in the bottle. Neck labels introduced later carried a vintage date. And back labels provided simplified maps of the region, various facts about the wine, anecdotal information and so forth.

NOTE: For quality products, the corks are often branded with the name of the vineyard and the maker of the wines.

The Place-Name Concept

Pinpointing a wine's origins is its place-name. The place-name idea was introduced in France early in the twentieth century as a way of combatting fraud. Unscrupulous vintners in Reims and Épernay had been using cheap grapes from the south to produce wines they labeled as Champagnes. The true growers, threatened with economic ruin, rioted, forcing the government to send in the troops. Subsequently, protective legislation delimited Champagne's regional boundaries and specified that a wine—to be called Champagne—had to be made from grapes grown in that demarcated region. This was the start of the Appellation d'Origine Contrôlée or AOC, the Controlled or Protected Place-Name.

The AOC not only provided legal authorization for a wine's regional, district or vineyard name, but eventually also spelled out which grapes could be planted, how the vines were to be grown, how many grapes could be picked and the quantity of wine that could be pressed from them. Place-name regulations may also govern how the wine is vinified—specify its characteristics, the proportions of various grapes in its blend, the requirements for its aging and so on. Wines that don't meet the standards of their locales are declassified, losing the right to their appellations. Although they're authentic products of their district or region, these wines are no longer permitted to carry their geographic names.

NOTE: French wines covered by these appellations constitute a relatively small proportion of the country's wines, only about 25 percent of its total output.

The basic premise of the appellation system is that the more precisely a wine's origins are pinpointed, the more authentic and better the wine is likely to be. This concept has been adopted in varying degrees throughout the world. However, minimum standards and controls differ greatly from country to country, and even within sectors of the same country. Government agencies regulate the labeling in some places while wine producers and merchants police themselves in others. In still other places, a coalition of private and public interests may supervise the labeling of the wine.

Estate-Bottling

Estate-bottling, associated with quality wines, is the most precise form of labeling. It specifies not only the smallest and most localized growing area—the vineyard—indicating that the grapes come from the owner's parcel of land, but also indicates that the owner himself is responsible for the wine's vinification and bottling. The

estate-bottling designation is based on the premise that the producer—to protect his own reputation—will do his utmost to guard
the individuality, distinctiveness and quality of his wine and that he
will pay close, personal attention to every phase of the grape
growing and wine-making process that is carried out on his property.

Second Labels

Second-label wines are those that do not measure up to the stan-
dards of the winery's main label. The idea originated when famous
Bordeaux vineyards began to bottle the earlier-maturing products
of their younger vines separately. Second labels have included
Carruades de Lafite (Château Lafite), Pavillon Rouge du Château
Margaux (Châteaux Margaux), Les Forts de Latour (Château
Latour), Hauts de Pontet (Château Pontet-Canet), Bahans Haut-
Brion (Château Haut-Brion), Château Potensac (Château Léoville-
Las-Cases), Comtesse de Lalande (Château Pichon-Longueville),
Château Marbuzet (Cos d'Estournel) and Château Haut-Bages
Averous (Château Lynch-Bages).

NOTE: Word in the Bordeaux trade is that wine from vines
twelve years or older goes into Lafite-Rothschild and from vines
seven to twelve years old into its Carruades de Lafite.

A number of California producers have adopted the second-
label idea. Hawk Crest is the second label of Stag's Leap Wine
Cellars. Liberty School comes from Caymus vineyards, while
Beaulieu vineyards second-labels three of its wines: Georges de
Latour Private Reserve, Beaulieu Rutherford and Beau Tour. Some
wineries even offer third labels to take advantage of surplus grapes
grown on their property or of grapes purchased from others.
(Château Lafite-Rothschild's third label is simply called "Pauillac,"
the name of its commune.)

Varietal Labeling

A varietal wine bears the name of its principal grape. That name is
most useful when the wine retains the distinctive character and
aroma of its specified grape. The best varietal wines are pressed
from such premium varieties as the cabernet sauvignon, pinot noir,

chardonnay and riesling.

In the past such labeling was the sole means of identifying a wine in the United States, since it had few geographical appellations until fairly recently. An American wine may be named for its grape if the blend includes at least 75 percent of that variety. (An earlier minimum was 51 percent.) Some vintners go well beyond the required minimum. Seeking to create wines of greater uniformity and overall quality, they may include as much as 90 to 100 percent of the grape named.

NOTE: When abundant vintages yield a substantial grape surplus, varietal wines may be offered at lower-than-usual prices. They are then called "Fighting Varietals."

Other countries have also adopted varietal labeling. It's now seen in Australia, New Zealand, Chile, Argentina and South Africa. But such labeling hasn't been much in evidence in Europe, where geographic names are generally used, and where law and tradition determine which grapes can be grown in the fine-wine districts. Alsatian wines are an exception. Because of that region's intermittent occupation by Germany, Alsace remained outside the French tradition of relating a wine's name to its place of origin. Alsatian wines were named for their predominant grape instead. Austrian wines also carry varietal names such as Veltliner, Rotgipfler and Walschriesling.

Some Europeans, however, have turned to varietal labeling to circumvent their country's tougher appellation laws. A French wine can carry a varietal label as long as it's made 100 percent from the grape named. Yet the grapes can be grown anywhere in the country and the quality of the wine depends largely on the individual producer. In Burgundy, for example, an Aligoté wine may be attractive in one place and coarse and acidy in another. A recent trend in the South of France has been to identify wines by their grape names rather than by their geographic areas, in an effort to make these wines seem more distinctive.

Proprietary Labeling

A proprietary label, which features a brand name, trade name or winery name, offers the wine maker the greatest degree of flexibility.

He does not have to identify his grapes or their source. He can blend the wine as he sees fit, using whatever grapes in whatever proportions he wishes. He is also free to alter the blend at will. The wine maker may draw his grapes from widely divergent sources, representing several sectors of a given country or perhaps more than one country. (The determining factor is usually the availability and price of the grapes.) Whatever components he uses, the wine maker can create a uniformity of style by adjusting his blending and other cellar treatment so that the wine displays the same taste and aroma year after year. (To achieve such a blend, some wine makers readily forgo their right to identify their product as a varietal wine.)

In Europe, proprietary labeling enables the vintners to get around tougher appellation restrictions. A number of proprietary wines in France are inexpensive blends produced by famous châteaus. Carrying such names as Mouton Cadet and Maître d'Estournel, they almost suggest second labels. One Bordeaux wine, initially made in Pauillac, became so popular that its producers had to reach for their grapes not only beyond Pauillac but beyond the Médoc itself. An even more extreme example was a white wine with a French-sounding name sold in England. Initially, the components had been French, but as grape prices rose, its makers turned first to Italian, then to Austrian sources. Although the wine's character kept changing, its name and label did not.

In the United States, proprietary labeling allows the vintners to bypass the varietal requirements. Proprietaries have become popular here, perhaps because brand-name recognition is a key characteristic of the culture. Such wines have begun to move into the premium field as well. California producers have developed quality wines for the upscale market with such names as Opus One, Dominus, Rubicon and Insignia. (The overall name used for this prestigious group is Meritage, signifying the best and usually the most expensive wines made by these wineries.)

Generic Labeling

Generic labeling technically indicates a wine's type or class, but more commonly refers to wines that have appropriated the name of either a European wine (claret, Chianti, port, Rhine wine or sherry) or a European locale (Beaujolais, Burgundy, Champagne, Chablis and Sauternes). These borrowings began innocently enough when nineteenth-century immigrants, newly arrived in America, attached familiar Old World names to the wines they were making at home. Subsequently this practice was perpetuated in commercial wine production.

With few exceptions, generics are little more than routine jug wines that bear little if any resemblance to their namesakes. The same grape varieties or production methods are rarely used. Even when they are, the soil and climate conditions of the original cannot be duplicated.

A true Burgundy is pressed exclusively from the pinot noir; a California generic may rely on such hot-climate varieties as the zinfandel, grenache, barbera, ruby cabernet and carignane. A true claret is a rich yet austere Bordeaux, whereas its generic can be a dry, sometimes tart wine that is usually is quite light in body. (American wine makers have been known to bottle generic clarets and generic Burgundies from the same vat.) True Sauternes, pressed from noble rot grapes, is a richly luscious wine, while the generic (which drops the final s) never employs botrytized grapes and is more often dry wine than sweet.

A true Chablis is characterized by a crispness, flintiness and bite, whereas the generics are usually soft and slightly sweet. (They may be red or pink as well as white wines and slightly fizzy as well.) A true Rhine wine is known for its splendid sugar-acid balance, whereas the generic version is generally quite tart. Although Mosel wines are celebrated for their delicacy and fragrance, generics that call themselves "Moselles" are usually quite bland.

Like its nominal prototype, a generic sherry may be pressed from raisined grapes; some are even inoculated with flor. But many are baked at high temperatures to re-create the characteristic nut-like or "rancio" taste of the original. They may also be filtered through wood chips to simulate the slow aging process that occurs in the solera.

Generic ports are sometimes pressed from low-quality grapes or even culls and are often lamentably raw. Whereas true tawny ports acquire their color by extended wood-aging, the generics may combine red and white wines. Or they may use less pigmented grapes or even coloring agents. As for generic Tokays, they often bear a closer resemblance to generic ports and sherries than to their Hungarian namesakes.

Generics have become a way for producers to market their surplus grapes or wines. In the United States, where only the vaguest regulations cover such wines, the use of borrowed names is permitted so long as a general place of origin is indicated on the label—as in a Napa Valley Chablis or a New York State Burgundy. Generics are also seen in Europe, Australia, South America and South Africa. Chile uses designations such as Tipo Borgana (Burgundy Type) and Tipo Chablis (Chablis Type), but confusingly employs Bordeaux grapes for its Burgundy-type wines. The Australians make a variety of generics including Moselle, hock (Rhine wine), Chablis, Sauterne, claret and Burgundy, as well as ports and sherries. A number of other countries, including Russia and the United States, produce generic ports and sherries, too.

European vintners have long sought to prevent the exploitation of their wine names. In 1916, an agreement between Britain and Portugal defined port as "a wine produced in the delimited Douro region," and specified that a wine could not be sold as port in Britain unless it was produced within those established boundaries. (Britain however allows the sale of generic ports that specify their country of origin—as in "Australian port" or "South African port.") Portugal itself had hoped to set true port apart from its imitators by creating an official "Oporto" designation, but since most of the wine is shipped out in bulk for bottling elsewhere, foreign shippers continue to use the more familiar "port" on their labels.

There have been other attempts to restrict wine names to their original locations. Early in the twentieth century, the Madrid Convention gave wine sources the sole right to their own geographic names. In the 1970s, the Common Market required that wines shipped by member nations be accompanied by certificates of origin, spelling out the source of their components. (When the wines of more than one country are involved, the label reads "Countries of the European Economic Community.")

The most freely appropriated name has been Champagne, which has been applied to white, red and pink wines pressed from a variety of grapes and made sparkling by the classic *méthode champenoise* or one of its alternatives. Trying to protect the exclusivity of the name, the Champagne industry has spent millions on lawsuits, fighting successful legal actions in Australia, Germany, Spain and Italy. By international agreements and Common Market regulations, the Champagne name is now restricted in Europe to French sparkling wines grown in the delimited Marne region around Reims and Épernay. Even the term *méthode champenoise* has been banned outside that region.

The United States however has never been a signatory to such agreements, and American courts have consistently rejected the claims of the French producers. They say the producers waited too long to sue, and that in the meantime the name has found its way into common usage. U.S. vintners can still call their sparkling wines Champagnes provided they indicate their geographic origin on the label—as in "New York State Champagne" or "California Champagne."

Some people believe that generic labeling should be discontinued because it misrepresents and debases the unique identity of the originals and in general deceives the public. Recommendations have been made in the United States that Barolo, Beaujolais, Frascati, Rhône, Rioja and Mosel labels be eliminated, while Champagne, Chablis, Madeira, Málaga, port and sherry labels be retained. American vintners are phasing out generic labeling to a degree. A number of northeastern wineries have combined varietal and generic names—as in "Diamond Chablis," "Dutchess Rhine Wine" and "Delaware Moselle." Other American wine makers are using proprietary or varietal names or simply labeling their table wines "red" or "white."

NOTE: When Australian producers replaced the familiar generic names with varietal ones, domestic sales fell. They now use generic labels at home while giving varietal names to the wines they ship abroad.

Vintage-Dating

A vintage date refers to the year when the grapes were harvested and made into wine. Any wine—good, bad or indifferent—can carry such a date if it is made from the grapes of a single year. Vintages first came into prominence with port wines and Champagnes. The port shippers would declare a vintage in splendid weather when the crop was excellent enough to stand on its own and when the wine demonstrated a fine potential for aging. Each firm made the decision individually. (Some shippers waited eighteen months after the harvest to see how the wine was coming along before declaring a vintage; others would wait thirty-four months.) In the Douro, a vintage is declared only three or four times in a decade and usually by a near-unanimous consensus.

In the Champagne region, declaring a vintage is often based on the recommendation of a growers' organization, the Comité Interprofessionel du Vin de Champagne (Interprofessional Committee of Champagne). Individual producers can follow suit if they wish; the region's variable weather gives them some leeway. More and more Champagne vintages however are being declared. (The prices fetched by vintage Champagnes are generally 25 to 50 percent higher than those of the nonvintage wines.)

NOTE: While vintage Champagnes represent the wines of a single harvest, nonvintage Champagnes can be better balanced since they represent the producers' blends. To create and maintain their own house styles, the producers blends and reblend a number of wines. For their nonvintage Champagnes, the best firms may combine as many as fifteen wines drawn from four or five harvests.

The vintage-dating of table wines did not begin until the mass production of glass bottles in the eighteenth century. The bottles, with their uniform apertures, could then be securely corked and their straight sides meant that the wines could be stored away horizontally for an extended period. Vintage-dating proved useful: It enabled wine makers to differentiate between their production of various years. It also provided consumers with the key to storing certain wines and helped them avoid wines that were too old.

NOTE: Vintage-dating is most significant in Northern Europe, particularly in the regions of uncertain weather such as Bordeaux and Burgundy in France, and the Rhine and Mosel Valleys of Germany.

Vintage-dating was not considered important for most other table wines however, until the twentieth century when a date on the label came to suggest status and prestige, due in part to an association with the laying down of fine wines and in part to advertising.

Vintage dates then became synonymous in the public's mind with superior quality. Capitulating to the public's insistence that a year be indicated on the label, many producers now vintage-date their entire production regardless of its quality. The majority of wines however remain nonvintage, giving their makers greater flexibility: They are free to blend the products of two or more years for maximum effect.

Vintage-dating differs with location. In the Northern Hemisphere, grapes are usually gathered between September and November. Below the equator, they are generally harvested six months earlier, between March and May. Although some Southern Hemisphere wines are already on the market while their Northern counterparts have not yet been vinified, both carry the same year on their labels. German Eisweins carry two dates to indicate that the crop was harvested one year, but not vinified until the next. Since sherries, Madeiras and Marsalas are blended in soleras—and combine a number of vintages—the dates on their labels indicate the year the solera began, not the year of the harvest.

FRENCH LABELING

In the eighth century, Charlemagne introduced laws regulating French wines; in the fifteenth, Charles VI specified where Burgundy wines could be grown. The nineteenth century saw the start of the *appellation contrôlée,* the controlled place-name system. In 1935, a semiofficial agency, the Institut National des Appellations d'Origine Contrôlée, or INAO, was created. Made up of civil servants and wine-industry representatives, its purpose was to classify French wines and determine which growing areas in the country should receive their own appellations.

The INAO set up three basic classifications for French wines: Appellation d'Origine Contrôlée (AOC), Vins Délimités de Qualité Supérieure (VDQS) and Vins de Pays. In addition, there are the ordinary table wines, the vin ordinaires, also known as the Vins de Table (VDT).

The highest rank, the AOC, covering wines from the better regions, guarantees that their grapes were grown in a specific locale and that the wines themselves were made under fairly strict conditions. The VDQS covers regional and district wines that are inexpensive blends, produced mainly in the Midi, Provence and Corsica. (Once an honorable category in itself, the VDQS has become a stepping-stone to an AOC.) The third classification, Vins de Pays (country wines), covers the blends from small off-the-beaten-track regions, many in the South of France. Its wines may bear the name of their village, county or grape variety, or receive elegant-sounding names such as Côtes du Rhône.

The French appellation system is, in effect, a series of geographical groupings that narrow down to smaller and smaller areas. Wines from the largest, least-precise areas are labeled "Produce of France." These are followed by such regional appellations as Bordeaux, Burgundy, Rhône Valley, Loire, Alsace and so on. Then come the districts within the regions, the villages within the districts, and finally—and most localized—the individual vineyards within the villages. The broadest grouping, the VDTs or vin ordinaires, are mostly nondescript jug wines that carry no geographic designation other than France itself. These may come from almost anywhere, including other countries. Among them is the *gros rouge* (fat red) of the Midi, once a staple of the workingman's diet. (Its cost is based on its alcohol level.) Also included in this VDT category are "zip-code wines," whose only indication of origin is the postal zone in which they were bottled.

The AOC regulations are periodically revised. New appellations have been created, among them the Côtes de Bourg and de Blaye, Cahors, St-Véran and Côtes du Ventoux, along with Minervois and Côtes-de-Provence. In the Rhône Valley, a separate Gigondas appellation was established to distinguish its wines from the more routine Côtes du Rhône products. And a special appellation has set Savennières apart from the surrounding Côteaux de la Loire. In Burgundy, a les Maranges appellation has been created, covering the marginal areas on the periphery of the famous Côte d'Or communes and including three small communes at the southern tip of the region.

French appellations do much more than indicate geography; they may specify production standards, along with crop yields and minimum alcohol levels. A wine that doesn't meet its AOC requirements is declassified and must be sold under a lesser label, either with a commune name or with an even broader district name.

Also declassified is a wine's overproduction. Growers who limit their yields generally produce richer and more intense wines, since they further concentrate the flavors in their grapes. Growers who overcrop or overproduce—who have pushed their vines beyond the allotted limits or squeezed more wine out of a given quantity of grapes—usually end up with thin, weak, watery products.

To bear the name of a vineyard, a wine must achieve a certain minimum level of alcohol. Wines registering less must carry a lesser name. If their alcohol level drops below a certain point, they must carry a more general regional appellation. (If they contain slightly more alcohol than their classification requires, they can be labeled "Supérieure.")

In poor years, the French estates exclude the wines that do not meet their standards; selling them off in bulk to shippers and others, who blend them with the discards of other estates, then label them as regional wines. (When completely anonymous grapes are involved, the wines are simply labeled "Vins de Table.")

Although their wine output is strictly limited by the AOCs, some growers in traditionally famous locations have exploited the marginal areas within their delimited boundaries by creating new vineyards. (They have bulldozed trees and smoothed out fields to do so.) In little more than a decade, the Champagne region has just about doubled its acreage. In Beaujolais, the success of the Nouveau wines has led to huge plantings in the less favored Bas-Beaujolais sector. In Chablis, because of an increased demand for white wines in general and for its wines in particular, the legal limits of its acreage have been expanded. (Once-banned grape varieties have also been incorporated into the Chablis blend.)

NOTE: Nature as well as law limits wine production. Having developed virtually every spare inch of land in their choice viticultural areas, the French have gone abroad to purchase vineyards, build wineries and participate in joint wine-making ventures. Owners of Bordeaux estates have invested in Chilean and American wineries, while Champagne producers are now making sparkling wines in California and Argentina.

Bordeaux Labeling

Bordeaux's appellations are Regional, District and Subdistrict. Regional applies to wines from any sector of the entire region. District applies to wines from its five main areas (Médoc, Graves, Sauternes, St-Émilion, and Pomerol). Subdistrict applies to wines grown in specific communes within the districts. The smallest and most precise locations are the individual vineyards whose wines carry their own names rather than an AOC as such.

Bordeaux labeling can best be understood if visualized as four concentric circles. The outer circle represents the most general area, the regional AOC, which encompasses all of Bordeaux. Its labels read "Appellation Bordeaux Contrôlée," and its wines can be drawn from anywhere within the vast Bordeaux region. These are generally undistinguished wines and include the millions of gallons produced by cooperative wineries.

The second circle, encompassing the five main districts, draws its wines from several communes within each district. The labels here read "Appellation Médoc Contrôlée," "Appellation Graves Contrôlée," and so on. (Second-label wines may use this designation, although third-label wines must carry a broader "Bordeaux" appellation.)

The third circle, encompassing the subdistricts, draws its wines from a number of vineyards within the borders of a single commune. Labels here read "Appellation Pauillac Contrôlée," "Appellation Margaux Contrôlée" and so on. (More than thirty communes in Pauillac, for example, are entitled to an "Appellation Pauillac Contrôlée.")

Wines from the fourth—the smallest and innermost—circle carry the name of a vineyard along with that of the commune or village. Labels here read: "Château Lafite-Rothschild, Appellation Pauillac Contrôlée"; "Château Carbonnieux, Appellation Graves Contrôlée." (One exception is the prestigious Château Haut-Brion in Graves, whose vineyard name is permitted to stand alone.)

To illustrate: Four Bordeaux red wines, representing the four concentric circles, would be labeled "Bordeaux AOC" (regional), "Médoc AOC" (district), "Pauillac" (commune), and "Château Lafite-Rothschild" (single vineyard).

NOTE: The bulk of the Bordeaux trade however is in shippers' wines, mostly anonymous blends that generally carry the shipper's name along with an appellation of origin. (The shippers usually buy their wines by the cask from a given township or region, then blend, finish and bottle the wines, selling them under their various labels.)

Because the Médoc is known primarily for its red wines, the white wines here—even from the top estates—can carry only the wider "Bordeaux" appellation. Graves, which is generally associated with red wines, must use a subappellation for its whites. As a result, the exquisite white wine produced by Château Margaux cannot carry the name of its celebrated vineyard; it uses a proprietary name instead. Subject to the same restrictions are the red wines grown in primarily white-wine regions. For example, the red wines of Entre-Deux-Mers must carry the wider "Bordeaux" designation.

The finest Bordeaux wines are the Vins de Château, which come from an officially demarcated vineyard under single owner- ship. The vineyard itself must possess the building and equipment to press the grapes and store and bottle the wines. Although *château* translates as "castle," only a few of the buildings are pala- tial structures; they may simply be cottages, farmhouses, ware- houses or even sheds. In Bordeaux, just about any wine-making operation—regardless of its size or character—can call itself a château. Most are little more than modest vineyards with wine cel- lars. Of the seven thousand or so châteaus, only about two hundred produce quality wines. (The legendary Bordeaux estates represent less than 2 percent of the region's acreage and produce less than 1 percent of its wine.)

NOTE: *Petit châteaus* are small, little-known vineyards situated on the fringes of the fine wine districts at lesser sites and on lesser soils. They usually produce simple and early-maturing red wines.

"Château-Bottled" or "Estate-Bottled" applies to a wine vinified in a structure attached to a specific vineyard, provided that the structure and the vineyard are mutually involved in its production. (Although French wine producers and shippers outside Bordeaux have appropriated the "Château-Bottled" designation, it lacks legal status elsewhere in the country.)

In Bordeaux, the following phrases establish the authenticity of estate-bottled wines:

- *Mis* (or *mise*) *en bouteilles au (*or *du) château* (Château-bottled)
- *Mise du château* (short form)

NOTE: These designations, along with the château name, may be branded on the cork as well.

In Bordeaux, the following designations have no legal standing:

- *Mis en bouteilles dans nos caves* (Bottled in our cellars)
- *Mis en bouteilles dans nos chais* (Bottled in our warehouses)

Those cellars and warehouses may be located anywhere in the country.

Other designations without official standing are:

- *Mis en bouteilles dans Château* so-and-so
- *Mis en bouteilles en Bordeaux*
- *Mis en bouteilles dans la region de production*

The first does not mean the bottler owns or controls the vineyard's production, while the other two do not claim very much.

NOTE: Bordeaux wines intended for export often carry the initials *ADEB* (Association pour le Dévelopement du Vin de Bordeaux), indicating the maker has voluntarily submitted his wine to a panel of experts for approval.

Burgundy Labeling

Burgundy's labeling system is based more on quality levels than on geographic distribution. It classifies the scattered parcels in the fragmented vineyards of the region down to and including the tiniest parcels. The wines themselves are divided into four categories: Region, Village, Premier Cru and Grand Cru. They are also best understood in terms of concentric circles narrowing down from the largest, most general growing area to the smallest, most precise plot of land.

The outer or regional circle encompasses the general blends whose grapes can be drawn from anywhere in Burgundy. Its labels read: "Appellation Bourgogne Contrôlée." The second or village circle includes the ordinary wines drawn from two or more vine-yards within a given commune or village. Labels here read: "Pommard," "Nuits-St-Georges," "Volnay," "Côte de Beaune-" and so on. (When preceded by a village name—as in "Santenay-Côte de Beaune" or "Monthélie-Côte de Beaune"—the wine comes from the indicated village.) This second circle also includes wines from secondary communes situated at either end of the Côte de Nuit such as Fixin, as well as wines from single but generally undistinguished vineyards.

NOTE: By law, Côte d'Or red wines must be pressed from the pinot noir grape and white wines from the chardonnay. Wines employing other varieties cannot carry a second-circle designation but must employ the broader "Appellation Bourgogne Contrôlée" instead.

The third circle represents the Premier Cru (First Quality Growth) wines. Grown in the better vineyards of each Burgundy commune, these carry on their labels both the commune and vineyard names. For instance, the village of Gevrey-Chambertin encompasses twenty Premier Crus, including Chapelle-Chambertin, Chambertin Clos de Bèze, Latricières-Chambertin, Charmes-Chambertin and so on.

NOTE: When a third-circle vineyard that is known primarily for its white wines produces red wines as well, the reds must carry the less specific designation of the second circle.

The fourth and innermost circle represents the highest-quality Grand Cru (Great Growth) wines. Grown mainly in the Côte de Nuits, these come from vineyards of superior soil and exposure. So esteemed are they that their labels need carry only their eminent vineyard names. These Grand Crus include Clos Vougeot, Chambertin, Montrachet and Musigny.

The smallest Grand Cru vineyard is the tiny two-acre Romanée-Conti, also known as the Domaine de La Romanée-Conti or DRC.

To summarize, Burgundy's quality levels are: 1) Regional, 2) Village, 3) Premier Cru, and 4) Grand Cru. For example, for a Gevrey-Chambertin wine, the lowest category is the regional "Appellation Bourgogne Contrôlée." The next level is the commune or village name, "Appellation Gevrey-Chambertin Contrôlée"; then comes the Premier Cru, whose label would read "Gevrey-Chambertin/ La Combe-aux-Moines" (the commune and vineyard names). The highest-ranking Grand Cru here would carry the name of an estimable vineyard such as "Le Chambertin."

Only a few Burgundian parcels are large enough to produce estate-bottled wines. Labels here bear not only the vineyard name but also the name of the owner, followed by the term "Propriétaire" or "Viticulteur".

The following phrases establish the authenticity of the estate-bottled wines in Burgundy, where a wine estate is known as a *clos* or a *domaine*:

- *Mis* (or *mise*) *en bouteilles au domaine* ("Bottled at the estate")
- *Mis au* (or *du*) *domaine* (short form)

Less frequently used but nevertheless authentic are:

- *Mis en bouteilles par le propriétaire* ("Bottled by the proprietor/grower")
- *Mis par le propriétaire* (short form)
- *Mis en bouteilles à la propriété* (Bottled on the property)
- *Mis à* (or *de*) *la propriété* (short form)

NOTE: These designations must appear in French and on the main label. If they appear in English or on the neck label, they are not valid.

Often seen on the labels of Burgundy shippers but lacking any official standing are:

- *Mis en bouteilles au mes caves* (Bottled in my cellars)
- *Mis en bouteilles dans nos chais* (Bottled in our wineries or cellars)
- *Mis en bouteilles à Beaune* (Bottled in Beaune)

The first may be a product of more than one vineyard, and the shipper's cellar might be located anywhere. The second may be bottled in a shipper's cellar located some distance from the vineyard. The third provides a commune name without any indication of where the grapes themselves were grown.

Vaguer still are:

- *Mis en bouteilles sous nôtre garantie* (Bottled under our guarantee)
- *Mis de l'origine* (Bottled at the place of origin)

• *Mis en bouteilles par les vignerons* (Bottled by the growers)

Although Burgundy uses uniform standards that are logically based and applicable to the entire region, its labeling has rightly been called a jungle. Much of the confusion was created in the nineteenth century. The Côte d'Or vintners, wishing then to increase the sale of their wines, had decided to associate them with the most prestigious vineyard in their village. With official approval, they added the name of a prestigious vineyard nearby to the name of their village, separated only by a hyphen. This composite name suggested that the wines of the village came from a quality location when in fact they were drawn from a much wider area. The public was beguiled; sales increased. Other Burgundy villages followed suit.

Gevrey rechristened itself Gevrey-Chambertin; Chambolle became Chambolle-Musigny. Morey-St-Denis expanded its name with a nod to Clos St-Denis. The little village of Aloxe appended the illustrious Corton name to its own, becoming the impressive Aloxe-Corton. Vosne-Romanée renamed itself for the eminent Domaine de La Romanée-Conti, and the adjacent communes of Puligny and Chassagne claimed the Montrachet name for themselves, since that prestigious vineyard straddled them both. They respectively became Puligny-Montrachet and Chassagne-Montrachet.

Adding to the confusion, some vineyards decided to append the name of the most notable nearby vineyard to their own. Eight vineyards in Gevrey-Chambertin appropriated the illustrious Chambertin name, becoming Chapelle-Chambertin, Chambertin–Clos de Bèze, Latricières-Chambertin, Charmes-Chambertin and so on.

Because the commune names and vineyard names sound so similar, it is often difficult to distinguish between the two. Yet the difference between their wines may be enormous. A Vougeot wine is a commune wine bearing little resemblance to the outstanding wine grown in the prestigious Clos Vougeot vineyard. A wine labeled "Beaune AOC" can easily be mistaken for a Côte de Beaune–Villages. (The former comes from the closely delineated and fine commune of Beaune; the latter, deriving from farther afield, is a blend of two or more wines drawn from secondary communes.)

Compounding the confusion has been the ongoing fragmentation of the Burgundy vineyards themselves. As their proprietors died off, the land has been divided into smaller and smaller parcels. Yet anyone who shares in a given vineyard can label his wine with the name of that vineyard whether his parcel is at the top, bottom or middle of the slope. Moreover, each owner cultivates and harvests that plot of land in his own way and makes his own special style of wine. In Burgundy therefore, the maker is as important as the wine.

The variations are many. The same vineyard might yield three distinct wines: one from a grower who produces, bottles and sells his own wine; another from a shipper to whom the grower has sold his raw wine; and a third from a shipper who owns a parcel there from which he produces his own wine. (A shipper who blends the wine of several owners may use the vineyard name but not if he draws his blends from several vineyards.) Depending on the shipper's skills, his blend may be better than an estate-bottled wine drawn from a plot owned by a single vintner.

Chablis Labels

Chablis wines are categorized as: Petit Chablis, Chablis, Chablis Premier Cru and Chablis Grand Cru. Most modest is Petit Chablis, a shipper's blend from lesser vineyards, also known as *Bourgogne des Environs de Chablis*. The blend must attain at least 9.5 percent alcohol and may include wines from outside Chablis. The next category, Chablis alone, possesses slightly more alcohol and richness while Premier Cru, produced in nearly two dozen small vineyards around the town of Chablis, must reach at least 10.5 percent alcohol. (Several of the Premier Cru vineyards are legally permitted to add the name of a famous nearby vineyard to their own, as in Chablis-Vaudésir, Chablis-Grenouilles and so forth.)

Grand Cru is reserved for the wines grown in the seven leading Chablis vineyards: Les Clos, Blanchots, Bougros, Grenouilles, Les Preuses, Valmur and Vaudésir. Their labels carry the vineyard name, often with the "Grand Cru" designation added. Their wines must attain at least 11 percent alcohol.

Beaujolais Labels

Only red wines pressed from the gamay grape may legally bear the Beaujolais name. Although the Chardonnay wines grown here have been called Beaujolais Blancs they are not, strictly speaking, true Beaujolais wines at all.

The appellations for Beaujolais wines are: Beaujolais, Beaujolais-Villages and Cru Beaujolais. Beaujolais alone comes from Bas-Beaujolais, the region's southern sector, where the terrain is flatter and the soil is a sedimentary clay. Required to attain at least 9 percent alcohol, the wine may be chaptalized to accomplish this. (For export, the wine's alcohol level is often increased to 11 or 12 percent.)

Beaujolais-Villages wines are drawn from thirty-nine communes in the Haut-Beaujolais sector. Sturdy and dependable, these wines usually demonstrate more character than Beaujolais alone. (Adding "Villages" to an appellation indicates a somewhat better product.) Although these wines are generally higher in alcohol, they are often also chaptalized.

The Cru Beaujolais are invariably darker, richer and fuller than the other Beaujolais wines. Produced in the top nine northern sectors and bearing a commune name rather than a vineyard name, they are: Moulin-à-Vent, Morgon, Chénas, Brouilly, Côte de Brouilly, Fleurie, Juliénas, Chiroubles and St-Amour. A tenth cru, Beaujolais-Régnié, added in 1988, is simply called Régnié. Whether grown on the largest vineyard estate or on the smallest parcel of land, all the Cru Beaujolais are equally entitled to bear the prestigious name of their commune.

NOTE: Beaujolais Nouveaus are made from Beaujolais alone or from Beaujolais-Villages wines, never from a top-ranking Cru Beaujolais.

Champagne Labeling

In and of itself, the Champagne name in France constitutes a guarantee of authenticity. Wines bearing the name must be grown in the strictly demarcated Champagne Délimitée zone and follow the classic méthode champenoise. They do not carry a vineyard name since they are pressed from purchased grapes. Instead, they are known by the name of their maker. The prestige Champagnes are usually made from the first pressings of the highest-rated grapes. These are either labeled Grand Cuvée (Great Blend) or Tête de Cuvée (Top of the Line). Others may combine several pressings but never the third or fourth alone. Special Cuvée indicates a producer's best wines, while Premier Cuvée refers to the best wine of a given commune.

NOTE: A one-year bottle-aging minimum is set for nonvintage (NV) Champagnes and a two-year minimum for vintage Champagnes. Some prime examples of the latter are not released until they're eight to ten years old.

Other terms seen on Champagne labels are Grand Cru, which refers not to the wine itself but to a quality vineyard in a famous village whose grapes have fetched the highest prices. RD, for *recemment dégorgé* (recently disgorged) refers to particularly fine Champagnes that are allowed to rest on their yeasty sediment several years longer than others, making them fuller and more flavorful. The British equivalent here is LD, for late disgorged.

RM stands for *récoltant manipulant* (grower and winemaker), CM for *coopérative de manipulation* (a cooperative that makes wine from its members' grapes), NM for *négociant-manipulant* (a Champagne house that buys grapes and makes wine) and MA for *marque acheteur* (purchaser's mark). Meaningless Champagne terms on the label are "Réserve," "Privat," and "Speciale."

NOTE: Authentic Blanc de Blancs Champagnes come from the delimited Côte des Blancs zone. Elsewhere the term *Blanc de Blancs* simply indicates a white wine made from light-skinned grapes. The term, although redundant and meaningless, is often employed outside the Champagne region by producers who think it endows their wines with a greater elegance and prestige.

Rhône Valley Labeling

Wine classifications in the Rhône Valley are: 1) Côtes du Rhône, 2) Côtes du Rhône–Villages, 3) Côtes du Rhône with a district or village name, and 4) Rhône wines with their own appellation.

Côtes du Rhône, which covers the entire Rhône region and

encompasses some one hundred and twenty communes, refers to the simplest and least-expensive wines. Literally millions of gallons of these are made each year, many produced by cooperatives. Most of these are sturdy and tasty but undistinguished. Slightly better are the *Côtes du Rhône-Villages* wines, produced mainly in the southern sector of the region. These representing blends drawn from one or several villages, these are also usually produced by cooperative wineries.

NOTE: Because the Southern Rhône is best known for its red wines, the highest appellation permitted the white wines is a Côtes du Rhône-Villages.

Côtes du Rhône with a district or village name covers wines drawn from a specified delimited locale—for instance, Côtes du Rhône-Chusclan and Côtes du Rhône-Ardeche. The highest-quality wines in the region carry their own appellation. Numbering less than twenty, they include Côte Rôtie, Condrieu, Châteauneuf-du-Pape, Château Grillet and Hermitage. (The Hermitage AOC covers only the prestigious Hermitage Hill; wines from the surrounding area carry a Crozes-Hermitage label.)

NOTE: Single vineyard names are rare in the Rhône Valley, but a number of producers are beginning to engage in estate-bottling and to feature their vineyard names on the labels.

Alsatian Labeling

Most French wines are named for their place of origin but Alsace, because of its recurrent occupation by Germany, did not come under French labeling laws until the 1960s. As a result, the best Alsatian wines carry varietal names rather than place names.

The wine categories here are: Grand Vin d'Alsace, Edelzwicker and Zwicker. Grand Vin, also known as Grand Cru or Grand Réserve, applies to wines grown in the best vineyards of the leading villages. These must be made 100 percent from their specified grape variety (riesling, gewürztraminer, tokay d'alsace, or muscat), employ only the first and possibly the second pressing, and attain a minimum alcohol level of 11 percent. The Grand Vin labels carry a commune or a village name—Guebwiller, Ammerschwir, Ribeauville and so on—along with the shipper's name and address.

NOTE: The Grand Vin or Grand Réserve designation has no official significance elsewhere in France.

Edelzwicker (Blend of Noble Grapes) refers to wines combining two or more of the better grape varieties. These—made from second and more likely third pressings—are generally served as carafe wines. Zwicker (Blend of Grapes) is a more commonplace product, combining chasselas and sylvaner grapes.

Cru Exceptionnel or Réserve refers to an Auslese wine, and a Vendange Tardive is a late-harvest wine. Grains Noble or Selections des Grains Nobles (Selection of Only the Ripest Grapes) refers to those rare wines made from individually picked noble rot berries. These are somewhat similar to the German Trockenbeerenausleses.

NOTE: Shippers' names and brand names are more common than vineyard names in Alsace, since few vintners own enough land to produce single-vineyard wines. (Special Reserve Selection refers to a single-vineyard wine.) To bear an estate name, the wine must come 100 percent from that source. Some Alsatian vintners are beginning to engage in estate-bottling, however, and to feature vineyard names.

Miscellaneous French Labeling

Authentic Pouilly-Fuissé always carries a vineyard name. When grown outside its delimited zone, the wine must be labeled "Mâcon-Fuissé." St-Véran, a relatively recent appellation, encompasses the wines of eight Mâconnais villages nearby. (Previously, the wine carried only a Beaujolais Blanc or a Mâcon Blanc designation.) Côte Châlonnaise wines are labeled Premier Cru (First Growth) when they're of officially recognized quality. In the Côtes de Provence, wines of officially recognized quality are labeled Cru Classé (Classified Growth) and they carry a vineyard name.

ITALIAN LABELING

Italy has named its wines for their place of origin (Chianti, Orvieto, Bardolino); for their grape varieties (nebbiolo, sangiovese, dolcetto); or for a combination of the two (Dolcetto d'Alba, Sangiovese di Romagna, Brunello di Montalcino). Some Italian wines may carry the names of their wineries or shippers, while others are fancifully labeled—as in Lacryma Christi and Est! Est! Est!

In 1963, Italy instituted its appellation system, the Denominazione Controllata (Controlled Place-Name), which now covers some 250 designated wine zones. Although nominally supervised by the Ministry of Agriculture, the system is actually administered by a committee made up of wine growers, producers, dealers, members of professional wine associations, state experts and others.

The Italian appellation system sets up three categories: 1) Denominazione Semplice di Origine (Simple Place-Name), 2) Denominazione di Origine Controllata or DOC (Controlled Place-Name), and 3) Denominazione di Origine Controllata e Garantia or DOCG (Controlled and Guaranteed Place-Name). In addition, there are the ordinary *vinos de tavola* or table wines.

The Simple Place-Name, which covers about 12 percent of the country's output, indicates the wine's general place of origin. The DOC, the main category, covers more than one hundred fifty wines from about seventy districts and designates the legally defined viticultural areas. It specifies that a wine may not be sold under a given name unless produced in a defined area from specified grape varieties and then bottled according to certain regulations. The DOC controls the production of wine, not its quality.

The DOCG, the highest category, is devoted to the country's finest wines and covers specific vineyards in nine districts. It establishes, controls and guarantees territorial zones of production; specifies which grape varieties can be grown; and sets their yields. It is meant to verify a wine's quality as well as its authenticity. Among the DOCGs are Chianti, Albana di Romagna, Vino Nobile di Montepulciano, Brunello di Montalcino, Barolo, Barbaresco, Gattinara, Carmagnano and Torgiano.

To earn a DOCG, the vintner must submit his wine to a panel of wine makers chosen from all over the country. The panel's members set the standards for taste, flavor, bouquet, color, acid content and so on; periodically retasting the wines and declassifying those that don't measure up.

Before Italy instituted its nationwide appellation system, *consorzios* (associations of local growers) established their own requirements. Operating on a self-policing basis, the winemaking consorzios created systems of quality control, established basic wine styles, and set production standards, along with alcohol levels and minimum aging times. They also monitored their members' cellars. Such growers' associations still oversee some of the country's strictest labeling regulations.

Best known is the Consorzio del Chianti Classico (Consortium of Classic Chianti Producers). Formed in 1920, it determined whether or not a given parcel could be turned into a vineyard, drew up the boundaries of the district and established Chianti's Zona Classico (Classic Zone). In 1933, the Consorzio's standards were enacted into law, and in 1976, the Zona Classico was officially designated. The Consorzio also issues a neck seal for the bottles of its members, featuring the Gallo Nero (Black Rooster)—the symbol of the Chianti League, formed in 1376 to defend the Florentine Republic against Siena.

Although more than two hundred classified vineyards produce classic Chiantis, the Consorzio now represents only about a fourth of the famous ones, since the others believe that their own names are a sufficient guarantee of wine quality. Growers in the immediate vicinity of the Zona Classico established their own conzorsio, which sets its own standards and also issue a special neck seal for the bottles of its members. That seal depicts a della Robbia cherub.

Adjoining the Zona Classico are six districts that are permitted to combine the Chianti name with their own. They are Chianti Montalbano, Chianti Rufina and the Chiantis Colli Fiorentini (Wines from the Florentine Hills). This group includes Colli Pisane, Colli Senesi and Colli Arentini.

NOTE: By law only Tuscan red wines may be called Chiantis. The region's white wines must be called Bianco Toscano (Tuscan White Wine) or Colli Toscani (Wine from the Tuscan Hills).

The Chianti blend, codified in 1967, included 50 to 80 percent of the red sangiovese grape, 10 to 30 percent of the red canaiolo and 10 to 30 percent of the white trebbiano. In 1984, the white-grape requirement was reduced to 2 percent and the red-canaiolo requirement to 5 percent. In addition, up to 10 percent of nontraditional grape varieties could be blended into the wine. Tuscan vintners have sometimes further altered their blends seeking to create richer, smoother, and more velvety wines. Some have eliminated the traditional white grapes altogether and used 100 percent sangiovese or its close relative, the sangioveto grosso, instead. Other vinters have made considerable use of such non-indigenous grapes as the cabernet sauvignon, merlot, and cabernet franc. Although the resulting blends are still grown in the delimited Chianti district and are of high quality, they do not meet the traditional DOC requirements and so cannot carry the Chianti name. These Tuscan wines are given such names instead as Carmagnano, Solaia, Tinscvil, Tignanello, Sassicaia, Ornellaia and Pomino. At first classified only as vinos de tavola, they have recently received a new designation to acknowledge their Tuscan origins, the *Indicazione Geographica Tipica* or IGT.

Veneto has set up a delimited Zona Classico for its Soave wines. (Its initially quite small acreage has been extended to meet the increased demand for white wines.) Another Zona Classico has been established for the Verdicchio wines of Marche. Guaranteeing their authenticity is the designation: Conzorsio dei Verdicchio dei Castelli di Jesi.

Estate-bottling is something of a rarity in Italy, practiced primarily by a few vintners in Chianti and Lombardy. A single-vineyard estate is known as a *tenuto* or *castello* and the labels for estate-bottled wines read:

- *Imbottigliato al tenuta*
- *Imbottigliato al castello*

Much vaguer designations are:

- *Imbottigliato ne'l origine* (Bottled at the place of origin)
- *Imbottigliato nella zona di produzione* (Bottled in the zone of production)
- *Meso en bottiglia del produttore al'origine* (Bottled with products from the place of origin)

Vintage dates generally appear on the labels of the better Italian wines. Other label terms loosely indicating age are Vecchio (old) and Stravecchio (older still). The wines may also carry such age designations as Riserva or Riserva Speciale, which differ in their significance from wine to wine. "Riserva" for a Chianti, Barolo, or Barbaresco indicates that the wine has spent three or four years in wood and another half-year or so in glass; "Riserva Speciale" is a few years older. For a Brunello di Montalcino to be called a Riserva, it must be aged for at least 5 years, with $4^1/_2$ in wood and the remainder in glass.

"Superiore" in Italy refers to a wine with a higher-than-normal alcohol level. Bardolino and Soave Superiores register at least 11.5 percent alcohol, and Valpolicella Superiores must reach 12 percent. "Liquoroso" indicates a wine with an alcohol level of 16 percent or more.

Guaranteeing that an Italian wine comes from where the label says it does is a red seal affixed to the cork. It bears the words: *Italia Marchio Nazionale* (National Italian Trademark). Another red seal bearing the initials *INE* attests to the wine's authenticity for export and is issued by the Istituto Nazionale per l'Exportazione (National Institute for Export).

SPANISH LABELING

Spain relies on geographic names for its wine labeling but much of it is based on brand names or producers' names rather than on appellations as such. In effect since 1933 has been the Denominación de Origen or DO (Name of Origin) system, which encompasses twenty-seven appellations, including Rioja, Jerez, Montilla-Moriles and Málaga. This system is administered by the Instituto Nacional de Denominaciónes de Origen (National Institute of Place Names).

Working through its Ministry of Agriculture, the Spanish government has created for each of the delimited regions a self-regulating control board, a Consejo Regulador de la Denominaciónes de Origen (Regulatory Council of Place-Names). Each board sets nominal vineyard standards for its region and collects wine samples, which it subjects to analysis. The approved wines are then given an official Denominación de Origen number, which usually appears on the back label. Wines approved for export receive a Garantia de Origen (Guarantee of Origin) designation, which usually appears as a paper sticker affixed to the cork. (As a rule, the consejo reguladors, or regulatory councils, lack strict enforcement capabilities.)

Applying somewhat stricter standards than most is the regulatory council in Rioja, which allows only a handful of grape varieties to be cultivated and sets specific aging requirements for the region's wines. Rioja classifies its wines as Viños de Crianza (with breeding) or Viños sin Crianza (without breeding). Those with breeding must spend at least one year in wood and one in glass. They're usually designated for export. Wines without breeding are regional wines, subject to neither barrel-aging nor bottle-aging requirements and generally consumed locally. In Jerez, the consejo regulador subjects the sherry wines to special regulations. It defines the zones of production, specifies the grape varieties that may be grown, sets minimum alcohol levels and so on.

Estate-bottling is rarely practiced in Spain. Known as *Embottelado de Origen* or *Gengarrafado de Origen,* it is occasionally seen in Rioja, where only a few of the better wines actually come from single estates. The majority of Rioja's wines are drawn from a number of vineyards, their blends generally combining the grapes of the grower or producer with those purchased from others. Vineyard names here are more like brand names. (Although *viña* stands for "vineyard," the appearance of the term on the label does not necessarily indicate the bottling from a single vineyard.) Sherry, the blended product of many vineyards, never carries a vineyard name.

Reserva in Spain generally refers to a red wine of a good vintage that is aged for a minimum of three years. Gran Reserva is a wine made in exceptional years and also aged for at least three years. The Reserva designation in Rioja is based on the assessment of the individual producer; if he doesn't think his wine merits this status after some wood-aging, he bottles it and ships it out forthwith. (Some of the older Rioja establishments age their Reservas for at least six years.) Gran Reservas spend a minimum of two years in wood and three in glass, although some of the older establishments age such wines for at least eight years.

The Spaniards don't take vintage-dating very seriously. The year on the label may reflect only the age of the oldest wine in the blend. (For sherry, the vintage date refers to the year the solera began.) *Cosecho* and *vendimia* both translate as "vintage" but are quite loosely used. *Años* ("years") preceded by a number indicates the time the wine spent in wood. *Vieja pasada* means "old" and *escogida,* "very old" or "selected." (For sherries, *pasada* refers to a superior old fino or amontillado.) Spanish sparkling wines or *viños espumosos* that meet certain production standards are given a Denominación Especifica. Those that follow the méthode champenoise are called *cavas;* those made by bulk fermentation are called *granvas.*

PORTUGUESE LABELING

Supervising wine regulations in Portugal is a semiofficial agency, the Junta Nacional de Vinho. The Junta has established a number of officially recognized regions and indicates a wine's authenticity by giving it a Denominacao de Origen (Place-Name) or a Selon de Origen (Seal of Origin). These designations, however, are not consistently applied.

The country's strictest regulations are seen in the Douro, the only region where vinho do porto (port wine) can be grown. There, the Instituto do Vinho do Porto (Port Wine Institute) samples, tests and analyzes the wine before it is blended and aged. Wines that meet the institute's established standards are awarded a Designacao de Origen (Certificate of Origin) and given a Vinho do Porto Garantia designation for export, which includes an individual testing number.

Estate-bottling, known as *Engarragado na Origen,* is not commonly practiced in Portugal. The best wines carry regional or brand names rather than vineyard names. Garrafeira, which translates as "Best Wine" or "Private Stock," refers to a premium wine that has been aged by its producer.

MADEIRA LABELING

Madeira's wines usually carry the name of their predominant grape. Traditionally, these were sercial, bual, verdelho and malmsey, but now other grape varieties are included as well. Since the blends usually represent several years, the date on the label does not indicate the vintage year but the year that the blending began. Wines aged for at least three years are labeled Choice, Selected, or

Finest. Reserve wines are aged for five years, Old Reserves for ten years and Special or Extra Reserves for fifteen years. Vintage Madeiras, the best wines of a single year, are made only from traditional grapes and spend at least twenty years in wood and two years in glass.

GERMAN LABELING

Germany labels its wines in a highly structured and consistent way, comprehensively demarcating its growing units for the entire country. The labels for quality wines provide in uniform order information on the vintage, growing region, commune or town, vineyard, grape variety, quality level and producer, while for regional blends involving lesser grapes, brand names are generally used .

Before 1971, there were about twenty-five thousand wine names and almost as many vineyard sites in Germany. Reform legislation that year reduced this unwieldy number to less than three hundred by setting a minimum size of 12.5 acres for each vineyard and by specifying that a site or district name could be used only if the wine was actually grown there. As a result, many secondary sites in each town were incorporated into two or three highly regarded vineyards. For instance, the famous Bernkasteler Doktor vineyard, previously confined to about three acres, was expanded to include some eighty other sites within a five-mile radius of the town of Bernkastel. (The best wines, however, continue to be grown at or very near the original site.) Piesporter Goldtröpfchen once referred to the wine of a single vineyard, but it now includes wines from a number of Piesport vineyards. The 1971 reforms also replaced the earlier categories of General Blends, Village Wines and Quality Wines with four new categories that represent areas narrowing down from the largest region to the smallest parcel of land. These categories are: Gebiet, Bereich, Grosslage and Einzellage.

The Gebiet represents an entire growing region, such as the Rheingau; a Bereich is a subregion within a Gebiet, such as Johannisberg. Each Bereich is divided into a number of Grosslagen (collective or composite neighboring vineyards), sharing a similar soil and climate and bearing the name of their best-known village.

The Einzellage is an individual vineyard site that covers at least 12.5 acres.

To merit a Bereich (subregion) designation, at least 75 percent of the wine must be grown in the named area. Grosslage (collective vineyard) wines may come from the named village or from several others in the vicinity. For example a Niersteiner wine may not only derive from the village of Nierstein itself but from any or all of the twenty or more vineyards located in fourteen nearby villages.

An *er* added to the village name converts it into a possessive—as in Niersteiner (From around Nierstein), Hattenheimer (From around Hattenheim), Piesporter (From around Piesport) and so forth. In Einzellage (individual vineyard) wines, the village name is followed by the vineyard name. Such wines include Hattenheimer Hinterhaus, Oppenheimer Herrenberg, Wehlener Klosterberg and so forth. Some Einzellage wines are so famous that only their vineyard names need appear on the label: In the Rheingau, these are Marcobrunn (in Erbach), Schloss Johannisberg (in Johannisberg) and Schloss Vollrads (in Winkel); in the Mosel-Saar-Ruwer, they are Josephshof (in Graach) and Scharzhofberg (in Wiltingen).

To summarize: If a label reads "Hattenheimer Wisselbrunnen, Schloss Rheinhartshausen," *Hattenheim* with an *er* is the Grosslage (village), *Wisselbrunnen* is the Einzellage (individual vineyard) and *Schloss Rheinhartshausen* is the specific site. If a label reads "Johannisberger, Schloss Johannisberg, Fürst von Metternich," *Johannisberg* with the *er* represents the Grosslage, *Schloss Johannisberg* the Einzellage and the proprietor is a member of the von Metternich family. (*Fürst translates as "prince."*)

Although the same vineyard name may appear on more than one label, the village name that precedes it will eliminate any confusion. The towns of Wehlen and Zeltingen both have within their boundaries a Sonnenuhr (Sundial) vineyard, but the wine of one is a Wehlener Sonnenuhr and the other is a Zeltinger Sonnenuhr. And while the towns of Graach and Zeltingen both have a Himmelreich (Kingdom of Heaven) vineyard, one wine is a Graacher Himmelreich, the other a Zeltinger Himmelreich.

Nevertheless, the name similarities can be confusing. In the Saar region, Scharzhofberg is the wine of an Einzellage (individual vineyard), but Scharzberg is the wine of a Grosslage (composite vineyard), while Wiltinger Scharzberg is a generic blend whose components may be drawn from anywhere in the region.

NOTE: Further efforts to simplify wine names and classifications have come up against Germany's strict wine laws. The labels for a number of lesser wines, however, feature only the names of the town and the shipper.

The 1971 reform legislation also set up three quality levels for German wines: 1) Deutscher Tafelwein, 2) Qualitätswein bestimmter Angaugebiete or QBA, and 3) Qualitätswein mit Prädikat or QMP.

Deutscher Tafelwein (German Table Wine), the broadest category, also known as Tischwein, covers the simple, light, pleasant wines best consumed directly from the cask. These carry the name of one of the country's five general regions: Rhein, Mosel, Oberrhein, Neckar, or Main. (At least 75 percent of the wine must come from the region named.) Tafelweins however need not involve any particular grape nor attain any specific level of alcohol.

NOTE: In 1982, a new regional category a step above Tafelwein was created. Called Deutscher Landwein (German Country Wine), it also covers light, uncomplicated wines meant primarily for domestic consumption.

At the next level is Qualitätswein, further broken down into two categories: Qualitätswein Bestimmter Anbaugebiete or QBA (Quality Wine from a Designated Region) and Qualitätswein mit Prädikat or QMP (Quality Wine of Special Distinction).

The QBAs come from approved quality regions known as Anbaugebieters (wine regions under cultivation), including the Rheingau, Rheinhessen, the Pfalz, Mosel-Saar-Ruwer, Nahe, Franconia, Ahr, Baden, Hessische Bergstrasse, Mittelrhein and Württemberg. The grapes involved here must ripen sufficiently to ensure that their wines will display the taste and style associated with their particular region.

The QMPs or Qualitätswweins mit Prädikat are grown in individual vineyards within the subregions. In addition to meeting the basic QBA requirements as to origin and legal approval, these are wines of the highest quality. Elegant and long-lived, they represent the best concentration of attributes, such as brilliance and breed. (In poor years, no QMP wines are produced.)

The QMP category is further divided into six quality levels, each denoting a higher degree of ripeness, an increased fullness of body and a greater concentration of flavor and sweetness. In their ascending order these quality levels are: Kabinett, Spätlesse, Auslese, Beerenauslese (BA), Eiswein and Trockenbeerenauslese (TBA).

Kabinett, the driest premium wine, is pressed from the first gathering of fully ripened grapes in a normal harvest. Slightly fruitier than a QBA, it is light, delicate and low in alcohol. Kabinett wines range from *trocken* (dry) to *halb-trocken* (half-dry).

NOTE: These wines acquired their name in the eighteenth century when vineyard owners would lock away in special cabinets, wines from superior vintages for their own use.

Spätlese (late-picked berry) is made from more fully ripened grapes, picked at least a week after the main harvest. Riper and more intense, more concentrated in depth and flavor, this wine averages 10 percent alcohol by volume and is vinified dry, medium-dry or sweet.

Auslese (specially selected late-picked berry) is made from a still-later gathering of extraripe grapes. Removed from each cluster are the blemished, unripe, or otherwise defective berries. Auslese wines, produced only in excellent vintages, are more intense in bouquet and flavor than the Spätleses, and usually sweeter as well. (They often serve as dessert wines.)

Beerenauslese or BA (selected picked-off berry) is made from specially selected, fully ripened, handpicked clusters, often affected by noble rot. Produced only two or three times in a decade, these sweet, luscious wines display honeyed, nectarlike flavors, flowery aromas and a superb concentration of fruit.

Trockenbeerenauslese or TBA (selected, dried, picked-off berry) is the rarest of the German wines, produced only once or twice in a decade and made from botrytized grapes. The grapes, left to shrivel on the vine until November, are then individually handpicked. Each yields a concentrated, syrupy drop of must. The sugars here are so dense that they cannot ferment out fully, leaving the wine intensely sweet and rich and relatively low in alcohol (about 7 or 8 percent). Phenomenally complex, Trockenbeerenauslese wines combine a fruity scent intermingled with a subtle suggestion of herbs and spices.

Between the BA and the TBA categories is Eiswein (Ice Wine), made from extremely late ripened grapes left on the vine until the first frost of December or January. The grapes, containing about 30 percent sugar and gathered berry by berry, are pressed while still frozen. The water in their must—now ice—is discarded, concentrating their grape sugars further. Eisweins are intensely sweet, but a ripe acidity balances out their rich fruit sugars.

NOTE: Some vineyards indicate quality grades (Kabinett, Spätlese, Auslese, and so on) by using different-colored foil capsules—blue, green, pink, gold, white, etc., covering the corks. The practice is not official, however, and varies from one wine maker to the next.

SUMMARY OF GERMAN WINE CATEGORIES

Geographical Classification	Quality Level
Gebiet (Region)	Tafelwein
Bereich (Subregion)	Landwein
Grosslage (Wine District)	Qualitätswein (QBA)
Einzellage (Vineyard)	Qualitätswein mit
	Prädikat (QMP)
	Kabinett
	Auslese
	Spätlese
	Beerenauslese
	Eiswein
	Trockenbeerenauslese

Chaptalization is permitted for some German wines but not for others. Even in good years sugaring is allowed for Tafelweins and Deutscher Landweins. (In poor years, their blends may also be balanced out with wines imported from other Common Market countries.) Bereich and Grosslage wines are generally sugared as well to bring their alcohol levels up to the desired minimum. QBA wines can be sugared if necessary, whereas QMP wines cannot; the latter must attain at least 9.5 percent alcohol naturally. An Einzellage (single-vineyard) wine cannot be sugared either.

For estate-bottled wines, the labels read:

- *Erzeugerabfüllung* (estate-bottled)
- *Erzeugerabfüllung aus eigenem lesegut* (estate-bottled by the producer from his own harvest)

Equivalent terms are *Schlossabzug* or *Schlossabfüllung* (bottled at the castle). The Schloss designation is similar to that of a château in Bordeaux and refers to the entire wine-making property, including the vineyards and the buildings. (Some of the larger estates in the Rheingau's feature actual castles or at least manor houses.)

The label terms Wachstum, Kreszenz, Gewächs and Eigenegewächs all refer to growth. A specific name following them indicates the vineyard's ownership. Erben, which translates as "heir," refers to wines sold under the name of the vineyard's original owners. When preceded by a proper name, it indicates that the vineyard is managed by the current generation of that family.

Bestes is the owner's best barrel. Fass, Fuder and Stuck all refer to the cask. Since for their best wines the Germans treat each day's pressing separately, a number is used to indicate the specific cask from which the wine was bottled. For example, "Fuder" followed by "109" indicates the 109th barrel put down that year. This enables the consumer to purchase more of a given wine if he or she wishes.

German quality wines receive an official testing number, which appears on the label. Known as the amtliche Prüfungsnummer (Official Testing Control and Registration Number), abbreviated to A.P. Nr. or Pruf Nr. or simply P.R., the number indicates that the wine has passed an objective three-part appraisal administered by an official government panel. Involved in this appraisal are an inspection of the applicant's vineyard and cellar, a chemical analysis of the wine and a sensory evaluation of its taste, color, clarity and bouquet.

Other German label terms include Weinbauort, which refers to a wine community, and Weingut (wine estate), which refers to a specific winery, including its cellars or vineyards. A Staatsweingut (state-owned vineyard) is the property of the German government, although it operates autonomously. (A crest on the label here features a stylized eagle.) Weinkellerei refers to a wine cellar;

Zentralkellerei to a central cellar. (The latter, combined with Staatsweingut, indicates a quality wine produced in a state-owned vineyard.) Abfüller (bottler) refers to a winery or a bottler. Winzerverein is a wine producers' association or a growers' cooperative. Verband Deutscher Prädikat Weinguter or VDP (German Association of Vineyardists of Distinction) is a wine growers' group. Deutsches Weinsiegal refers to a wine seal.

Germany's sparkling wines are known as *sekts* or *schaumweins;* the finest examples are labeled with a specific place of origin. Qualitätsschaumwein indicates that their grapes were grown in a designated area. Prädikat Sekt signifies that at least 60 percent of the wine is of German origin; the remainder may come from Italy or France. Sekt alone indicates that the sparkling wine is most likely an import.

Despite Germany's tight labeling laws, certain well-known wines seem to have geographic names but in fact do not. Zeller Schwartze Katz (Zell's Black Cat), which takes its name from the town of Zell, may once have come from a number of vineyards there, but is now an undistinguished blend drawn from unknown sources. (It's usually classified as a Bereich or a subregional wine.) The origins of Krover Nacktarsch are somewhat vaguer. Moselblümchen (Little Mosel Flower) is the trade name of a wine drawn from lesser Mosel vineyards. (A regional blend, it does not merit a specific geographic designation.)

Liebfraumilch is the generic name for a number of extensively blended Tafelweins ranging from decent to poor. Its a generally haphazard, heavy and sweetish blend of low-acid wines drawn from various regions. The wine was first grown in a monastery vineyard on the outskirts of the Rheinhessen town of Worms and known as Liebfrauenstift ("The Church's Endowment"). Replacing the monastery chapel in the fifteenth century was a Gothic church, the Liebfrauenkirche ("Church of the Beloved Lady" or "Holy Virgin"). A nearby vineyard, which decided to call its wine Liebfraumilch ("Milk of the Beloved Lady"), found that the name greatly increased the wine's popularity. Soon other vineyards in the vicinity were adopting the name.

Initially pressed from the riesling, Liebfraumilch is now made from müller-thurgau or sylvaner grapes. When sold in Europe, it is fairly certain to be of German origin—usually from the Rhineland. When sold in the United States, Canada, South Africa or Australia, the wine may not be of German origin at all.

AMERICAN LABELING

Regulating wine labeling in the United States is a federal agency, the Bureau of Alcohol, Tobacco and Firearms (BATF). A division of the Treasury Department, it is primarily responsible for overseeing the taxation of wines and spirits. (At the state level, agricultural inspectors may measure grape-sugar levels and set minimum alcohol levels.)

American wines are classified as table or dinner wines when their alcohol level is below 14 percent, and as dessert wines when their level is between 14 and 24 percent, although the latter may not be sweet at all. The word, *fortified,* is not used on the labels because when Prohibition ended certain wines were promoted for their high alcohol content, and government officials—concerned that "fortification" might imply the potential to intoxicate—banned the term, hoping to discourage excessive wine consumption in the country.

American wines are usually generics or varietals, and frequently combine both generic and geographic names—as in New York State Champagne and California Port. As a rule, though, winery names predominate and serve in effect as brand names.

Two quality grades are generally recognized in the United States: standard and premium. Both are largely defined by price. Premium—also known as Special or Select—refers to the higher range wines. (Superpremium and Ultrapremium are priced progressively higher.) A wine aged longer than usual is labeled a Reserve. These various terms are not consistently applied, however, and differ from one winery to the next.

In recent years, some regions have been given American Viticultural Appellations or AVAs. Created by the BATF, these AVAs are based on the region's geographic features, its climate and history of local grape production. In some cases, they formalize existing place-names. In others, the grape growers petitioned for the naming of their areas.

The first AVA was approved in 1983. More than a hundred others have since been created. In California, these include Howell Mountain and Los Carneros, along with Amador in the Sierra foothills; Edna Valley, Paso Robles and York Mountain in San Luis Obispo and Cuenoc Valley in Lake County; also Shenandoah, Santa Cruz Mountain, Yolo and Pope Valley. Napa Valley has a number of sub-AVAs; a recent addition is Stag's Leap.

In the Northeast, the AVAs include the Finger Lakes district, Martha's Vineyard and the North Fork of Long Island. A Lake Erie appellation, cutting across several states, encompasses Ohio, Pennsylvania and New York. A Southeastern New England appellation covers Connecticut, along with Rhode Island, and southern Massachusetts.

NOTE: Winery owners in the West have requested for a tristate Pacific Coast appellation that would encompass California, Oregon and Washington State. The labels for these blends would list the percentage of grapes drawn from each state. At present they can carry only a general "American Wine" designation.

Critics of the AVAs note that although their aim is to define quality areas, the system is vulnerable to political pressures. They also note that a viticultural area may be highly regarded because it includes one or two prominent wineries while it producing generally mediocre wines overall. The critics believe that the AVAs should be defined by soil characteristics and weather patterns, not—as some are—by roads or other readily identifiable physical boundaries that have nothing to do with viticulture. They add that while in Europe the AOC laws usually specify the grapes that can be planted, the yield per vine or per acre, the style of the wine and so on, American AVA designations carry no such quality requirements.

When a vineyard name is specified on an American label, 95 percent of the grapes must derive from that source. When the term estate-bottled is used, the grapes must come from a vineyard owned or controlled by a winery located in an AVA. Such estate-bottling is indicated by:

• Grown, produced, and bottled by so-and-so
• Produced and bottled by so-and-so

If the label reads:

- Perfected and bottled by so-and-so
- Perfected and bottled in our cellar
- Blended and bottled by so-and-so
- Made and bottled by so-and-so
- Cellared and bottled by so-and-so

Only 10 percent of the wine need come from the maker's own production; the rest can be purchased from other sources. The producer may have given the wine cursory treatment here or only arranged for its final blending, or he may have contracted for others to make the finished product. Or he may have bought the wines in bulk and not kept them separate from other lots fermented in his cellars. (Large wineries have been known to exchange wines with one another to balance out their inventories.)

A label that read "Produced by so-and-so" indicates that the wine was probably not made from grapes grown in the vineyard listed on the label. A label that reads "Bottled by so-and-so" gives no indication as to the origins of the wine. The winery may have used purchased grapes, then finished and bottled the wine itself; or it may have only bottled the wine.

On American sparkling-wine labels, "Fermented in the Bottle" indicates the *méthode champenoise;* "Fermented in this Bottle" refers to the transfer method; and "Charmat process" or "Cuvée Close" indicates that the wine was made sparkling by bulk fermentation.

LABELING IN OTHER COUNTRIES

In 1959, Argentina's Congress set up the Instituto Nacional de Vitivinicultura, or INV, and gave it jurisdiction over the country's grape-derived products. Australia doesn't have an appellation system as such but indicates the wine's general origins with these geographic abbreviations: VIC (Victoria), NSW (New South Wales), SA (South Australia) and WA (West Australia).

In Austria, the quality-wine labels—which are about as detailed as the German ones—include regional, village and vineyard names and employ such terms as Qualitätswein, Kabinett, Spätlese, Auslese, Beerenauslese (BA) and Trockenbeerenauslese (TBA). A uniquely Austrian category, Ausbruch—somewhere between a BA and a TBA—covers wines made in vintages with a high incidence of noble rot. Austrian wines that meet established prerequisites and are true to type are given a Weingutessiegel Osterreich (Austrian Quality Seal). Those that pass an official tasting examination—somewhat like the German P.R. appraisal—are given a Wein aus Osterreich (Austrian Wine) seal.

Canada's best wines carry a Vintners' Quality Alliance (VQA) designation on their label or neck capsule, indicating that the grapes are from a specific area and that the wine's quality has been attested to by a panel made up of vintners and sommeliers. For its quality wines, Chile carries both a brand name and a place of origin on its labels, which may also specify the grape variety, vintage year and vineyard name. The age of a Chilean wine is indicated by four government-controlled categories: Courant, Especial, Reservado, and Grand Vino, referring to wines aged one, two, four and six years, respectively.

Greek wines were once typically blends drawn from sizable areas involving different regions of the country, a practice currently banned. Some wines that were initially named for their general place of origin—Crete, Sámos, and so on—may now carry more specific place-names, such as Peza and Archanes in Crete. In 1969, an appellation control system created twenty-eight official Greek wine regions. (They represent about 11 percent of the country's vineyards.) Greek labels are generally not very informative. Some employ the vague French phrase "Produit de Region Determinée" (product of a selected region) or the equally vague English phrase "Appellation of Origin of High Quality."

Hungary usually names its wines for the districts in which they are grown; seventeen of these districts have been officially classified. (Adding an *i* to the place-name converts it to an adjective, as in Balatoni for Lake Balaton, Tokaji for Tokay and Egri for Eger.) The grape variety—kadarka, furmint, rizling—often follows the place-name. (For noble rot Tokays, a special neckband indicates the number of puttonyos included in the blend.) Hungarian wines designated for export bear a seal of authenticity issued by Monimpex, a state-run agency. Israel has phased out generic wine names in favor of varietal ones and generally markets its wines under their winery names.

South Africa's Origin of Wine law requires that to bear a place-name, a wine must be drawn 80 percent from the defined area; to carry a varietal name, it must derive 75 percent from that grape. Exercising considerable power over which wines are made in the country, and who makes them, is a cooperative wine growers' association commonly known as KWV, an abbreviation of its Afrikaans name. The KWV banned the use of French wine names on South African labels in the 1930s as part of deal struck with the French government. (In return, France agreed to import South African lobsters.) Wines from the former Yugoslavia are usually named for their hometowns, districts or grapes. *Sortno* on the label followed by a year indicates their vintage, while *stolno* refers to a blend of most likely lesser wines.

LABEL DECEPTIONS

Despite varying degrees of official and semiofficial control, no wine-producing country is immune to label deceptions. A number of isolated abuses have been reported in a number of places. Vintners have claimed that their product is of a specific origin, although the blend includes wines from elsewhere. Wine makers have created the impression that their wine comes from a desirable geographic sector or even from a particular vineyard, when in fact it is a regional blend. Vintners have also used elegant names to suggest certain styles and qualities and deceive the unwary. (In France, wineries have in part appropriated the names of famous estates such as Maître d'Estournel in Bordeaux, reminiscent of the highly ranked Cos d'Estournel and Mouton Cadet, echoing the estimable Mouton-Rothschild.) Wine makers, too, have copied the label styles of prestigious and expensive wines. Or they've claimed a wine was from a vintage other than its own. Or they have incorporated grape names into brand names even though these grapes weren't used in the wines at all.

NOTE: Wineries have also been known to withdraw products that do not sell, then give them new names and put them back on the market.

Another form of deception is "baptizing" or transferring a prestigious name from a small quantity of good wine to a greater quantity of a cheap one. Early in the twentieth century, wine makers were pasting Bordeaux labels on bottles of largely Mediterranean wines. More recently, a Burgundy shipper tried to pass off as an elegant Côte d'Or wine some five thousand bottles of a simple red. And Californians have been known to present South American wines as their own.

Wine makers have tampered as well with documentation for export. In the 1970s, French government inspectors, checking a Bordeaux cellar, discovered vats of red wine carrying the notation "Can be used as Beaujolais in America." A complicated scheme involving a lesser French product called for shipping the wine in bulk to the Netherlands, where it was bottled; then sending it to England, where it was labeled "Pouilly-Fuissé"; and finally shipping it to the United States for sale.

Unscrupulous vintners have also "stretched" or extended their wines by blending them with wines from other regions and even from other countries. Two hundred years ago, pale Bordeaux wines were regularly bolstered with reds from the Rhône or Cahors. Burgundy shippers, unable to find good inexpensive wines locally, have added mediocre bulk wines to their prestigious blends. The popularlity of Pouilly-Fuissé has prompted its makers to seek out increasingly anonymous components—in one case, a Beaujolais Blanc. In California, North Coast wineries have trucked in cheaper products from the state's more prolific regions, blending them with their quality wines. Some stretching combinations are curious. A German riesling—an aristocratic grape in its own right— was blended into a French white wine from Graves.

Vintners have also sold more wine than their vineyards could possibly produce. Great quantities of Chablis are marketed every year despite the region's limited acreage and problematic weather. (Although Chablis is a white Burgundy, a white Burgundy claiming to be a Chablis may not always be one.) The phenomenon has also been observed in the Pommards and Beaujolais of France, and in the Chiantis, Barolos, Barbarescos and Frascatis of Italy. In Champagne, when their supply of grapes ran short, a number of famous houses purchased already-made and -bottled wines from the region's big producers and cooperatives, then labeled and marketed them as their own.

Notoriously difficult to monitor are the "improved" wines of lesser years. An undistinguished Beaujolais was trucked to the Côte d'Or in the dead of night to bolster the wine of a poor vintage. High-alcohol wines from the Midi, the Rhône, Algeria, Morocco, Corsica, Italy and Portugal have been added to pale, thin Burgundies, making them uncharacteristically big, full-flavored and coarse. Warm-climate products from the South of France and Italy have made weak Beaujolais wines more robust. Monitoring is always difficult in Burgundy because of the characteristic fragmentation of its vineyards here. (The vintners here usually produce their wines away from their small parcels of land.) High-alcohol imports have also compensated for the shortcomings of German wines in poor vintages. In the northeastern United States, vintners in certain years have added to their blends inexpensive wines or wine concentrates from California, Spain and elsewhere to their blends.

Also difficult to monitor is chaptalization, which boosts the wine's alcohol level by adding cane or beet sugar during fermentation. Although the law permits Beaujolais producers to increase the alcohol level of their wines by 2 percentage points for export, some have increased the level by 4 percent or more.

Wines can be altered in other ways. A cheap white can be added to a heavier red to simulate the color, body and bouquet of a premium product. Coloring agents can be used to brighten wines. Charcoal filtering can render a white wine disarmingly pale. Overly acid wines can be salvaged by burying them in other blends. A wine can be sweetened with chemicals or have its definition sharpened with citric acid.

SOME LABEL CAVEATS

Appellation Contrôlée: In France, an appellation guarantees only the wine's origin, not its character or its quality. (It does not govern bouquet, flavor or any of a wine's finer characteristics.) As a result, inconsequential products can carry a distinguished AOC and command higher prices while wines from lower-ranked areas—if made by more-skilled vintners and treated with greater care—may actually be higher in quality. In Italy, critics charge that the DOCG classification, supposedly reserved for the country's finest products, has been too widely awarded and now includes a number of mediocre wines as well.

Estate-Bottled: Estate-bottling, although theoretically reserved for the unblended wines of great vineyards, does not guarantee excellence. The wines may include grapes grown in the vicinity of the named vineyard as long as the proprietor of record finishes and bottles them. Even when he uses his own grapes exclusively, if his approach is casual rather than dedicated he may still turn out a mediocre product. The reverse is also possible: Vintners who don't qualify for an "Estate-Bottled" designation may buy their grapes or wines from good outside sources, then finish their wines with great care and skill.

In Bordeaux, "Château-Bottled" is an assurance of authenticity but not necessarily of quality. A grower here can register a château name for any piece of land he owns, and label his wine "Château-Bottled" whether it's good, bad or indifferent. And any company in Bordeaux can call itself a château, even if it produces and bottles imported blends. (Producers have also been known to incorporate "Château" into their trade names or to sell wines under the name of a nonexistent château.)

Second Labels: Second labels were originally applied to the products of younger vines grown in prestigious vineyards. Now they can also apply to wines that don't meet the standards of the first label. Second labels came into prominence in the 1980s when, after a series of successful vintages, the top châteaus became more and more selective about what went into their wines. The wines from their "rejected" vats that they didn't wish to discard or sell off to shippers were included in their second-label category as well. And in abundant years, second labels have become a way for producers to market their overproduction. (In poor years, the great French estates may offer less than half of their wines under their own vineyard names, and the rest under a second label.) In some cases, though, the cuvées that don't make it to the first label may be very fine indeed.

Place of Business: A French label can state that a wine was bottled in a given village but provide no indication as to where its grapes were grown. An American winery can indicate its principal place of business on the label, provided the wine was bottled there. A number of establishments in Northern California have left their original sites while retaining headquarters offices and bottling plants there. Their labels can thus imply that the more prestigious address is the source of their wines—even though they have actually drawn their grapes from elsewhere. To prevent such misleading labeling, a Napa Valley ordinance requires that all of its wines bottled here include at least 75 percent of valley-grown grapes in their blends.

Varietal Labeling: In the United States, a wine containing 75 percent of a given grape is permitted to carry a varietal name. The remaining 25 percent can consist of whatever grapes the wine maker chooses; they need not meet any particular standards or come from the best vineyards or the best soils. And even when 90 or 100 percent of the named grape is used, that grape can be grown anywhere in the country.

Vintage-Dating: As a rule, a vintage-dated wine need not come 100 percent from the year indicated. Vintners are always permitted to top off their casks or tanks with a small amount of wine from other years; the minimums, however, differ from country to country and wine to wine. The Champagne region requires that at least 80 percent of the wine come from a single year. Germany sets a 75 percent minimum, whereas a vintage wine in the United States must be at least 95 percent from the year specified.

NOTE: Because of the public's demand for vintage-dating, wine makers have taken a variety of measures to bring their products up to par in poor years. In Bordeaux, in bad vintages, the grapes might once have been left on the vines to rot, but now selective harvesting and modern equipment have made it possible to produce drinkable wines every year. Most commonly used in improving wines is chaptalization, which increases the alcohol level and viability of the wines.

Overproduction: In the Champagne region overproduction has been legalized to a degree. In certain years vintners here are permitted to use in their nonvintage blends their excess production, which is known as blocked stock.

Superior: The term *Supérieur* (French) or *Superiore* (Italian) is not in itself an indication of excellence, but refers to a wine whose alcohol content exceeds the minimum level required by local standards. A mass-produced wine from a lesser district can therefore be labeled "Superior" if it is higher in alcohol than usual.

OTHER CONSIDERATIONS

Wine making can involve an estimated forty chemicals, including sulfiting agents, fungicides, preservatives, food colorings, and so on. Some are natural products of fermentation, whereas others are added to stimulate fermentation, aid in clarification, improve the bouquet or preserve the wine.

Most widely employed in stabilizing a wine is sulfur dioxide or SO_2. Used to keep down unwanted yeasts and bacteria, it protects newly picked grapes from mold during shipment and destroys spoilage microbes during the wine's transportation, storage and aging. SO_2 can also help keep a wine sweet by halting its fermentation. (The wine retains more of its grape sugar this way.)

The majority of commercially distributed wines contain sulfites in one form or another. (Even so-called organic wines generate some of these naturally.) Although usually harmless in the amounts normally employed, sulfites can produce severe reactions in individuals allergic to them, particularly in those who have asthma. Since 1987, warning labels have been mandatory in the United States for wines containing more than 100 parts of SO_2 per million. (The legal limit is 350 parts.) Their labels read: "Contains Sulfites." Wine makers who don't employ SO_2 can state on their labels "No Added Sulfites."

For some time, American consumer groups have been requesting full label disclosure of the ingredients or substances in wines. The Food and Drug Administration (FDA) has also sought such a disclosure. Wine-industry representatives, however, have resisted these requests, maintaining that the fermentation process substantially transforms the wine's basic ingredients and additives. They also say that any FDA involvement is unnecessary since wines and other alcoholic beverages are not consumed for their nutritional value.

7

BUYING, STORING, AND AGING

BUYING WINE

There are currently an estimated three thousand wines on the market. The array of their bottles and labels in the wine shop can be bewildering. Distinguishing between the excellent and the commonplace is often daunting. Some suggest that you cast about until you find a wine merchant who can offer knowledge and patience when assisting you with your purchase.

More than four decades ago, a British wine enthusiast described the ideal merchant as one who will provide you with selected wines of good quality to suit your palate and your pocket, who will take back a wine that doesn't satisfy you and provide something else in its place, who will always be glad to taste a wine with you and discuss its particular characteristics as well as its virtues or defects before you buy it and who will provide you with a carefully selected yet moderately inexpensive wine collection on which you can depend with confidence for all occasions, replenishing it as you require.

Such merchants—if they exist at all anymore—are few and far between. There are no shortcuts to learning to buy wine today. Only by experimenting and tasting over a period of years can one acquire a deep and practical knowledge of the subject. One needs to approach wine in the spirit of adventure, leaving oneself open to discovery and surprise, finding out where one's personal preferences lie through trial and error. An eminent collector likened the process to the princess who went around kissing frogs. "Kiss enough of them," he said, "and you'll find a prince."

In making their selections, some people look for a clue—any clue. Perhaps a name enchants or a fragment of advertising comes to mind. Perhaps they respond to the color of the wine, the name of the grape, the shape of the bottle. Or they might base their choice on the wine's place of origin or its price. Many people find a few wines they like and stick with them. Others are willing to sample the less known wines as well as the more publicized ones. They will try bottles from Australia, Chile, Switzerland, Hungary and so on.

There are a number of ways to learn about wine: one can look through newspaper ads and wine-shop catalogs, or read specialized wine publications or books on the subject. Browsing is of major importance. The best times to check out the wine shops are Mondays through Thursdays, when they are less crowded and their salespeople are more accessible. The ideal time is in summer, the quietest wine-buying season of the year. The worst time is between Thanksgiving and New Year's Eve, which is the busiest season.

While browsing, one can observe if the table wines are presented horizontally (as they should be) or stood upright (as they should not). And one can note whether the bottles are displayed in the shop window, exposed to heat and light (as they should not be). After several visits, one can also get some idea of the stock on hand, as well as a sense of its turnover. Dealing with more than one shop can provide the opportunity to ask more questions and also compare notes.

Common sense is the key to intelligent buying. Before embarking on the costlier wines, it's best to sample the more affordable ones in the same category, to become accustomed to them. Price, however, isn't always a clue to quality: Plenty of good wines are available at reasonable prices. And high prices should not be equated with merit. Some people think if a wine costs a lot, it must be the best. Yet in some professional tastings, lower-priced wines have tied for first place with higher-priced ones.

Wine pricing is as much an art as a science. It is based on

image, ego and tradition, as well as on market conditions. The high prices set for premium wines often have little to do with their actual production costs. (Some owners of prestige wineries acknowledge that their prices are based primarily on what the market will bear.) Scarity also determines some prices when little of the wine is produced. Since the most prestigious Bordeaux wines establish the prices for premium wines elsewhere, top California producers use them as a benchmark. They believe that their best Cabernets equal or surpass the best of Bordeaux and so merit equal or higher prices.

Wine bargains on the other hand should be approached with caution. A wine offered at a price that seems too good to be true is best avoided. It may have been mishandled in shipping, stored too long in an overheated warehouse, or frozen as it sat on a landing dock. Or the wine may simply be too old. (Last year's Beaujolais Nouveau is no bargain even at a special price.)

Some consumers like to buy their wine in quantity, saying it prevents the frustration of seeing it disappear from the shelves. (It's always a good idea however to sample a bottle first.) When making quantity purchases, one should ask about discounts by the case and the cost of home delivery, if any.

NOTE: A number of serious collectors rarely buy their wine in quantity, declaring that such purchases take away the risk and the adventure of the wine experience.

Wine is distributed through a three-tier system involving the winery, the wholesaler (shipper, importer and distributor) and the retailer who deals directly with the public. Wineries invariably release their wines young, seeking to recoup their costs as soon as possible. (Holding a wine until it's ready to drink is an expensive proposition; wines aging in winery cellars do nothing for the cash flow.) Wholesalers and retailers generally sell the wines young as well. (They don't want to tie up their own capital waiting for the wines to mature.) As one retailer said, "If you're not selling them, you're not getting paid for them." As a result, fine red wines are relatively inexpensive shortly after their release, while mature reds command premium prices.

NOTE: When buying a mature red, it's important to know the retailer. A few years of inept handling can age a wine too rapidly and hasten its demise.

Bordeaux vintners learned that if they sold off their entire vintage at once and then wine prices rose, the middlemen and not themselves would reap the benefits. Therefore, each year the vintners hold back a certain percentage of their production, then release it gradually in batches—perhaps a fourth of the vintage at a time. (Each lot is known as a *tranche* or "slice.") If the premiere tranche is well received, the second batch can be offered at a higher price.

The best Bordeaux wines are rarely ready to drink when they come on the market. (They are at their best when either too costly or no longer available.) When the region's first growths were released, British connoisseurs and collectors would buy them and then age them in their own cellars. To cover the cost they would sell off part of their purchase, retaining the rest for their personal use. (In effect, they acquired their drinking wines free and clear.) Nowadays, speculators often buy up such wines, cellar them for a few years, then cash them in. Their interest in consuming the wines is peripheral at best.

NOTE: Investment-grade wines include less than a dozen top Bordeaux châteaus, some leading Vintage Ports and a few California wines.

Another form of investment is the wine future—a contract to buy a wine for future delivery. The wine is usually sold in case lots, although a rare few examples are only available as single bottles. Their price is announced six months after the harvest. The winery keeps the wine in wood for about two years, then bottles and ships it out. Further aging is always required here. (In years when the wines produced are light and early-maturing, there is no futures market.)

Most of the futures market is in first-growth red Bordeaux, but contracts have also been offered for French Burgundies, premium Italian reds and some California Cabernet Sauvignons.

Futures were initially bought by wine merchants to ensure their supply, but are now offered to the general public as well. Dabbling in futures has become a form of prestige, an ego trip for those with discretionary income. They like to tell their friends they are laying down some claret.

The wineries sell these contracts for future delivery to shippers, who sell them to importers. The contracts reach the consumer by way of the retailer. On signing the contract, the consumer usually pays in full, making a long-term commitment to finance the maturation of a wine that may not be drinkable for a decade or so. Meanwhile, the seller receives an interest-free advance on the developing wine.

Although futures have been promoted as a way of locking in advantageous prices, they generally amount to a wager that the wine's value will increase by the time it matures. Yet wine prices can remain unchanged or even drop, if the supply exceeds the demand, or if serious fluctuations occur in international currencies. In a depressed economy, the mature wine may sell for less than its original cost. The contract holder then finds himself committed to a wine he can buy locally for less. Or perhaps a better vintage comes along while his funds are tied up. Had the contract holder put his money into a conservative, short-term investment instead, he might have accrued enough interest to cover the cost of the mature wine if its purchase still seemed desirable.

NOTE: "Futures" seem to suggest that there are regulators to enforce the guarantees the purchaser receives when he signs the contracts. There are no such legal safeguards however. If the firm becomes insolvent, its customers have little recourse in recovering their investments. Potential purchasers would be wise to check out the stability of the source that offers the wine futures.

Wines can also be bought at auctions. These create a lively secondary market where collectors and others with excess inventory can sell their wines outside the normal commercial channels. Wine auctions are conducted in London, Paris and elsewhere. (In Britain, during the post–World War II years, selling off the contents of their wine cellars was a noteworthy way for old families to pay their estate taxes.) In the United States, auctions have generally been banned. The wine-and-spirits trade there maintains that they would compete unfairly with retail sales. Auctions are permitted as charity events, however, but they are not true auctions, since many of the wines are donated. Moreover, the high prices they often bring reflect more on the generosity of the bidders than on the value of the wines that are offered.

Some auctions feature ancient wines whose significance lies in their labels and their provenances. Wealthy enthusiasts eagerly spend thousands of dollars on such bottles. But the chance of these wines being drinkable is extremely remote and the bottles themselves are rarely uncorked. Some people buy the wines as investments, hold them for a few years and then auction them off again. Successful bidders have often been restaurateurs or people in the wine trade who acquire the bottles in order to generate some publicity for their enterprises.

NOTE: In the United States, some states are looking into the possibility of letting professional auctioneers sell off private wine collections. (Restricting such sales to private collections prevents importers, distributors and retailers from using them to move their excess stock.) New York State now permits such auctions, provided they are conducted by licensed retailers of long standing and that the wines they offer have already matured.

STORING WINE

A wine cellar is both a collection of bottles and the place where they are stored. It can be a short-term cellar, meant for day-to-day drinking or a long-term cellar, meant for aging as well as storing the wines.

For short-term storage, no more wine should be acquired than can be consumed within a few months. Virtually any storage space will do here: a shelf in a cupboard, cabinet, or bookcase; a file drawer; a countertop; even a corner of the floor. The collection might include a dozen or so relatively uncomplicated wines: eight table (red and white), three fortified (dry and sweet) and one sparkler. The fluctuating nature of this cellar encourages experimentation and variety. Its nicest feature is its convenience; one needn't dash out at the last minute to search for a bottle for an evening meal or a spontaneous celebration.

A long-term cellar is best begun with a few bottles. It takes years of buying, culling and tasting to assemble a collection that reflects one's personal tastes and interests. The cellar might include wines from various countries or might concentrate on one country, one region or even one town. The most specialized have concentrated on a single vineyard.

The better the wine, the more sensitive it is to its environment. Red wines need temperatures of about 55°F. The more delicate whites and sparkling wines require slightly lower temperatures; fortified wines do best at 60 to 65 degrees. If stored at sustained high temperatures white wine will darken and take on the taste of overripe grapes and caramel. On the other hand, sustained low temperatures will numb the wine and damage its taste.

Wines, such as red table wines, set aside for aging develop best at relatively low and constant temperatures. At sustained high temperatures, they lose their freshness and vitality, becoming flat, brownish and unpleasant. Long-term storage should not be contemplated if the wine will be exposed to high temperatures over time or to marked fluctuations in temperature. (Such conditions age it faster by increasing the wine's reaction rate, and expanding the bottle microscopically, which produces a bellowslike effect that draws in unwanted air.) However, temperatures that hold at 65 to 70 degrees are acceptable for wines meant for consumption within a few months. And seasonal fluctuations need not cause serious concern either as long as they are neither abrupt nor drastic.

NOTE: It is essential that wines be kept away from boilers, water heaters and the like. Hardest on them are furnaces that turn on during the day and build up heat, then turn off at night, causing the temperature to fall sharply.

For its proper development in long-term storage, a wine needs to remain serene. It needs to be kept safe from vibrations and shock. Sustained jostling or similar disruptions will alter its breathing pace, causing it to throw off its sediment too soon and accelerating its aging process. (Some of the best-preserved wines have not been moved in years.) Heavy street traffic or nearby construction can stir up a wine. When the Paris subway was being built, an elderly gentleman living in the vicinity of l'Étoile stopped storing his clarets at home. He feared they would become "too bubbly."

Wine should also be kept away from the vibrations produced by frequently run washing machines, humming refrigerators, noisy air conditioners and loud-playing stereos, along with perpetually slamming doors and heavy foot traffic. Storing the bottles under the stairs is not a good idea, either. They will be subjected to frequent footfalls.

Darkness is also necessary. Exposure to bright light over an extended period accelerates the wine's aging process and generally damages it. Although the bottle's tinted glass offers some protection, it doesn't filter out all the harmful ultraviolet rays. Direct and sustained fluorescent light is particularly destructive since it can discolor the wine, make it dull and cloudy and impart a musty or off taste. Also required is a fairly stable humidity level— about 60 percent. Too little moisture will dry out the corks. Too much will encourage the growth of mold and fungi, which might penetrate the corks.

Winery cellars provide ideal storage conditions. Some are natural caves with never-changing temperatures. Others are dug deep into rock or chalky subsoil; the surrounding tons of stone and earth create an excellent insulation for the wine. In the Champagne region, the cellars are located in limestone quarries dating back to Roman times. Some reach depths of three hundred feet and are linked to the surface by elevators. (They are so extensive that trains run through them.) Vaults in Rioja have been carved seventy feet down in the chalky subsoil. In Vouvray, the vineyards are sited atop a great limestone cliff, while cut into the chalk below is a deep honeycomb of caves. Some of California's oldest cellars were dug by Chinese laborers working with picks and shovels. (They had originally come to America to work on the transcontinental railroad.)

The cellars of other wineries are located above ground. Among these are the long, low shippers' lodges of Oporto, whose earthen floors and few windows help to maintain reasonable interior temperatures year-round. In Andalusia, the whitewashed sherry bodegas shield their tiny windows with straw mats that keep out heat and light while admitting the circulating air. Modern aboveground cellars rely on air-conditioning and special insulation to stabilize their temperature and control their humidity.

In a private home, a section of the basement can serve as a long-term wine cellar, provided that its temperature is cool and fairly even, that its humidity is sufficient and that there is general serenity. If not, air-conditioning can stabilize its temperature and insulation can cushion the wine against excessive vibrations. (The designated space should also not be too cramped to allow for the wine cellar's expansion.)

NOTE: Whether or not to store wine in an apartment depends on the specific circumstances. A reasonably quiet hall closet can serve if its ventilation is good, if its temperature is relatively consistent and if the vibrations in the vicinity are not excessive.

Despite the convenience it provides for serving, the kitchen is too bright and busy a place for extended wine storage. The stove continually creates extreme fluctuations of temperature. The various appliances and general household activity produce too many vibrations. Unsavory fumes and sharp penetrating odors, which the wine can absorb, float in the air. Unless the space is fairly large and well ventilated, and unless the bottles are rotated frequently, wines stored in the kitchen will lose their freshness in a matter of weeks.

NOTE: Under no circumstances should wine ever be kept near vinegar. Its bacterial agents will quickly convert the alcohol into the astringent acetic acid that is better known as vinegar.

Some people prefer ready-made cellars for storing their wines. These are self-contained units that range from cabinets holding three dozen bottles to walk-in chambers with a thousand-bottle-or-more capacity. Refrigeration enables them to maintain a basic temperature of 52° to 55°F. (Some units provide additional compartments for chilling or for keeping the wines at room temperature.) The more elaborate examples feature absorption systems to minimize vibrations and carbon filters to absorb extraneous odors.

Also available for wine storage in some large cities are warehouses with special temperature-controlled vaults, maintained at an optimal 55°F. A monthly fee is charged for each case stored. Availing themselves of these facilities are restaurateurs, retailers and serious collectors; for the more modest collector, rental fees tend to be prohibitive.

CARING FOR WINE

Good wines demand thoughtful care. If treated with respect they can last a long time. If stored carelessly or indifferently, they will peak too soon or turn to vinegar.

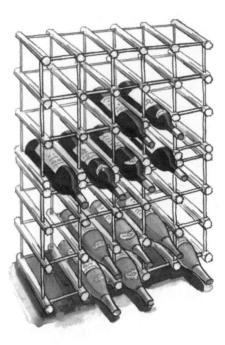

Horizontal storage

It was once thought that the cork was sufficiently porous for tiny quantities of air to enter the bottle and that the limited oxidation that occurred allowed the wine to breathe gradually, enhancing the aging process. It has since been found that the cork's cellular structure seals out the air. Yet the wine does breathe and develop in the bottle because air is already present. (It's inevitably introduced during bottling in the form of a bubble.)

The cork is the wine's main defense against the deterioration and, to do the job properly, needs to be kept moist, supple and expansive. Horizontal storage makes this possible. Placing the bottle on its side shifts the air bubble from the top to the center, allowing for direct and moistening contact between the cork and the liquid. Storing the bottle upright causes the bubble to float to the top, creating an air space between cork and wine, and causing the cork to dry out so that it shrinks away from the sides of the neck. This creates the danger of leakage and—more significantly—allows air to penetrate the bottle. Even in minuscule amounts, the additional air will overoxidize the wine, rob it of its character, benumb its vitality, age it prematurely and encourage the vinegar-makers to proliferate. For a sparkling wine, a shrinking cork will not only speed up its deterioration but also cause its effervescence to dissipate, leaving a flat, insipid liquid behind.

Horizontal storage is therefore essential for table and sparkling wines. Suitable for such storage is the wooden crate or cardboard carton in which the bottles were shipped. The box is simply set on its side and the bottles arranged cork-side-out, so that any signs of shrinkage or other deviations in the corks can be noted. Individuals with large collections often use diamond-shaped bins stacking the bottles one atop another in staggered rows. Some collectors have their racks custom-made and designed to fit a given space. Others turn to free-standing ready-made wood, bamboo, metal or plastic racks, which are available in modular or stackable units and come in various sizes and shapes. (Whatever the material or style, the rack should be at least fourteen inches deep, to accommodate the bottles comfortably; and the compartments high enough to let air circulate around the bottles so the wines are less susceptible to changes in temperature.)

Because heat rises, the most delicate wines should be stored closest to the floor—the lowest tiers of the rack reserved for sparkling wines. Positioned directly above them are the white table wines; then come the rosés, the lighter red table wines, and finally, the sturdier reds. Fortified wines, which need neither horizontal storage nor lower temperatures, can be stored upright at the top of the rack. (Their higher levels of alcohol will protect them).

It is best to separate the wines according to their country of origin, grape variety, vintage and so on, and to mark the racks, shelves or compartments accordingly. One can also keep a cellar book spelling out the locations of the bottles. This might take the form of a simple loose-leaf folder, an elegant leather-bound volume or a computer disk. Columns on the left-hand page can include the name of the wine, the date of purchase, location in the cellar, country of origin, vintage, shipper, retailer, quantity purchased and the price paid. Columns on the right-hand page might include the date of uncorking, tasting notes, and perhaps even the menu for the meal at which the wine was served, along with a list of the guests who were present. Some people incorporate wine labels into their cellar books; others paste their labels in special scrapbooks, organizing them country by country like a postage stamp collection.

NOTE: Most wine labels will peel off after a bit of soaking. For those that prove recalcitrant, the bottle can be filled with warm water and placed in a narrow container to which ordinary household ammonia has been added. (Rubber gloves should be worn for this.) After about an hour, the label will generally come loose; if necessary a razor blade can further assist in its removal.

A wine that has been stored away in a large cellar with its label not readily visible can easily be forgotten and lose its charm—if not its life. To make its contents known at a glance, the bottles can be fitted with a plastic tag placed over the neck and marked with its name and vintage. (Sold in wine shops, these tags come with pens that feature erasable ink and are reusable.)

To prevent overlong storage and the resulting decline in quality, the wine should be checked at intervals. Its color should be monitored from time to time for brownish traces of maderization. And its corks should be checked for signs of shrinkage or other deviations. A bulging cork, for example, indicates that excessive heat or cold has pushed it out. Wine bleeding through the cork signals the seepage-in of too much air. (Such corks are called "weepers.") A loose cork usually means the bottle was stored too long in an upright position.

Even under the best of conditions, corks shrink over time, and their cellular structure breaks down. The life expectancy of a good cork is about twenty-five years. (Most major châteaus recork their wines every fifteen to twenty years.) In addition, slow evaporation can markedly reduce the fill level of the bottle. Some collectors prevent any overoxidation by topping off their bottles with additional wine, preferably of the same vintage or at least of the same decade. A number of experts object to such recorking and refilling, however. They point out that opening the bottles will expose fragile old wines to too much air, putting them at risk. They note that very old wines still sealed with their original corks have been found to be in excellent condition.

Very slow evaporation need not damage the wine. Wines older than fifteen years are often perfectly good, even when reaching only midway up the bottle's shoulder. For young wines, the liquid level should reach the neck or be close to it. A catalog announcing the sale of a restaurant's wine cellar included bottles of Bordeaux that had never been refilled. It described them as "HSF," "MSF," and "LSF," referring to their high-, mid- and low-shoulder fill levels.

VINTAGE CHARTS

Vintage charts are designed to rate wines and provide an overall sense of how they fared in given years. (In some places, only one year in every three is good.) Vintages mean the most in places where no two crops are alike and where splendid back-to-back years are rare. They're of little consequence in the more southerly regions whose climate is generally consistent and whose sun shines with regularity.

The farther north a wine region is located in Europe, the more significant its vintages. They're most important in areas of unpredictable weather, where even minor variations result in markedly different wines. In years of volatile weather, the differences can be spectacular.

Vintages have long been influential in Bordeaux, in Burgundy's Côte d'Or and Chablis district, in Champagne and in the Rhineland of Germany. In some places, only one year in every three is good. California has begun to keep vintage charts, although the somewhat variable weather of its North Coast region doesn't begin to compare with the volatility of Northern Europe. (California's vintage charts generally cover Napa, Sonoma and Mendocino Counties, along with Santa Clara to the south.)

Vintages are considered great when all the wine's elements come together—when its color, personality and character cannot be improved on. Red wines, because of their higher tannin content levels, are more dependent on the quality of their vintages than are white wines. In good years, the tannin levels rise; in poor years, even the quality grapes do not acquire enough tannin to hold their wines together. In good years, the sugars are also higher. In poor years, when there isn't enough sugar, the grapes don't mature properly; they yield coarse and overly tart wines.

NOTE: In all but the most disastrous growing seasons, vintners can compensate for the shortcomings of nature. By employing modern viticultural and vinicultural techniques, they still can manage to produce reasonably good wines.

The rating scales that vintage charts employ are neither uniform nor consistent. They range from 1 to 10 and 1 to 20, all the way to 1 to 100. One 10-point chart rates 1 as acceptable, 2 as bearable, 3 inoffensive, 4 fair, 5 average, 6 good, 7 very good, 8 excellent, 9 outstanding and 10 extraordinary. In another 10-point chart, 1-2 represents a less-than-average vintage, 3-4 average, 5-6 good, 7-8 very good and 9-10 exceptional. In still another, a defective wine is rated 0-1, a clean but not special wine 2-5, a good and harmonious wine 6-9 and a noble ripe wine 9-10.

Some experts believe that the 20-point system associated with France is comprehensive enough to cover all of a wine's nuances and gradations. One such system rates poor wines as 0-9 and fair ones as 10-12, while 13-15 signifies good, 16-18 very good and 19-20 the best. Another 20-point system uses 1-10 to indicate an outright failure to barely passing, while a 10-11 wine is sound and acceptable with no defects, a 12-13 is fair, a 13-16 is sound with some personality, a 16-17 is memorable and an 18-20 represents a great wine.

The United States sometimes uses a 100-point system—which is in effect a 50-point system, since the lower half indicates only the worst ratings. One such vintage chart ranks poor wines as below 60, average wines 70-79, very good wines 80-89 and excellent wines 90-100. Another chart uses 75-79 to signify average wines and 96-100 the extraordinary ones. Some charts use letters rather than numbers to indicate quality levels. One such chart lists the top wines as AAA, followed by those rated AA, A, B, C and D.

NOTE: Whatever the rating system, the charts are based on the premise that the wine was in good condition when purchased and that it was stored in a relatively cool, vibration-free, odor-free cellar whose humidity was sufficient to keep the corks from drying out.

Vintage charts also employ letters in conjunction with the numbers to track the wine's development and the pace of its aging. The letters indicate when a wine is not ready to drink; when it is drinkable but with its potential still unrealized; and when it is fully ready to drink. In one system, *A* indicates the wine would be best with further aging, *B* that it can improve with additional aging and *C* that it's ready to drink, while *D* advises caution about further aging and *E* indicates that the wine may already be over the hill. In another system, *C* is for caution (the wine may be too old), *E* is for early maturing (the wine may be drunk now but has not yet reached its peak), *T* is for tannic (the wine needs further aging) and *R* is ready to drink. Another vintage chart uses *D* to signify that the majority of wines of a particular year are ready to drink, *A* that on average they are still immature and *U* that they're unavailable because they are still aging in the winery cellars.

Vintage charts can serve as a rough guide to buying and storing wine if their limitations are understood. The main limitation is that they tend to oversimplify. They are essentially a collection of generalities, lumping together all of a region's wines for a single year. Yet a stormy spring can damage early-ripening grapes while leaving later-flowering varieties largely untouched. Or if some grapes are picked before a rain and some after, the the vintage can be mixed. Also, natural cataclysms—heavy rain, hail and drought— rarely affect every area of a region equally; one sector might experience good weather while another encounters devastating conditions. In short, no summary can capture the many variations possible in a single year.

And not all wines from great years are necessarily great; bottle variations make some better than others. Even when the vintages are good, indifferent or poor wines are inevitably made. (There are always the incompetent or greedy producers who will turn out thin, dull wines without any character.) Conversely, in lower-rated years, a skilled wine maker may produce a decent enough wine, or a secondary vineyard may produce a better wine than its more distinguished neighbor. Given the differences in wine quality not only from year to year but from region to region, vineyard to vineyard, cellar to cellar, grape to grape and even bottle to bottle, some people think that it's presumptuous to spell out the drinkability of a wine.

NOTE: Assessments of a wine's potential are subject to change as well. A vintage sandwiched between two highly regarded years may be overlooked in its youth only to be discovered years later. Or good wines will occasionally lapse into dullness for several years and then surprisingly regain their attractiveness.

Vintages are a significant factor in merchandising. The whole-saler—to even out his income from good to bad years—may exaggerate the virtues of a lesser vintage while deliberately underestimating the quality of a better one. To create more recep-tivity to the wines of relatively unimpressive years, he may keep them off the market until the more popular vintages are gone. And for the wholesaler, a series of good years creates its own problems. It makes it difficult for him to sell his remaining inven-tory at a profit.

The relationship between the wholesaler and the retailer can also be problematic. The wholesaler may ask the retailer to accept a certain number of bottles—including the château wines of a bad vintage. The retailer will put those bottles on his shelves, fearing that he might otherwise be left out of the distribution channels he wants to ensure delivery when a high-quality vintage is released or when a rare bottle of wine is allotted. For example, for an importer to qualify for a single bottle from the prestigious Domaine de La Romanée-Conti, the Burgundy shipper might demand that he also buy large quantities of the shipper's other wines.)

AGING TIMES

Even when the site, soil and variety are the same, variations in weather can cause the grapes to mature at different rates from vin-tage to vintage and the wines differ accordingly in their aging char-acteristics. Some vintages hit their peaks sooner, others later. (The wine of one year may be better for immediate drinking, while that of the previous year is best consumed a decade later.) As a general rule, red wines from relatively light low-tannin vintages should be drunk before the reds of heavier years.

Ninety percent of the world's wine is meant to be drunk with-in a year or so of its production. (It is bottled within months of the harvest.) After a year or so, it begins to deteriorate, losing color and bouquet, becoming flat and dull. The remaining 10 percent of the world's wine has the ability to age gracefully. These are the cel-larable wines that gain value with time. Meant for extended aging are the outstanding tannic reds: the best French Bordeaux and

Burgundies, the premium Italian wines, some California Cabernet Sauvignons and others.

NOTE: To recoup their costs, producers usually sell their quality red wines long before they reach their peaks, generally releasing them at about age two. The best reds, however, may not appear on the wineshop shelves for three to seven years.

The dynamics of a fine wine's aging are not fully understood. Its development has been likened to the stages of human growth, evolving from childhood and adolescence to maturity and old age. A young wine is one that has not yet reached its peak and is still improving. A mature wine has developed richness, softness and refinement, while an old wine has passed its peak and is declining.

Determining when a wine reaches its peak and how long it remains there are its origin, the quality of its vintage, its storage conditions, the size of its cask or tank, the extent of its oxidation, and so forth. Crucial too is the vinification method and the personal style of the vintner.

The more slowly a fine wine develops, the longer-lived it may be. Wines with an unmistakable concentration and depth are rarely drinkable early on. Closed-in, rough and unfocused at first, they need the time to open up and express their subtleties. With bottle-aging, they can acquire added stature. Developing finesse and complexity, they can demonstrate an unexpected range of tastes and aromas that younger wines cannot match.

Some collectors who purchase wine by the case buy an extra bottle to sample after a number of years in order to judge the wine's progress. Others experiment with a few bottles to determine how soon to open the wine. Only by tasting can the consumer determine how a developing wine is coming along. If one bottle and then another shows signs of excessive age, it's a warning to drink up the remainder as soon as possible.

Then there are the collectors who keep their wines too long, who save them as a comfort for their old age, treating them as objects of art to be preserved and cherished. A wine past its prime will become brown and dried out and acquire a dry-leaf odor and an oxidized taste. Some ancient wines that were drinkable when first uncorked proved so fragile that they faded within minutes. A century-old bottle of Lafite yielded a pale brown liquid tinged with scarlet and exuding a dim bouquet of violets. Tasting only vaguely of grapes, it was so thin on the palate as to be almost watery. Jonathan Swift once refused a venerable wine, saying, "Sir, I drink no memories."

Although the red wines capable of maturing should be aged further, most consumers cannot resist the temptation to uncork the bottles at once. They assume that the wines are ready to drink when purchased. (It is estimated that about 95 percent of all wines are consumed within a day or so of leaving the shop and most within a week. Most of the better vintages are consumed prematurely. As one wine maker said, "The average person has never aged a wine and so he doesn't know the difference." Drinking a good wine too soon has been called "a form of infanticide."

It was once believed that to be truly great, a red wine had to be undrinkable for the first decade of its life. Yet few reds are now vinified to mature for the length of time of which they're capable. Most are made ready to drink in five years or less. Some of the finest reds peak after about ten years. And the rush is on to produce them lighter, fruitier, and quicker-maturing, and to make them "friendlier" sooner. The speeded-up wines that are ready for consumption two or three years after the harvest, may be charming in youth but quickly deteriorate and fade; most languish and die within a couple of years.

White wines, which are negligible in their tannins, need little aging. (The wineries generally bottle and ship them out as soon as they are bright and stable.) Their greatest charm is an engaging freshness. Most white wines are meant for consumption on their release and keep only a year or two. A rare few have the potential for graceful aging. As their youthful fruit abates, they become more complex and rounded. With additional time in the bottle, they acquire deeper flavors and a more desirable bouquet. Among these are the noble rot Sauternes, the great white Côte d'Or Burgundies, and the fine German Rieslings.

Blush wines and rosés are also best enjoyed in the freshness of their youth. They should as a rule be consumed within two years of the vintage; generally turning dangerous by age three and over the hill by age four. Sparkling wines are not meant for aging either; their freshness and vivacity tend to diminish with time.

Champagnes have already been bottled-aged by their makers and are ready to drink when sold. (Vintage Champagnes, once made in a richer fuller style, could remain bubbly for a decade or more.) Sparkling wines sold in larger-than-standard bottles—in magnums, jeroboams, and so on—should be consumed as soon as possible. Their transfer to oversized bottles has increased their oxidation and reduces their staying power.

Fortified wines generally benefit little from bottle-aging but, because of their higher alcohol content, can be stored away for extended periods. The lighter, drier sherries, however—the finos and manzanillas—and the ruby and tawny ports are best soon after they have been bottled. Vintage Ports, which need years in the bottle to evolve, possess great keeping powers. The finest have improved for thirty, forty, and even fifty years. The current trend however is to make them drinkable within fifteen or twenty years. Madeiras are among the longest-lived of the fortified wines; the rarest retain their vitality and fruit for sixty years or more. (Accounting in part for their extraordinary longevity is their complex volcanic soil and their estufa baking process.)

The criteria for aging a wine is based on its source, grape variety, quality of its vintage, and style of vinification, as well as on its condition when purchased and on the available storage facilities. A few wines are still vinified in the slower-developing older style; but most are now made in the newer earlier-maturing style.

The following is a general guide to the keeping and aging of wines, assuming they have been properly cellared and cared for:

French Wines

Bordeaux:

Médoc reds of good provenance and vintage, characteristically firm and hard in youth, once needed decades to reach their peak and could survive a quarter-century or more. The French, now reflecting the current view of earlier drinkability, have come to prefer their wines—even the greatest of them—relatively young. The average for the finest Médocs had been up to fifteen years of aging and five to ten years for most of the others. Some now reach their peaks in eight to ten years, hold that level another five years or so, and then begin a slow decline. Others are ready to drink in three to seven years. Gascony wines take two to three years to soften up, while those from the Petit Châteaus are generally at their best soon after bottling. Second-label wines are also meant to be taken young.

St-Émilions and Pomerols, less tannic than the Médocs, are ready in five to eight years at their finest. (Rare examples can be aged ten to twelve years.) The long-lived St-Estèphes once needed more than five years to become smooth and attractive, but some are drinkable at age two or three now. Among Bordeaux's white wines, Château d'Yquem ages beautifully. (Some examples have survived for more than five decades.) Most of the region's other whites are meant for immediate consumption.

Burgundy:

Red Burgundies pressed from the pinot noir usually mature faster than the Cabernet Sauvignons of Bordeaux and are generally are not expected to last as long. Fine Côte d'Or wines once reached their peaks in eight to ten years; some survived for two decades. Most are now ready to drink by age five. Lesser red Burgundies ripen in about eighteen months.

Among the Beaujolais wines, Moulin-à-Vent generally ages best; its finest examples can improve for eight to ten years. Morgon, Fleurie and Chénas can last for five years or more. Most of the other crus usually ripen in three to four years. A St-Amour can be drunk within two years of the vintage. As for the ordinary Beaujolais, they soon lose their attractive grapy color, flavor and fragrance. It is said of them:"Drink the wine of the preceding year, no older." Beaujolais Nouveaus usually crumble in about six months and are best taken by Christmas of the vintage year. They should generally be avoided after the following March or April. (Preservatives often prolong the life of those designated for export, however.)

Among the white Burgundies, the most magnificent from the Côte d'Or can remain at their peaks for four to six years, while the region's more typical wines go off in three years or so. A Grand Cru Chablis is usually at its best by about age four. Other good examples generally retain their youth and fragrance for two or three years; lesser examples last only a year or two. The better Côte de Beaune whites usually run their course in a year or so. The sooner the regional Bourgogne Blancs are consumed, the better.

Rhône Valley:

The best Hermitage reds once needed decades to reach their maturity, but are now made drinkable by about age ten. Some need only six years in the bottle. The Cornas and Gigondas reds can benefit from five to ten years while the Crozes-Hermitage should keep three or four. The best Côte Rôties once needed six years or so to blossom but now reach their heights in three or four years.

The red wines of the southern Rhône are generally softer and faster-maturing. The best Châteauneufs once needed a decade to reach their peaks but now are ready to drink at age five or less; the lightest examples can be drunk in a year or two. Côtes du Rhône wines, meant for consumption when bottled, are best taken within a year or so.

Among the Rhône whites, the top-ranking Château Grillet has the greatest potential for aging, reaching its maximum drinking level at about age five. Other whites such as Condrieu are best taken young. Muscat Beaumes-de-Venise can be drunk after a year or so, but with a degree of bottle age more subtle secondary aromas can replace its fresh flowery appeal.

Loire Valley:

Most reds from the Loire Valley are ready to drink when released. In superior vintages, those from Chinon, Bourgueil and St-Nicholas may improve for a few years in the bottle. Among the Loire whites, the finest Vouvrays can take long cellaring without any loss of verve; rare examples have remained fresh and youthful for five decades. Noble rots from Bonnezeaux and Quarts de Chaume have also survived for half a century. Sweet luscious Anjous can take a few years of aging. Some highly acid Savennieres are not worth considering until they're about age five. Best taken within a year of their release, however,—and no more than two years—are Pouilly-

Fumé, Sancerre, Quincy and Muscadet wines. By age three or four, these wines become tired and disappointing.

Alsace:

The finest Alsatian white wines require some bottle-age to achieve their depth and complexity. The Special Reserve Selections need several years. The greatest vendange tardives (late-harvest wines) don't reach their peaks for five or six years and can last ten to fifteen years. Most other Alsatian wines are ready to drink when shipped.

Other French Wines:

Cahors, once dark harsh and unyielding, needed a decade or more to develop. Now vinified for earlier maturity, it is drinkable in about five years. Moulis reds are generally ready to drink at about age five and can improve for about a decade. Some of the best Bandols and the Rully and Givry reds are ready to drink in two or three years. Among the Mâcon whites, Pouilly-Fuissé is best taken by age two or three and should be avoided after age five. Other Mâcon whites are meant for immediate consumption; they fade in about a year.

Italian Wines

The great Barolos, once robust, tannic and long-lived, didn't reach their peaks for two decades or more. (A rare few survived nearly a century.) The best are now drinkable after ten years or so; most others are ready to drink in six to eight years, although a few mature somewhat sooner. The most extraordinary Barberas possess ten to fifteen years of life, while others are ready to drink within four to eight years, and some by age three. A Barbaresco can mature in six to ten years, while a good Gattinara needs about five years.

Amarone once needed a decade or two to reach its peak but is now vinified to be drinkable by about age five. Brunello di Montalcino famed for its intensity, once needed more than two decades to achieve finesse and balance. (Some examples aged well for half a century.) Now made less tannic and more accessible, a Brunello can mature in six to ten years. The lighter Rosso di Montalcino, Brunello's younger brother, is ready to drink when released.

Classic Chiantis from great vintages once needed a decade or two to work off their tannins. Some can now be enjoyed after five or six years. Simple fruity Chiantis are meant to be taken within a couple of years of the vintage, while still light and fresh. Rubesco is ready to drink when released but can keep for several years.

Valpolicellas are drinkable in three years or so. The lighter-bodied Bardolinos and Dolcettos, maturing early and fading soon, are best taken by age one or two. (For the most part, they're over the hill by age three.) Freisa di Chieri, ready to drink on its release, can shed its rough tartness after a couple of years and acquire a remarkable bouquet. The best Taurasis are relatively long lived; they reach maturity at about age ten.

Most Italian white wines—Soave, Verdicchio, Vernaccia di San Gimignano, Cortese, Pinot Grigio, and so forth—are best taken as young as possible, preferably within a year of the vintage.

Spanish Wines

Rioja's outstanding red Riservas are capable of graceful aging; those from exceptional vintages come into their own at about age ten, reaching their peaks at age fifteen or twenty. (A rare few have survived for thirty and forty years.) The more typical Riojas and other Spanish reds are generally ready to drink when released at age four or five. Vega Sicilia's Gran Riservas are ready after ten years, as are the finest Ribera del Dueros. (The Riberas from light vintages can be taken at about age five.) Spanish white wines are meant for immediate consumption.

Portuguese Wines

Highly tannic Colares red wines need a decade or more to mature. Fairly tannic too are the Reserva Dãos from top vintages, which can last two decades or more. Other Dão reds usually mature in five to ten years. The white Dãos are best consumed within a year. Also meant to be taken young and sprightly are the Portuguese vinho verdes; they should be drunk within a year or so.

German Wines

Good German Rieslings are ready to drink when released but, because of their excellent acid balance, can age superbly. Those from the richest vintages acquire their subtleties and nuances until about age ten, becoming dull and murky by their fifteenth year.

QBA and Kabinett wines reach their fullest flavor within five years. The Spätleses, enjoyable when young, generally peak in five to ten years. The Ausleses require two to three years of bottle age and can continue to develop in glass for at least a decade. Although the BAs, TBAs and Eisweins peak in seven to ten years, they can usually remain fresh and intriguing for decades. The more modest German white wines, ready to drink when shipped, are best consumed by age two.

American Wines

Most Cabernet Sauvignons from California's Napa Valley are at their best between the ages of five and eight; superior examples can continue to improve until about age fifteen. (Many are now vinified for earlier consumption, however, and are ready to drink when released, but they can acquire additional complexity if laid down for two or three years.) Fine California Merlots can be laid down for seven or eight years; lesser examples for four to six years or less. Zinfandel reds may be taken youthful or mature depending on where they were grown and how they were vinified. The richer fuller examples can be aged profitably for a decade; the most tannic need ten to fifteen years in the bottle. Others are ready to drink by age seven or eight, while some are approachable at about age two. The finest California Chardonnays are ready for consumption when released but can demonstrate a greater complexity of bouquet and flavor after three or four years. Some can be aged for eight to fifteen years. (One thirty-year-old was still in superb condition when tasted.) Most Chardonnays however should be consumed within a year or two.

In the Pacific Northwest, Cabernet Sauvignons from good vintages have lasted as long as a decade. The Pinot Noirs from Oregon's Willamette Valley are generally meant for consumption within three or four years. Other northwestern reds are generally ready to drink when released. New York State's red wines are usually ready to drink when released as well.

Other Countries

Many Australian red wines are ready to drink when bottled. Although the tannic reds can age well, acquiring a rounder finish, their true potential is often sacrificed for the softness of early maturity. Swiss white wines are intended for immediate drinking and should generally be consumed within three years of the vintage.

8

SERVING

WINE TEMPERATURES

To demonstrate its finest qualities, a wine should be served at its proper temperature. For some, room temperature is ideal; others need cooling or chilling. As a rule, the more substantial the wine, the warmer its temperature should be; the sweeter the wine, the cooler. Another consideration is the time of year. In summer, a wine can be served a few degrees cooler than in winter. (Warm weather makes a Cabernet Sauvignon taste somewhat flabby.) Considered as well should be the point in the meal at which the wine is presented: When taken as an apéritif, it should be a bit cooler than when accompanying the main course.

There are four basic temperatures at which a wine can be served: room temperature, cellar temperature, light chilling and sharp chilling.

ROOM TEMPERATURE

The idea of serving wine at room temperature originated in Europe before the advent of central heating, when indoor temperatures in cool weather registered 60 to 65°F. (Interiors today are about 10 degrees warmer and, as a result, so are most room-temperature wines.)

Sixty degrees or so is best for a tannic red; the elements responsible for its taste, aroma and bouquet are most active then. A few minutes in the refrigerator can cool it sufficiently. When served at 70 degrees or more, a robust red will lack the necessary astringency and its alcohol becomes dominant. Losing its vigor, the wine will take on a semistewed flavor, making it seem formless, flabby and oppressively heavy. On the other hand, serving a sturdy tannic red wine too cool—at 50 degrees or so—will deprive it of its taste, aroma, and most of its bouquet, making it seem far more astringent than it actually is.

Best served at room temperature are the more substantial Bordeaux and Burgundies (including the Beaujolais Grand Crus); Hermitage and Côte Rôtie wines from the Rhône; Barolos, Barbarescos and Riserva Chiantis from Italy; and the heavier California Zinfandels, Cabernet Sauvignons and so forth. Room temperature is suitable as well for medium-rich fortified wines, including sherries, Madeiras, ports, and Marsalas.

CELLAR TEMPERATURE

Cellar temperature ranges from 50- to 60°F (as if the wine had just emerged from a cool underground cellar). It is best for uncomplicated wines, characterized by irrepressible fruit: for the lighter reds, the blush wines, and the rosés. Cellar temperature enhances their freshness; its slight cooling removes their typically sharp edges, yet lets their crisp acidity, piquancy and flavor come through. (Room temperature would throw their sweetness and acidity out of balance and make the wines seem dull and flat.)

Best served at cellar temperatures are most Beaujolais. (The heavier examples—Moulin-à-Vent and Morgon—are more pleasant when served a bit below room temperature.) Cellar temperatures are also appropriate for the lighter reds from the Rhône's Côtes du Ventoux; the Chinons and Bourgueils from the Loire; the Italian Bardolinos, Valpolicellas, and Dolcettos; along with the Spanish Valdepenas and California's lighter Zinfandels. Cellar temperatures are suitable as well for generic Burgundies and clarets and for the sweeter fortified wines.

LIGHT CHILLING

Light chilling, which ranges from 45- to 55°F, can enhance the crisp flavor of a white wine, accentuate the delicacy of a rosé and refresh an unpretentious young red. It can also reveal the lovely subtleties of a drier fortified wine (served as an apéritif) and show to greater advantage a sweeter, heavier-bodied dessert wine. Light chilling is appropriate for most white wines, including fine white Burgundies and top-quality German and Alsatian Rieslings and for the fuller-bodied, fuller-flavored Chardonnays from California and Australia.

Light chilling is also suitable for light-bodied, sometimes lightly sweet red wines made to be drunk young, including the Beaujolais Nouveaus, Côtes du Rhône wines, Loire Valley Cabernet Francs, and lighter Italian Chiantis and Spanish Riojas. Light chilling is suitable as well for lighter fortified wines served as apéritifs. These include fino and manzanilla sherries, light tawny ports and dry vermouths, as well as Sercial and Verdelho Madeiras. It is also appropriate for the richer Madeiras, oloroso sherries, Málagas, Muscatels and Tokays.

SHARP CHILLING

Sharp chilling, which ranges from 35- to 45°F, brings out the flavor of a sparkling wine. It also keeps CO_2 in solution, reducing the bottle's internal pressure and prolonging the life of the bubbles. (Higher temperatures would stimulate the wine's molecular activity and expand its CO_2, creating a greater propulsive force behind the cork and making the wine go flat much sooner.)

Sharp chilling also counteracts the assertive sweetness of luscious white wines and offsets their possible cloying. It is particularly suited to botrytized wines, including the French Sauternes and Barsacs. (Bottles of Sauternes have been chilled almost to the freezing point by encasing them in blocks of ice.) Other wines that can benefit from sharp chilling are Beaumes-de-Venise, Italian vin santos, and German Eisweins, Ausleses, Beerenausleses, and Trockenbeerenausleses.

The manner in which a wine is brought to its proper serving temperature should always be gradual. A red wine—allowed to become warm naturally—will open up fully, displaying its bouquet and lingering flavor. Red wines carried up from cool cellars were once set on a sideboard for a while so they could reach room temperature slowly. (This is known as *chambrer; chambre* in French translates as "room.") If the temperature of a red wine were raised abruptly—by plunging the bottle into hot water, setting it in front of an open fire, or placing it near a radiator—the wine would be thrown off balance and would breathe off most of its bouquet.

NOTE: If time is short and the wine is too cool, a hand cupped around the glass along with the room's ambient temperature should warm it sufficiently.

White wines need an hour or so in the refrigerator, assuming they are reasonably cool at the start. Red wines need only about twenty minutes. For sharp chilling, a wine requires two or three hours in the refrigerator. Champagnes and other sparkling wines—bottled in thicker, more stress-resistant glass—require about two hours. Wines in oversized bottles—in magnums and jeroboams—need additional time.

NOTE: When the bottles are too large or too numerous to fit into the refrigerator, they can be placed in sturdy plastic bags and packed with ice, or they can be arranged horizontally in the bathtub, topped with a layer of ice cubes and then immersed in cold tap water. (The water, encouraging the ice to melt, makes for a more efficient surface contact with the bottles.)

Generally, the better the wine, the less chilling it will need; cold can mask its subtle flavors and aromas. Overchilling can damage the wine's quality, impair its bouquet, and dull its flavor nuances. It can even paralyze the wine, freezing the taste out of it, and turning it into the equivalent of ice water. As the wine warms up during the meal, it will lose whatever sprightliness, freshness, and charm that remains. Rarely does the last glass taste as good as the first.

Wine should be chilled no more than a few hours in advance. Left in the refrigerator overnight, it will never regain its earlier charm. (Champagne particularly develops an odd, flat, unpleasant smell and taste.) If the bottle has been chilled but not opened, it is much better to return it to the cellar and then rechill it before serving. (Wines stored in the refrigerator for extended periods are in a state of suspended animation and do not evolve as they should.)

Like warming, chilling should not be hastened. Placing a bottle in the freezer subjects it to a sharp, swift drop in temperature, shocking the wine and dulling its personality. The extreme cold might also expel the cork or crack the bottle. Nor is it a good idea to put the glasses themselves in the refrigerator, to fill them temporarily with ice cubes, or to set them upside down in an ice bucket. The moisture that is then introduced will inhibit the evaporation needed to release the wine's bouquet and aroma. In sparkling wines it also destroys their effervescence. (Drying the glasses only rewarms them with the heat of the hand.) Placing ice cubes directly into the glass will dilute a wine and damage its flavor beyond recall and should never be done with good wines.

Wine can also be chilled in an ice bucket. Cracked or crushed ice is more efficient than ice cubes in the bucket. A half-ice, half-water mixture is even better. Making more surface contact with the bottle, it will lower the wine's temperature sooner. (If the bucket in a restaurant contains only ice, one can ask the waiter to add water or simply add some oneself.) After about twenty minutes the bottle should be fairly icy to the touch. Most ice buckets are not deep enough however to accommodate the long-necked flute-style bottles associated with German, Austrian and Alsatian wines. Upending these bottles for a few minutes in the bucket will make their necks feel as icy as the rest. Sparkling wines, bottled in thicker glass, need thirty to forty-five minutes in the bucket to chill.

NOTE: Although ice buckets are useful for retaining the chill of a white wine or for prolonging the sparkle of a Champagne during a leisurely meal, they are generally superfluous if the wine has already been chilled.

Ice buckets can also be used for red wines in summer if they seem too warm on the tongue. (Chilling such wines lightly for ten or fifteen minutes will make them taste livelier.) Or adding very cold water but no ice to the bucket will cool the red wine down sufficiently in half an hour or so.

Casual wines, meant to slake the thirst, can be cooled more casually. Jug wines can be taken "on the rocks" and may in fact taste better since the colder temperatures will mask their imperfections. For picnics, the wines can be chilled in the refrigerator, then transferred to a thermos jug or an ice chest. In summer, in southern France, Italy, Spain and Greece the ordinary red wines are often diluted with water. Inexpensive white wines and rosés may also be cut with water or combined with ice cubes and club soda for a refreshing drink known as a "spritzer."

UNCORKING THE WINE

Once the wine has been brought to its optimum temperature, the bottle can be uncorked. Some people prefer doing this beforehand in the kitchen so they can try the wine themselves before serving it to others. By sampling a quarter-glassful in advance, they can check on the wine's soundness and catch any stray particles of cork. They then securely recork the bottle until serving time.

When serving wine at a dinner party or other gathering, it's important to have a corkscrew you are familiar with and feel comfortable using. The better the wine, the more carefully the bottle should be opened. This is the recommended method:

1. Using the point of a knife or the corkscrew, score the foil capsule covering the cork and bottle neck all the way around the first ridge. Strip off the top of the foil, exposing the cork. Wipe the cork, neck and bottle rim with a clean, dampened cloth or paper towel to remove any traces of mold or residue.

2. Holding the bottle firmly by the neck, insert the corkscrew. Turn until it almost fully penetrates the length of the cork.

3. Ease the cork out and inspect it. It should be moist, firm and clean-smelling, not discolored or emitting a musty or otherwise objectionable odor.

4. Carefully wipe the lip of the bottle inside and out to remove any traces of mold or residue.

5. Pour the wine—without resting the bottle on the rim of the stemmed wine glass. (Its high center of gravity makes the glass susceptible to spills.)

6. After pouring, use a slight twist of the wrist to send the last few drops of wine back into the bottle neck. This will prevent dripping.

Never fill the glasses to the brim but leave a space at the top to let the wine's volatile substances and evaporating ethers collect, allowing the bouquet and aroma to develop. Since red wines need the most aeration, their glasses should be filled about half full. For white, rosé, and sparkling wines, their glasses are filled about two-thirds full.

Wine is served clockwise around the table. (Port is traditionally served counterclockwise.) If the guests are to serve themselves, place the bottle in the center of the table or else ask them to pass it along.

NOTE: Do not discard the cork. At slow, leisurely meals, recorking the wine between courses will keep it from overoxidizing; the cork will also be required if any wine is left over. When serving more than one bottle, pour wine from the second bottle into fresh or at least empty glasses in case it differs substantially from the first wine.

Should the cork prove balky and difficult to extract, set the bottle on the floor and press down on it with one hand for greater leverage, while pulling up steadily on the corkscrew with the other hand. Should the cork break off midway, reinsert the corkscrew at a slightly more diagonal angle and begin again. Should the cork be inadvertently pushed into the bottle, do not try to retrieve it. Instead, strain the wine at once into a clean container through a cheesecloth-lined sieve. Should the cork crumble, push the remaining section into the bottle, then immediately strain the wine into a clean container.

CORKSCREWS

Before the invention of the corkscrew, corks were tapered and projected over the rims of the bottles. (A strong set of teeth was required for their removal.) With the introduction of the corkscrew, straight-sided corks became possible with tops that were flush with the rims of the bottles.

The traditional corkscrew features a metal shaft or worm and some form of leverage. Preferable is a helix-shaped worm with an outside diameter of $3/8$th of an inch and at least six spirals. (Solid augers with straight shafts that look like wood screws do not get a

good grip, and their sharp edges can split or shatter the corks.) A crossbar provides the necessary leverage by intensifying the worm's twisting action. A modern corkscrew features a plastic sleeve that grips the bottle neck and centers the worm precisely. Its extralong stainless steel helix, coated with Teflon, makes the cork's extraction virtually effortless. (This modern device is particularly good for extracting corks that are broken, dried out, or too tight.

A variant of the traditional corkscrew has a pair of vertical wings that raise up laterally as the worm penetrates. Returning the wings to their vertical position exerts a strong upward pull on the cork. Another variant, called the "waiter's friend," is a compact folding corkscrew that looks like a penknife. A lever at one end is braced against the bottle's lip and acts as a fulcrum. Also often seen in restaurants and wine bars is a heavy-duty corkscrew installed on the bar itself. It features a pair of hinged arms that grip the bottle firmly, a wooden lever, a sharply pointed worm and a stainless steel barrel. Two smooth, swift motions remove the cork: the first action, a twist of the wrist, activates the lever and forces the worm into the cork; the second reverses the lever, extracting the cork and ejecting it out the other end of the stainless steel barrel.

Nontraditional cork extractors dispense with the worm entirely. One is a two-pronged cork puller featuring a pair of tines attached to a small handle. The tines are inserted on either side of the cork and the handle is gently and steadily twisted to bring out the cork, unpierced and intact. (This is particularly useful for soggy or crumbly corks, which a conventional corkscrew would demolish.) Another nontraditional decorker injects compressed air or CO_2 through a hollow, needlelike probe into the cork. Building up in the space between cork and wine, the air or gas pushes the cork upward until it exits. This is not suitable, however, for bottles made of thin or uneven glass; the pressure might cause them to shatter.

OPENING A BOTTLE OF CHAMPAGNE

Champagnes and other sparkling wines should be well chilled before their bottles are uncorked, not only to bring out the wine's inherent flavor but also to reduce the propulsive pressure behind the cork. The wine glasses should be set out in advance and the bottles opened at the very last moment in order to preserve as much of the lively effervescence as possible.

Particular care must be taken in opening the Champagne bottle. Any undue shaking or agitation can expel the cork prematurely. Flying out suddenly, it can careen around the room at high speed, or ricochet dangerously off the walls. When opening the bottle, the cork's likely trajectory must always be kept in mind; the neck of the bottle pointed away from one's body, face and eyes, as well as from those of others in the vicinity. It should also be pointed away from such breakable objects as mirrors, lamps, clocks, glass-framed pictures, window panes and so on.

The safest device for extracting the mushroom-shaped cork is the human hand, which is capable of exercising the greatest degree of control. A corkscrew, knife or similar implement should never be used, except for removing the foil capsule that covers the cork.

This is the recommended method for uncorking a bottle of Champagne:

1. With the point of a knife, incise the foil capsule, scoring it all the way around about $1^1/2$ inches from the top. Strip a way the foil to expose the wire hood that anchors the cork.
2. Untwist the bottom loop of the hood and lift it off. Remove any metal scraps that can taint the wine during pouring.

3.   Tilt the bottle away from the body at a 45-degree angle and grasp the cork's mushroom-shaped dome firmly between thumb and forefinger. With the other hand, rotate the bottle slowly by its base, turning it in one direction a quarter-turn at a time. Always turn the bottle, not the cork. (The bottle is rotated out from under the cork, rather than the cork being twisted out of the bottle.)

4.   With thumb and forefinger, guide and control the cork's emergence, rocking it gently to let a little CO_2 escape so that some of the pressure behind the cork is dissipated.

5.   When two-thirds of the cork has emerged, smoothly ease out the rest. The cork should exit with a muted sound, accompanied by a slight wisp of vapor. (The louder and more explosively it departs, the faster the CO_2 will rush out, taking valuable wine with it.)

6.   To prevent any foaming over, pour each glass one-third full; then, a moment later, pour the wine two-thirds to the top. (Filling the glass to the brim only invites spilling.)

NOTE: If the cork does not move out on its own, continue to rotate the bottle by its base. If the cork remains stubborn, run a stream of hot water over the bottle neck for a few seconds. If the cork breaks, cover it with a cloth and hold the bottle neck under tepid water until the cork works itself loose. If the cork does not come out, do not try to remove the remaining stem with a corkscrew. Instead, lay the pressure-filled bottle on its side until it can be returned to its place of purchase. (A reputable wine shop will replace the bottle.)

BREATHING

A wine's breathing is simply its exposure to air. The aeration can be brought about by uncorking the wine in advance or by letting it sit for a while in its glass. Breathing is essential for some wines and unnecessary for others. For still others, it can have disastrous results.

The wines that benefit most from breathing are the tannic reds, which come to life and release more of their subtle flavor in contact with the oxygen in the atmosphere. Among them are the best Bordeaux and other good Cabernet Sauvignons; high-caliber Burgundies; many Spanish and Portuguese reds, and Italian Barolos, Gattinaras and Spannas, as well as classic Chiantis and Brunellos di Montalcino.

Since most mature reds have already resolved their tannins, about half an hour of breathing is usually quite sufficient for them. Additional exposure to air would risk the loss of their fruit and much of their character. After an hour or so, the wines would not be as fresh and vigorous as they once were; after two or three hours, they are likely to deteriorate. (There are some exceptions, however; certain sturdy Barolos have been uncorked twenty-four hours in advance.)

Breathing is most beneficial for young, tight and seemingly unyielding reds. The more sharply tannic they are, the more positively they respond. Softening their tannins, the aeration modifies their inner hardness, rounding off their roughness and sharp edges. After an hour or so, these wines become softer, fuller and more generous. (Some tannic young California Cabernets have benefitted from several hours of breathing.)

NOTE: If time is short, the wine's oxidation can be hastened by pouring it into a glass to expose more of its surface to air. Swirling or rotating the wine slightly in the glass further intensifies the aeration. And inexpensive red wines can be helped to absorb more oxygen from the air by transferring them back and forth several times between the glass and another container.

NOTE: A wine opened five years too soon may need twice as much breathing as its properly matured counterpart. Although the aeration seems to speed up maturation, it is no substitute, however, for normal aging. A well-made red wine achieves its highest potential only by its slow and gradual development in wood and glass.

For venerable and delicate old reds, to breathe is to die. Such wines should not be opened until the last moment. The older and more fragile they are, the shorter their life expectancy once they have been uncorked. The wines may taste fine when first sipped, but can fade rapidly. Some crumble on contact with the air, literally disintegrating in five or ten minutes. Tragic tales are told of uncorking old wines in advance only to discover that their long-developed flavors have floated away. Whatever breathing an old wine needs best takes place in the glass, where the wine can be monitored and consumed before it falls apart.

Advance aeration is not advisable for lighter red, rosé or white wines either, since they possess fewer tannins. Opening their bottles ahead of time to let them breathe would cause the wines to lose the fresh, fruity character and aroma that constitute their greatest charm. Breathing is also out of the question for sparkling wines; their lively bubbles would vanish into the air. It is unnecessary for fortified wines as well—with the exception of some Vintage Ports. A fifteen- to twenty-year-old Vintage Port can benefit from a few hours of aeration, but the older examples should not be uncorked in advance.

DECANTING

As they age in glass, most fine wines throw a degree of deposit. Although it's harmless, the sediment can muddy the wine and—if allowed to float free—can obscure its color and produce an odd, somewhat furry sensation on the palate.

To leave the unwanted sediment behind and serve only the bright, clear liquid, one must decant the wine or transfer it to another container. That container, known as the decanter, might be a vessel with a stopper, an open-necked carafe, a pitcher, a jug, or simply an empty, well-washed-and-dried wine bottle. The pouring, which is done slowly and carefully, stops as soon as the first trace of sediment appears. Done properly, decanting can draw off all but about half an inch of clear wine. When poorly done, it can leave behind as much as two or three inches of a liquid laden with sediment and not very drinkable.

The wines most in need of decanting are the mature tannic, powerful, well-made reds which throw a considerable deposit in the bottle. They include the high-caliber reds from Bordeaux and Burgundy's Côte d'Or, Hermitage wines from the Rhône and such full-bodied Italians as the Barolos. Vintage Ports also throw a heavy deposit during their extended periods of bottle-aging.

NOTE: Red wines, aged primarily in wood, rarely need decanting Since they undergo frequent racking in the cask, which removes most of their sediment before they are bottled.

Lighter red wines and rosés need no decanting at all; they have a negligible sediment. Nor do many modern, speeded-up wines, which have already been clarified by filtration. Fortified wines, other than Vintage Ports, need no decanting either. Since their bottles are generally stored upright, their deposit—if any—settles to the bottom and is easily left behind.

Exposure to air during the decanting process—transfer from one container to another—may be beneficial or hazardous, depending on the wine. Tight tannic young reds can be decanted well in advance to accelerate their breathing and soften their rough edges. Mature well-made reds should be decanted no more than an hour ahead. A venerable old red is best poured directly into its glass at the very last minute.

NOTE: One can also decant by setting out the glasses beforehand in a neat row, then pouring the wine smoothly into them in an unbroken stream. Particular deftness is required here, since any abrupt midstream interruption might rouse up the sediment.

The decanting process can be vertical or horizontal. Vertical decanting stands the unopened bottle upright for a time, allowing the sediment to drift slowly down to its base. (Depending on the degree of deposit, this may take several hours or several days.) For the decanting itself, the foil capsule covering the cork is completely stripped off, allowing an unobstructed view of the bottle neck. A light source is then set up to illuminate the neck. (This can be a candle, a not-too-glaring flashlight or a light bulb.) The light is concentrated on the neck with the bottle positioned three or four inches away. With the bottle resting lightly on the decanter's rim, pouring begins. When the first sign of sediment appears in the neck, the pouring stops and the wine is served.

For horizontal decanting, the bottle is gently transferred from its horizontal storage rack in the cellar to a wine basket and carried horizontally to the table. As the bottle reclines in the basket, it is tilted slightly so that its cork can be extracted, then it's lifted by its base to enough of an angle so that the slow and smooth pouring can proceed. Some people miss the point of horizontal decanting entirely. They carry the bottle to the table horizontally in its basket, then stand it upright to pour—distributing the sediment throughout the wine. Or else they use the basket for wines with a negligible or nonexistent sediment.

NOTE: In both vertical and horizontal decanting, the bottle must be handled gently. Any twisting, jiggling or jerky up-and-down movements can stir up the sediment.

Should the heavy sedimentary interior crust of a Vintage Port become dislodged, the bottle should not be opened but stood upright for about twenty-four hours, letting the loose particles drift to the bottom. Then the bottle is uncorked and the wine strained into a decanter through a cheesecloth-lined sieve.

GLASSWARE

Glasses that are pleasing to the eye and feel good in the hand enhance a wine's loveliest qualities and stimulate the anticipation of sipping. The glass itself should be uniform, with no distracting bubbles, striations or irregularities. Clear, unadorned glass shows off the wine's color and highlights to advantage. (Etched, frosted or tinted glass tends to detract.) Thinner, more delicate glass that has a smooth, finely polished rim with little or no bead or thickness around the edge seems to make the wine taste better. Coarser glasses, with their thickly rounded, obtrusive rims interfere with the wine's pleasures. As a French restaurateur said, "A grand Bordeaux in a bad glass is no longer a grand Bordeaux."

The components of the wine glass are its bowl, its stem and base. The bowl should have a 10- to 12-ounce capacity, allowing for enough breathing space above the wine so the bouquet and aroma can develop. Huge, oversized bowls may look dramatic but tend to distort the bouquet. Small bowls allow little breathing space and are usually overfilled, making them prone to spillage. Best are the glasses whose bowls are shaped like partially opened tulips, ballooning out in the middle and tapering gently inward at the top. Their narrower diameter at the top concentrates the bouquet and aroma at the point where the nose meets the glass. As one wine maker noted, "When wine is served in a water glass, it is pretty hard to catch a noseful."

The stem raises the glass and isolates the wine from the hand. (A hand on the bowl would obscure the view and warm a wine meant to be taken cool.) The stem also makes twirling and swirling possible, further releasing the wine's bouquet. Creating a higher center of gravity, however, the stem makes the goblet inherently unstable, so that spillage is always a possibility.

NOTE: When a white wine is spilled, club soda should be poured on the tablecloth as soon as possible. When a red wine is spilled, the spot should be daubed with white wine or sprinkled with salt. The cloth is then rinsed in cold water before its regular laundering.

Specially designed glasses—varying in shape, size and height—are available for Burgundies, Bordeaux, Rieslings, Chardonnays, Chiantis and other wines. Simplifying matters however is the all-purpose wine glass, which stands six to eight inches high. It has about a three-inch stem and a bowl about three inches in diameter. Its capacity is about 12 ounces.

The wine according to type is poured into the goblet at different levels: half-full for red wines and two-thirds for white, sparkling and rosé wines. (The latter need less aeration.)

NOTE: Casual table wines with straightforward fruity flavors can be served in ordinary water tumblers. (These include light Zinfandels, light Chiantis, lesser Beaujolais, and Chenin Blancs, as well as jug wines.) For picnics and large informal gatherings, where not-very-high-caliber wines are served, plastic glasses might be used.

Preferred for Champagnes and other sparkling wines are the tall narrow, tapering V-shaped glasses known as flutes. Their narrower tops not only concentrate the bouquet but also provide less surface area for evaporation. And by preventing the quick dissipation of the bubbles, the flutes prolong the lively sparkle of the wine.

NOTE: Often associated with Champagnes and other sparkling wines are squat, short-stemmed, wide-mouthed glasses called coupes. These however warm the wine too quickly, diminishing its bouquet. And they expose too much of the wine's surface to air, increasing the flow of bubbles and making the wine go flat in record time. Moreover, their shallowness encourages spilling.

Sherries are traditionally served in copitas, which are narrow short-stemmed, tulip-shaped glasses with a 3- or 4-ounce capacity. Other fortified wines are served in short-stemmed chimney-style glasses with a 4- to 6-ounce capacity. Port is often served in good-sized brandy snifters that are filled about one-third full.

CARING FOR GLASSWARE

Stemmed wine glasses are best stored by suspending them upside down, with their bases set in slotted racks, so air can circulate around their bowls while their interiors remain free from dust. Otherwise, the stemware should be stored on its base, not on its fragile rim. (Storing them on their rims also allows stale air to become trapped inside the bowl. And the rim coming into direct contact with a wooden shelf can pick up the distracting odor of the wood.)

Wine glasses are best washed in very hot water, swabbed with a brush, then dried thoroughly with a lint-free cloth. Soap or detergent can leave a microscopic residue that creates an off-flavor in the wine and impairs the effervescence of a sparkling wine. Decanters should be washed and dried in the same manner.

MISCELLANY

Various artifacts, gadgets and paraphernalia are available for serving wine. There are decanters with special built-in ice compartments to chill the wine; terra-cotta coolers, which must first be soaked in water; iceless chillers with insulated sides; and reusable gel-packs kept in the freezer, which are then slipped sleevelike over the bottle.

There are wine cradles meant to ensure more precise control in decanting. There are also glass and crystal ice buckets that allow the bottle and its label to be seen. For leftover wines, there's a gadget that vacuums out most of the air to slow down spoilage. There are special pouring spouts that prevent dripping by sending the last few drops of wine back into the neck. And there are special coasters on which to set the bottles so they won't leave a ring on the tablecloth.

9

TASTING

There are certain basic requirements for any wine. It should be attractive to look at and pleasant to smell. It should demonstrate fruit and roundness as well as a reasonable degree of acidity. If we approach a wine with our senses alert, we will become aware not only of its appearance and aroma but also of its tactile quality, its "feel" or texture. We can sense its inner structure as well, its very "bones," as it were. The finer the wine, the more deliberately it should be tasted. Tasting involves looking at and sniffing as well as sipping the wine.

JUDGING A WINE

LOOKING AT THE WINE

One of the loveliest attributes of a wine is its color. Color is often a key to its health and age as well . To observe the color, we pour some wine into an unadorned goblet. Holding the glass against a white background (a tablecloth, a napkin, or even a sheet of paper), we tilt the bowl at a 45-degree angle so the liquid forms a neat, oval pool. Then we look down into—not up at—the wine, noting the color from the shallower edge to the center.

The color in a young red wine should be bright, even and con-sistent; in an older red, it will be tawny. A rosé should be pinkish in hue; a yellowish cast or an overly pronounced orange tinge may indicate a defect. White wines range from pale ash to amber, they sometimes also display tints of green or silver. A slight brown edge in either a red or a white wine suggests overoxidation; a stronger brown indicates excessive age.

Clarity is another key to soundness; the wine should be clear and even throughout. Any hint of haziness, cloudiness or murkiness signals a problem—although this may be temporary if the bottle has been agitated and its sediment roused up. Before any final judgments are made, the wine should be given the chance to rest and settle down.

NOTE: Clarity was once a reliable clue to a wine's health and stability, but filtering can now make any wine look startlingly clear.

In addition to the wine's color, we consider its body or substance and its viscosity. Holding the stem of the glass between thumb and forefinger, we tilt the bowl slightly, spinning the glass gently. As the wine swishes up the sides of the bowl then trickles back down, it forms streaks or paths, called "legs." The more slowly the legs descend, the fuller the body. When fairly uniform, they indicate a thicker wine; when unevenly spaced, a thinner one. In wines of considerable viscosity, the trickle-down patterns are slow and graceful, creating the nearly perfect arches that the Germans call *kirchenfenster* ("church windows").

SNIFFING THE WINE

Sniffing is an integral part of tasting. To bring out the wine's innate vapors, we fill the glass half-full so that the aromatic compounds— the essences and ethers—can collect in the space above the liquid. (Filling the glass to the brim would cause the bouquet to float off in all directions and disappear into the air.) We spin or swirl the glass to speed up the release of these aromatic elements. By aerating the wine, swirling opens up its volatile components and thrusts its aromatic elements upward toward the nose for our fuller appreciation. The French say that swirling makes the wine "waltz."

The finer red wines, richest in their aromatic compounds, benefit most from swirling. The lesser reds, rosés and whites, possessing fewer compounds, need little or no swirling. Champagnes and other sparkling wines are never swirled; any spinning would destroy their already fragile bubbles.

No instrument is as sensitive to a wine's nuances as the human nose. Although most people believe that the sense of taste is confined to the mouth, taste is intrinsically linked with smell. Seventy-five percent of a wine's enjoyment comes from its smell. As we sniff the wine, its aromatic vapors travel up behind the soft palate at the back of the mouth. On entering a narrow cavity high in the nostrils, they encounter the olfactory receptor cells. There, nerve endings pick up the aromatic message, transferring it directly to the olfactory bulb of the brain, which in turn converts that message into electrical signals. These signals are then interpreted by the brain.

To sniff the wine, we lower the nose into the glass and then inhale quickly and rather sharply to carry the wine's fragrance to the nerve endings high in the nostrils. If we sniff just after the wine has been poured and sniff again after a few seconds of swirling, we can detect a world of difference in the aroma and bouquet.

NOTE: To understand the role of the nose, we take a sip of wine and, holding it in the mouth for a moment, pinch the nostrils shut. The flavor then disappears. When we release the nostrils, the flavor returns.

In considering the wine's aroma and bouquet, we ask ourselves: Is the odor fresh and clean? Is the scent aromatic or flowery? Does it suggest herbs, earth, or fresh hay? Is the fragrance spicy, smoky, woody, or musky? Does the wine smell of fruit as it should? If it's a varietal wine, can we recognize the character of its predominant grape?

NOTE: Sniffing can also reveal wine's defects such as corkiness, moldiness and mustiness, along with vinegary or perhaps chemical smells.

SIPPING THE WINE

After sniffing, we pause for a few moments to let the nose recover. Then we sip the wine. Holding it briefly in the mouth, we note its general shape and temperature. We consider its viscosity, along with its texture, weight and consistency. Then we slowly roll the wine about in the mouth turning it over and over to reach as many taste buds as possible. (The taste buds are sensitive to the four basic tastes: sweet, sour, bitter and salty; wine involves only the first three.) We perceive the wine's sweetness at the tip of the tongue, the acidity in the middle and the bitterness at the back. In a good red wine, the sensation might at first be soft and nearly sweet, followed by some acidity, and then by the slightly bitter taste of the tannins.

As we sip, we ask ourselves: What is the wine like to taste and drink? Does it feel good in the mouth? Is the taste simple or complex? Dull or stimulating? Does the flavor confirm what the aroma indicated? We also consider the sugar-acid balance. (A tart wine needs a bit of sweetness for balance. A sweet wine needs a degree of acidity so that it isn't cloying.)

And we consider the wine's various flavors. Simplest and most immediately appealing are the fruit flavors reflecting the grapes. Some wines actually taste grapy, while others suggest cherries, raspberries, peaches and so on. A definite grapiness indicates extreme youth, while a more vinous taste suggests the wine's greater maturity. A wine aged extensively in wood may exhibit the flavor of oak. Some wines taste of eucalyptus, mint or peppers. Others reflect the flavor of their soil—as evidenced in the earthiness of a Burgundy or the tanginess of a Chablis.

After swallowing, we pause to note the aftertaste, or how long the bouquet remains on the palate. Most desirable in a wine is a long, lingering and memorably flavored aftertaste..

NOTE: Experts generally consider red wines more significant than whites. The reds, fermented on their skins, generate more tannins and acids; acquiring at their finest a richly concentrated fruit, a fine nose, a sturdy backbone and a greater potential for aging. White wines—which as a rule require less processing—are characterized at their best by a delicate aroma and bouquet and by a pleasantly crisp acidity. However, the most notable can be as complex and nuanced as the finest reds. They include the majestic white Burgundies, the great German Rieslings, the exquisitely luscious noble rots and other rare sweet white wines.

The sequence of looking, sniffing and sipping is not fixed but can be varied in any way one wishes. After sniffing, one might reappraise the color, then spin the glass again and take another sniff. The emphasis should always be on the sensory rather than the cerebral. (Too much analysis diminishes the here-and-now pleasures of wine.) Although the tasting ritual can intensify a wine's charms, some people dispense with it entirely. As one fellow declared, "I don't care much about a wine's nose or its legs or even its full body. I just like the taste."

JUDGING A SPARKLING WINE

The key to evaluating a sparkling wine is its base wine—not its bubbles. No amount of bubbles can improve a mediocre wine. And inferior wines only worsen when made effervescent: the bubbles emphasize their flaws and make their defects more readily evident.

Sparkling wines range from light and delicate to full-bodied and strongly flavored. Some exhibit a dry elegance and finesse; others are luscious and creamy. The driest need the best base wines, since there isn't any sweetness to mask the flaws. The marks of a good Champagne are its pronounced acidity and a delicate bouquet. Red and pink sparklers are more strongly flavored and fuller-bodied by nature. For them, a delicate bouquet is less important.

After evaluating the wine's taste and aftertaste, we consider the character of its bubbles. More than a visual delight, the bubbles play a significant role in our appreciation of the wine. Quickly carrying the aroma and bouquet to the nose, the bubbles clearly reveal the flavor and enhance the desirable characteristics of the wine. We look for tiny, persistent bubbles that gently prick the tongue. They should be neither too few, making the wine flat, nor too many, making it frothy. (Bigger bubbles are not desirable, since they burst out too explosively and soon vanish.)

GOOD, GREAT AND POOR WINES

Some claim that the key to a wine's greatness is climate and weather. Others maintain that "soil speaks"—that a wine's distinctiveness comes from the soil in which its grapes are grown. Discussing the matter, one vintner said, "We seek to find harmony between the grape and its soil so we can create the best aromatic expression of the wine." Yet paradoxically, the wines that demonstrate the greatest depth and complexity are those associated with barren soils and harsh climates. A great wine is almost always made under difficult conditions. (There is an axiom in the wine business that the very best wines are made from grapes that are "stressed.") When the vine's very existence is challenged, it seems to develop a greater tenacity and stamina. The harder the vine has to struggle, the more likely it is to yield a splendid wine.

Wine quality begins with the selection of the grapes. (Mediocre grapes never make great wines.) Associated with excellent wines are the cabernet sauvignon, pinot noir, chardonnay and riesling. The wine's refinement comes from the talent, judgment and skills of the wine maker, and from his intense desire to create something that is fine and enduring.

Quintessential wines have always come from small growers, who are able to devote close personal attention to their products. They can give their wines the thought and respect they demand. They can be unstinting in their dedication to every aspect of the vinification process. The design of the winery itself is secondary. As one distinguished wine maker said, "You don't need all that fancy equipment. It just needs to be good and clean."

In a great wine, all the elements come together; all the components are in exactly the right proportions. Its color, personality and character cannot be improved upon. Great wines are also endowed with the strength for a long life. Impressive and memorable, they combine the splendid freshness of youth with the grandeur of age, displaying an extraordinary finesse, a tremendous concentration of ripe fruit, a lovely bouquet and wonderful nuances of style. Each wine is fascinating and alive, differing subtly from bottle to bottle, glass to glass, sip to sip. The flavor lingers. Such wines are meant to be savored. "So much is happening," one oenophile said, "you practically have to pick your way through."

Other wines may initially look good, smell good and taste good, yet lack an internal structure, a firmness, or texture. They don't hold our interest. Demonstrating little bouquet, breed or subtlety, they are meant for casual consumption. Then there are the wines that aren't very good to begin with. (They may have been made from immature vines or from overcropped grapes.) Excessive character may make some wines too assertive; too little character makes others dull and monotonous.

Finally, there are the outright poor, out-of-balance wines. They may be too bland or bitter; excessively earthy or musty. Too much acidity may make them thin and tart or sharp and unpalatable. Too little may make them fat and flabby. Insufficient alcohol may make them meager and watery; too much may make them hot, heavy and clumsy.

An incorrectly made wine may be cloudy and short-lived, disagreeable in taste, unpleasant in bouquet and unclean or "off" in its odor. A wine supposed to be dry may be almost sickeningly sweet. A wine ruined by a bad cork will develop a moldy smell. Wines that are overly oxidized or too long past their prime may prove to be undrinkable.

Another problem might be an overdose of sulfur dioxide. (SO_2 is widely employed as an antioxidant and as a preservative.) Used in moderation, the SO_2 imparts no smell or taste of its own. At a higher level, however, its presence may be felt as a light prickly sensation in the nose or as a dried-out and faintly pasty impression at the tip of the tongue. In excess, sulfur dioxide can overstimulate the nerve endings, anesthetizing the nose and inducing both sneezing and a scratchy throat. It can also produce an acrid metallic odor and a noticeably unpleasant taste. (Sparkling wines are particularly susceptible here since their bubbles carry the odor of the SO_2 quickly to the nose.)

PROFESSIONAL TASTING

Tasting is an essential tool for vintners, shippers, wholesalers, wine merchants, restaurateurs, and those who regulate labeling. In Bordeaux, the brokers taste the wines of their region to decide which they will buy and which they won't. They begin their tasting in the spring, before the wood extracts from the casks begin to permeate the wines.

Wine makers taste their still-fermenting wines at intervals. One, monitoring his wine's progress, said, "I taste it every fourteen days to see how the wine is coming along. I wait until the sweetness and acidity are in harmonious balance." Vintners sampling a six-week-old wine can tell if it has the staying power needed for special aging. And they taste representative samples periodically to see if the wine is receiving enough time in wood and glass.

Tasting is also an indispensable tool in blending. One Beaujolais shipper tastes hundreds of wines in order to create his own distinctive blends. Sherry makers sample and grade their wines to determine which are to be designated for special soleras and which are to go into general blends. And for the great Champagnes, one of their secrets is the selection of only the best batches for the final assemblage.

The professionals, who taste a grower's or shipper's product every day, evaluate the wine not in relation to other wines but in terms of how it measures up to its own type. They become particularly sensitive to the aromas and flavors of the wine, acquiring a built-in memory of its bouquet and body. Concentrating on a narrow range of wines, they may know little about these outside their own area of expertise. When presented in a blind tasting with a wine out of context, they may be unable to distinguish a Pomerol from a Médoc, a California wine from a French wine or even an unfamiliar red wine from a white.

WINE THIEVES AND BARREL TASTINGS

Wine thieves are devices designed to withdraw small quantities of wine from barrels, vats or tanks for sampling. The earliest device was most likely a hollow reed inserted into the bunghole of a cask. (A finger placed over the reed's upper end held the wine inside. When the finger was lifted, the wine was released.) Currently in use are siphons, pipettes and so forth. Sherry makers employ a unique wine thief, a *venencia*—a long, flexible shaft with a cup at one end. The *venenciado,* its operator, dips the cup into the cask, filling it with wine and then with a flourish, raises the shaft high in the air to pour an accurate and steady stream of wine into the several small glasses he holds in his other hand. This gives the sherry, which thrives on oxidation, a maximum exposure to air in a minimum amount of time. Barrel tastings sample the still-developing and -unfined wines, which tend to be rough and murky. One wine merchant called these tastings "a lonely dirty business," adding that "someone has to do it."

NOTE: Professional tasters spend much of their time in the semidarkness of bone-chilling cellars subject to such occupational hazards as deadened palates, swollen tongues and mouths that feel like sandpaper from the tannins they encounter.

A *venencia*

TASTING COMPETITIONS

Tasting competitions are designed to evaluate and promote certain wines. Serving as judges for them are retailers, restaurateurs, wine consultants, wine writers and so forth. The tastings are generally

292 • THE GIFT OF WINE

blind so that the wines will be judged on their own merits; pre-
conceptions tend to influence judgments. (Knowing what one is
drinking inevitably affects one's response.)

In a blind tasting, the wine's label is masked with a taped-on
paper rectangle, or the bottle is wrapped in foil. If the shape might
be a giveaway, the bottles are covered with corrugated cardboard
cylinders or with uniform bags (paper or plastic) taped shut at the
neck. A number is assigned to each bottle. If the wines are to be
poured out in advance, the glasses are numbered to correlate with
the numbers on the bottles.

Professionals wine tasters seldom swallow. They don't want
their ability to make distinctions blurred by the alcohol; they need
to retain their objectivity. Excessive intake would numb the olfactory senses and upset the brain's delicate balance. The wine's alcohol would release the mechanisms that inhibit those parts of the
brain responsible for recording new information and for exercising
judgment. (And the judges take no food during these sessions,
although wine is generally meant to accompany food.)

Professional tasting involves swirling, sipping, chewing and
spitting. After swirling the wine, the judge holds his nose four or
five inches away from the glass and inhales the fragrance at the
rim. Swirling again, he lowers his nose into the glass for a second
sniff. (He paces the sniffs about half a minute apart so as not to dull
the olfactory nerves.) Then he takes a good mouthful of wine—at
least half an ounce—and rolls it around in his mouth, swishing it
over his gums, teeth and palate, while intermittently pressing his
tongue upward against the hard palate so that he seems to be
chewing. As he balances the wine in his mouth, he sucks in a little
air through slightly pursed lips as though whistling inward; this
aeration releases the wine's flavor further. As the warmth of his
mouth brings out the aromas and volatile compounds, the taster
intensifies the experience by breathing down his nose. Enabling
the vapors to pass through his olfactory bulb once more, he
extends the moment when the wine, air, nose and palate all come
together.

Tasting competitions usually involve large numbers of wines,
which are generally divided into more manageable groups of ten
or so. The judges first evaluate the wines for their overall quality,

rarely needing to sample them all since they can eliminate those inadequate in bouquet and aroma simply by sniffing. Then they rate the remaining wines according to their strengths and weaknesses.

A wine judging is at best an inexact exercise—a series of essentially fleeting impressions. The individual responses are always subjective and highly ephemeral. Asked to taste the same group of wines two weeks apart, even professionals may contradict themselves. Moreover, individual judges differ in their approaches, temperaments and perceptions. They also vary in their thresholds of sensitivity and in their ability to taste the wine's various compounds. Some judges are more sensitive than others as to how a wine opens in the glass; they are more receptive to its subtlety and additional nuances. A wine that seems dry to one may appear sweet to another. One judge may find the acids crisp and delicious while another considers them sour and painful. One may find the tannins obnoxious, while another sees them as important and profound. One might find high levels of alcohol to be rich and lush while another considers the wine harsh and out of balance. In sampling the same wine, one taster said it had "heavy, meaty, earthy flavors"; another called it "superbly elegant."

NOTE: In reviewing a Napa Valley Chardonnay, one wine publication called it "smooth, concentrated and well-behaved ... [with] deep fruit flavors and a sense of intensity"; another review described the wine as "bitterly acid, austere and lean ... [with] no character and no soul."

Judges have good and bad days. Influencing their responses is the time of day, their physical condition and what they had eaten or drunk earlier. Although they taste only tiny quantities of wine and seldom swallow, they are nevertheless susceptible to sensory overload, and palate fatigue will affect their judgment. A judge can effectively deal with only a limited number of wines. (Two or three hours of concentrated tasting will numb even the best of palates.) Yet experts are often called on to sample more than a hundred wines in four hours with only brief intervals of rest. (They may be able to eliminate about half of them by smell alone.)

In tasting competitions, wines with lush, rich, fruity qualities and an intensity of alcohol often push the more elegant and subdued examples into the background. The winners are not necessarily desirable for drinking, however, nor do they always go well with food. As one observer noted, "Too much wine these days is being made to be tasted and not drunk."

A blind tasting is required as part of an examination given annually by the Company of Vintners, a London guild. The examination—which lasts four days—includes written tests, essays and an oral examination on enology, viticulture, marketing and retailing. (Candidates must have five years of experience in working with wines and spirits.) For the tasting, each candidate is presented with a group of wines—three reds, two whites and a rosé—arranged in pairs. He is informed that one wine from each pair is from a known French district while the other is not French. After identifying the French wine and its district, he must accurately describe its quality, area of production, vintage, state of maturity and the grape variety or varieties in its blend. For each non-French wine, the candidate must name its country of origin. Those who pass this demanding examination are awarded a "Master of Wine" certificate.

PLANNING A TASTING

Group tastings are a good way to learn about grapes, vintages and wine-producing countries. They permit many wines to be sampled in a short period of time. There is much to be learned at a tasting. When one considers a number of wines side by side, not only do their obvious similarities and differences become apparent, but their more subtle distinctions are revealed as well.

A tasting can be held to instruct or entertain. (The first doesn't involve swallowing; the second does.) To keep matters manageable, the number of participants should be limited to six or eight. To prevent sensory overload, the number of wines should be limited to five or six. The wines themselves may be red or white, sparkling or fortified. They should be in the same category or of equal quality since there isn't much point in comparing a Burgundy with a Mosel or a port with a Bordeaux wine.

The tasting should be held after a stretch without food to keep the nose and taste buds undistracted by other tastes and smells. And avoided beforehand should be anything that might inhibit the ability to taste—such as acidy juices or highly seasoned or palate-numbing foods. To be avoided as well is anything that might detract from or interfere with the wine's bouquet, aroma and flavor. Included here are cooking odors, the smell of flowers, heavy perfumes, colognes, aftershave lotions, cigars, cigarettes, pipes and so forth. (Serious tasters have been known to sniff the inside of the wine glass before the wine is poured to detect lingering detergent odor, if any.

NOTE: To eliminate as many distractions as possible, participants at a serious wine tasting say little and speak only in moderate tones. To eliminate the power of suggestion, they avoid frowning, smiling, or engaging in similar responses until all the wines have been sampled.

A tasting generally lasts two or three hours. Professional tasters find midmornings, about 10 A.M. best; the palate is at its freshest then. Social tastings can be scheduled as lengthened cocktail hours running from 5:30 to 7:30 in the evening, or as afterdinner events. The earlier tasting might be preceded by a bowl of bland soup with some plain crackers so as not to startle the empty stomach with a succession of wines. Accompanying the tasting itself neutral breads or crackers and palate-cleansing bland cheeses—such as a Gruyère or mild Cheddar—that leave no significant aftertaste. Since the earlier participants will have gone for some time without substantial food, an assortment of hors d'oeuvres, pâtés, cheeses, and nuts can be served afterward. Sessions held later in the evening might be followed by tea or coffee along with a good, rich cake.

The bottles for the tasting should all be uncorked at the same time. (The most practical method for distributing the wines is to let each guest pour his or her own.) The wines should be set out in the sequence in which they will be tasted: white wines preceding the reds, dry wines before the sweet and light-bodied before heavier bodied. The position of each wine is important, since one set of impressions can distort the next. A hard wine can make the one that follows seem softer than it is. A concentrated wine can not only overshadow a more delicate one but also dull the palate. Younger wines should generally be tasted before older ones. (The

assertive nature and stronger taste of a younger wine can overwhelm an older, smoother counterpart.) When the wines are of the
same age, the least expensive should be tasted first. Yet there can
be exceptions: an elegant wine is more likely to create a good
impression if sampled earlier.

The wine tasting may be horizontal (comparing a number of
wines from the same year) or vertical (sampling the same wine
from a number of years—that is, comparing recent vintages with
older ones). When wines from different countries are to be tasted,
it's better as a rule to concentrate on those pressed from one
grape, in order to detect more readily the variations produced by
climate, soil and style of vinification. In any case, the wine tasting
should always have a unifying theme to give it focus.

SOME THEME POSSIBILITIES

1. Compare red or white table wines from several countries made from the same grape and within the same price range, such as Cabernet Sauvignons from California, Romania, Israel and Australia, or Rieslings from Germany, Alsace, Chile and New York State.
2. Compare a group of white wines from a single country, such as Italy (Orvieto, Soave, Verdicchio, Frascati, Lacryma Christi) or France (an Alsatian Sylvaner, a Muscadet, a Pouilly-Fumé, a white Bordeaux). Or compare a group of red wines from Italy (Valpolicella, Barbera, Barolo, Chianti and so on).
3. Compare several wines from one geographic region, such as the Chiantis of Tuscany, the Riojas of Spain, the Zinfandels of Northern California or the Rieslings of the Rheingau.
4. Compare three or four white or red French Burgundies from the same vintage but from different communes.
5. Compare a group of red California varietals, such as Zinfandels, Pinot Noirs or Cabernet Sauvignons, made by different producers. Or similarly compare a group of California white varietals, such as Chenin Blancs, Sauvignon Blancs, Chardonnays or Johannisberg Rieslings.
6. Compare three of New York's red or white varietals with three of its red or white generics.
7. Compare three or four California sparkling wines with three or four French Champagnes.
8. Compare several vintage Champagnes, made by different producers, with several nonvintage Champagnes.
9. Compare a group of white wines representing different German regions (Rhine, Mosel, Nahe and so forth).
10. Compare the Bordeaux wines of one region, such as the Médoc, with those of another, such as St-Estèphe, Pauillac, St-Julien or Margaux.
11. Compare a varietal, such as a Cabernet Sauvignon,

from different Northern California counties (Napa, Sonoma, Mendocino, and Santa Clara).

12. Compare the wines of a single vintage from several vineyards in a major Bordeaux commune, such as St-Émilion, Pomerol, Graves, St.-Julien, St-Estèphe, or Pauillac.

13. Compare three Auslese wines from the same vineyard region in Germany, but from three different growers.

14. Compare two or three white Burgundies from the same vintage and the same vineyard or commune, but produced by different shippers.

RATING SYSTEMS

Various rating systems have been devised to tabulate the judgments of the eye, the nose and the palate. Listed on a tally sheet, these ratings assign a specific number of points to each characteristic. The sheet may also permit a descriptive word or two, since jotting down any special impressions can heighten one's perceptions and make the responses to the wines more precise. The systems are based on either a 10-point or a 20-point scale; the latter allowing for more nuances in the distinctions that are made.

A 10-point scale assigns one point to each of the following wine characteristics: appearance, color, aroma, volatile acidity, total acid, sugar-acid balance, body, flavor, bitterness and general impression. A 20-point tally gives up to 2 points for color, 2 for appearance, 6 for olfactory characteristics (aroma and bouquet), 2 for flavor, 5 for gustatory characteristics (sweetness, bitterness, acidity), 2 for overall quality and 1 for "feel" or texture. A wine scoring 9 to 12 points here is considered acceptable, 13 to 16 average, and 17 to 20 outstanding. Another 20-point system gives up to 5 points for flavor, 4 for bouquet, 4 for general quality, 3 for balance, 2 for clarity, and 2 for acidity.

One specific 20-point scorecard reads:

> **APPEARANCE:** Brilliant—2, Clear—1, Cloudy—0.
> **COLOR:** Correct—2, Somewhat off—1, Distinctly off—0.
> **AROMA and BOUQUET:** Varietal—3, Distinct but not

varietal—2, Vinous—1. (One can add 1 point for bottle bouquet and subtract 2 points for any odd or off-odors.)

SWEETNESS: Normal for wine type—1, Too much or too little—0.

TOTAL ACIDITY: Normal for wine type—2, Somewhat high or low—1, Too high or low—0.

FLAVOR: Desirable for wine type—2, Deficient or slightly off—1, Distinctly off—0.

ASTRINGENCY and BITTERNESS: Normal—2, Slightly high—1, Distinctly high—0.

BODY: Normal for wine type—1, Too much or too little—0.

TEXTURE: Satisfactory—1, Unsatisfactory—0.

OVERALL QUALITY: Impressive—2, Slight—1, Undistinguished—0.

NOTE: Although these various systems seem to suggest that wine quality is precisely identifiable, the conversion of sensuous experience into quantifiable data is more of a personal response than a scientific one.

Since the primary function of a tasting is to decide which wines are liked most and which are liked least, the group may be polled by a show of hands to find out which wines were the favorites and which were the least preferred. Or the participants might vote for their favorites in order of preference: 3 points for first place, 2 for second, and 1 for third. At a blind tasting, the voting should be done when all the wines have been sampled, but not yet identified. The coverings of the bottles are then removed to reveal the labels, and a list of the wines, keyed to the numbers on the bottles, is distributed to the participants.

INGREDIENTS AND SUPPLIES FOR A WINE TASTING

1. The wines to be sampled.
2. A good-sized table or a series of smaller tables to hold the bottles.
3. White cloths to cover the tables.
4. One or more reliable corkscrews.

5. Stemmed wineglasses.
6. Glasses and pitchers of drinking water, or bottles of mineral water, to clear the palate between sips and to relieve palate fatigue.
7. Pitchers of water to rinse out the glasses and a large bucket for discarding the rinse water.
8. Paper napkins for drying the rinsed glasses and a trash basket for discarding them. (The supply of paper napkins should be ample, in case of spills.)
9. A spittoon bucket if the wine is not to be swallowed.
10. Neutral bread, bread sticks, melba toast or water crackers.
11. A bland cheese. (If it is not presliced or diced, knives and cutting boards should be provided.)
12. Bland soup to serve with crackers before the tasting for early sessions and/or hors d'oeuvres, coffee and cake to serve afterward for later sessions.
13. Pencils and tally sheets or small pads of paper for note-taking, to be distributed before the tasting begins.
14. A list of the wines presented, to be distributed after they have been rated. The list should provide such pertinent details as the wine's full name, its producer, shipper, vintage year, shop where purchased, and the amount paid.

NOTE: For a blind tasting, the supplies will also include paper rectangles to mask the labels, or aluminum foil, and corrugated cardboard cylinders or uniform bags, to cover the bottles. Also needed are tape to fasten the coverings in place and felt-tipped pens for numbering the bottles.

To determine the amount of wine needed for the tasting, count on each bottle to provide six to twelve samples, depending on the wine and whether or not it's to be swallowed. (An ounce of wine is just enough for a few swallows, although 2 ounces may be better.) Some suggest allowing about half a bottle per person of all the wines combined. Others say plan on a whole bottle for each eight to ten participants. (It has been noted that twelve sips can add up to a respectable glass of wine.)

Glass stemware is best for tastings. (It can be borrowed, rented or bought.) Provide a glass for each participant or separate glasses for sampling red and white wines. (The goblets can be labeled with the guests' names at the base to avoid any confusion.) The glasses should be uniform in size and shape so as not to introduce extraneous elements into the comparisons. If they do vary in size, the larger glasses can be used for red wines, and the smaller ones for white wines.

To defray the cost of the tasting, a BYOB (Bring Your Own Bottle) event can be organized. Here, the host or hostess sets the theme and asks each participant to bring one or two bottles representing a given country, vintage, or price range. (To avoid duplication, a list is made of the individuals who will be responsible for each wine.) The participants must then deliver the bottles sufficiently in advance so the red wines can settle down and the whites can be properly chilled.

In a BYOB variation, each participant contributes to a dinner by preparing a dish and providing the accompanying wine. To round out the meal, the host or hostess provides a dessert wine or perhaps a bottle of Vintage Port. To avoid duplication and to ensure variety, the details of the menu should be worked out well in advance.

NOTE: People have also organized themselves into wine-tasting clubs that meet regularly at one another's homes on a rotating basis, either once a month or once every other month.

THE DEVELOPMENT OF TASTE

Wine has inspired a wide range of personal preferences. Some people like their wines red, others white; some dry, others sweet. Some prefer them assertive, others like them milder.

Habit and culture play their part in the establishment of personal preferences. The Spaniards, who take their sherries with food, like them light and dry. (Their sweet sherries are meant mainly for export; brown and cream sherries were specifically created for the Anglo-Saxon market.) The Spanish say, "We ship them sweet but drink them dry." On the other hand, the Italians vinify their Orvietos dry for export but take them semisweet at home. And the French drink the luscious Beaumes-de-Venise as an apéritif while other nationalities consider the wine more suitable as an after-dinner drink.

The development of individual tastes is an evolutionary process. Fine wines are subtle and demanding; they take time to appreciate. The beginner needs to work his way up to them gradually. At first he wants his wines immediately accessible, preferring his reds robust, full-bodied and slightly sweet, and his whites and rosés fruity. As his palate develops, he becomes more accustomed to the idea of complexity. He begins to find that a degree of dryness is necessary and desirable. As he moves on from the simpler to the more intricate, he comes to appreciate the tartness and moderate bitterness produced by the wine's tannins and other compounds.

Yet a wine needn't always be dry to be good. Sweetness in a wine is considered a valuable asset in France and Germany. The Germans base their quality ratings on the grape-sugar levels; the sweeter the wine, the more expensive it will be. And among the most expensive French wines are the sweet, luscious noble rots.

There are also different kinds of sweetness. Harvesting some grapes late concentrates their sugars and results in richer-tasting wines. And the extraordinary botrytized wines, produced in a number of countries, are notable for the intriguing interplay of their intense sweetness and their balancing acidity. Lesser wines however may be sweetened artificially and can create a sticky, unpleasant feeling in the mouth.

NOTE: What is perceived as sweet can differ from what is actually sweet. A wine with 1.5 percent residual sugar may not seem sweet at all if its acidity balances out its grape sugars.

American tastes can be contradictory. People talk dry but often drink sweet. Accustomed to the taste of soda pop, they seem to prefer a degree of sweetness in their wines. (The most popular wines in the United States all contain some residual sugar.) Yet at the same time, many Americans turn away from openly sweet wines, equating sweetness with self-indulgence and a lack of personal character. To accommodate them, French vintners have begun to reduce the sugars in some of their wines. They have picked their grapes prematurely in Entre-Deux-Mers, Monbazillac and Jurançon to make the wines lighter and crisper. The Germans, also wishing to appeal to the large American market, have vinified some of their wines *trocken* (dry) or *halb-trocken* (half-dry), fermenting out all the sugar in the former and leaving behind an almost imperceptible degree of sweetness in the latter.

In the United States, red wines were more popular than whites before the 1980s. Since then, a preoccupation with fitness and health has stimulated an interest in lighter beverages, leading to an increased emphasis on white wines. Various countries, wishing to take advantage of the trend, have increased their white-wine production in areas normally known for red wines. Recent reports, however, citing the benefits of red wine on the heart and on general health, are reversing this trend.

Because white wines appear to be lighter than the reds, they seem to be less fattening. However a wine's calories come primarily from its alcohol, not from its pigmentation so that a white wine can in fact be more fattening than a red. To establish the calorie count, the alcohol content is multiplied by 2. Since 0.5 percent alcohol represents 1 calorie, an ounce of table wine with 12.5 percent alcohol contains 25 calories; a $3^1/_2$-ounce glass adds up to about 80 calories. Fortified wines, which are higher in their alcohol, average 44 to 55 calories an ounce, but are generally consumed in smaller quantities. Depending on the fortified wine, a 3-ounce serving can range from 120 to 170 calories.

NOTE: Lighter-calorie wines have been developed for the diet-conscious. Their grapes are either harvested early, while the sugars remain low, or are allowed to ripen fully. Some of the alcohol is then processed out of the wine. In either case, the wine's character and flavor are compromised. (Wine enthusiasts who wish to reduce their caloric intake would do better to eliminate any extra fats, sugars and starches from their diets.)

10

MATCHING WINE
WITH FOOD

GENERAL
CONSIDERATIONS

Wine and food are a great combination, with each bringing out the best in the other. There are, however, certain requirements in matching the two. Their relationship should be balanced: they should complement, not compete, with one another. A key to their compatibility is the character of the wine, not its color. While conventional wisdom calls for pairing white wines with white meat, fish, and poultry, and red wines with beef and lamb, this approach is too rigid; it narrows the options too much.

The primary requirement in matching food and wine is common sense. Dry wines are generally more appropriate with meals since their higher acidity will stimulate the palate and cleanse it between bites. Sweet wines, on the other hand will appease the appetite and are usually best served with desserts or else on their own. Lighter wines are best served at the beginning of the meal; heavier ones at the end. Light wines call for light dishes; delicately styled wines for delicately flavored ones. Full-bodied wines can hold their own with assertively flavored foods; they are able to cut across the richness of robust dishes. The heavier the dish, the heavier the appropriate wine.

NOTE: A delicately nuanced light red wine would be overwhelmed by a platter of barbecued ribs but can nicely accompany lobster. A light white wine, fine for a mild-flavored fish, would be wiped out by a dark pungent pot roast, but a sturdy full-bodied white can be paired with game birds and even steak.

Areas producing primarily red wines serve them not only with rich meats, game and sausage, but also with fish and seafood. Regions known mainly for their white wines often match them up with heartier meat and game dishes. The residents of the Rhône Valley pair their robust full-flavored whites with full-bodied spicy dishes and pungent cheeses. In Burgundy, a rich Meursault has been served with beef. The Germans take their white wines with lamb chops, bacon, ham and sausage. In Alsace, where white wine also predominates, full-bodied Gewürztraminers have accompanied strong savory dishes of ham and roast goose. In Reims and Épernay, it is not unusual for Champagne to be served with every course.

The Corsicans take rosés with their highly seasoned fish dishes. In Bordeaux, where red wine is king, people often drink it with fish-based meals. The French use red wines in sauces for salmon, tuna and halibut; in St-Émilion, a robust red is a key component in a typical sturgeon dish. On the Spanish coast, red wines are taken with fish and shellfish, while in Portugal, robust red wines are paired with sturdy sardines.

Regional dishes have been developed with local wines in mind. A Sancerre innkeeper says, "We make very light sauces for our meat and fish dishes so that our light local wines go with everything." In Greece, the piquancy of the retsinas makes them the perfect foil for the richness and spiciness of the food. In Spain, the brisk light nutty flavor of a fino sherry combines well with a range of tapas and other local specialties. Mediterranean dishes, characteristically featuring garlic, herbs and olive oil, are well suited to the wines of southern Italy, France and Spain.

Consideration in the pairing can focus on the key ingredient of the dish or its sauce, marinade, stuffing, etc. A chicken prepared with mushrooms can be matched with an earthy Pinot Noir; a chicken prepared with dill can take an herbal Sauvignon Blanc. Delicate sauces require light-bodied low-alcohol wines, while richer sauces need more assertive ones. The intense, spicy brown sauce of a robust dish, for example, requires a wine with more body. A highly acid tomato sauce calls for a wine relatively high in acid. A heavy cream sauce needs a dry, high-alcohol wine, whereas a slightly sweet sauce (made from meat stock or a reduction of butter and cream) does best with a wine that isn't austerely dry.

NOTE: Dishes cooked with wine should be accompanied by a wine of a similar style: a red Burgundy served with boeuf bourguignon, a Madeira with a sauce madère, and a red Bordeaux or other Cabernet Sauvignon with dishes featuring a bordelaise sauce.

Other considerations are the cooking method used, the time of the year and the character of the meal. With steamed foods, lighter wines are served; with grilled or barbecued foods, fuller wines. Summer's characteristically lighter foods can be accompanied by tart white wines or rosés. For bigger and richer winter meals, heartier red wines are often the best choice. More splendid and complex wines are required for formal occasions, while simple ingenuous wines are most suitable for picnics and casual get-togethers.

Red wines range from light and fruity to medium, and on to full-bodied, strong, robust and assertive. The lighter-bodied reds, minimal in their tannins, go best with blander meats such as pork and veal. Medium-bodied, more elegant reds are suitable for most meat dishes and can also accompany sauced poultry, rich vegetable dishes and fresh cheeses. Moderate to robust reds go well with beef or lamb and are suited to duck and goose, casseroles, ragouts and cassoulets as well. Rich concentrated reds need substantial foods—such as steaks, roasts and game—to complement their assertiveness.

White wines can be simple, light and refreshing or big, robust and powerful. They range from the dry and delicate or crisp and tart to the medium-dry with moderate acidity, on to the sweet and full-bodied. Light dry white wines with delicate flavors can be enjoyed on their own as apéritifs or as sipping wines. When crisp and pleasantly acid, they go well with light fish preparations, light pastas and other light foods. Fruity white wines with more body are meant for richer pastas, sauced or grilled fish and for simply seasoned poultry. Those with good acidity can freshen the flavors of pork or veal. Although most whites tend to lose their charms when paired with robust foods, the wines with a fair amount of body and a more pronounced character can stand up to and enhance fairly heavy dishes or highly seasoned ones.

Fruitier, sweeter white wines have proven compatible with highly seasoned or spicy foods. (Such foods would destroy the delicate nuances of a dry subtle white wine.) Best for spicy Mexican and Indian dishes, and for the slight sweetness of certain Chinese and Thai dishes, are off-dry whites such as Rieslings, Gewürz-traminers and Chenin Blancs. Fino sherries also go well with spicy foods.

As a rule, sweet luscious whites—the Sauternes, late-harvest German and California Rieslings and Italian vin santos—are best served with desserts or on their own. Yet the balancing acidity of the sweet noble rots makes them more versatile than one might expect. They can also go well with foods that complement their sweetness, such as a pâté de foie gras, served at the start of the meal.

When all is said and done, the best wine to accompany a meal is the wine you feel like drinking. The object is to enjoy the meal, to drink what you like with the food you like. Only through experience—only through simple trial and error—is it possible to discover which combinations will work best for you.

THE ALL-PURPOSE WINE

Although rosés and sparkling wines have been called "all-purpose," they are not flexible enough to be served throughout a meal. Rosés, often the choice of those reluctant to decide between a white wine and a red, are more of a compromise than a solution. Their lighter-colored, lighter-bodied examples can be taken with hors d'oeuvres, fish dishes and lightly flavored foods. But the darker, fruitier, heavier-bodied rosés that go well with lighter meats don't do much for the heavier ones.

And while the crisp clean dryness of a brut Champagne goes well with canapés and brings out the brininess of oysters, it is generally too acid for most dishes and hardly suitable for roasts or game. While a medium-dry sparkler with a fresh lively taste and crisp fruit can complement fish and shellfish—as well as ham, turkey, lamb, duck and chicken dishes with rich but delicate sauces—it doesn't work well with meat dishes of greater richness and gravity. Those dishes call for fuller-bodied Champagnes with big weighty flavors, such as a Blanc de Noirs. Most appropriate with light desserts and delicate cheeses are the smooth, aromatic, extradry Champagnes demonstrating a degree of sweetness. As for the sparkling rosés or pink Champagnes, the more substantial among them can be paired with heavier dishes such as a rack of lamb, while the lighter examples are best served at the end of the meal since they're particularly amenable to fresh fruit and light creamy cheeses.

WINE AND FOOD

BEFORE THE MEAL

There are two schools of thought on serving spirits before a meal that will feature wine. One school maintains that a cocktail before dinner will give the guests a lift and make them more receptive to one another and to the food and wine that follow. (Cocktails laden with fruit and sugar however can take away the desire for food and make a dry wine taken afterward taste harsh and bitter.)

The other school holds that grape juice and malt spirits are incompatible; that hard liquor will numb the palate and dull the senses, impeding a wine's appreciation. As a famous French restaurateur once noted, "After a cocktail or two, one couldn't possibly tell a great Bordeaux from a bottle of red ink."

A more appropriate introduction might be a well-chilled, low-alcohol table wine (dry or medium-dry); a dry sparkling wine; or a crisp fortified wine with a lively assertiveness, such as a vermouth or a fino sherry. Priming the palate, these will prepare it for the foods to come. Other possibilities are not-too-sweet rosés, or appetite-whetting wine-based apéritifs that are characterized by a certain tanginess.

WITH HORS D'OEUVRES

Desirable accompaniments for hors d'oeuvres are wines that enhance the appetite. Always appropriate are light-bodied, crisp and dry but not fruity Champagnes and other sparklers. These wines can complement the savory appetizers without overshadowing them. Their fresh acidity goes particularly well with the smoky, salty foods served before dinner, nicely setting off the richness of caviar, for example. Also appropriate are dry white wines, characterized by a crisp acidity, a steely quality or a bone-dry tang.

The nature of the hors d'oeuvres will determine the most suitable wine. Raw vegetables can take a light white wine—a Chenin Blanc or a Pinot Grigio. Light canapés such as cheese puffs or quail's eggs go well with a crisp light white wine. Fish-based appetizers generally call for crisp fruity, dry whites, while meat-based appetizers go well with light reds such as a dryish or a moderately sweet rosé. Harmonizing with stuffed mushrooms, salami, salted almonds and ripe olives are the dry fortified Madeiras and vermouths. A fino or amontillado sherry goes well with Spanish tapas, featuring tidbits of sausage, ham, prawns and mussels along with olives; while an oloroso is formidable with more aggressively flavored tapas such as smoked squid.

WITH THE FIRST COURSE

Suitable for oysters on the half-shell, for countering their salinity and rounding out their acidity, are full but dry table wines. The stony flavor and flinty bite of a fine Chablis, for example, provides a wonderful contrast to the brininess of the oysters. Other good raw shellfish accompaniments are a brut Champagne, a musky Muscadet, a St-Véran, a crisp white Graves; a Sauvignon Blanc, Sémillon, Aligoté or Pinot Gris. Refreshing with steamed mussels or clams are Portuguese vinho verdes, Italian Vernaccias and manzanilla sherries. Paired with smoked salmon may be a dry white, a light red or a dry sherry, Madeira or Marsala. (Some people prefer a rich Sauternes with their smoked salmon.)

Suitable for the rich pâtés that precede the main course are dry-to-fullish white wines, moderate in their acidity. Good with duck and rabbit pâtés are dry white Swiss wines; suitable as well are light-bodied reds and rosés. Pâtés also respond to the intensity of an older, sweeter German Riesling—a Spätlese or an Auslese. Providing the necessary counterpoint to a foie gras is a sweet

Beaumes-de-Venise. Some maintain that the only way to moderate a pâté's excesses is with the intense sweetness of a luscious Sauternes.

WITH SOUP

Soups, which range from light broths to almost-stews, can be accompanied by a variety of wines. For consommés and most clear light soups, a wonderful partner is a medium-dry Champagne. Appropriate too are dryish fortified wines, such as a fino or amontillado sherry or a Sercial Madeira, that are served at cool cellar temperatures. A light white wine can accompany a pumpkin soup; a medium-dry white can be matched up with a rich oyster-spinach broth. A medium sherry or a tawny port is fine with onion soup. The wine for a rich *bouillabaisse* (fisherman's stew) might be a weighty white, a light to medium red or a dry rosé. Other fish-soup possibilities are fortified fino or amontillado sherries and Verdelho Madeiras. Paired with a lobster consommé or a cream-based soup might be a not-too-dry sparkler or a medium-bodied white such as a Chardonnay. Appropriate with thick, hearty soups can be a Pinot Noir or other dry red wine.

WITH FISH AND SEAFOOD

Fish dishes generally need a wine with some acidity to cut through their oiliness. White wines—which tend to be more acidic than the reds—have a special affinity for seafood. Most suitable are the crisp, clean and tangy or somewhat flinty whites with a degree of fruitiness. Other good accompaniments are light- or medium-bodied sparkling wines and dry fino and manzanilla sherries. (A fino served ice cold can add a bracing bite to the fish's flavor.) Although strongly tannic red wines and rosés clash with fish and seafood, fruity reds can accompany their strongly flavored dishes.

Depending on the specific character of the fish and how it is prepared, the accompanying wines might be light and delicate or full-bodied and vigorous. For light and simply broiled, or grilled, baked or steamed fish, the wine might be a crisp dry Aligoté, a Sauvignon Blanc, Chardonnay, Riesling, Chenin Blanc, a

Swiss Chasselas, Seyval Blanc, vinho verde, or a Muscadet. Or the wine might be a Verdicchio, Sancerre, Chablis, Champagne, Pouilly-Fuissé, or German Spätlese. Big-flavored saltwater fish—salmon, swordfish, halibut, monkfish and bluefish—require flavorful wines that are on the mellow but not on the sweet side. These include fruity young reds such as a light Pinot Noir, Sangiovese, or a Beaujolais-Villages and sturdy whites such as a Chablis or a Pinot Gris. Rich seafood dishes with thick sauces and more complex seafood stews need assertive wines that exhibit a fair amount of fruit and body. A fish in cream sauce can find a perfect partner in a high-alcohol Chardonnay with plenty of body and flavor. A grilled salmon in a béarnaise sauce can be paired with a big-bodied white wine or a lighter red from the Rhône.

For oyster and shellfish dishes, a fine accompaniment might be a Sauvignon Blanc, Sémillon or Pinot Gris; a Chablis, Sancerre or white Graves. Mussels, clams and shrimp can take a Muscadet, an Aligoté or a Verdicchio. Grilled shrimp and vegetables go well with a Greek retsina or an Italian Soave. Suitable for shellfish in tomato-based sauces are red wines and rosés. Needed to bring out the rich, subtle sweetness and buttery flavor of lobster are high-acid, full-bodied wines. These might be a California Chardonnay, a German Riesling, a Gavi dei Gavi from the Piedmont, a Chablis or other fine white Burgundy or a light red wine with some degree of substance.

WITH PASTA

Determining a suitable wine for a pasta are the components of the dish and the seasonings in its sauce. Appropriate wines here range from medium-dry whites to lighter and fuller reds, and might even include medium-bodied sparklers. Seafood pastas and those topped with light cream or cheese sauces can take dry to medium-dry white wines and medium- to full-bodied reds. For linguine with a tomato-based seafood sauce, a Lacryma Christi can provide a fine combination of dryness and acidity. For savory pastas topped with rich, pungently flavored meat sauces, a robust assertive red—such as a Chianti Classico or a Barbera—is needed.

WITH POULTRY

Grilled or roast chicken can take anything from a crisp dry white, to a light red or a sturdy rosé, on to a fuller, moderately luscious even robust red. Other good companions are white wines with smoky flinty flavors, such as a Pouilly-Fumé from the Loire, a white Burgundy, a lean American Chardonnay or a German Riesling. Roast poultry with a fairly simple stuffing calls for a light red wine, while a bird with a richer stuffing requires a weightier red. The wine for poultry prepared with a cream or a fruit sauce can be a full white such as a gently fruited Vouvray or a Chenin Blanc. Poultry with a tomato or a spicy brown sauce might be accompanied by a fruity young red such as a Beaujolais. Cornish game hens can be paired with a Riesling, a Chardonnay or a Pinot Noir, among others.

Suitable for fuller-flavored, more pungent poultry—turkeys, game birds, ducks and geese—are red or white wines exhibiting good body, a pronounced taste and a complex personality. Turkey can be accompanied by a medium-rich to fullish white with good fruit and low acidity, such as a California Chardonnay, an Alsatian Riesling, Pouilly-Fumé, white Rhône or white Burgundy. To complement turkey with a rich spicy stuffing, the wine might be a robust flavorful red from the Rhône, Beaujolais or Provence; an intense French Bordeaux or other Cabernet Sauvignon; a Spanish Rioja; or an American Zinfandel. Another wine of choice here might also be an earthy Burgundy, an Oregon Pinot Noir, a dark muscular Barolo, a fino or a medium-dry amontillado sherry.

Duck can be partnered with either a red or a white wine that is intense and fruity enough to cut through its richness, such as a medium-bodied, dry tannic red or a fruity and flowery white. Well suited to duck prepared with oranges or cherries are such red wines as a California Merlot, a Bordeaux or a Rioja. Appropriate whites with duck are German Spätleses or even a luscious Sauternes or a vin jaune. Admirably holding their own with assertive dishes such as turkey and game birds are German wines of appreciable sweetness; the more concentrated examples can harmonize beautifully with the full flavors of roast goose as well. Roast goose can also be matched with a gutsy red wine such as a Châteauneuf-du-Pape, St-Émilion or Pomerol, a Côte de Nuits Burgundy, a Chianti or a Barolo. Lightly smoked goose breast might be paired with a Muscat Beaumes-de-Venise. Right for roast goose with an apple-sausage stuffing is an Alsatian Pinot Gris or an Alsatian Tokay. The richness of squab calls for a mellow Riesling, a Chardonnay or a Barolo. For richer-tasting game birds (pheasant, partridge, grouse, guinea hen, quail and wild duck), more assertive and robust red wines are generally best, among them are the big Burgundies, Amarones and Zinfandels.

WITH MEAT

The lighter, fairly delicate meats such as veal and pork can be paired with wines that are neither too acidy nor overly sweet, be they red, white or rosé. Depending on the meat's preparation, the wines may be light or medium-bodied, semidry or moderately luscious. (For highly or richly seasoned meat dishes, the accompaniments can be full-bodied reds.) Some people prefer a medium-bodied sparkler, to let the taste of the veal and pork come through.

For veal in a light cream sauce, the wine might be a fresh Swiss white and for veal in a spicy brown or tomato sauce, a fruity young red such as a Merlot. Richly roasted or braised veal calls for a more concentrated red such as a Rioja, a Cabernet Sauvignon, or a Pinot Noir, while a veal cutlet Milanese can be paired with a Chianti Classico. Osso buco needs a full-flavored red wine with the body to match the weight of the meat and the acidity to cut through its richness.

Fresh ham, pork chops, pork loins and simple pork roasts go well with fruity young red wines or with deep-bodied, not-too-dry whites. The red wine might be a Bandol from Provence or a Beaujolais; the white, a Swiss or a German wine. Wines of bright acidity, such as rosés and light reds, are needed to balance out the saltiness of smoked hams. Glazed hams can take sweeter white wines, such as German Spätleses, or rosé wines. Paired with smoked pork chops might be a drier Gewürztraminer.

An old adage recommends claret with lamb. Yet lamb can be accompanied by a white as well as a red wine. Tender young lamb is best with a medium-bodied red or a richer white; more pun-gently flavored older lamb calls for more mature and complex reds. Suitable for grilled lamb chops, crown roast, rack of lamb or leg of lamb are medium- to full-bodied reds with substantial alcohol. They include a Médoc or Pomerol, Fitou, Hermitage, Rioja, or Barolo; a Cabernet Sauvignon, Merlot or Pinot Noir. Roast rack of lamb tarragon might be served with a white Fumé Blanc or a red Côtes du Rhône. Lamb stews do well with fresh lively red wines such as Italian Dolcettos. A roast leg of lamb can be paired with a dry, light or medium-light sherry.

Beef dishes—steak tartare, baby ribs, and calf's liver—call for medium-bodied reds and rosés. Appropriate with beef stew might be a red Rioja, a Bandol rouge, a full-bodied Italian Dolcetto or a California Zinfandel. Heavier red meats—steaks, chops, prime ribs, or roast beef—require fuller-bodied, robust reds with enough tannin to hold their own. Suitable for grilled steaks are good earthy Burgundies, forceful Bordeaux, Portuguese Dãos or solid northern Italian reds. Matching the robustness of roast beef might be an Amarone, Rubesco, Hermitage, a Cahors or a Pinot Noir. Although an entrecôte of beef is usually paired with a red wine, it has on occasion been served with a luscious Sauternes. Beef stew can take a Zinfandel, a Beaujolais or a Côtes du Rhône. Recommended for stews, roasts and other hearty fare are sturdy Portuguese table wines from the Douro. And served with pot roast might be a full-bodied Zinfandel or a Petite Sirah from California, a French Châteauneuf-du-Pape or an Italian Barolo.

Heavy, dark game meats such as venison and boar, which are pronounced in taste, robust in texture and powerful in intensity, demand complex red table wines. These might be rich Riojas, Rubescos, Amarones, full-bodied Rhône reds (Hermitage, Châteauneuf-du-Pape), Barolos, Petite Sirahs, or certain Zinfandels. The perfect match for some game dishes, depending on their sauces and seasonings, might be a full-bodied Riesling—a Spätlese or an Auslese—or a late-harvest Pinot Gris from Alsace.

With Salads

Traditional wine-oriented meals rarely include a salad course. (When salad is served at formal dinners, it is often accompanied by a glass of water.) The vinegar in the salad dressing would bring out the wine's latent acids, distorting its flavor and the acetic taste might linger disturbingly in the mouth. Some people substitute lemon or lime juice or mustard for the vinegar in the dressing. Others maintain that a fairly light salad dressing—consisting of 1 part vinegar to 5 or 6 parts oil—will hardly affect the wine. A good accompaniment to such a salad, they suggest, might be a chilled spicy wine such as a Gewürztraminer.

WITH CHEESE

Cheese and wine go well together; the alkalinity of the cheese complements the acidity of the wine. The milder and more delicate the cheese, the more delicate and fruity the wine should be; the stronger and older the cheese, the more robust and rich the wine. (The most assertive, sharp-flavored cheeses require the most assertive, full-bodied wines.) Neutral harder cheeses find a good match in fruity, low-alcohol wines, while softer cheeses generally call for richer, riper wines.

Suitable for simple, unaggressively flavored, everyday cheeses —provolone, Monterey Jack, Bel Paese and muenster—are fruity wines, either red or white, that are light to medium in body. A Chenin Blanc can go with a mild white cheese; a dry Gewürztraminer with a muenster. Slightly sweet unripened cheeses, such as mozzarella or ricotta, can take dry fuller-bodied whites or light reds and rosés. Savory soft creamy cheeses— Camembert and Brie—pair well with medium-dry white wines with body, such as a Chardonnay or with light to medium red wines, such as a Dolcetto or a Beaujolais.

Appropriate for mild, semifirm cheeses—Swiss, Jarlsberg, Emmentaler or Gruyère—are light dry white wines; fruity aromatic and full-bodied reds, or sherries that are medium in body. Other semifirm cheeses—Edam, Gouda, fontina, Cheddar—call for weightier wines. A rich, sharp Cheddar can be accompanied by a dry fruity, medium-bodied red or rosé, a medium-bodied white, or a port or sherry.

Strong brash, brawny and pungent cheeses—Danish blues, Roqueforts, gorgonzolas, and Stiltons—go well with young fruity medium-bodied reds (Zinfandels, Merlots, Petite Sirahs). Sweet white wines are also good. A great Sauternes provides an intriguing contrast to a strong Roquefort; the wine's sweetness balancing out the powerful taste of the cheese. The bigger wines—German Ausleses and Beerenausleses—are splendid with richer blue-veined cheeses; their appreciable sweetness blends well with the pungency of those cheeses. Paired too with Gorgonzola and strong blue cheeses can be a Recioto della Valpolicella, a Barolo or a Barbaresco. Fine as well with pungent cheeses are amontillado and oloroso sherries, ports, Madeiras and Marsalas. Vintage Port has traditionally been paired with Stilton cheese, as have ruby and LBV Ports.

Some Bordeaux vintners recommend that goat cheeses and blue-veined cheeses be taken with their oldest red wines; others maintain that such cheeses are too sharp-tasting to show off their high-caliber wines to full advantage. They suggest that milder less competitive cheeses be served instead.

NOTE: Any inexpensive red wine will do for lesser, ripe-flavored cheeses such as Limburger or Liederkranz.

WITH DESSERT

Still, sparkling or fortified wines can accompany the dessert course. Lighter desserts call for lighter wines; more substantial cream-based confections need richer heavier ones. Because sweet foods can make a wine taste relatively bitter, the dessert should be a little less sweet than the wine that accompanies it.

The tartness of such fruits as apples, plums, pears, apricots, peaches and so on, matches well with rich, sweet wines. Particularly good with fresh-fruit desserts are Muscat wines, Asti Spumantes, rich Alsatian Gewürztraminers and the less concentrated noble rots. Accompanying fresh strawberries and poached fruit might be sparkling wines on the sweet side.

Paired with light desserts can be full-bodied rosé or pink Champagnes. Fine with ice cream, sherbet, fruit tarts and light cakes are sweet sparklers. Also suitable with cakes, tarts, pastries, flans, custards, mousses, crêpes, rich creamy desserts and puddings are late-harvest and noble rot wines. Custards, baked fruit soufflés, fruit tarts or rich mince and pumpkin pies can highlight the power and elegance of a rich Sauternes.

Served as well with the dessert course can be port, Marsala, Madeira (Bual or Malmsey), or an oloroso sherry (amoroso or cream). Nutmeats can be accompanied by a dry fino or amontillado sherry or a Sercial Madeira. Sweet sherries have been served with fresh fruit, banana tarts, mince pies and cheesecakes. Paired with rich ice creams and caramel desserts have been supersweet, superdark pedro ximénez sherries.

WINE FOR OTHER OCCASIONS

Suitable for light lunches, brunches, summer picnics and lawn and beach parties are casual light-bodied wines. For elegant buffets—featuring quiches, fondues, cold cuts, pasta salads, smoked fish, lobster and seafood salads—the accompaniments might be rich but somewhat dry white wines (a Sauvignon Blanc, a Vouvray or a Savennières from the Loire, a German or an Alsatian Riesling).

Suitable for assorted cold cuts and cheeses are uncomplicated, light to medium red wines such as Italian Barberas and semidry rosés. Traditionally taken with brunches or buffets of cold meat and fowl are delicate Champagnes and other sparkling wines. Some people like to serve a fino or a medium-bodied sherry with a sweet tang at their brunches and buffets.

While omelettes and quiches can take a white wine, more heartily seasoned egg dishes respond best to a light fruity red such as a rosé or a Beaujolais. Accompanying grilled hamburgers might be a Chilean Merlot, a modest California Cabernet Sauvignon or a Beaujolais. Just right for pungently barbecued meat can be a Petite Sirah or a Zinfandel with rich spicy fruit. Other possible accompaniments are a Côtes du Rhône, Chianti, Valpolicella or a Barbera. Holding their own with chilis and pizzas can be a lesser Chianti wine or a Petite Sirah.

NONFRIENDLY FOODS

Foods that don't lend themselves readily to accompanying wines are artichokes, asparagus, citrus fruits, and those involving chocolate. Artichokes can make a wine taste metallic or cloying, while asparagus tends to dull the senses. Citrus fruits and fruit cocktails also have a deadening effect because of their great acidity.

NOTE: Although chocolate interferes with the taste of most wines, sweet Champagnes, sweet California Muscats and sweet fortified wines have accompanied cakes and desserts featuring it.

Meals served with wine should generally avoid uncommonly strong flavored or highly seasoned foods as well. Overpowering a wine will be foods pickled in vinegar or seasoned with condiments such as horseradish, cloves, capers, mint, some mustards and hot peppers. Also to be shunned are pungent cocktail sauces, dips that contain Tabasco or Worcestershire sauce, spicy salsas and hot curries.

NOTE: Delicate sparkling wines are generally risky with foods involving a considerable amount of garlic, forceful spices or other aromatics—although robust everyday table wines can usually hold their own with them.

WINE TAKEN AFTER DINNER OR ALONE

Some wines are so rich, intense and complex that any food—no matter how good—will only detract. Such wines are best taken as an experience in themselves, so that they can be given the attention they deserve. They are meant to be sipped and savored in a relaxed leisurely manner, accompanied perhaps by a biscuit or a sweet cracker.

Among these sipping libations are fortified wines (semisweet sherries and Malmsey Madeiras, along with Vintage, tawny, and ruby Ports), luscious late-harvest wines (the great Hungarian Tokays and the highest-caliber French Sauternes, German Eisweins, Beerenausleses and Trockenbeerenausleses). Included here as well are the rich Gewürztraminers and vins de paille, along with the great full-bodied Italian reds such as the Barolos and Brunellos di

Montalcino in their prime.

NOTE: Often more suitable as sipping wines are some of the bigger, fuller-bodied California Chardonnays—which can be a bit overwhelming with food.

SERVING SEVERAL WINES AT A MEAL

At a dinner party or other formal occasion, where several wines are to be served, a dry sparkler might be presented as the apéritif, a red wine might accompany the meat course and an even better red might be paired with the cheese. When two main courses are served, a lighter red can accompany the poultry and a heavier red the roast. After dinner, an oloroso sherry can provide the comfort and solace of a brandy, although some consider a Vintage Port the only fitting conclusion to a memorable meal.

When several wines are to be served, as much thought should go into their sequence as into their selection. Ideally, each wine should build up to the next: a white followed by a red, a dry followed by a sweet, a young by an old, a lighter-bodied by a fuller-bodied, a cool wine by one at room temperature and an inexpensive wine by a more costly example.

NOTE: Wines served at either end of the meal need not follow this pattern; both the apéritif and dessert wine can be older or younger than those following or preceding them.

Some say that the last wine should be the finest to provide a fitting climax to the meal. Others don't believe in saving the best for last. As one oenophile said, "I like to drink the rare wines while my palate is still sharp enough to appreciate them." And at a special Bordeaux luncheon, the host informed his guests, "We are going to drink what I consider the good wines first and then drink the younger wines afterwards."

These are some examples of multiwine meals:

- At a French-oriented dinner, Champagne was served with the terrine de foie gras; a red Burgundy accompanied the red snapper prepared with red wine and leeks; and a red Bordeaux was paired with the saddle

of venison with wild mushrooms. The salad was
unaccompanied. Served with the rhubarb tart
topped with vanilla ice cream was a Beumes-de-
Venise—a muscat wine.

- At another French-oriented meal, Corton-
Charlemagne was served with the oysters, and
Château Cheval Blanc accompanied the capon
stuffed with sausage and steamed morels. Taken after
various cheeses was a Grand Cuvée Champagne
served with a rich dessert of *feuilles d'automne.*

- At an all-Champagne dinner, the wines increased
progressively in sweetness as they accompanied the
hors d'oeuvres, salmon fettucine, goat cheese salad
and red snapper. The sweetest of all was served
with the *crème brûlée.* Another all-Champagne dinner began with a Blanc de Blancs, moved on to a
nonvintage brut, then to a vintage brut and finished
with a sparkling rosé.

- At an all-Bordeaux meal, a white Graves accompanied the poached salmon, a St-Émilion was paired
with the stuffed guinea hen and a luscious Barsac
was served with the dessert. Another all-Bordeaux
dinner featured wines from the same St-Émilion
estate but representing several vintages.
Accompanying the pâté, coq au vin and Stilton
cheese, they increased progressively in age.

- At a meal featuring Italian wines from Tuscany, a
Vernaccia di San Gimignano served as the apéritif, a
Chianti Classico accompanied the pappardelle with
dried tomatoes, a Chianti Classico Riserva was paired
with the seared tuna, and a Brunello di Montalcino
accompanied the grilled sirloin steak.

- At an all-Chilean meal, a Chilean Chablis accompanied the shellfish and a Chilean Cabernet Sauvignon
was paired with the steak and potatoes.

- At an American state dinner featuring California
wines, a Chardonnay accompanied the Maine lobster
medallions and a Cabernet Sauvignon was paired

with the roast fillet of beef. Concluding the meal was a sparkling Blanc de Noirs served with the dessert of lime sherbet and fresh raspberries.

Other multiwine meals have been international in their style:

- At a spring dinner in a private New York club, a sparkling Alsatian Crémant accompanied the oysters, a Verdelho Madeira the curried soup of mussels and shrimp, a white Burgundy the carpaccio served with green mustard and red caviar, a red Burgundy the pheasant served with morels, asparagus and baby carrots. And a late-harvest Alsatian Gewürztraminer accompanied the dessert of sherbet and caramelized pears.
- At a London banquet, a German Auslese Riesling was served with the poached salmon, a French red Bordeaux with the lamb-and-chicken mousse and a moderately sweet Champagne with the dessert of peaches and coffee ice cream.
- At an even more international dinner, an amontillado sherry accompanied the consommé, a dry American Chardonnay the poached salmon, an Italian Barolo the cheese course and a French Beaumes-de-Venise the rich fruit pie concluding the meal.

SERVING GREAT WINES

A great wine should be the centerpiece of the meal, not its accessory. The more serious the wine, the less fussy the food paired with it should be. To show off the wine's subtleties, the accompanying dishes should be kept simple and their sauces lightly seasoned.

Served with the finest red wines might be a simple roast chicken, a game bird, grilled steak, roast beef or lamb chops. Served with the finest white wines might be a steamed or a simply prepared fish with a delicate hollandaise sauce. Accompanying the meat or fish might be a few modest vegetables. Served too should be a loaf of good bread and—to conclude the meal—a cheese that's neither too bland nor too sharp. (Flowers should be omitted from the table, since their aroma can interfere with the wine's bouquet.)

LEFTOVER WINE

Ideally, a bottle of table or sparkling wine should be consumed in its entirety. Once uncorked and exposed to air, the wine soon loses its character and quality. The more quickly and securely recorked it is, the better its chances for short-term survival. The wine should then be refrigerated to keep its flavor and aroma from deteriorating too rapidly. (Leaving it in a fairly warm place will encourage microbial action and speed up its spoilage.) A table wine, if properly cared for, can remain drinkable for about twenty-four hours, although it won't taste quite as good the second time around. A wine left in the refrigerator more than a day or so will become discolored and exhibit a musty aroma and a flat taste. Some claim that most red wines will last three or four days in the refrigerator, while a white wine can survive for about a week but the sooner either is consumed, the better.

NOTE: About two hours before serving, a red wine should be taken from the refrigerator and allowed to return gradually to room temperature. A white wine or a rosé, normally taken chilled, is best served directly from the refrigerator.

The ancient Romans protected their wines by pouring a thin layer of vegetable oil over the surface, then flicking it off just before serving. There are now various ways to exclude the outside air. Leftover wines can be decanted into smaller bottles, or their ullage can be displaced by adding glass marbles—of the sort that children play with—to the bottle. More elaborate methods call for blanketing the unfinished wine with an inert gas; vacuuming out the air with a special hand pump; or suspending a balloonlike pouch inside the bottle, which expands as the wine is poured.

NOTE: If glass marbles are used, they must first be sterilized in boiling water and care must be taken when pouring so that the marbles don't chip the goblets. Also, recycled bottles must be thoroughly washed and rinsed so that no trace of their previous contents remains. The bottles should then be air-dried or dried in a slow oven for about half an hour.

Fortified wines, consumed in smaller quantities, are invariably left unfinished. Because of their higher alcohol levels, they're in less danger of spoilage, but they do oxidize and evaporate. The finer the fortified wine, the sooner it should be consumed. Lighter, drier sherries go off rapidly and are best refrigerated and finished within the week. (A fine fino should be consumed within a day or two.) Sturdier, sweet sherries generally keep somewhat longer in the refrigerator, as do Málaga wines; the optimum time for preserving their flavor is about a month. Ruby and tawny ports soon lose their freshness. Old Vintage Ports should be decanted and consumed within a day or two, but some Madeiras can remain noble for months when they are decanted.

Leftover wines have various uses. Some people keep a special vinegar keg on hand into which they toss their odds and ends of wines. Leftover Champagne can be combined with orange juice, corked well and refrigerated, and then served as an apéritif the next day. After a party, the tail ends of sparkling and/or table wines can be combined and served as a punch the following day, garnished with fresh fruit.

Leftover wines can also be used in other beverages, fresh fruit concoctions and desserts. And they can serve as marinades, meat tenderizers and sauce ingredients. Tannic reds are good for marinades, while not-too-acid reds and whites are suitable for sauces. (Wine, after all, is an integral part of both coq au vin and boeuf borguignon.)

The leftover red wines used in cooking should be young and full-bodied; the leftover whites should be dry and preferably strong. The heat of the stove will evaporate out some but not all of their alcohol—anywhere from 5 to 45 percent may remain. (In cooking, wines are used for their flavor, not their alcohol.) Sparkling wines lose their bubbles when heated, but not their ability to flavor the food.

NOTE: Any leftover wine should be tasted before it's used. If it isn't any good on the palate, it won't be improved by cooking. And if the wine is poor, it can spoil the dish.

ORDERING WINE IN A RESTAURANT

In a restaurant, most people choose the food first, then consider the wine list. Others select an entrée only after they've chosen the wine. Before making their selection, however, the diners should look around to see how the restaurant stores its bottles. Lesser wines or those with a quick turnover may not be harmed if kept in a too-warm dining room, but serious wines should not receive such treatment.

Many diners are hesitant about ordering wine with their meals. Finding the wine list intimidating and afraid of making a mistake, they often turn to something familiar such as a Beaujolais, a rosé or a Chardonnay; or else they ask the waiter for his recommendations. (When requesting the waiter's assistance, one should specify the price range preferred.)

A wine list can be classic or innovative, cautious or daring, depending on the restaurateur's temperament and expertise. Wine lists range from handwritten slips of paper to computer printouts. Some are bound "books" with thick covers, with the actual labels pasted in.

A good wine list can be short or long. The best are for the most part found in restaurants with a large-enough and knowledgeable-enough clientele to make the investment in storing and aging premium wines worthwhile. Such lists offer small but meaningful selections appropriate to the menu and the setting. And they're frequently revised to reflect changes in the menu, the wine market and the restaurant's inventory. Some restaurants offer two wine lists: a shorter, abridged version for most customers, and a special list, for wine enthusiasts, generally higher in its price.

Many wine lists leave much to be desired. They offer vintages that are too young for consumption or depend on faster-maturing regional wines or on speeded-up products. Other lists omit the vintage year. (One doesn't know if the wines are from a good or a poor year, or if they're too young or too old.) And some lists aren't revised often enough to reflect the changes in the stock on hand.

A number of establishments try to make the selection process less stressful by indicating specific wines on their menus to accompany their entrées. The restaurant might suggest two or three wines, at different price levels, for each dish. One menu lists four reds suitable for steaks and chops, and five whites for fish, oysters and other shellfish. The list of another restaurant breaks down the choices into red and white categories, then divides them further into light-, medium- and full-bodied wines. Some establishments offer a wine of the week and suggest the dishes to go with it.

Other restaurants place a bottle on the table before the diners are seated, offering them a sample of the wine. The diners pay only for what they drink or—if they wish—can purchase the entire bottle. Still other establishments offer a *menu de dégustation* (tasting menu), which matches the food to the wine. One place offers a fixed-price dinner that includes four wines: a Champagne, a California Chardonnay, a white Burgundy, and a red Bordeaux. The diner can sample one or all of these wines and pour as much as he wishes. Other restaurants sponsor special dinners—often in conjunction with a wine maker, importer or distributor—that include a wine with each course, and cover everything from the apéritif to the digestif.

Wine can be ordered by the half-bottle, carafe or glass, as well as by the bottle. Lesser quantities might be the answer when the food the diners select is so varied that it's difficult to choose a bottle suitable for everyone. Moreover, ordering wine by the glass encourages greater experimentation.

NOTE: When ordering a house wine by the glass or the carafe, it's a good idea to ask what the wine is and where it comes from.

On occasion, one may wish to bring a special bottle of wine to the restaurant. Establishments that don't serve alcohol generally permit this, but may charge a small corkage fee. Others usually discourage the practice, since it cuts into their profits. (They may be obliging however if the request is made well in advance, but will most likely charge a considerable corkage fee for the privilege.)

Restaurants mark their wines up a minimum of $2^1/_2$ times the wholesale price; more often they mark them up 3, 4, and even 5 times. High prices have contributed to wine's aura of elitism and exclusivity and to the commonly held belief that wine is mainly the province of connoisseurs and gourmets. (A true enthusiast however likes a wide range of wines and chooses them for themselves rather than for their cost.)

There seems to be a psychological factor in wine pricing, however. Some proprietors believe a wine should bring whatever the traffic will bear. And then there are the customers who think that only expensive wines are worth drinking; they equate high price with merit. Great wines are often ordered by those who care little about the taste and who drink such wines indiscriminately. They are more exhilarated by the notion of drinking something costly than by the wine itself. According to one restaurateur, they miss the point entirely. "If you drink only the best," he notes, "you have no way of knowing it is the best."

Then there are those who won't choose the least-expensive wines—no matter how highly recommended they are—for fear of looking cheap. As one proprietor said, "I have to push people to drink the inexpensive wines. They always want to pay more." Other restaurateurs have stories to tell about good but inexpensive wines that didn't sell until their prices were raised. Yet more and more restaurants are trying to include at least one or two inexpensive bottles on their lists to encourage more active wine consumption.

When the waiter brings the bottle, there is usually the ritual of showing the label, extracting the cork, pouring a little wine into the glass, waiting for a response and, finally serving the wine. Before the bottle is uncorked, the diner should have the opportunity to inspect the label and the vintage date to see if this was indeed the wine that he or she had ordered. If the bottle arrives covered with a napkin, the diner should ask to have it temporarily removed so the label can be seen. (If the wine has been completely decanted and is presented only in its decanter, it may not always be the wine that was ordered.)

NOTE: If one chooses the wine of one vintage and the waiter uncorks the wine of another year, the diner has a right to protest. If he has not been informed of the change in the wine list, the restaurant owes him the chance to select another bottle.

Some restaurants employ a sommelier or a wine steward to look after the wine cellar and to assist the diners in choosing the wines for their meals. His symbol of office is a silver chain worn around the neck with a *tastevin* (tasting cup) attached. An attentive sommelier will select the wine, decant or chill it, and then see that it's properly served. (Since decanting provides the opportunity to impress the diners, some wine stewards tend to overdo this.)

NOTE: For those sommeliers who are genuinely helpful, the rule of thumb is to tip at least 10 percent of the cost of the bottle. If the sommelier does nothing more than hand the diner the wine list, pour the first round, then set the bottle down and vanish for the rest of the evening, no special gratuity is warranted.

Being served a bad bottle of wine in a restaurant is a rarity. When it does occur, a degree of courage is required to send the bottle back. Even those who are knowledgeable about wine hesitate to complain. Yet a cloudy wine is unacceptable, as is one that emits an off-odor. So is an overoxidized table wine that tastes more like a sherry or a Madeira. Also unacceptable are moldy wines or those smelling or tasting of vinegar.

When served a wine that is unpleasant to smell or taste, the diner can consult the captain, sommelier or waiter to enlist his assistance. The diner might say, "It took me a moment to realize it, but I think something is not right with this wine." He might add, "Try this wine. I think it may be off." If this does not get the desired results, he might say, "I'm sorry, but I must ask to try another bottle." Or, "I want this bottle replaced even if I have to pay for it." (A responsible restaurateur will replace the bottle and probably send it back to the distributor or wholesaler, who will have to take the loss.)

More commonplace when dining out is a wine that disappoints. When a customer is not pleased with a relatively inexpensive wine, one proprietor says, "We bring him something else that is similar in price and character but never the same wine." A diner who orders an expensive old wine that has been resting in a restaurant's cellar for many years may be told that the bottle will be opened only at his own risk. Rare is the restaurateur willing to assume the responsibility for an ancient bottle.

11

CONSIDERING ALCOHOL

Wine's positive effects are enormously appealing. In moderation wine provides a form of mental and physical relaxation. It induces feelings of life enhancement and conviviality. Long before the development of pharmaceutical tranquilizers, wine was seen as a vital restorative; an antidote to stress, anxiety and tension; a tonic against fatigue. Because wine's acidity resembles that of the gastric juices, it also has a gently stimulating effect on the salivary glands, whetting the appetite and improving the digestion. As an eighteenth-century man of science said, "Wine stimulates the stomach, cheers the spirits, warms the body, raises the pulse and quickens the circulation."

Wine has been used to provide a psychological lift to convalescents and the aged, the weak and the irritable. It also lends interest and flavor to their diets. In European hospitals, many older patients are allotted a small ration of wine with their meals and physicians have prescribed Champagne after surgery.

Medical evidence seems to indicate that consumers who are temperate enjoy a healthier life and greater longevity than those who don't drink at all. A number of long-term studies suggest a link between moderate alcohol consumption and reduced coronary disease. Mainstream authorities have cautiously endorsed the idea that moderate drinkers experience fewer cardiovascular problems, suffer fewer heart attacks and have less risk of stroke than teetotalers.

This may be because moderate drinkers appear to have higher

levels of protective HDL (high-density lipoprotein) and lower levels of LDL (low-density lipoprotein). HDL, the so-called good cholesterol, is thought to cleanse the coronary arteries of accumulated fatty deposits, which can block the heart and cause heart attacks. LDL is viewed as the dangerous cholesterol because it has artery-clogging properties.

A report in France indicated that drinking red wine as part of a regular diet has helped to keep down the incidence of heart disease. Red wine is known to raise HDL levels while lowering those of LDL. Studies indicate that the wine inhibits LDL's oxidation and so reduces the accumulation of cholesterol on arterial walls. It is also believed that the tannins in red wines slow down the formation of blood clots, which can close off the arteries that feed the heart. (Blood clots are a major factor in heart disease.) One study showed that only wine—not beer or hard liquor—was associated with a longer life and that its apparent protective effect was far greater than had been observed elsewhere.

NOTE: Diet is also a significant factor in heart disease. In countries whose citizens consume fewer fruits and vegetables and more animal fats, the death rate is higher for coronary disease.

Alcohol does not need to be digested. On entering the digestive tract, it goes directly to the stomach where about 20 percent of it is neutralized by a special enzyme and broken down into intermediate acids and toxins. Passing through the stomach wall, the remaining alcohol is filtered and metabolized by the liver. It then enters the bloodstream, which transports it to the parts of the body containing water. As the alcohol travels through the body, it affects every biological pathway and every cell, but under normal conditions, its impact on the psychomotor and other systems is only temporary.

The rate of the alcohol's absorption into the bloodstream largely determines one's feelings of intoxication. (Champagnes and other sparkling wines increase the absorption rate somewhat, since their CO_2 content produces a vasodilation, or a widening of the blood vessels.) A slower rate of absorption is most desirable. It is believed that the alcohol in wine is absorbed more slowly than the alcohol in distilled spirits because of the buffering effect of the grape elements. Food further slows down the absorption; a full stomach can delay complete absorption. Most effective here are the foods dense in carbohydrates, which also replenish some of the blood sugars that the alcohol depletes. Food, however, cannot prevent intoxication when too much alcohol has been consumed. Too much alcohol also has a dehydrating effect. (Water or plain soda can be taken to help replace the body's fluids.)

The body needs about an hour to metabolize the alcohol in a drink. If one sips slowly and waits that length of time before taking a second drink, this will allow time for the return of normal concentration and muscular coordination. In the case of excessive consumption, the effects will eventually taper off, but the drop will be slow. About eight hours is generally needed for the body to eliminate the alcohol entirely. Time is the only effective remedy for clearing the blood.

A hangover is the toll that consuming too much alcohol takes. According to popular theory, a hangover is a rebound phenomenon—the withdrawal syndrome that is experienced as the alcohol leaves the system. Over the course of an evening of heavy drinking, the brain becomes somewhat tolerant of the alcohol; the next morning when it leaves the brain, the rebound occurs. Hangover symptoms include a headache and an acid stomach, among others. The recommended treatment is aspirin and a mild antacid along with some physical activity to increase the body's circulation and produce more adrenaline. Some suggest that spicy and peppery foods can increase the metabolism and help the body rid itself of the intermediate acids and toxins.

The blood alcohol concentration or BAC is the amount of alcohol by weight in a given volume of blood. After the last drink has been consumed, it takes at least twenty minutes for the BAC to reach its peak. In the United States, the legal definition of intoxication is the point at which the BAC reaches 0.10 or one-tenth of one percent. In many states, an automobile driver is considered legally drunk when his blood alcohol level registers this percentage. Some states have lowered the permissible BAC level for motorists to 0.8 percent, while more restrictive states set it at 0.05 percent.

NOTE: Studies have shown that drivers with a BAC level of only 0.04 percent are more likely to have accidents and that, even at 0.05 percent, their ability to drive a car is questionable.

Recognizing these hazards, U.S. Federal regulations require that a warning appear on wine labels stating that the "consumption of alcoholic beverages impairs the ability to drive a car."

Alcohol is a mind-altering drug. The more alcohol in the bloodstream, the more can reach the brain and affect its natural functioning. Excessive intake can slow down reaction times and cause drowsiness and a loss of alertness and concentration. It can also disrupt visual ability, reduce peripheral vision, blur eyesight and cause double or multiple vision. Interfering with reflex responses and coordination, excessive alcohol intake can affect one's muscular actions as well—making voluntary movements clumsy, staggering the walk and slurring the speech. And alcohol dulls the areas of the brain that enable people to make sensible decisions; their judgment is impared.

A standard drink is defined as the equivalent of 1/2 ounce (12 grams) of pure alcohol. This can take the form of 5 ounces of wine, 12 ounces of beer or 1 1/2 ounces of an 80-proof spirit. Light drinking involves the consumption of one to ten drinks a week. Moderate drinking has been defined as one to three drinks a day, or from ten to twenty-nine drinks per week. (This generally accepted definition of moderate drinking is based on the daily amount of alcohol that an average, healthy adult can consume without untoward effects.) Heavy drinking involves thirty or more drinks a week, while binge drinking refers to downing five consecutive drinks or more at a single sitting. Generally recommended by American health experts is one to two drinks a day because the evidence shows that those who consume this quantity have a lower risk of mortality. Other studies suggest that two to six drinks a week for men and one to three drinks for women are more ideal.

An individual's response to alcohol—the speed of its processing—varies according to age, body weight, metabolism and gender. Even within the same range of age and weight, many variations are possible. They are based on the individual's chemistry, his previous drinking experience, physical health, whether he has eaten, how fast he drinks and how much he has consumed in a given period. In people who are tired, anxious or depressed the response to alcohol may be exaggerated.

Weight is a key factor in determining how quickly the body

can metabolize and clear alcohol from the bloodstream. The heavier the individual, the greater the capacity for alcohol. Men—because of their generally larger body mass, characterized by more muscle and less fat—can handle relatively more alcohol than women. (The same amount of alcohol in a smaller body mass is proportionately greater in its potency.) As a result, one drink for a woman can have the effect of two drinks for a man. (Studies have suggested that most women can safely drink only about half as much alcohol as men.)

Women can become intoxicated faster than men for other reasons. They seem to have less of the special stomach enzyme that processes and helps neutralize the alcohol. This allows more of the alcohol to pass directly into their bloodstreams. And alcohol has ramifications during pregnancy as well. Crossing the placenta freely, it can affect the developing fetus. Although some experts maintain that the mother's blood alcohol needs to reach a certain threshold before the fetus is at risk, many doctors' groups recommend that women abstain entirely from drinking during pregnancy. They say that drinking at even a social level during the first month or two can affect the child. They maintain that moderate drinking will impair the child's intellectual ability and its ability to concentrate, while heavy drinking can result in fetal alcohol syndrome, whose symptoms include mental retardation, abnormal facial features, central nervous system problems, growth deficiencies and behavioral difficulties.

One's ability to absorb alcohol decreases with age. Total body water diminishes as one grows older, while body fat increases. And the liver no longer processes alcohol as efficiently. According to scientists and other experts concerned with the effects of alcohol on the health of the elderly, small amounts may be helpful, but heavier use may lead to physical and mental impairment and to a worsening of chronic ailments. Also affected can be the liver, pancreas, intestines, and blood and nervous systems. (In older people, signs of alcoholism such as problems with memory, balance or sleep are often incorrectly assumed to be natural consequences of the aging process or the effects of chronic illness.) Experts recommend that older people limit their alcohol intake to one drink a day.

NOTE: Since the elderly often take various medications, they also need to be aware of possible interactions between alcohol and the drugs prescribed for them.

The line dividing drinking and problem drinking is often blurred. Drinking to excess has been described as drinking to get drunk, or as being unable to remember what happened after one has been drinking. A problem drinker has been defined as anyone who drinks enough for it to interfere with his physical or social functioning. He has also been described as someone who has been drunk at least six times during the previous year or has had serious difficulties during that time as a result of his drinking. According to one expert, the central questions are: How much and how often does the person drink? When does he drink? Is this accompanied by difficulties on the job or with his family?

An alcoholic has been described as a person whose behavior is determined by alcohol, for whom alcohol has become a physiological or a psychological necessity, whose dependency overwhelms his judgment, and yet who continues to drink nevertheless. In other words, alcoholism is characterized by either a continuous or periodic impaired control over drinking, a preoccupation with and the use of alcohol despite its adverse consequences. In 1966, the American Medical Association recognized alcoholism as a disease.

NOTE: Experts who treat alcoholism say that those closest to the alcoholic are often the last to acknowledge the existence of the problem. Family, friends and coworkers tend to minimize the serious repercussions of alcohol abuse and alcoholism, perhaps in part because of the general climate of denial that surrounds the subject. They prefer not to confront the situation.

The physiology of the alcoholic differs from that of the social drinker. Excessive intake over an extended period can cause anemia and such other blood abnormalities as low white cell or platelet counts. It can also promote malnutrition. (Although alcohol itself contains a small amount of carbohydrates, which provide the elements necessary for quick energy, it is not sufficiently nutritious to serve as a substitute for food.) Alcoholics not only tend to eat less but also experience an impaired ability to absorb food.

Commonly associated with alcohol abuse and alcoholism is cirrhosis of the liver. Under normal circumstances, the liver burns fat as fuel and clears the body of many toxic substances—including alcohol. But when alcohol is present in the bloodstream, the liver burns that alcohol instead, causing the fat to accumulate. Cirrhosis refers to a fatty liver, a liver that has become thickened and scarred. This condition interferes with its usual filtering function so that it can no longer remove as much alcohol from the blood. As a result, more of the alcohol reaches the brain and other organs. Moreover, there's build up in the body of acetaldehyde, the toxin produced by the normal breakdown of alcohol, creating a decreased tolerance for alcohol and finally a general loss of various control mechanisms.

The special stomach enzyme also works even less in alcoholics; the alcohol they consume is not properly metabolized. Alcoholic women may be so lacking in this enzyme that, even if they consume less alcohol than men, they are more likely to develop liver disease. (Women who drink heavily are also more likely to develop gynecological problems.)

On a more superficial level, alcohol dilates the subcutaneous blood vessels, causing the blood to rush to the skin. In long-term excessive drinking, the blood vessels that feed the facial skin dilate and contract so frequently that the smaller ones become fragile and rupture. (They appear as blotchy red spots on the face and cause the eyes to puff up.)

Alcohol may protect the heart when consumed in small quantities, but does nothing to prolong life when taken in large quantities. Studies indicate that alcohol abuse can be a major contributor in cardiovascular disease and strokes. (Among the dangers of chronic overuse is muscle weakness, including a weakness of the heart muscle—which can lead to heart failure.) Alcohol abuse also increases the chances of an early death from cirrhosis of the liver or from accidents. Heavy drinkers are subject as well to an increased risk of hypertension, gastrointestinal bleeding and cancer of the liver and pancreas. Excessive use can also cause other organic complications, sometimes involving the brain.

Scientists generally accept the notion that alcoholism is a multifaceted disorder based on complex genetic, social and cultural factors. They have discovered that the blood chemistries of some individuals make them especially vulnerable to alcohol's side effects and more prone to addiction. According to one study involving male twins, a strong genetic influence was evident in those who developed drinking problems before the age of twenty, while in those who developed drinking problems in adulthood, environmental factors seemed to be the stronger influence.

NOTE: Researchers have also found that women share the same genetic susceptibility to alcoholism as men.

The predisposition to alcoholism seems to run in families. It has been estimated that the children of alcoholics have three to four times the risk of developing alcoholism than do the offspring of nonalcoholics. (The children of alcoholics are also at a generally greater risk of having physical, mental and emotional problems than their peers.) Counselors recommend that people with a family history of problem drinking avoid drinking alcohol every day, that they avoid it when they are alone or depressed and perhaps that they even avoid alcohol altogether.

Wine drinkers are more likely to drink moderately and to consume alcohol with their meals than other drinkers. Wine tends to work best in a social or a family setting. As one oenophile pointed out, "Wine is a drink that simply does not work if you sit down and try to drink a bottle all by yourself." Researchers have found that alcoholism is less of a problem in cultures that encourage the responsible consumption of wine. Such cultures seem to find the balance between the advantages of moderation and the problems of overconsumption. As one researcher stated, "It may in fact be better to have a culture that views alcohol as part of daily life than one that prohibits it, because forbidding children to have any experience with alcohol may leave them unable to control their drinking as teenagers." Abstention, he pointed out, gives children the message that drinking is a kind of evil, making it virtually impossible for them to deal with alcohol in moderation.

According to most findings, parents play a major role—either directly or indirectly—in determining the patterns of alcohol use in their children. It isn't what the parents say but what they do that influences whether or not their children will become alcohol misusers. Children tend to follow the drinking patterns of their parents. Experts have found that children exposed to alcohol abuse early are more likely to become alcoholics themselves. And when parents drink every evening to relieve feelings of stress, their children learn that lesson. "Youngsters do what parents do," another observer said. "If the parents drink a lot, the kids do, too."

The best parental role models are those who treat wine as a natural component of a meal, who present it in an unglamorized family setting, and who demonstrate in their own lives that moderate consumption is the key to the pleasures and benefits of wine. Children who have never been taught moderation at home or who consider drinking an indulgence often view alcohol consumption as a rite of passage into adulthood. (Binge drinking is most often seen among those emerging from their teens.) "The message young people need to receive," one observer said, "is that while alcohol should be drunk only by adults, drinking does not make you an adult."

NOTE: Researchers have found that while peer group influences on behavior predominate during the midteen years, parental influences tend to be longer-lasting; they dominate earlier, then reassert themselves as the children become older.

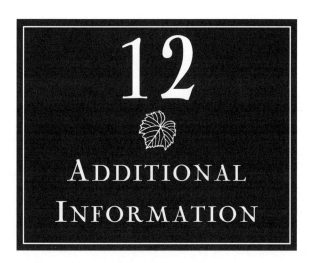

12

ADDITIONAL INFORMATION

THE VOCABULARY OF TASTE

Characterizing the taste of a wine is not a simple matter. Certain aspects are easier to describe than others. Sweet, sour and bitter can be defined more readily than can fruity or flowery. But for describing taste and smell, there is no accurate language, no clear-cut linguistic rules. Wine professionals have been trying for years to establish a standardized terminology, but they haven't been able to agree on the fine points.

Wine descriptions are often overblown or precious or both. Wines have been said to exhibit "a savage primordial character," to display a "bricky taste" a "whiff of tar," or to possess the "lacy nose of licorice." Writing about a group of wines, one critic said, "They grab you by the palate, swing you around, give you a bone-cracking massage and leave you limp with an almost silly grin on your face." A Frenchman, encountering a fulsome description, declared, "Delicate and elegant I can swallow, but when I read that a wine is also coaxing, purring and tender, I'm not sure whether to drink it or marry it."

Until a greater degree of standardization develops, the following terminology might prove useful in registering one's own responses.

ACIDITY: The natural tartness or bite of a wine, produced by its nonvolatile acids and felt lightly on the tongue. When properly balanced by grape sugar, it gives the wine a refreshing and necessary piquancy.

NOTE: Acidity in a wine should not be confused with the sour pungency that vinegar produces.

AFTERTASTE: The sensation that lingers on the palate after the wine is swallowed; the echo of its bouquet and flavor. Depending on the length of the aftertaste, a wine is said to be long or short. In a great wine, the aftertaste can persist fifteen minutes or more.

AROMA: The unique grapy fragrance associated with fresh, young wines; it is less apparent in the light, dry ones.

ASTRINGENT: A rough, coarse quality, produced by the wine's tannin, more related to its feel than to its taste. Is detected as a puckery sensation in the mouth, similar to that produced by a cup of strong tea. The astringency, cleansing the palate, makes the last sip of wine taste as good as the first. Can also be an indication that the wine will be long-lived.

NOTE: Red wines require astringency in moderation, but when it's excessive, they taste bitter.

AUSTERE: A dry crispness, seen in restrained and subtle wines. Associated primarily with high-caliber Cabernet Sauvignons, this characteristic is also evident in some white wines, such as a fine Chablis. Can also refer to the excessive and sharp tightness of a red wine in need of breathing. (See also Closed-in.)

BALANCE: The proper proportions of the various components in a wine whose relationship is harmonious and which complement rather than overwhelm one another. The components include physical elements (body and color), taste elements (sweetness and acidity), and less tangible qualities such as character and finesse.

BARNYARD: A wine smelling unpleasantly like wet hay.

BIG: A wine's unusual strength and power. Refers to the intensity of its flavor, the assertiveness of its aroma and bouquet. Is generally applied to highly tannic red wines possessing more body and alcohol than most others. Is often a code word for high alcohol content, but can also refer to a heavy wine lacking subtlety and refinement.

BITTER: A harshness related to the wine's tannin level, usually perceived in the aftertaste. A characteristic that usually disappears with age.

BODY: A wine's substance or degree of concentration, reflecting its nonsugar solids in solution. Red wines tend to be medium to full in body, whereas white wines are typically lighter.

BOUQUET: The enhancing fragrance or scent of a wine; a distinctive and subtle mingling of its diverse odors. Originates in the deepest levels of the earth to which the vine has penetrated. A more complex characteristic than aroma, bouquet develops largely during bottle-aging. (While aroma is seen in young wines, bouquet is a characteristic of older ones.)

BREED: The obvious superiority of a wine as demonstrated by the harmonious balance of its bouquet, complexity and flavor. Is the hallmark of wines made from aristocratic grapes grown in the finer viticultural districts.

BRUT: A mark of extreme dryness, indicating the wine's negligible retention of grape sugar. Initially used to describe Champagnes, it can now refer to still wines as well.

BUTTERY: A richness of flavor, a creamy lusciousness, associated primarily with California Chardonnays.

CHARACTER: The definite, unmistakable quality of a wine that possesses in full degree the color, taste and bouquet associated with its type.

CHEWY: A full-bodied, textured quality that makes a wine feel good and rich in the mouth, a characteristic associated with fine red wines.

CLEAN: A pleasing palatability and soundness that is sensed as a refreshing purity in the mouth after the wine is swallowed.

CLOSED-IN: A tightness indicating that the wine has not matured enough to fully express its flavor or bouquet. Is also associated with tannic young reds that improve with breathing.

CLOUDY: A wine's lack of clarity, its haziness or muddiness. May be caused by poor fermentation, agitation of the bottle or bottle-sickness. If the condition does not clear up with rest, the wine may prove undrinkable.

COARSE: A heavy heartiness, a lack of depth and finesse; generally seen in full-bodied but otherwise ordinary red wines.

COMPLEX: A multiplicity of stimulating and pleasing flavors and aromas; a characteristic of fine wines.

CORKY (Corked): A wine tainted by a dried-out, moldy or

defective cork whose generally disagreeable smell and taste suggest rotting wood or damp basements. Can first be detected by sniffing the moist end of the cork. (The condition is generally attributed to a chemical compound formed by the interaction of moisture, mold, and the chlorine used in bleaching the corks.)

NOTE: If the corkiness doesn't quickly dissipate, the wine should be tasted before serving to see if it's palatable.

CRISP: A clear-cut briskness produced by the wine's acidity. Is seen primarily in white wines, which are generally more acid than the reds.

DELICATE: A light elegance, sometimes a fragility, associated with good white wines; the opposite of sturdy, big or coarse.

DRY: The absence of residual grape sugar in a wine; the opposite of sweet. (See also Brut and Residual Sugar.)

DUMB: A young wine that lacks the characteristic taste or smell of its type.

EARTHY: The unmistakable character of the warm, sweet-smelling earth, perceived as an attractive wine taste and aroma. A characteristic of wines grown in alluvial or predominantly clay soils. Is seen in sturdy, no-nonsense reds from the Rhône and the Loire Valleys. Can be disagreeable when too pronounced. (See also Goût de Terroir.)

ELEGANT: The finesse and balance that give high-caliber red or white wines their complexity and interest.

FAT: A heaviness in a wine; a positive attribute in big, generous reds and richly luscious whites.

FINESSE: A wine's style and polish; the combination of its delicacy, strength and body, joined together in successful harmony.

FINISH: The taste that lingers after the wine has been swallowed. Is most desirable when it leaves a pleasant feeling of warmth in the mouth. (See also Aftertaste.)

FIRM: A wine's sturdiness or backbone produced by its high levels of tannin. Is an indication of the wine's keeping qualities. (May also be a polite way of saying the wine is harsh.)

FLABBY: A lack of firmness or structure caused by insufficient acidity in the wine.

FLAVOR: The actual taste of the wine, which, along with aroma and bouquet, reveals the wine's complexity or the lack of it.

FLINTY: A clean, sharp, almost austere attractiveness; a characteristic of fine, dry white wines grown on a chalky soil, such as a Champagne or a Chablis.

FLOWERY: A bouquet that evokes the soft scent of violets, lilacs, honeysuckle and so forth. Is associated with white wines grown in cooler districts on stony soils, such as Rieslings from the Mosel and northern Italian wines.

FORWARD: A red wine that has become soft and pleasant before its time, a characteristic seen in wines from lesser vintages that lack the potential for much aging.

FOXY: A strong, pungent flavor, a fruity tang and a rich, distinctive muskiness; associated with wines pressed from labrusca grapes. (The labruscas were once called fox grapes.)

FRAGRANT: A pronounced and agreeable bouquet or aroma.

FRESH: The liveliness of fragrance and taste in a young wine—often its most charming and appealing quality. Usually disappears with bottle age, although mature, high-caliber wines retain this quality to a considerable degree.

FRUITY: An unmistakable, grapy aroma and flavor that combines tartness and sweetness. Suggests the taste of ripe fruit, and may be reminiscent of apples, pears, apricots, peaches, blackberries, black currants and so forth.

GENEROUS: A rich, hearty quality generally associated with red wines that are full-bodied and full-flavored.

GOÛT DE TERROIR (Taste of the Soil): An elusive, almost rustic earthiness evident as a fairly high acidity that dominates the fruit elements of the wine. Associated primarily with fine red Burgundies, it is not only related to the soil in which the wine is grown but to the total environment nurturing it.

GRAPY: A sweet aroma and a pronounced fruit flavor imparted by certain grape varieties, particularly the muscat and concord. Is not highly regarded as a rule since it tends to diminish the subtlety of the wine.

GRASSY: See "Herbaceous."

GREEN: The generally disagreeable acidity of a wine pressed from unripe fruit. It can also refer to the appealing freshness of a wine pressed from prematurely picked grapes, as in Portuguese vinos verdes and French Muscadets.

342 • THE GIFT OF WINE

HARD: A lack of suppleness due to a wine's excessive tannin, which changes to firmness with age. Is an indication of the wine's potential longevity. Generally seen in austere reds, it is also evident in high-acid, extremely dry whites wines from Chablis and the Saar Valley.

HARSH: A roughness or overastringency associated with immature red wines that usually disappears with age.

HEAVY: A fullness of body and a high degree of alcohol that is not accompanied by a corresponding richness of flavor. Often a characteristic of chaptalized or sugared wines.

HERBACEOUS: Vegetablelike flavors and odors in a wine. Agreeable when grassy and when it evokes tea or eucalyptus, but harsh when it suggests bell peppers, artichokes or asparagus. (The harshness may be caused by the vine's improper trellising, the grape's inadequate ripening or perhaps a problem in vinification.)

INTENSE: The concentrated and well-defined taste and texture of a wine that sets the best examples apart from the others.

LIGHT: A wine low in body and alcohol. (This is a physical and not a quality characteristic, since a light wine can be charming or quite dull.)

LIQUOREUX: The luscious viscosity of a fine, rich wine. Refers more to its unctuous, velvety body than to its sweetness. Is associated with noble rot wines and other good dessert wines.

LONG: The ability of a wine to persist on the palate for some time after it has been swallowed. (See also Aftertaste and Finish.)

MADERIZED: A chemical deterioration caused by a wine's prolonged aging or its exposure to heat. Acquiring a hint of burned taste, the wine may be palatable at first, but then becomes flat and musty. Before turning to vinegar, it emits a distinctly "rancio" odor or else smells like rotting hay. Maderization also affects a wine's color, causing the reds to fade and the whites to turn brown. (See also Oxidized and Rancio.)

MELLOW: The soft, ripe lusciousness of a wine, implying a degree of sweetness. It is generally associated with mature reds but can be seen as well in chaptalized or sugared wines.

MOLDY: An unpleasant flavor and a fetid odor caused by a wine's excessive aging or by a defective cork. (See also Corky.)

NOSE: A wine's scent, a composite of all of its fragrances.

Ranging from light and delicate to deep and complex, it may reflect its predominant grape or suggest almonds, cloves, black pepper, cherries, vanilla, or a hint of the salt sea. A good nose refers to a considerable aroma and a pleasing flowery bouquet. A big nose refers to a rich, complex bouquet that fills the room when the bottle is uncorked. A sophisticated nose indicates a layered complexity produced by years of bottle-aging. An off-nose refers to a wine that doesn't smell right.

NUTTY: A wine's pleasant, pungent aftertaste that's reminiscent of almonds, walnuts, hazelnuts and so forth. Is associated with fortified wines such as sherry and Madeira.

OAKY: An attractive, vanillalike aroma and taste imparted by the wood during cask-aging. Can also be produced by barrel-fermentation.

NOTE: The oakiness in some Chardonnays can be an overwhelming characteristic that overpowers the taste of the fruit. A number of Americans, however, seem to prefer them that way.

OXIDIZED: An overexposure to air that increases a wine's volatile acidity and causes it to lose freshness and color. (The wine may develop a cooked taste.) Is most prevalent in old bottled wines but may also be responsible for the premature aging and deterioration of other wines. (See also Maderized.)

PAPERY: The odor of dry leaves, a characteristic of old wines that shed most of their tannin as they age.

RAISINY: A sweetish flavor associated with hot-climate wines that are pressed from overripe or shriveled grapes.

RANCIO: A gently bitter, nutlike taste and odor caused by the wine's partial oxidation is considered a desirable characteristic in fortified sherries, Madeiras and Marsalas. . In table wines, it is unpleasant.

RESIDUAL SUGAR: The sugar that remains after fermentation, accounting for the wine's natural sweetness.

RICH: A fullness of body, a density of flavor and a generosity of bouquet in a wine.

RIPE: A mellowness in the wine; it refers to those showing no trace of harshness or greenness.

ROBUST: A sound and sturdy heartiness; a well-developed body and flavor in a wine.

SCENT: A wine's aroma. In young wines, the flowery scents of roses, violets and magnolias are not uncommon. In older red wines, the scents may be of chocolate, clove, cinnamon, wood smoke, toast or truffles.

SHARP: See Acidity.

SOFT: An ingratiating sensation related to the maturity of a wine. (Can also refer to wines lacking in character.)

SHORT: Refers to wines that do not linger on the palate because of their lack of acidity and firmness. (See also Aftertaste and Finish.)

SOUR: A disagreeable acidity seen in wines on their way to becoming vinegar. They may have been poorly made, improperly stored or else sealed with defective corks.

SPICY: A piquant, attractive flavor suggesting nuances of mint, herbs, pepper and so on. Is seen in fruity young wines.

STALKY: A somewhat unpleasant odor, suggesting twigs or green wood, found in tannic but underripe red wines. It is a characteristic that usually diminishes with age.

STEELY: An austere tartness, even an extreme hardness, associated with well-made wines from the Saar Valley and Chablis. It produces a fresh, attractive, metallic sensation on the tongue. (See also Flinty.)

STEMMY: A harsh greenness generally associated with wines fermented on their stems. Is considered a desirable quality in wines such as the grassy whites of Sancerre.

STRUCTURE: A wine's armature or backbone, based largely on its tannin content. Is an assurance of the wine's strength and longevity.

SWEET: The presence of discernible sugar in a wine. (See also Residual Sugar.)

TANNIC: A wine's slight astringency or bitterness. Deriving from an assortment of organic compounds found in grape skins, seeds and stalks. Sensed as a stimulating puckery feeling in the mouth, similar to that produced by a strong cup of tea, it is associated with full-bodied red wines that become rich and mouth-filling with age.

TART: A somewhat sharp, refreshing quality that reflects a high degree of fruit acid in a wine (not to be confused with either a harsh greenness or a vinegary sourness).

TEXTURE: The tactile quality or feel of a wine in the mouth, a reflection of its grape solids. Is usually associated with red wines that are fermented on their skins..

THIN: A somewhat watery quality seen in wines deficient in body or alcohol.

TIRED: A wine whose charm has passed—one that should have been consumed young but wasn't.

UNCTUOUS: A great full-bodied fatness in a wine, produced by its high levels of glycerine, a characteristic of noble rot wines. (See also Liquoreux.)

VANILLA: A mild flavor produced by vanillin, a substance found in oak and imparted to the wine during wood-aging. It's apparent in the nose and aftertaste. Is associated with mature Bordeaux and Burgundy reds and with some Chardonnays.

VEGETAL: A wine's negative herbaceous smell and taste, caused by excessive irrigation or improper trellising. At its worst it suggests rotting vegetables. Is seen in some red Bordeaux and in some California Cabernet Sauvignons. (See also Herbaceous.)

VINOUS: The concentration or essence of a wine's good qualities. Can refer to its alcoholic strength as well.

WITHERED: A wine's desiccation—the loss of its freshness and fruit—caused by excessive oxidation. Is seen in wines left in uncorked bottles or stored in their casks too long. (See also Woody.)

WOODY: A musty, overbearing flavor and aroma in a wine. Is caused by storing it in wood too long or by a defect in the cask.

YEASTY: The taste and odor of a wine just as it emerges from fermentation. Obscuring the nose at first, it generally disappears with age. (If the yeastiness persists, the wine may have been improperly vinified.) Is considered a desirable characteristic in wines bottled soon after fermentation, such as Champagnes, Muscadets and some Swiss wines.

GRAPE VARIETIES

Some grape varieties are cultivated throughout the world, others only in restricted areas. Earlier-maturing berries are needed for the more northerly regions with their lower temperatures and briefer growing seasons. Their preeminent grapes are the red cabernet sauvignon and pinot noir, the white chardonnay and riesling. Warmer climates need grapes that can resist sunburn and shattering, yet retain a fair degree of acidity. Their most notable varieties are the red syrah, carignan, grenache and zinfandel, and the white muscat, trebbiano, french colombard and green hungarian.

Wine makers once employed only native grapes, showing little interest in those grown outside their own regions. (A number of vintners still use local grapes as much as possible to preserve the specific characteristics of their locales.) But now vines that have adapted to specific places over the centuries are being uprooted and replaced with those of distant origin. Certain grapes have been transplanted more and more; the cabernet sauvignon and chardonnay have become particularly ubiquitous.

Traditionalists view the trend with alarm. They see it as the first step in the eventual homogenization of wine styles. They warn that varietal names will lead consumers to expect the same taste in the wines regardless of where the grapes are grown. Yet the source of the grapes always matters. Although a number of varieties are adaptable to a wide range of conditions, their wines are never quite the same from one place to the next. Each wine is modified by its immediate environment, by its unique combination of site, soil, sunshine and rainfall. Transferring a grape from one region to another, even within the same country, will produce markedly different wines even when the methods of cultivation, harvesting and cellar care are identical.

NOTE: Different countries and even different sections of the same country may use different names for the same grape varieties. Grapes have also been misnamed; they've been called "pinots" or "rieslings" when they are not those varieties at all.

The following is a sampling of some of the world's grapes:

ALBANA: Italian white grape grown in Emilia-Romagna. Yields a rather high alcohol wine with a distinctive aroma, which is vinified both dry and sweet and made sparkling as well.

ALBARIÑO: Spanish white grape; the most important variety in Galicia. Produces a rich, floral wine that is often naturally pétillant. Similar to the riesling, the grape is said to be of Rhine Valley origin, although some believe it originated in Portugal.

AGLIANICO: Red grape grown in southern Italy. Yields an intense, well-structured wine that shares the elegance and longevity of those made from the country's better-known grapes.

ALEATICO: Italian red grape from Elba that may be a relative of the muscat. Yields a fairly sweet wine with a pronounced spicy flavor. (Aleatico di Portoferraio is a much-prized example.) Is cultivated all over Italy, most successfully in Tuscany, Umbria and Corsica. Brought to California nearly a century ago, the grape is used there in blending and as a dessert wine. (An off-white version, made by removing the grape skins before fermentation, is vinified dry.)

ALICANTE: See Grenache.

ALICANTE BOUSCHET: High-yielding red hybrid widely grown in California's Central Valley. Produces a sturdy and somewhat coarse high-sugar wine, best suited to bulk blending. Serves as a varietal as well. Because of its intensely colored pulp and juice, the grape also acts as a *teinturier* (dyer) to darken the state's paler red wines.

ALIGOTÉ: French white grape cultivated on the lower slopes of the Côte d'Or. Employed as a varietal, it yields a fresh, crisp wine, medium in body and with good fruit. Once considered a second-class grape in Burgundy , it came into its own when the chardonnay was in short supply there. (When overcropped, the aligoté yields generally thin and acidic wines that are used in the region's lesser blends such as the white Beaujolais.) Is also grown in California, the Russian Federation, Bulgaria and other countries where it serves both as a varietal and in blending.

AURORA: White hybrid grape extensively cultivated in New York's Finger Lakes region, where it does well in the short growing season. Yields a light, crisp, fragrant white wine that is made both dry and semidry. Serves as a component in sparkling wines as well. Is also cultivated in Switzerland.

AUXERROIS: See Malbec.

AZAL: Indigenous Portuguese white grape; a component of vinhos verdes.

BACCHUS: White hybrid grape grown in Germany; a cross between the riesling, sylvaner and the müller-thurgau. Is similar to but more prolific than the müller-thurgau.

BACO NOIR: Red hybrid grape that is early bearing and moderately frost resistant. Cultivated primarily in the American Northeast, it yields light- to full-bodied wines, some young and fruity like a Beaujolais, others with some potential for aging. Is also grown in France.

BARBERA: Red grape widely cultivated in northern Italy. Yields a dark, tannic, full-bodied, and somewhat astringent wine with a robust bouquet, good fruit flavors and a woodsy aroma. Is widely planted in California's Central Valley because of its high acidity and its resistance to sunburn and shatter. Once considered a second-rate grape—best suited to blending with the region's flabby, low-acid jug wines—it is now enjoying new popularity in California as a hearty varietal that's rich and fruity. Also is cultivated in South America.

BEAUNOIS: See Chardonnay.

BLANC FUMÉ: See Sauvignon Blanc.

BLAUBURGUNDER: See Pinot Noir.

BLAUFRÄNKISCH: Austrian red grape related to the gamay.

BOUSCHET: Also called Gros Bouschet. See Cabernet Franc.

BRETON: See Cabernet Franc.

BRUNELLO: Italian red grape, a subvariety of the sangiovese. Cultivated in Tuscany, it is responsible for Brunello di Montalcino, one of Italy's finest red wines. (See also Sangiovese.)

BUAL (*Boal* in Portuguese): White grape cultivated in Madeira whose luscious, somewhat sweet wine bears its name.

BURGER: Productive but poor-quality white grape, whose cultivation is no longer allowed in the better French vineyards. In Germany, it's used in lesser blends. In California, it serves as a blending wine and in the bulk production of sparkling wines.

BURGUNDER: See Pinot Noir.

CABERNET D'ANJOU: See Cabernet Franc.

CABERNET FRANC: French red grape closely related to the cabernet sauvignon but less tannic and more productive. Yields a rounder, faster-maturing wine with a fruitiness reminiscent of cherries, blackberries or blueberries. Widely cultivated in the Médoc and Graves, it's used there to soften and balance out the more astringent cabernet sauvignon. The predominant grape in St-Émilion, where it's known as the bouschet, it reaches its peak in the estimable wine of Cheval Blanc and is also grown in Pomerol. In the Loire, where it's called the breton, the grape is responsible for the crunchy wines of Chinon and Bourgueil, and is employed as well in Cabernet d'Anjou and Cabernet de Touraine wines, along with a number of rosés, including the Cabernet Rosé de Saumur. Is also cultivated in northeastern Italy and on the East and West Coasts of the United States. In California, the grape serves as a varietal and is also used in high-level proprietary wines.

CABERNET SAUVIGNON: Classic red grape of France; the aristocrat of Bordeaux. Yields lean, complex, full-bodied, tannic wines in the Médoc. Displaying a hardness, even an astringency, in youth, and needing plenty of time to become drinkable, its wines become soft, velvety, aromatic and complex with age. Incomparably balanced, at their finest they demonstrate strength, character, elegance and longevity.

The cabernet sauvignon is also grown elsewhere in France—in the Loire Valley and in Provence. Its popularity is increasing in Italy, where it's cultivated in Tuscany, the Piedmont and other regions. (It is either blended with traditional Italian grapes or vinified as a claret-style varietal.) Considered America's most popular red varietal, the cabernet sauvignon is grown extensively in California, where its more rapidly developing wines tend to show off well in youth. They are characterized by fruitiness and a fleshy style. Some are rich and robust, others are less tannic and light-bodied, while still others are soft and flabby. The finest examples come from Napa Valley; other good wines come from Sonoma and Santa Clara Counties. The grape is also grown in Australia, Chile and Rioja; in the latter they're called Claretes. Their wines are generally softer and easier drinking than the French. The grape is cultivated as well in Bulgaria, Hungary, Israel, Romania, the Russian Federation, South Africa and the former Yugoslavia.

CANAIOLO: Italian red grape whose soft, fragrant, and somewhat sweetish wine is used as a varietal, and in Chiantis and other blends.

CANNONAU: See Grenache.

CARIGNAN: High-yielding French grape best suited to warm-climate cultivation. Produces a sturdy, agreeable, high-alcohol wine known for its firmness and color. In the Rhône Valley and Provence, it's used as a varietal and in blending. In Italy, it's called the gragnano, and in Spain, the cariñeno—although it's known as the mazuelo in Rioja. In California, where it's called the kerrigan or carignane with an *e*, it was initially dismissed as a lesser grape. Finding greater favor there now—along with other Rhône varieties—it serves as a robust varietal and is used also in generic Burgundies and in fortified wines.

CARMENERE: French red grape employed in various Bordeaux blends; may be related to the cabernet sauvignon.

CARNELIAN: Red hybrid grape a cross between the grenache, cabernet sauvignon and carignane. Grown primarily in California's Central Valley, it yields light-colored and quick-maturing wines.

CATAWBA: Hardy, productive and vigorous red hybrid; discovered growing on the banks of the Catawba River in North Carolina. It is believed to be the result of chance pollination between a labrusca and a vinifera vine. One of the first American grapes to be developed commercially, it is now widely cultivated in New York State, Ohio and California. Is employed in various red and white blends ranging from dry to sweet. Also serves as a sparkling-wine component.

CHARBONO: Red grape grown in California and believed to be Italian in origin. Yields an extremely dark, full-bodied and flavorful, but somewhat rough wine, similar in style to a Barbera. It is employed as an inexpensive varietal and in generic Burgundies.

CHARDONEL: White hybrid grape grown in the Finger Lakes region. A cross between the chardonnay and the seyval blanc, it's more cold-resistant than the chardonnay. Yields a light, fruity, delicate wine that is vinified both dry and sweet, and also serves as a sparkling-wine component.

CHARDONNAY: Premium French white grape. One of the easiest of the noble varieties to grow; its vine is particularly vigorous and its berries ripen early. Yields fresh, clean, crisply dry, and fine-textured wines that are intensely flavored and characterized by a certain flintiness. Is used in virtually all the best French white wines, including those from the Côte d'Or and the Rhône and Loire Valleys. Is employed exclusively in the great white Burgundies, which range from the finest steely Chablis (where the grape is called the beaunois) to the soft, delicate, flowery, aromatic Meursaults and big, chewy Montrachets. Is also the basic white grape of Champagne, where it yields a firm, full, strong yet unbelievably light wine that displays extraordinary delicacy and finesse. Is also associated with such Mâconnais whites wines as Pouilly-Fuissé and St-Véran. Has recently become a fixture in the vast vineyards of the Midi, where it serves as a varietal.

Thriving under a variety of climatic and geographic conditions, the chardonnay has been planted all over the world: in Italy, Spain, Portugal, Russia, Bulgaria and the Czech Republic; in Australia, New Zealand, South America, South Africa and the United States. Italy grows the grape mostly in its northern provinces although the cultivation has lately been moving south. In the Piedmont, the grape is known as the pinot d'alba and in Alto Adige, as the weissburgunder (white burgundian). In Spain, the chardonnay enjoys considerable success in the Penedés region. Is edging out the sémillon in popularity in Australia, where its wines—depending on the growing region—range from big, fruity and often high in alcohol with a rich buttery texture, to the more austere examples. In New Zealand, the wines are leaner and more acidic.

The chardonnay, considered America's most successful white varietal—having supplanted the chenin blanc, colombard and others—is the grape of choice in at least fifteen states, including California, Oregon, Washington and New York. American Chardonnays run the gamut from fruity and uncomplicated to rich and complex. They range from the leaner, lighter, more delicate and elegantly styled to the big, mouth-filling and opulent. At their finest, the wines display a delicate, fragrant bouquet and a lightly toasted, creamy flavor. (Many however are flawed by too much body and oak, making them seem more like dessert wines than table wines.) In the more rigorous growing conditions of the Pacific Northwest and in New York's Finger Lakes and Long Island, more acidic, taut and lean wines are produced. They share some of the French intensity and fragrance. The grape is also used in generic wines and for blending in the United States.

NOTE: Initially known as the pinot blanc chardonnay, the grape was believed to be a white-fruited version of the pinot noir. When it was subsequently found to be a separate and distinct variety, most labels dropped the pinot designation, but the French still occasionally refer to the chardonnay as the pinot blanc.

CHASSELAS: Productive, early-ripening white grape; the dominant variety in Switzerland. Yields a mild, fresh, sturdy wine that at its finest is lively and often slightly pétillant. Appears in various Swiss districts under different names: as the fendant in western Valais, the dorin near Lake Geneva and the markgrafler in the east. Is also widely cultivated in France, where it produces such light, attractive wines as the Pouilly-sur-Loire and the Crepy of Savoie. Was the traditional grape in Alsace, until superseded by the gewürztraminer and other varieties, but is still used there for carafe wines and other ordinary blends. Is also grown in Germany, where it's known as the gutedal.

CHASSELAS DORÉ: See Palomino.

CHAUCHE GRIS: See Gray Riesling.

CHELOIS: Red hybrid grape grown in the Finger Lakes region of New York, the midwestern United States and Canada. Yields a dry, full-bodied vinous wine that displays a pleasant flavor and a subtle bouquet.

CHENIN BLANC: White grape that originated in Hungary and was introduced to France in the twelfth century by the monks of Angers. The principal grape of the Middle Loire, it yields a soft, flowery, fragrant wine with a melonlike succulence. It is responsible there for the finest Vouvrays; the wines of Touraine, Anjou and Savennieres; and the sparkling wines of Saumur, which at their finest retain some natural sweetness while their excellent acidity gives them a clean, crisp, lively finish.

The predominant grape of South Africa, where it's called the steen, the chenin blanc is employed there in table wines, dessert wines, generic sherries and ports. In California's Napa Valley, it yields a fresh, full, fruity wine that displays an agreeable sweetness with a nice touch of acidity. In the Central Valley, its wines are generally bland and undistinguished but with a touch of sweetness. Also serves in California as a sparkling-wine component.

NOTE: Although the chenin blanc is sometimes called the pineau blanc or pineau de la Loire and is known in Argentina and Chile as the pinot bianco, it isn't related to the pinot blanc and in fact is not a true pinot at all.

CINSAULT: Red grape that thrives in warmer climates and is grown in southern France, South Africa and California. Yields a robust wine, characterized by a certain spiciness and intensity, that adds warmth, fullness, scent and color to various blends. Cultivated extensively in the lower Rhône Valley, it serves as a component of Châteauneuf-du-Pape wines. In California, it's used in Rhône-style blends. In South Africa, where the cinsault is known as the hermitage, it's responsible for some of that country's best red wines.

CLAIRETTE: French white grape planted extensively in the Rhône Valley and in the South of France. Is employed in various blends and in the sparkling Clairette de Die.

CLEVNER: See Gewürztraminer.

CLINTON: Red hybrid grape grown in Italy. Was brought there from the United States about a century ago. Produces a popular aromatic red wine in eastern Veneto.

COLOMBARD: White grape grown in France. Yields a pale, fresh, lively wine whose acidity is balanced out by a touch of sweetness. In the Cognac region its rather acid wine is best suited to distillation and is made into brandy. In California's Central Valley, it is known as the French colombard. Its rather dry, neutral wine there is employed in blending and also goes into lesser sparklers, inexpensive table wines and generic jug wines. A few California wineries feature the grape as a varietal.

COLORINO: Highly pigmented Italian red grape grown in Tuscany and used primarily to heighten the color of Chianti wines.

CONCORD: Hardy, productive, early-ripening labrusca grape, initially cultivated in Concord, Massachusetts. Now the predominant commercial grape grown east of the Rockies, it yields a dark purple, full-bodied, aromatic, high-sugar wine with a distinctive foxy flavor. Is employed as a varietal and in various blends, including generic Burgundies and Champagnes. Also serves as a component in semisweet and sweet fortified wines. Tolerant of a wide range of growing conditions, the concord is cultivated extensively in Arkansas, Missouri, North and South Carolina, Kansas, Nebraska, Iowa, New York, California, the Pacific Northwest and elsewhere.

NOTE: Extremely versatile, the concord also serves as an eating grape and in wine concentrates, grape juice, jams and jellies as well.

CORTESE: White grape grown in Italy's Piedmont. Yields a fresh, light, dry wine with a mild fruity bouquet. Its best-known example, the Cortese di Gavi, displaying a sharp but balanced acidity, is somewhat reminiscent of a crisp, dry Chablis.

COT: See Malbec.

CRIOLLA: See Mission.

DE CHAUNAC: French-American red hybrid grape grown in New York's Finger Lakes region and on the Niagara Peninsula in Canada. Its rich, soft, claretlike wine is characterized by considerable color and substance, and is employed in various blends.

DELAWARE: Sturdy, productive red grape, discovered in New Jersey and transplanted to Delaware, Ohio. Is thought to be a complex hybrid resulting from chance pollination between labrusca vines and vinifera vines of German and Italian ancestry. Yields a pale, well-balanced wine that displays a fresh, clean, fruity taste, a pleasing flowery bouquet and a definite, but not-too-strong, foxy flavor. Is used to add body, richness and bouquet to various red and white blends and also serves as a medium-dry varietal and as a sparkling-wine component.

DIAMOND (Moore's Diamond): American white grape developed in the nineteenth century by Jacob Moore and believed to possess some European ancestry. A vigorous grower with excellent cold-weather hardiness, it is cultivated primarily in the northeastern United States, where it yields a pale, tart, delicate, almost austere wine that combines fruitiness, piquancy and great subtlety with a pronounced aromatic bouquet. Is employed both as a varietal and in table-wine and sparkling-wine blends.

DOLCETTO: Productive red grape grown in northwestern Italy; the quickest-maturing of the Piedmont reds. Yields a fragrant flavorful, medium-bodied wine with good color and plenty of fruit. (Dolcetto roughly translates as "sweet little thing," although the wine is dry.) Best known is the Dolcetto d'Alba, grown in hilly country around the city of Alba.

DORIN: See Chasselas.

DURIFF: Red grape named for the nurseryman who propagated it late in the nineteenth century. Yields a full-bodied but undistinguished wine used primarily in blending. Was once widely planted in the Rhône Valley. Is grown in California, where it's called the petite sirah.

DUTCHESS: Red hybrid grape grown in the northeastern United States and believed to be a cross between a concord, a delaware, and some vinifera grapes. Yields a light, dry, rather clean wine with a generous bouquet and no trace of foxiness. Is employed both as a varietal and in blending.

EHRENFELSER: White hybrid grape; a cross between the riesling and the sylvaner. Grown in Germany, it's popular in the cooler districts because of its ability to produce higher yields of quality fruit in a relatively short growing season. Serves as a blending grape.

ELVIRA: American white grape; discovered in Missouri and now also grown in New York State. Relatively low in sugar and medium in acidity, it yields a fresh, attractive, spicy and somewhat foxy wine used in various blends.

EMERALD RIESLING: White hybrid grape; a cross between the johannisberg riesling and the muscadelle. Developed for California's warm climates, it has been increasingly cultivated in the Central Valley. Its rather soft, light, semisweet wine with an agreeable bouquet is employed as a varietal and in various blends. Is also grown in Israel, where it produces a charming, flavorful wine.

FENDANT: See Chasselas.

FLORA: White hybrid grape developed at the University of California; a cross between the gewürztraminer and the sémillon. Yields a spicy wine, somewhat similar to a Gewürztraminer, employed as a varietal and in various blends. Also serves as a component in sparkling wines.

FOLLE BLANCHE: White grape widely cultivated in France. Known as the gros plant in the Loire Valley, it yields a light, dry wine there that's thinner and sharper than a Muscadet. In the Cognac region, its light-bodied, high-acid wine is best suited to distillation. In Armagnac, where the grape is called the picpoul, its wine is also distilled into brandy. Is grown in California's North Coast counties as well, where it serves as a varietal wine and in generic Chablis blends.

FRANKEN RIESLING: White hybrid grape grown in California; a cross between the sylvaner and the mainriesling. Yields a pale, dry, delicate and fairly fruity wine that is used as a varietal and in generic Rhine wines.

FREISA: Italian red grape, vinified both dry and semisweet. (It is somewhat tart when young.) Best-known examples are Freisa di

Chieri and Freisa d'Asti. Is also used as a component in sparkling wines. In California, it serves as a blending grape.

FRENCH COLOMBARD: See Colombard.

FURMINT: White grape grown extensively in southeastern and Central Europe (Hungary, Germany and Italy). Yields a wine with an almost herblike aroma whose best-known example is the sweet luscious, golden Tokay of Hungary.

GAMAY: French red grape prized for its easy-growing, quick-maturing qualities. Cultivated extensively in Beaujolais, it yields a medium-bodied wine with a distinctive fruitiness, a fresh, light, enticing flavor and a wonderful sprightliness. Elsewhere in Burgundy, its wines are commonplace. Barred from the best Burgundian vineyards, the grape is used primarily in regional blends. The gamay is also grown throughout the Loire Valley, in certain sectors of the Northern Rhône and in Switzerland. In California, it is used in a varietal wine.

GAMAY BEAUJOLAIS: Red hybrid grape initially thought to be a gamay but now believed to be a lesser clone of the pinot noir or an obscure grape from the South of France. Grown widely as well in California's North Coast counties, it yields a generally fruity wine there. Is variously employed as a varietal, in rosés and in generic Burgundies.

GARGANEGA: Italian white grape grown in Lombardy and Veneto. Serves as a component in Soaves and other white-wine blends.

GARNACHA: See Grenache.

GEWÜRZTRAMINER: White grape, which is a selected strain or clone of the traminer and named for Tramin or Termeno, its village of origin in the Italian Tyrol. (Although traminer and gewürztraminer are technically interchangeable, the latter—which translates as "spicy traminer"—supposedly yields a more intense and flavorful wine.) The gewürztraminer is grown in Alsace, elsewhere in Europe and in the United States. In Alsace, its distinctive wine displays an infectious floral bouquet, an intensely fruity taste, a slight sweetness and a concentrated pungent flavor that is evocative of herbs and spices. Yet despite its rich, flowery bouquet, the wine is quite dry. Is also cultivated in Germany, where it's known as the clevner; in Switzerland, where it's called the heide; in the Italian Tyrol, where it's called the traminer aromatico; as well as in Austria, Eastern Europe and California. (Outside Alsace, the spiciness of the wine is muted.) In California, the wine is heavier and more alcoholic than in Alsace.

GRAGNANO: See Carignan.

GRAUERBURGUNDER: See Pinot Gris.

GRAY RIESLING: French white grape, also known as the chauche gris. Grown in Alsace, it yields a fresh, clean wine with a flowery fragrance. Despite its name, it is not a true riesling.

GRECHETTO: Italian white grape; the basic component of Orvieto. Is also blended with the chardonnay to create an earthy white wine.

GRENACHE: French red grape; a principal variety in the Rhône Valley. Lightly pigmented and high-yielding, it produces a fairly assertive, occasionally hard wine that serves as a traditional component in Châteauneuf-du-Pape and the region's heavier blends. Is also grown in the Loire Valley and in the South of France, where it's known as the alicante. Yields a good dessert wine in Banyuls, adds strength and fruitiness to Provençal blends and is responsible for some of the best rosés of Tavel and Lirac. Serves principally as a blending grape in Rioja, where it's called the garnacha, and in Sardinia, where it's called the cannonau. In California, it serves as a varietal that at its finest is redolent of fruit and spices. In the Central Valley, it's a workaday grape that yields large quantities of light-colored, full-bodied, generally undistinguished wines. It is used there in various table-wine blends and in generic ports. Is also grown in Australia.

GRIGNOLINO: Italian red grape grown in the Piedmont, particularly in Asti. Yields a dry, rather high alcohol wine, light to medium in body, with a flowerlike aroma, an almost imperceptible touch of bitterness and a slightly sharp aftertaste. Also serves as a component in sparkling wines. The grignolino in California yields a pleasant varietal and is used in rosé wines as well.

GROS LOT (Grolleau): Productive French grape grown in the Loire Valley, whose fair-quality wine is often vinified to retain a degree of sugar. Is also employed in ordinary Anjou rosés and in lesser table-wine blends.

GROS PLANT: See Folle Blanche.

GRÜNER VELTLINER: Austrian white grape yielding a fruity, delicate, and lively wine. Is extensively cultivated in Italy and California as well.

GUTEDEL: See Chasselas.

HEIDE: See Gewürztraminer.

HERMITAGE: Australian red grape; an offspring of the cinsault. (Named for a famous Rhône Valley vineyard whose primary grape is the syrah, not the cinsault.) Yields a sturdy red wine with great staying power.

HUNTER VALLEY RIESLING: White grape grown in Australia. Despite its name, it is not a riesling at all but a sémillon. (See also Sémillon.)

IONA: American red grape named for an island in the upper Hudson River where it was first grown. Cultivated extensively in the Finger Lakes region now, it serves as a component in white-wine blends there.

ISABELLA: American red grape; one of the country's first commercially grown grapes. Yields a full-bodied, slightly dry wine with a distinctive foxy flavor that has been employed as a varietal, in various red and rosé blends and in generic champagnes. Considered an inferior variety now, it is no longer much grown.

IVES: American red grape related to the concord and believed to be an accidental hybrid. Is named for Henry Ives, who grew it from seed on the banks of the Ohio River. Its coarse, heavy wine with a strong, foxy flavor is particularly valued for its deep red color. It is employed in generic Burgundies, in still and sparkling wines and in sweet fortified blends.

JAQUEZ: White grape grown in Madeira. More disease-resistant than other local varieties, it is frequently included in blends bearing the names of the island's better-known grapes.

JOHANNISBERGER: See Sylvaner.

JOHANNISBERG RIESLING: See Riesling.

KADARKA: Hungarian red grape similar in style and color to the Italian grignolino. Is believed to be Albanian in origin. Serves as the principal grape in Hungary's Egri Bikavér (Bull's Blood) wine.

KERRIGAN: See Carignan.

KLEVNER: See Pinot Noir.

KNIPPERLÉ: Alsatian white peasant grape whose generally

undistinguished wine is used in lesser blends.

LAGREIN (Lagarino): Red grape grown in the Italian Tyrol and employed there in light red and rosé blends.

LAMBRUSCO: Italian red grape grown in Emilia-Romagna whose light-colored wine is somewhat fizzy and not entirely dry. Is also employed in blush wines and in white-wine blends.

MAINRIESLING: White hybrid grape; a cross between a true riesling and a sylvaner. Is employed in various blends.

MÁLAGA: Prolific California red grape employed in various blends. (It is not related to the Málaga wines of Spain.)

MALBEC: French red grape, once widely planted in Bordeaux. Its rich, full, moderately tannic, and relatively quick maturing wine is used to soften the more astringent Cabernet Sauvignon. It's now primarily the grape of choice in Cahors, where it is called the cot or the auxerrois. In southern France, it's known as the pressac. In Argentina—where its name is sometimes spelled "malbeck"—the grape yields a supple, medium-bodied and popular varietal. Is also cultivated in California's Napa Valley and is a rising star in Long Island vineyards.

MALVASIA (Malmsey): White grape originating in Crete and now grown principally in the South of France, most notably in Banyuls and Roussillon, where it is blended with the grenache and other varieties to produce both apéritif and sweet dessert wines. Also widely grown in Italy, it adds a slightly broad style and aroma to Est! Est! Est! and Frascati wines, and is employed as well in Verdicchio and Chianti blends. In Sicily, its rich, liquoroso wine is responsible for the sweet, golden Malvasia di Lipari, one of the country's best dessert wines. In Madeira, it makes a rich, sweet, aromatic wine called Malmsey. In California, its wines are undistinguished and employed in various still-, sparkling-, and dessert-wine blends.

MALVOISIE: See Pinot Gris.

MARÉCHAL FOCH: Red hybrid grape cultivated in the northeastern United States. Winter-hardy, it requires only a brief growing season. Yields a dry, fairly sturdy, berrylike wine, somewhat reminiscent of a Burgundy.

MARKGRÄFLER: See Chasselas.

MARSANNE: White grape of the Northern Rhône Valley,

employed in Hermitage Blanc wines. In California, it has become an increasingly important variety.

MATARO: See Mourvèdre.

MAZUELO: See Carignan.

MERLOT: Early-maturing French grape, widely planted in Bordeaux. Its supple, medium-bodied wine with accessible tannins and a berrylike taste is routinely used to soften the more astringent Cabernet Sauvignons. In St-Émilion and Pomerol, the grape constitutes about 80 percent of the blend and at Château Pétrus—where it is used exclusively—it yields a full-bodied wine unmatched in its excellence.

Softer and rounder than the cabernet sauvignon, the merlot has been increasing in popularity. It is now cultivated in the South of France, Italy, Spain, Switzerland, Hungary, Romania, Bulgaria, the former Yugoslavia, South America (Argentina and Chile), Australia, New Zealand and the United States. In Italy, where it's grown from the Alps to the tip of the boot,the merlot yields wines ranging from inexpensive jug wines to rare and expensive ones. In northern Italy, particularly in Veneto, the grape does extremely well, yielding a rich, chewy wine with good fruit and a seductive aroma. Elsewhere in Italy, its wine is generally soft and bland. The merlot also serves as a key component in Hungary's Egri Bikavér and in Spain's Vega Sicilia. It is bottled as a varietal in Australia and is also used in blending there. In Napa and Sonoma in California it makes for a soft, plummy varietal and is also used to soften Cabernet Sauvignon wines. The merlot has been successfully cultivated on Long Island as well.

MEUNIER: Productive French red grape. Is traditionally combined in Champagne with the pinot noir and chardonnay. In Alsace and the Loire, it yields pleasant rosé wines. In California, it serves as a blending grape. Fermented away from its skins there, it produces a white wine.

NOTE: The meunier, a subvariety, is sometimes confused with the point noir.

MISSION: Red grape believed to be of Spanish origin and initially called the criollas. Brought to California from Mexico by Franciscan monks in the eighteenth century, it became the first vinifera to be cultivated in America. Yields a fruitful and vigorous wine but one lacking in color and acidity. Although no longer highly regarded, it is still cultivated by bulk producers in Southern California, where it's used in table-wine blends, in generic ports and sherries and in sweet dessert wines.

MISSOURI RIESLING: Indigenous American white grape resembling the elvira. Despite its name, it is not a true riesling at all.

MOORE'S DIAMOND: See Diamond.

MOURVÈDRE: Warm-climate red grape that originated in Spain, where it is called the mataro. Yields a dry, astringent wine with hard tannins used primarily in blending. In France, particularly in the Southern Rhône, it adds finesse to Châteauneuf and Côte du Rhône blends. In the South of France, it's combined with the grenache and cinsault to produce the fine red wine of Bandol. In California, where it's called the mataro, it yields a dry and flavorful vin gris.

MÜLLER-THURGAU: Prolific, hardy, early-ripening white hybrid grape developed in the nineteenth century by a Swiss scientist who left no written record of his work. Was at first believed to be a cross between a riesling and a sylvaner, but is now thought to be a cross between two riesling clones. Designed for difficult climates, it is able to withstand harsh winter weather and to achieve a highly reliable yield in a relatively short growing season. Less acid than the riesling and the most widely planted grape variety in Germany, the müller-thurgau is responsible for vast quantities of mild, middle-range wines—soft-scented with a flowery bouquet and a slight muscat flavor. (Some, however, are undistinguished and flabby.) The grape serves as a component in various blends, including Moselblümchens and sparkling sekts. It is cultivated as well in Austria and central Europe.

MUSCADELLE: French white grape grown in the sweet-wine districts of Bordeaux. Generally blended with the sémillon and sauvignon blanc in Sauternes and Barsac, it imparts a faint, agreeable muscat flavor to their wines.

MUSCADET (Melon de Bourgogne): French white grape initially grown in Burgundy, where its wines were of little quality or interest. Transplanted to Brittany, it yielded a light wine with a faint muscat flavor that made the region famous. Is now cultivated extensively in the lower Loire. In California, where it's known as the pinot blanc, it yields a heavier, fruitier wine.

MUSCADINE: A subgenus of the *Vitis* rotundfolia. (Also see Scuppernong.)

MUSCAT: One of the oldest grape families; some believe the Vitis viniferas are its direct descendants, is thought to have been either grown by the Phoenicians, Greeks and Romans in what is now southern France, or else transplanted there by the Crusaders on their return from Corinth and Cyprus. Cultivated more widely than any other species, its grapes are variously called muscatel, muscadelle, moscatel, moscat, muskat, moscat ottonel and so on. High in sugar and low in acidity, the grapes yield characteristically rich wines with a pronounced flavor and scent, and a powerful fruity bouquet. Exhibiting a distinctive honeysuckle taste and a certain muskiness, they usually show to best advantage in dessert wines, although some are served as apéritifs. The Muscat grape is particularly useful in blending as well because of its great ability to knit other wines together.

There are perhaps hundreds of subvarieties, ranging in color from pale yellow to reddish amber, on to almost black. They are grown in Italy, France, Spain, Portugal, Greece, Hungary, the United States, Australia, and the islands of Cyprus and Sardinia. The wines themselves vary in style from country to country, ranging from light to heavy and from completely dry to intensely sweet. One of the best examples, Muscat d'Alsace, is a full-bodied, dry and aromatic wine with a spicy bouquet. (It serves as an apéritif.) From the Mediterranean region of France comes the sweet fortified Muscat Doré de Frontignan. Italy is also known for its sweet Muscats: its Moscato d'Asti, Moscato di Canelli, Moscato del Trentino, Moscato Siracusa, and so on. The United States produces a Muscat Blanc and a Muscat Canelli, among others. Australia is particularly known for its Brown Muscat.

MUSCATEL: See Muscat.

MUSKAT: See Muscat.

NAGYBURGUNDI: See Pinot Noir.

NAPA GAMAY: See Gamay Beaujolais.

NEBBIOLO: Italian red grape whose name derives from *nebbia,* which translates as "fog" and refers to the early-morning mist clinging to the Alban hills during the harvest season. The wine, sturdy, chewy, and full-bodied, fairly high in alcohol and intensely flavored, exudes the aroma of dried fruit. The nebbiolo is associated with the Piedmont's greatest wines: its most powerful Barolos, its most refined Barbarescos, its Gattinaras, Infernos, Sassellas and Grumellos, along with other still and sparkling wines. In parts of the Piedmont, the grape is known as the spanna. In Valtellina, it is called the chiavennasca. And in California's Central Valley the nebbiolo has become an increasingly popular variety.

NIAGARA: Versatile white hybrid grown on the Niagara Peninsula, a stretch of land shared by Canada and New York's Finger Lakes region. Its fruity wines range from fresh and clean, with a distinctive foxy flavor, to rather sweet and bland. The niagara is employed in a semidry varietal and in various fortified blends, including generic sherries.

PALOMINO: Spanish white grape cultivated on the chalky soil of Jerez; the great grape of sherry. Is also grown in California's Central Valley, where it serves as a component in dry table wines and in sweet fortified blends, including generic sherries. (In California, it's known as the chasselas doré or "golden chasselas," although it isn't a chasselas grape at all.)

PARELLADA: A white grape from Catalonia in Spain. In California, it's used in chardonnay blends.

PEDRO XIMÉNEZ (PX): Spanish white grape widely grown in Jerez. Yields a thick, highly aromatic wine with concentrated flavors that suggest prunes, coffee or chocolate. Adds depth, color and sweetness to sherry blends.

PETITE ARVINE: Swiss white grape that supposedly traces its lineage back to the Roman legions.

PETITE SIRAH: Red grape initially believed related to the Rhône Valley syrah but now said to be the duriff. Yields a big, rough, full-bodied, tannic wine better known for its strength and vigor than for its elegance. Long popular as a blending grape in California, it adds color and body to generic Burgundies and to various jug wine blends there. Now made as a varietal as well, it yields a full-bodied, intensely colored wine, with soft, fruity flavors that becomes rich and generous when oak-aging has smoothed out its tannins.

PETIT VERDOT: French red grape whose characteristically acid and assertive wine adds body to Bordeaux blends. Some wine makers in California are using it in their Cabernet Sauvignon blends.

PICPOULE: See Folle Blanche.

PINEAU DE LA LOIRE: See Chenin Blanc.

PINOT: A noble grape family whose name derives from pine cone—a reference to the shape of its clusters. Known for yielding wines with breed, the pinot is widely planted in many of the world's best growing regions. Its subvarieties include the red pinot noir and pinot meunier and the white pinot blanc and pinot gris.

PINOTAGE: Red hybrid grape; a cross between Burgundy's pinot noir and the Rhône Valley cinsault. Developed in South Africa in the 1920s, it yields soft, round, fruity wines with some refinement that resemble the Rhône wines.

PINOT BLANC: French white grape widely grown in Burgundy. Yields light-textured, agreeably dry and fruity wines of some character and class. One of the best, a soft wine from Alsace, exhibits intense flavors, a beautiful bouquet and a touch of spiciness at its finest. In the Loire, the grape is called the melon de bourgogne, better known as the muscadet. It's grown as well in Italy, Germany, Austria, and the United States. In California, it's made as a crisp, dry, fruity varietal and also serves as a component in still and sparkling wine blends.

NOTE: Once an important component in Champagnes and other blends in France, the pinot blanc has been largely supplanted there by the chardonnay.

PINOT GRIGIO: Italy's most popular white grape, grown mainly in the northeast. Almost identical to the French pinot gris, it yields a pleasant, dry, fruit-scented wine that is vinified both light, fruity and crisp, and richer and more full bodied. The best examples, soft, fruity and fragrant, come from the Friuli region. In the United States, the grape produces a popular but undistinguished wine.

PINOT GRIS: French white grape grown in cool climates whose sturdy, dry wine characteristically displays a fullness and a slight fragrance. In Alsace, where it's called the tokay d'alsace, its wine is high in alcohol and austerely dry with very round flavors.

Grown in various countries, the grape is known as the pinot grigio in Italy, the malvoisie in Switzerland, and the rülander and grauerburgunder ("gray burgundian") in Germany. Thriving in the American Northwest, it yields a wonderfully fruity yet dry wine, particularly in Oregon.

PINOT MEUNIER: See Meunier.

PINOT NOIR: Extremely dark purple—almost black—grape, believed to have been brought to Gaul by the Greeks. Finicky, troublesome, and hard to grow, it does best in chalky soils and in cool climates with long growing seasons. The principal red grape of Burgundy, it produces wines, which range from light and charming to big and mouth-filling. It's responsible for the great, subtle, and splendid reds of the Côte d'Or, which are rich in their alcohol and strength and distinctively fruity and velvety. They are also characterized by a deep, elegant bouquet and the ability to age well. Also yields excellent full-bodied rosés in Burgundy that have a lovely pink hue. (When transplanted south to Beaujolais, its wine disappoints.) Is a key component as well in Champagne blends. In Alsace, it makes for light, pleasant red wines. It's also grown in the Loire Valley.

Hundreds of pinot noir clones are now cultivated in Germany, Austria, Italy, Switzerland, Hungary and the former Yugoslavia, as well as in South America (Chile), Australia, New Zealand, South Africa and the United States. Known as the spätburgunder ("late burgundian") in Germany, it yields the country's best red wines, characterized by a fine bouquet and a piquant spiciness. Is responsible for good German rosés as well. In Austria, where it's called the spätburgunder or blauburgunder (blue burgundian), its wines tend to be rather thin and commonplace. In Switzerland, where it's called the bourgogne or burgunder in one district and the klevner in another, it yields a deep-colored, full-bodied varietal with a good potential for aging. Blended with the gamay in Valais, it produces the fine red wine called Dole. In Hungary, where the grape is called the nagyburgundi, it yields a highly valued wine.

In northern Italy, where it's known as the pinot nero, it yields smooth, full-bodied, full-flavored wines that serve as components in Asti Spumante blends. In California, the grape is employed in varietals and in the better sparkling blends. Its wines there are drier and less complex than the French, with many of them relatively light bodied. The pinot noir does particularly well in Oregon, where its varietals are closer in character and style to their Burgundian prototypes. In Long Island, the grape has been used in sparkling red wine blends.

PINOT ST. GEORGE: Red grape grown in California's North Coast counties. Yields a thin, somewhat astringent wine employed in various generic and other table-wine blends. (Is not a true pinot at all, but a lesser variety.)

PLANT D'ARBOIS: See Poulsard.

PORTUGIESER: Prolific, early-ripening red grape, the mainstay of Germany's red wines. Widely planted in Rheinhessen and the Pfalz, it yields light-colored wines, somewhat sweeter than the Spätburgunders and with less body. In Austria, the grape is known as the blauer portugieser.

POULSARD: French red grape, also known as the plant d'arbois. Grown in the Jura, its light-colored wines are the best reds of the region.

PRESSAC: See Malbec.

PROCANICO: See Trebbiano.

PROSECCO: Italian white grape grown in Veneto. Yields a light, dry, pleasant wine, occasionally vinified semisweet; that also serves as a sparkling-wine component.

RAMISCO: Hardy Portuguese red grape, grown near the coast in Colares and yielding a dry, fruity red wine. Is able to withstand the ravages of salt water and wind and can also resist phylloxera when planted deep in sandy soil.

RAVAT: See Vignoles.

RED PINOT: Lesser California grape whose wine is used in blending. (Despite its name, the grape is not a true pinot.)

RIESLANER: German white hybrid; a cross between the riesling and the sylvaner. Grown in the Pfalz, it is used in various blends.

RIESLING (Johannisberg Riesling): Hardy and frost-resistant German white grape; one of the noble and classic varieties. Is believed to have come from an ancient, wild Teutonic vine. Flourishes in Germany's northernmost vineyards, where it is the source of virtually all fine Rhine and Mosel wines. Can ripen steadily to high levels of sugar while retaining the acidity that gives its wines an unanticipated life expectancy. A modest bearer, the grape combines the highest possible quality with the smallest yield. It is also particularly suited to late harvesting and is one of the few varieties susceptible to noble rot.

Riesling wines range from light and crisply acid to sweet and unctuous. At their finest, they are distinguished by a harmony of tartness and sweetness, a sharp, crisp taste and a flowery bouquet. Elegant with a touch of dryness, together with a discreetly perfumed fragrance, they demonstrate breed, character, and an uncommon depth.

The riesling grape is grown elsewhere in Europe—in France, Switzerland, Portugal, Italy, Austria, the former Yugoslavia, Bulgaria and so forth—as well as in the United States, South America, Australia and New Zealand. In Alsace, its wine is dry and well structured, with steely flavors, firm fruit and an unusually excellent balance. Known as the wälschriesling in Austria and Eastern Europe, the grape there is more productive and yields a lighter, slightly coarser wine. Called the weisser riesling in South Africa, it is responsible for a steely dry wine resembling a Muscadet from the Loire. In Chile, its light, crisp, attractive wine serves both as a varietal and as a component in sparkling-wine blends. In California, where it's known as the johannisberg riesling or white riesling, its wines range from the dry and refreshing to the somewhat flowery and not-too-dry, and feature a fruity aroma and a mild bouquet. The grape also thrives in the Pacific Northwest.

NOTE: A number of varieties bearing the riesling name are not rieslings at all. Among these are the gray riesling, missouri riesling, paarl riesling, emerald riesling, franken riesling, mainriesling and hunter valley riesling.

ROUSSANNE: French white grape grown extensively in the Rhône Valley. Yields fresh fragrant wines; some full in body and rather pronounced in character. Is used in various blends along with viognier and marsanne grapes. Is also employed in St-Peray and other sparkling wines, in the white Seysalls, and in the regional Roussette de Savoie. Grown now in California, the roussanne produces Rhône-style wines there.

RUBY CABERNET: Red hybrid; a cross between the carignane and the cabernet sauvignon. Designed to withstand a hot climate, it's grown extensively in California's Central Valley, where it's used mainly as a blending wine. Also yields a fruity, dry varietal with good color, acidity and flavor.

RULANDER: See Pinot Gris.

ST-ÉMILION: See Trebbiano.

SANGIOVESE: Italian red grape; second only to the Barbera in popularity. Yields lively, full-bodied, tannic and somewhat astringent wines. In Tuscany, it's combined with the trebbiano and malvasia in Chianti blends. In Emilia-Romagna, it's made as a varietal that's somewhat harsh in youth but whose bouquet intensifies with age. In California, it serves primarily as a blending grape but is now made as a varietal as well. In the Napa Valley, its wine—less sharply defined than in Italy—is bigger and softer, with abundant fruit. The sangioveto, a smaller, more intense version yields richer and longer lasting wines.

SANGIOVESE GROSSO: Italian red grape, a clone of the sangiovese. Is responsible for Brunello di Montalcino, one of Italy's prized red wines. Is also grown in California, where it's blended with the cabernet sauvignon.

SAUVIGNON BLANC: French white grape; the principal grape of the Loire Valley, where it's known as the blanc fumé. Increasing in popularity, it has been superseding the chenin blanc there. The grape of Pouilly-Fumé, Quincy and Reuilly, it yields a sprightly, fresh and fruity, lean and austerely dry wine with a slightly herbaceous or grassy taste and a long-lasting finish. Vinified as a sweet wine in Bordeaux, it is responsible for the luscious and memorable wines of Sauternes and Barsac there. In graves it is better suited to dry wines.

Is also grown in Italy, Cyprus, Austria, Australia, New Zealand, South America (Chile and Argentina) and the United States. In cooler regions, it yields intensely flavored wines; in warmer regions, softer, flabbier ones. A mainstay of the California vineyards, it is vinified in a variety of styles there, ranging from light and fruity to the rich and oaky. Is generally called fumé blanc when made as a drier-style varietal (similar to a Pouilly-Fumé) and called sauvignon blanc when vignified in a somewhat sweeter style. California uses the grape in generic Sauternes as well.

SAUVIGNON VERT: California white grape grown in the North Coast counties. Its harsh, bitter wine is used to offset the blandness of the generic Sauterne and Chablis blend.

SAVAGNIN: French white grape believed to be of Hungarian

lineage; it may have been transplanted by a returning Crusader. Serves as a component in vin jaune and in vin de paille blends.

SCHEUREBE: Sturdy German white hybrid; a cross between sylvaner and riesling grapes. Resistant to cold and disease and more prolific and easier to cultivate than the riesling, it is grown in the Pfalz and in Rheinhessen. Its wines can be hard and acidic at first, but take on fruit and finesse after a few years. When very ripe, the grape yields semidry and sweet dessert wines with a lush black currant flavor. It is also receptive to noble rot. The scheurebe is now cultivated in California's Napa Valley and in Washington State and Oregon as well.

SCHIAVA: Italian red grape grown in the Tyrol and on the western shore of Lake Garda. Yields a light red wine, used in Caldaro and Santa Maddalena blends.

SCUPPERNONG: American white grape, the best-known variety of the muscadine species. Thrives in the warm, humid climate of the southeastern United States, where it yields an amber-colored, rather full bodied wine that is usually quite aromatic and sweet. Is also grown in the Midwest.

SÉMILLON: French white grape cultivated extensively in Bordeaux and throughout the wine-growing world. Its rather rounded and velvety wines are noted for their fragrance. Serving as the base of the great white Bordeaux, it is traditionally blended with the sauvignon blanc and, to a lesser extent, with the muscadelle. Susceptible to noble rot, it is a major component in the luscious wines of Sauternes and Barsac. Blended with the sauvignon blanc in Graves, it produces a soft-bodied wine, balanced by a clean, crisp grassiness and a fruity bouquet. Is also used in the drier white wines of Entre-Deux-Mers and Monbazillac. It's cultivated as well in the United States, South America and Australia. It is an important varietal in Australia, where it's known as the hunter valley riesling. In California and Washington State, it appears both as a light, dry wine and as a sweet varietal. Is also used in various American blends, including the best generic Sauternes.

SERCIAL: White grape grown in Madeira. Of unclear origin, although it's thought to be a descendant of the riesling. It's employed in the dry Madeira wine that bears its name.

SEYVAL BLANC: French-American hybrid grape developed to

survive the harsh growing conditions of the northeastern and midwestern United States. Yields a high-quality, full-bodied, and well-balanced white wine, displaying a delightful bouquet and a clear crisp finish. (Is similar in style to the Sancerres and other French wines based on the sauvignon blanc.) Is responsible for some of the best wines in New York State and is also used there as a late-harvest grape there and as a component in sparkling wines. Is cultivated in France and in Canada as well.

SHIRAZ: See Syrah.

SPANNA: See Nebbiolo.

SPÄTBURGUNDER: See Pinot Noir.

STEEN: South African white grape; initially thought to be a cross between a riesling and an indigenous variety, but is now identified as the chenin blanc. Yields sweet, light, fragrant, and fruity wines. Is sometimes late-harvested as well.

STEUBEN: American red grape that serves as a component in various blends. Its wine is more delicately flavored than that of the concord's.

SYLVANER: German white grape that is faster-ripening and more productive than the riesling. Planted principally in Rheinhessen and in the Pfalz, it is responsible for a large proportion of Germany's fair to ordinary wines. Considered a superior variety in Franconia, it yields a wine that is light, fresh, and unusually mild at its finest, with a slight touch of acidity.

The sylvaner is widely cultivated in many parts of Europe—France, Switzerland, Austria, the Italian Tyrol and Hungary—and in the United States and Chile. In the Valais district of Switzerland, it is known as the johannisberger and in Austria as the osterreicher. Its wine in Alsace is charming with a clean, refreshing bouquet.

SYMPHONY: White hybrid grape developed in California and involving the muscat of Alexandria. Yields a wine similar to a Gewürztraminer whose flavors and aromas recall flowers, oranges and spices.

SYRAH: Slow-maturing French red grape, initially believed to have been introduced to France in the thirteenth century by Crusaders returning from Shiraz in Persia (now Iran). Scholars now think that the Phoenician seamen who founded Marseille brought the grapes from Asia Minor around 600 B.C. Its powerful, intense, tannic and deep-colored wine displays a smoky licoricelike quality and a memorable bouquet. The grape—in conjunction with the white viognier and marsanne—is responsible for the great red wines of the Rhône, which include the Hermitage, Châteauneuf-du-Pape and Côte Rôtie. It also provides the structure and backbone for other Rhône wines and adds robustness, color and bouquet to the blends of Provence. The syrah has become an important grape in California, where it serves as a varietal and in Rhône-style blends. Called the shiraz in Australia, it was widely planted there in the nineteenth century. Now the country's dominant grape, it yields a fruity, full-bodied, tannic wine, with a rough, spicy character, that is sometimes blended with the Cabernet Sauvignon. The syrah cultivated in South Africa as well.

TEMPRANILLO: Red grape believed to be a strain of the pinot noir, brought to Spain centuries ago by the monks of Cluny. Now the principal grape of Rioja, it yields a soft, spicy, moderately acid wine with a full, rich quality, a chewy texture and a lingering finish. Is employed there both as a varietal and in blending. Is also grown in La Mancha, where it is known as the cencibel, and in the Duero, where it's called the tinto fino. Elsewhere in Spain, the tempranillo is called the tinto del pais. Now cultivated in California as well, where it's called the valdepeñas.

THOMPSON SEEDLESS: California white grape grown extensively by the state's bulk wine producers. Its nondescript, rather neutral, low-acid wine is used in generic Rieslings and in various table- and jug-wine blends. Also serves as an eating grape and as a source of raisins.

TINTA: Portuguese red grape whose deep-colored, full-bodied wine is employed mainly in port and Dão blends. It is also grown in Madeira. Cultivated in California's Central Valley, it's generally used there for sweet fortified wines, including some of the better generic ports.

TOCAI: Italian white grape that yields a fairly full bodied, dry wine with a delicate aroma and a slightly bitter aftertaste.

TOKAY: California red grape said to have originated in Algeria and used as an eating rather than as a wine grape. (Is not related to the Tokay wines of Hungary, which are pressed from the furmint grape.)

TOKAY D'ALSACE: See Pinot Gris.

TORRANTES: Algerian white grape whose spicy, dry wine is somewhat reminiscent of an Alsatian Gewürztraminer.

TRAMINER: See Gewürztraminer.

TREBBIANO: Widely cultivated Italian white grape; the source of most of the country's white wines. Yields a luscious, fruity, definitely scented, and fairly assertive varietal in Tuscany. Elsewhere in the country its wine is generally bland and unimpressive, and serves as a component in Orvieto, Frascati and Chianti blends. The trebbiano di soave, a subvariety, yields a wine with some character that is used in the best Soaves. The trebbiano toscano, coarser and more prolific, yields a blander wine. In Umbria, the grape is known as the procanico.

The trebbiano is cultivated in other parts of Europe as well. Known as the ugni blanc in the South of France, it produces generally uninteresting wines, except for the fresh whites of Cassis. In the Charente, where it's called the St-Émilion, it yields a high-acid, low-alcohol wine that achieves greatness when distilled as cognac. In California, it yields an agreeable but neutral wine that is almost always employed in blends, although occasionally made as a varietal.

UGNI BLANC: See Trebbiano.

VALDEPENAS: See Tempranillo.

VALPANTENA: Italian red grape named for a region in Verona; its wine is employed in Valpolicella blends.

VELTLINER: See Gruner Veltliner.

VERDEJO: Spanish white grape that yields light, aromatic wines.

VERDELHO: Spanish white grape believed to derive from the pedro ximénez. Cultivated extensively in Madeira, it is employed in the somewhat sweet fortified wines that bear its name. In Portugal, it serves as a component in white ports.

VERDICCHIO: Italian white grape grown in Marches on the Adriatic coast, where it yields a pleasant, dry varietal wine. (The grape is also known as the grechetto.)

VERDOT: French red grape grown in Bordeaux. Its deep-colored, full-bodied, fruity and tannic wine serves as a component in claret blends.

VERGENNES: American white grape grown in New York State. Its very dry, exquisitely flavored wine is employed there both as a varietal and in blends.

VERNACCIA: Italian white grape grown in Tuscany. Yields a fresh, fruity, full-bodied wine that exhibits good acidity and sometimes earthy nuances, and is vinified both dry and sweet. Best known is the Vernaccia di San Gimignano, grown around the ancient town of that name. In Sardinia, the grape produces a very dry wine with an intense almondlike aroma resembling an unfortified sherry.

VIDAL: American white hybrid; a cross between traditional European viniferas and native labrusca grapes. A relatively early ripener, it's grown in the Finger Lakes region of New York State, where it yields an excellent and naturally sweet wine.

VIGNOLES: French-American white hybrid, winter-hardy and rapidly maturing. Grown in the Finger Lakes region of New York, it yields a fairly full wine with a distinctive bouquet that serves as the base for sparkling wines. Sometimes late-harvested as well, the grape is also known as the ravat.

VIOGNIER: French white grape, originally transported to Marseille by the Greeks, then brought north to the Rhône Valley. Yields a wine with a flowery perfume and a crisp but fruity flavor. Reaches its peak in Château Grillet and is responsible for the rare white wines of Condrieu as well. Is added in small quantities to the the grape red wines of the Côte Rôtie to soften them and make them less astringent. Is also grown in Languedoc-Roussillon. Now cultivated in California, it yields an intensely fruity, spicy wine there that is mainly used in blending. It is also grown in a number of other American states, and experimental plantings are currently under way in Italy and Australia.

VIURA: Spanish white grape grown in Rioja. Yields a light, aromatic wine, displaying an excellent crispness.

WÄLSCHRIESLING: See Riesling.

WEISSBURGUNDER: See Chardonnay.

ZINFANDEL (Zin): Reliable, sturdy, tough-skinned and prolific red grape, characterized by high sugars and tannins. It has been called a "truly American grape," but is of unknown origin. Similar to the primitivo of the Apulia region in southern Italy, it also genetically resembles some grapes from Hungary and the former Yugoslavia. Appearing in California in the nineteenth century, it may have been brought there by Agoston Haraszthy, who had imported thousands of European cuttings. Or it may have arrived with the waves of European immigrants at the time of the Gold Rush. Early in the twentieth century it was the favorite grape of eastern wine makers because it could survive the long train trip by boxcar from California better than most other viniferas could.

The grape yields an intensely flavored wine with depth, good color and a rich, full berrylike taste that can register as much as 15 percent alcohol. Initially a workaday blending grape—the source of California's mostly rough, mass-produced wines—it gave body and color to generic, low-acid clarets, Chiantis and Burgundies, and also served as a sparkling-wine component. In recent years, the zinfandel has come into its own as a varietal. A marvelously adaptable grape, the wine it yields can be made in a multitude of styles and strengths, ranging from smooth, silky and elegant to big, powerful and rough-edged, and from soft and unassuming to tannic and assertive. Some of the wines are fresh, fruity, and light—like a Beaujolais—whereas others are medium-bodied, smooth, elegant, and later-maturing—like a Cabernet Sauvignon. Still others are rich and heavy with a touch of earthiness. The best examples, produced in California's North Coast counties, are full-bodied and rich but not too heavy; rather they are open textured, lively, fruity and agreeable, with a rich berrylike fruitiness, a slightly tart quality, a distinctive—almost spicy—bouquet and a long finish. When late-harvested, its robust and intensely sweet wine resembles an after-dinner port.

A White Zinfandel—actually a blush wine that's pale pink or salmon-colored—is made by separating the color-laden grape skins from the clear juice early in the fermentation process. It's a generally light, bland and low-alcohol wine to which the chenin blanc and other grapes may be added for flavor. A touch of sugar may be added to produce a slight sweetness and a bit of carbon dioxide injected to make the wine slightly fizzy.

GLOSSARY

AMARONE: See Recioto.

ANGELICA: Amber-colored, fruity and somewhat sweet fortified wine, pressed from mission, grenache and other grape varieties. The better versions are blended and aged like sherries; the
lesser are little more than grape juice bolstered with brandy.

AQUATA: See Piquette.

ARMAGNAC: A brandy made in Gascony in southwestern
France. It is more robust than Cognac, because it is made by a single-
distillation method that retains more of the sturdy grape elements.

BOURGOGNE PASSE-TOUT-GRAINS: See Passe-Tout-Grains.

BRANDY: A spirit made from high-acid wines that are distilled
and then aged in oak.

BYRRH: An aromatic fortified wine made in southern France.
A proprietary product characterized by an appetite-whetting taste
of quinine, it is served as an apéritif.

CLARET: The traditional British name for the red wines of
Bordeaux. In the twelfth century, when Gascony was a possession
of the British Crown, these wines were mostly pale-colored and
called *clairet* or *clarret* then, deriving from *clair* ("light" or "clear").
"Clarret wines," it was said, "be fair coloured and bright as a rubie,
not deepe as an ametist." Claret is now a generic name for any red
table wine, but it is no longer much used.

COGNAC: A double-distilled brandy produced in the Charente
region of western France.

COLD DUCK: A combination of red and white sparkling wines.
Initially known as Kalte Ende (Cold Ending), it grew out of the
thrifty German custom of serving wines left over at the end of a
party as a chilled punch. Because of either a deliberate pun or a
typographical error, the punch came to be called Kalte Ente (Cold
Duck). It has been made available in bottles, with some versions
combining generic sparkling Burgundies and generic Champagnes,
and others involving carbonated wines.

COOKING WINE: Wine made unsuitable for drinking—to
exempt it from taxes on alcoholic beverages—by the addition of
salt. Somewhat acrid in taste, it is not as good for cooking as an
ordinary wine.

DUBONNET: A semisweet proprietary red wine made aromatic with herbs and somewhat astringent with quinine. Serves as an apéritif and a cocktail component. Initially produced only in France, it is now licensed for production in the United States and elsewhere. (Each country uses a domestic wine as its base.) A somewhat drier white version is known as Dubonnet Blonde.

FOLK WINES (Specialty Wines): Wines made from ingredients other than grapes. They're generally produced in regions unable to grow their own grapes and involve various fruits, vegetables and other ingredients, including cherries, peaches, blackberries, currants, elderberries, plums, gooseberries, loganberries, strawberries, apples, rhubarb, apricots, pineapple, cranberries and so on; also used are parsnips, potatoes, dandelions and even the sap of the silver birch tree.

GRAPPA: Clear, colorless Italian brandy distilled from pomace (the pressings left over after wine making, which include the grape skins, stems and seeds). Described as "the last element of wine," grappa was initially a harsh, raw, potent and generally fiery spirit, coarse in texture and smelling of earth and hay. It is now made in several styles, some distilled directly from the grape, others flavored with fruit, flowers or herbs. The best examples are made from single grape varieties, with their delicate and discreet flavors rounded out by wood-aging. (See also Marc.)

NOTE: Grappa may be the shortened form of the Italian *grappolo di uva,* which translates as a bunch of grapes.

JUG WINES: Generally inexpensive and unobtrusive wine blends that undergo shorter fermentations and briefer aging periods than most others. Bottled in gallon jugs or magnums, they are produced in France, Italy, Spain, the United States and so forth.

KIR: An apéritif that combines a table wine (originally a white Burgundy) with crème de cassis (a black currant liqueur) in a ratio of 3 or 4 parts to 1. Introduced in Burgundy, it was originally known as Vin Blanc de Cassis but renamed Kir after World War II to honor Felix Kir, the mayor of Dijon and a hero of the French Resistance. (The white wine now used now is an inexpensive Aligoté or a Muscadet.)

NOTE: Variants include Kir Cardinal, which replaces the crème de cassis with Beaujolais; Kir Rabelais, which replaces it with the sturdy red wines of Cahors; and Kir Royal, which replaces the still white wine with Champagne or another sparkler.

KOSHER WINE: Wines made in conformity with Jewish dietary laws and originally intended for sacramental use. (The entire wine-making process, from crushing to bottling, is carried out by observant Jews working under rabbinical supervision.) Products meeting these requirements carry a "U" inside a circle on their labels (standing for the Union of Orthodox Jewish Congregations), or have Hebrew lettering on their capsules and corks.

Traditional kosher wines, made principally made from concord grapes, were heavy and cloyingly sweet red wines. They now may be red or white, still or sparkling, varietal or generic. They may be pressed from vinifera, labrusca or hybrid grapes. (Their varieties have included the gamay, gewürztraminer, merlot, petite sirah, pinot blanc, pinot noir, riesling, shiraz and zinfandel.) Some of the wines are bone-dry, others are honey-sweet. Among the most popular are blush wines and rosés, which represent a transition between the traditional sweet wines and the drier ones more suitable with food. Kosher wines are produced in Israel, Italy, France, the United States and elsewhere.

LIGHT WINES: Wines subjected to special processing in order to reduce their alcohol content. (See also Nonalcoholic Wines.)

LILLET: Proprietary French wine flavored with herbs, fortified with brandy, and served as an apéritif. It's available in both red and white versions.

MÁLAGA: A dark amber and generally sweet fortified wine produced in southern Spain and named for the port from which it was first shipped. Pressed principally from sun-dried PX and muscat grapes and blended and aged in a solera, the wine is characterized by an unusually fragrant bouquet.

MARC: Clear, colorless brandy distilled from the grape pressings (pomace) that are left after wine making. A somewhat coarse and rough spirit with a woody, strawlike taste and a pungent aroma, it is also known as burning water (called *trinkbrandtwein* in Germany, *aguardiente* in Spain and *agurdente* in Portugal.) A notable example is Burgundy's Marc de Bourgogne, flavored with oranges, lemons and herbs. (See also Grappa.)

MAY WINE: German white wine flavored with the sweet, aromatic leaves of the woodruff plant. It is traditionally served in summer as a punch garnished with fruit. It has been marketed as a bottled product in Germany and the United States.

MEAD: An ancient beverage, produced by the fermentation of honey. (It is not a wine.)

MUSCATEL: A generally poor quality California wine pressed from muscat grapes.

NONALCOHOLIC WINES (Soft Wines): Wines—red, white or rosé, and still or sparkling—whose alcohol has been removed by special processing. However, as much as 0.5 percent may still be retained. (Those retaining no alcohol at all are labeled "Alcohol-Free.")

ORDINAIRE: See Vin Ordinaire.

ORGANIC WINES: Wines made from grapes grown without the use of chemical fertilizers, fungicides, or pesticides. (There are however no universally accepted standards as yet as to what constitutes an organic wine.)

PASSE-TOUT-GRAINS: A light red Burgundy; a blend of pinot noir and gamay grapes. Designed to stretch the region's limited pinot noir supply, it needs to involve only 30 percent of this variety whose grapes are generally drawn from the lesser Côte d'Or communes.

NOTE: Since a red Burgundy by law must be pressed exclusively from the pinot noir, Passe-Tout-Grains is not technically considered a Burgundy wine.

PIQUETTE: Thin, tart, low-grade wine made from pomace and containing only 3 to 4 percent alcohol. It is generally served free to winery workers in France, where its commercial sale is illegal. The Italian version is known as Aquata.

POP WINES: Wines or wine-based beverages bottled and marketed under brand names. Usually transient in popularity, they have included wine coolers, Cold Duck, Kir, Sangria, Apple Wine, May Wine and so on.

PUNT È MES: Italian proprietary wine; a combination of vermouth, bitters and sweetening. Originating near the stock exchange in Milan, it took its name from a stockbroker's term translating as "Point and a Half." It is served as an apéritif.

RAKI: A grape-based distillate flavored with anise and generally taken with water in a ratio of half-and-half. Produced in Turkey, it is similar to—although somewhat drier than—the Greek ouzo or the French pastis.

RECIOTO: Full-bodied high-alcohol Italian wine—red or white—that is sweet, spicy and unctuous, with great depth and complexity. Made from rich grapes picked from the uppermost part of the cluster, it is then raisined to further concentrate their sugars. Best known is the red Amarone of Veneto, characterized by a full, warm taste and a delicate aroma. (Its grapes are dried up to six months and the wine is aged for about three years.) A sweeter version is the Recioto della Valpolicella. A sparkling Recioto is also made.

ROSÉS (Vins Rosé): Wines pressed from red grapes whose skins are withdrawn when the desired shade of pinkness is achieved. Rosés are made in every wine-producing country, including France, Italy, Spain, Portugal, Greece, Morocco, Algeria, Israel, Germany, Austria and the United States. The grape varieties employed have included the grenache, gamay, pinot noir, cabernet franc, cabernet sauvignon, petite sirah, grignolino, cinsault, carignan and so forth, as well as the pinkish gewürztraminer. The wines themselves have run the gamut from light and pale to darker and more full bodied. The best examples are relatively low in alcohol and exhibit a richness of color, a fine fresh fruitiness and a bit of residual sugar. Nicely modifying their sweetness is a touch of sharpness, which makes the wines seem drier than they actually are.

The classic examples are pressed from moderately pigmented grapes—the grenache and the gamay. The finest come from the South of France, from Tavel and Lirac. Also well known is the Loire's Rosé d'Anjou. One of Italy's best rosés is a light, fresh Chiaretto grown at the southern end of Lake Garda. Spanish Rosados are pressed from the garnacha (grenache); some of these are full-bodied, others are fresh, delicately fruity and elegant. Germany produces an extremely pale pink Weissherbst pressed from the pinot noir. The most notable American rosés are grown in California's North Coast. Pressed from the grenache and gamay, they are fairly pale, fruity and somewhat crisp.

NOTE: Most rosés hover between 11 and 12 percent alcohol, but a muscular Cabernet from California can reach 13 percent or more.

SAKE: Japanese beverage made from fermented rice. Sometimes added are alcohol, sugar, yeast and other ingredients. Although appearing to be a white wine, it is in fact an uncarbonated beer that averages about 6 percent alcohol. Various versions are produced; some are somewhat sweet, others display a slightly bitter aftertaste. Traditionally taken warm in tiny cups, sake is now served chilled as well.

SANGRIA: Red-wine punch that originated in Spain. (Its name derives from *sangre* or blood and refers to the wine's strong ruby color.) It was initially a harsh, dry red wine modified with oranges, lemon juice, sugar and soda water. Now the wine may be garnished with pineapples, cherries or berries, or have brandy or cinnamon added. A white-wine variant is also made.

NOTE: Bottled versions of Sangria are produced in Spain and California.

SFURSAT: A concentrated Italian red wine pressed from nebbiolo grapes that have been left to dry in airy lofts for up to two weeks after the harvest.

TOKAY: Hungarian white wine named for Tokaji, a village in the Carpathian Mountains. Pressed from the furmint grape, the wine ranges in color from pale straw to amber and in taste from dry to sweet. Some examples are crisp and dry; others are full-bodied and fiery.

VIN DE PAILLE (Straw Wine): French wine produced in the Jura. Pressed from raisined grapes and fermented slowly, it is golden, sweet, thick, strong and inordinately rich, exhibiting a somewhat spicy character and an unusually high level of alcohol. Switzerland and Italy also produce straw wines.

VIN GRIS (Gray Wine): A remarkably hardy and refreshing dry French white wine pressed from red grapes and—like a blush wine—displaying only a slight trace of pinkness. The term generally refers to the pale rosés made from pinot noir grapes in Alsace and Burgundy. Other versions are produced in the Jura and Morocco.

NOTE: Vin gris has been applied as well to pinkish red-and-white combinations made elsewhere in France and in Central Europe.

VIN JAUNE (Yellow Wine): A deep golden, exceedingly dry, high-alcohol French wine made in the Jura. Pressed from late-gathered grapes and growing a florlike yeast, the wine is left to age in small casks for five to ten years.In the process, it acquires a highly developed and intensely fragrant bouquet, a pleasantly oxidized edge and a vaguely nutlike flavor that is reminiscent of a sherry. It is served both as an apéritif and as an afterdinner drink.

VIN ORDINAIRE: A commonplace blend of French red or white wines that may also include wines from North Africa, Greece or Spain. (It often isn't bottled at all.) In Portugal, ordinary wines are called *vinhos do consumo;* in Spain, *viños de pasto,* and in the United States, jug wines. In Britain, the wines are known as *plonk.*

VIN ROUGE: An undistinguished French red wine, often originating in the Midi and usually strengthened with domestic or foreign wines. Unless the label reads "Product of France" or its equivalent, the wine may not be French at all.

VIN SANTO: A rich, sherrylike Italian wine made from late-gathered grapes that have been partially dried indoors for some months, then slowly pressed. Their thick, concentrated juice is left to ferment in small oak casks sealed with cement or wax for three to six years or more. Kept in an attic or in another uninsulated space, the casks are subjected to extremes of weather. The resulting wine—sweet, intense and potent—generally ranges from 14 to 17 percent alcohol and is served as an afterdinner drink. Some versions combine a spicy, honeyed sweetness with a delicate flavor and a distinct pleasant dryness in the finish. Others are almost dry on the palate and exude an aroma of hazelnuts and almonds. Most notable is the Tuscan version made in the vicinity of Florence. A dry version is also made.

VINHO VERDE (Green Wine): Tart, low-alcohol, faintly fizzy Portuguese wine—red or white—pressed from underripe grapes. (The "green" alludes to the bracing acidity of the wine and the fact that it's bottled while still young.) To preserve its fruitiness and to keep it pleasantly refreshing, most producers ferment the wine in stainless steel or in glass-lined cement vats rather than in wooden barrels. Vinho verdes, made from a number of grape varieties, range in style from dry to semidry and generally average 9 percent alcohol (against the usual 12 or 13 percent for other Portuguese table wines). To re-create their youthful fizziness for export, some of the wines are injected with carbon dioxide.

WEISSHERBST: See Rosés.

WINE: Wine is the fermented juice of grapes, composed primarily of water, 7 to 15 percent alcohol and a small percentage of organic solids. Much more than a dilute solution of alcohol, it contains hundreds of compounds, including sugars, acids, sulfates, phosphates, mineral salts, esters, aldehydes and so forth. Some of these compounds derive from the grape itself; others are created by fermentation and aging. They differ in proportion from one wine to the next, determining the uniqueness of each.

WINE COOLERS: Hybrid products combining nondescript wines with fruit juices and carbonated water. The wines are usually whites, although reds and rosés have also been used. (Wine coolers may also be sweetened and colored.) They range in alcohol from 4 to 6 percent and are sold in small bottles like beer.

MISCELLANEOUS TERMINOLOGY

ABBOCCATO: Italian for semisweet. Literally translating as "mouth-filling," it refers to wines that retain a degree of unfermented sugar—usually 1 to 3 percent. The term is applied to Orvietos and other wines made in a soft and slightly sweet style.

ABOCADO: Spanish for semisweet.

ADEGA: Portuguese for a wine producer's cellar or warehouse; the equivalent of a Spanish bodega.

ALMACENISTAS: Spanish for storekeeper or stockholder. Refers to privately held lots of high-quality sherries purchased by established sherry houses from small growers who cannot afford to bottle and ship the wines themselves. The wines, without further blending, are labeled "Almacenistas." (They may be identified by a number to indicate their original producer.)

AMABILE: Italian for semisweet; somewhat sweeter than abboccato.

AMPELOGRAPHER: A specialist in grapes and wines.

AMPELOGRAPHY: The study and classification of grape varieties.

APÉRITIF: A light beverage, usually a fortified wine, flavored with herbs and other botanicals, which generally displays both acidity and sweetness. It's taken before meals to stimulate the appetite and prepare the palate for the foods to follow. Apéritifs include dry sherries and vermouths and such proprietary cocktail wines as Cinzano, Dubonnet, Lillet and so forth.

APERITIVO: Italian for apéritif.

ASCIUTTO: Italian for dry; interchangeable with *secco.* It refers to a wine that retains up to 1 percent unfermented sugar.

ASSEMBLAGE: The final blending of a wine; a term generally associated with Champagne.

BALLON: A large wineglass.

BARREL-FERMENTATION: The fermentation of a wine in wood, generally oak.

BISTRO WINES: Light, fruity, generally undistinguished wines intended for casual sipping.

BODEGA: Spanish for a producer's establishment. It may be a winery, a wine cellar or a small wine shop.

BROKER: A middleman in Bordeaux who serves as the liaison between the négociant (shipper) and the château (winery).

BULLETS: Bunches of hard, acid-tasting, smaller-than-normal grapes unsuitable for wine. They are caused by an early spring frost that damages the buds as they are about to open.

CANNELINO: Italian for sweet. Refers to a wine that retains 3 to 6 percent unfermented sugar.

CANTINA: Italian for a winery or a cellar.

CARAFE: Wide-necked, clear-glass container used in serving wine. (It also refers to a wine intended for early consumption.)

CAVE: French for a winery cellar, usually located underground. It also refers to a wine cellar in a restaurant or a private home.

CELLAR RATS: The winery workers who lug the hoses and clean the tanks.

CÉPAGE: French for grape variety. (*Cep* translates as "rootstock" or "individual vine.")

CHAI: French for an aboveground wine-storage space. Associated with Bordeaux, it may be a winery, a warehouse or even a shed.

CHAIR: French for a wine's body or fullness.

CHAPTALIZE: The practice of adding sugar to a wine during fermentation to balance out its acidity, mask its coarseness or modify an excessive foxiness. (In some cases, 17 grams of sugar may be added to a liter of wine to raise its alcohol level by 1 percent.) The added sugar ferments out at the same time as the natural sugar and does not sweeten the wine.

CLARETE: Spanish for a light red wine. It refers to certain Riojas that receive little wood-aging.

CLIMAT: A parcel of land in a Burgundian vineyard owned by one proprietor or several.

CLONE: A grape subvariety bred to be identical to its parents, although it can vary from them in fruit quality, disease resistance and longevity.

CLOS: French for enclosure. Originally referring to a vineyard surrounded by a stone wall, as was the monastic custom during the Middle Ages. Now refers to a vineyard in Burgundy, often of the highest rank.

CLUSTER-SELECTED: The delayed picking of grape clusters for late-harvest wines; a term seen on wine labels.

COMITÉ INTERPROFESSIONEL DU VIN DE CHAMPAGNE: The wine industry's professional and promotional organization in Champagne.

COMMUNE: French for parish. It refers to a town or village and the land surrounding it.

CORSÉ: French for a full-bodied wine.

CÔTE: French for a slope or hillside on which grapevines are grown. (The plural is *coteaux.*)

COUNTRY WINES: Anonymous wines made in many wine-producing countries. In France, the term covers not only unknown wines from the more obscure districts but inexpensive Bordeaux and Muscadets as well.

COURTIERS: Brokers in Bordeaux who act as middlemen between château owners and shippers.

CRU: French for growth. The term, referring to a particular parcel of land and its wine, implies quality. In Burgundy or Bordeaux, a Grand Cru (Great Growth) represents a high-caliber vineyard or wine. Elsewhere, the term may be a label embellishment of no significance.

CUVÉE: French for the contents of a cask or vat. In Champagne, it refers to the blending of wines pressed from several grape varieties. (See also Assemblage.)

DÉGUSTATION: French for a sampling of wines or a wine tasting. In a restaurant, a *menu de dégustation* (tasting menu) pairs appropriate wines with special dishes.

DIGESTIF: A beverage, usually sweet, taken at the end of the meal. It is designed to soothe the stomach and aid in digestion while complementing the dessert course. Included here are cream sherries, ports, Madeiras, noble rot wines and so on.

DOLCE: Italian for sweet. (See also Cannellino.)

DOMAINE: Holdings that constitute a vineyard property or estate under one management. In Bordeaux, the term can refer to a single unified property, provided the wine was actually produced there. In Burgundy, the parcels of land may be located in different communes and have different names.

EDELWEIN: A late-harvest wine made in California from botrytized grapes.

ÉLEVEUR: See Négociant.

ENCÉPAGEMENT: French for a blend of grapes. (See also Cépage.)

ENOLOGIST: A master wine maker or wine scientist.

ENOLOGY: The science and study of wine and wine making.

ENOTECA: Italian for wine library. The term usually denotes a wine shop, which may include a wine bar. It can also refer to a restaurant that serves local dishes to match local wines.

ENOTECHE: Italian for wine shop.

FRECCIAROSSO (Red Arrow): Italian term initially referring to wines grown in a Lombardy village of that name, but now the proprietary name for certain Lombardy wines.

GEMEINDE: The German name for a delimited township and its surrounding land; the equivalent of a French commune or parish.

GOULAYANT: French term for a wine's general goodness.

GOÛT D'APPELLATION: French for the taste of origin. In Burgundy it refers to the commune where the wine originated.

GOÛT DE GRÊLE: French for taste of hail. It refers to a wine whose grapes were bruised by a hailstorm. The condition may be evident as a slight taste of rot in the finished wine.

GRANDE MARQUE: French for a major label. It implies quality in a Champagne but is without significance for other wines.

HALB-TROCKEN: German for half-dry.

HAUT: French for high or elevated and it meant to suggest wine quality. While the Haut-Médoc is a particularly high-quality area in Bordeaux, the term has been somewhat loosely applied elsewhere: in Burgundy, the Haut Côte de Nuits and Haut Côte de Beaune are minor areas, which produces light, undistinguished wines.

HOCK: The British name for Rhine wines; an abbreviation of Hochheim, a village in the Rheingau.

HORIZONTAL BLENDING: The combining of wines of several properties from a single vintage.

LAGE: German for a vineyard or a specific parcel; the equivalent of a French climat or cru.

LESE: German for harvest. (*Spätlese* means late-harvest.)

LIEBLICH: German for a mild wine with a touch of sweetness—a wine that is somewhat sweeter than halb-trocken.

LIQUOROSO: Italian for liqueurlike. Refers to rich, sweet dessert wines.

MAÎTRE DE CHAI: French for cellarmaster; a term associated with Bordeaux.

MARQUE DEPOSÉ: French for registered trademark; appears on labels accompanied by a trade name or a coined name.

MENU DE DÉGUSTATION: See Dégustation.

MILLÉSIME: French for vintage.

MONOPOLE: French for a shipper's private brand. Although implying exclusivity, it does not indicate a monopoly. (The wine may come from a vineyard owned by a shipper or from elsewhere.) Now generally refers to diverse blends bottled by big firms.

NÉGOCIANT: French for a shipper, wholesaler or wine merchant who buys grapes and wines from others, then produces his own blends.

OENOLOGIST: See Enologist. (The name derives from the Greek *oinos,* translating as "wine.")

OENOPHILE: A lover of wine; a wine enthusiast.

ORGANOLEPTIC: The application of the senses in evaluating wines.

PARISH: A French commune or township.

PASADO: A Spanish term describing a superior old sherry—a fino or an amontillado.

PASSITO: An Italian sweet wine made from overripe or raisined grapes. Such wines vary in style and flavor according to their region of production. A prime example is Tuscany's vin santo.

PIERRE À FUSIL: French for gunflint. Refers to a wine's aroma or flavor, which evokes the sharp smell of flint struck with steel. (The term is used to describe the bouquet of a fine Chablis.)

PREMIUM: Refers to wines produced in limited quantities. Although intended to suggest high quality and exclusivity, it has been so loosely applied as to be virtually meaningless.

PROPRIÉTAIRE: French for a vineyard owner or grower.

PROPRIÉTAIRE-RÉCOLTANT: French for a vineyard owner-manager.

QUINTA: Portuguese for farm. It refers to a vineyard estate.

RÉCOLTANT: French for the person who grows and harvests his own crop.

RÉCOLTE: French for a vintage or harvest.

REDUCTIVE: The retention of the zesty fruitiness of a white wine by keeping it in stainless steel rather than in wood so that oxygen cannot get at it and reduce its fruitiness.

RÉGISSEUR: A French term that translates roughly as general manager. In Bordeaux, it refers to the individual who supervises the vineyard and the making of its wine.

RESERVE: A reference to a wine's age. Although implying special attributes and some degree of exclusivity—as if the wine were held in reserve until it was ready to drink—the term generally has no official standing. It can be defined in any way the producer or shipper chooses.

RHINE WINE: German white wine produced in the Rheingau, Rheinhessen, the Pfalz or Mittelrhein. It has also become a generic name for white wines produced in California and elsewhere.

RIPASSO: Refers to steeping ordinary Valpolicella wines in casks that contain a rich residue of Amarone to give them additional color and an extra depth of flavor.

ROSATO: Italian for rosé wine.

ROSSO: Italian for red; a name given to not entirely dry, red California wines.

ROUTE DES GRAND CRUS: French for Road of Great Growths, a famous Burgundy wine road that begins a few miles south of Dijon and winds its way through the important Côte d'Or vineyards. (See also Weinstrasse.)

ROUTES DU VIN: French for wine roads. Refers to areas in the Médoc, Burgundy and Alsace characterized by a high concentration of vineyards.

SACK: The British name for sherry; now a registered trademark for a private brand of amoroso sherry.

NOTE: *Sack* once applied to fortified wines from the Canary Islands as well, but these are hardly produced anymore. (The wine industry there never quite recovered from the phylloxera invasion of the nineteenth century.)

SEC: French for dry, but when applied to Champagne, it indicates a degree of sweetness.

SECCO: Italian for dry; the opposite of *abboccato* or *amabile*.

SÉCHÉ: French for dry; refers to withered or desiccated wines.

SÉLECTION DU GRAINES NOBLES (SGN): A very late harvest Alsatian wine characterized by great concentration and aging power; the equivalent of a fine Sauternes. (Is usually sold in half-bottles.)

SINGLE-VINEYARD: Wine made from grapes grown on a vineyard plot owned by one wine maker.

SPITZENWEIN: German for a sweet, luscious wine. Refers to high-quality wines pressed from botrytized grapes.

SPRITZER: A drink combining wine and club soda, often in equal parts.

STRUCTURE: The backbone of a wine. It is associated with tannic red wines.

SUPÉRIEUR: French term referring to a wine's higher-than-normal level of alcohol, not to its superiority.

SUPERMARKET VINTAGE: Bordeaux term referring to wines sold through channels not normally used in distributing fine wines.

TERROIR: French term for soil but meaning much more than soil: it refers to the unique characteristics of the place where the wine is produced—its specific vineyard site—but involving its entire ecosystem as well. The term integrates site, soil and climate with the vines, rootstocks and grape varieties, and also relates to the role of man in grape growing and wine making.

NOTE: In Burgundy, where the focus is primarily on the soil, *le terroir* is usually defined as a vineyard site or parcel.

TÉTE DE CUVÉE: French term signifying top of the line. The term once had legal significance, but is now used loosely on wine labels.

TINTO: Spanish for red wine.

TONNELIER: French for cooper, the maker of barrels.

TROCKEN: German for dry; also refers to withered or desiccated wines.

UVA: Spanish for grape.

V.D.P.: An organization set up in Germany to ensure high standards for the country's quality wines.

VENDANGE TARDIVE: French for late harvest. It is associated with Alsace, whose botrytized wines are rich in fruit although not always sweet. Also refers to French and American wines whose fermentation is halted before all the sugar has been converted out.

VERAISON: The start of the grape's maturation; the point at which the berry's initially green color changes and its opacity becomes translucent.

VERJUS: French for the unfermented, sweet-tart juice of unripe green grapes. A nonalcoholic product, it is used in making marinades and in sauces for cooking.

VERONESE: Fresh, light jug wines produced in Italy.

VERTICAL BLENDING: The combining of the wines of two or more vintages from one property.

VIEILLES VIGNES: Old vines whose grapes yield wines of generally greater complexity.

VIGNERON: French for grape grower. Although he may supervise the work of others, he more often is simply a skilled vineyard worker.

VIN DE GLACE: French for ice wine.

VINS DE CÉPAGE: French term for varietal wines.

VINTNER: See Wine Maker.

VITICULTURE: The science and art of grape growing.

WEINGUT: German for vineyard property. It can refer to a winery and its wine as well.

WEINSTRASSE: German for wine street or wine road. One notable example extends from the Pfalz, west of Mannheim, south to Schweigen at the French frontier. (See also Routes du Vin.)

WINE MAKER: The individual who oversees all phases of wine making, from cultivating, picking, crushing, fermenting and pressing the grapes to fermenting, racking, aging, blending and bottling the wine.

QUANTITIES AND MEASUREMENTS

The sizes of the wine bottles are based on the metric system, whose cornerstone is the liter at 33.8 ounces. The liter is the equivalent of 2.11 pints, 1.06 quarts, and 0.26 of a gallon. When the United States adopted the metric system in 1979, the conversion of bottle sizes presented no serious problems. Since the quart at 32 ounces is 1.057 liters, the 33.8-ounce liter is a touch more than a quart, making the difference between a fifth (at 25.6 ounces) and 3/4 of a liter less than a quarter of an ounce.

The American conversion to the metric system established the following bottle sizes:

- The *split* (6.4 ounces) became 3/16 liter (187 milliliters, 18.75 centiliters) or 6.3 ounces.

- The *tenth* (12.8 ounces), also known as the *half-bottle*—which is 1.10 gallon or 2/5 of a quart—became 3/8 liter (375 milliliters) or 12.7 ounces.

- The *fifth* (25.6 ounces), which is 1/5 of a gallon or 4/5 of a quart, became a 3/4 liter (750 milliliters, 75 centiliters) or 25.4 ounces.

- The *quart* (32 ounces) became 1 liter (1,000 milliliters, 100 centiliters) or 33.8 ounces.

- The *magnum* (51.2 ounces) became 1 1/2 liters (1,500 milliliters, 150 centiliters) or 50.73 ounces.

- The *jeroboam* (102.4 ounces) became 3 liters (3,000 milliliters, 300 centiliters) or 101.46 ounces.

NOTE: Although the quart measurement in the United States is a fourth of a gallon or 0.946 liters, it is 1.39 liters in Great Britain.

By law, the standard wine bottle in the United States is three-fourths of a liter (750 milliliters or 75 centiliters). In Europe, wine-bottle sizes vary from country to country and even from region to region. Some have been shrinking in recent years. They've been reduced from 75 or 80 centiliters down to 73, 72, or even to 70 centiliters.

Half-bottles hold 375 milliliters or 12.7 ounces. Half-bottles have their pros and cons. Some say they're generally adequate for two diners, while others maintain they offer too little wine for two people. Half-bottles are a convenient way of becoming acquainted with different wine, however, but offer no savings. They usually cost proportionately more than half the price of a full bottle, since they cost almost as much to fill, label and ship. (They need special bottling lines, bottles, corks and so forth.)

NOTE: Certain wines, such as late-harvest wines, are invariably sold in half-bottles. These rich, almost syrupy wines are meant to be taken in smaller quantities per serving.

Another bottle size, introduced by the Germans, contains amounts somewhere between those of the traditional bottle and the half-bottle. It holds two-thirds of 500 milliliters or nearly 17 ounces, giving two people two glasses of wine each. Its acceptance by the public, however, has been poor. Another size is the 187-milliliter bottle, sealed with a twist-off cap; the airlines use these for their mealtime service. Some restaurants are now offering wines in such bottles as well as in the more conventional ones.

A single serving of wine averages 4 ounces. A standard 75-centiliter bottle, containing about 25 ounces, is enough for six servings. Some calculate 5 ounces for a single serving so that there are five drinks in a 750-milliliter bottle; ten drinks in a 1.5-liter bottle, and twenty drinks in a 3-liter bottle. Determining how much will be consumed generally depends on the occasion and on the type of wine served. At lunch, one or two glasses per person should be sufficient. At dinner, a person usually drinks two or three glasses or 8 to 12 ounces of wine, making the norm about half a bottle per person.

A meal featuring several wines should provide about one-fourth bottle of each wine per person. A convivial group can easily put away more if a white wine is served as the apéritif, another white wine with the fish course, followed by a red wine with the meat course, and perhaps a glass of port after the meal. Some suggest allowing at least one bottle per person if you count on a glass or two as an apéritif or with the first course, and a glass or two with the main course. (At informal dinner parties, guests will probably consume more than expected due to the casual nature of the event.)

For parties and receptions, the rule of thumb is about two glasses of wine per person per hour. (During the first two hours, one can count on eight glasses for four people and twelve glasses for six people.) At longer-lasting events, somewhat more wine will be required. For eight to ten serious wine-drinking guests, thirty-two glasses—about a gallon, or 3.785 liters—should be sufficient.

The serving quantities for Champagnes and other sparkling wines are much the same as for still wines. About six bottles should be allowed for every ten guests. If the wine is to be used only for toasting, a case should be enough for about a hundred people. If it is to be served as a dessert wine, one bottle should be sufficient for every four guests.

NOTE: It's important to have enough wine. Nothing is more awkward than running short in the midst of the festivities. With enough bottles on hand, one can open a few more if necessary. (They should not be uncorked, however, until they're required.) Some people feel that counting on a whole bottle for each guest at a social gathering is a wise precaution. (Caterers estimate that 100 guests require six cases of table wine and two of Champagne.)

Because rich dessert or fortified wines taken after dinner are consumed in much smaller quantities than table or sparkling wines, they go two or three times as far. (An average serving is 2 to 2 1/2 ounces.) Sauternes and other noble rots are so concentrated and intense, that one small glass is sufficient and a bottle can serve eight guests or more. The half-bottles in which many late-harvest wines are sold generally provide four to six servings.

When one is entertaining large groups, the magnum—which provides approximately twelve 4-ounce glasses—is more festive, practical and economical than two standard bottles. Some connoisseurs collect magnums not only for their dramatic impact at a dinner party but because the wine ages more slowly in these larger bottles and also keeps better.

The following information on bottle sizes and on the number of servings in each might prove useful when planning a dinner or a party:

SIZE	FLUID OUNCES	SERVINGS PER BOTTLE	
		Table or Sparkling	Fortified
$^3/_{16}$ liter (split)	6.4	2	—
$^3/_8$ liter (tenth) or half-bottle	12.7	2–3	4
$^3/_4$ liter (fifth) or standard bottle	25.4	4–6	8–10
1 liter (quart)	33.8	6–8	10–12
Half-gallon	64	12–16	20–30
Gallon	128	24–30	40–60
Magnum (1.5 liters), equivalent of two bottles	50	8–12	—
Double magnum (3 liters), equivalent of four bottles	101	16–25	—
Jeroboam (5 liters), equivalent of six bottles	169	30–45	—
Imperial (6 liters), equivalent of eight bottles	202	32–58	—

NOTE: There are six magnums, three double magnums or one imperial to a case.

Champagnes are bottled in a greater variety of bottle sizes than table wines:

SIZE	FLUID OUNCES	SERVINGS
Split or quarter-bottle (187 milliliters)	6.3 ounces	1$^1/_2$ glasses
Half-bottle or pint (375 milliliters)	12.7 ounces	3 glasses
Full bottle (750 milliliters)	26 ounces	7 glasses
Magnum—2 bottles (1.5 liters)	52 ounces	15 glasses

SIZE	FLUID OUNCES	SERVINGS
Jeroboam—4 bottles (3 liters)	104 ounces	30 glasses
Rehoboam—6 bottles (4.5 liters)	156 ounces	45 glasses
Methuselah or Imperial —8 bottles (6 liters)	208 ounces	60 glasses
Salmanazar—12 bottles (9 liters)	312 ounces	90 glasses
Balthazar—16 bottles (12 liters)	416 ounces	120 glasses
Nebuchadnezzar— 20 bottles (15 liters)	520 ounces	150 glasses
Sovereign—36 bottles (27 liters)	936 ounces	270 glasses

NOTE: The oversized bottles are quite heavy, requiring strong arms to lift and a steady hand to pour. The largest are meant primarily for show; the nebuchadnezzar, holding 15 liters, is rarely seen and usually not exported. The sovereign, standing three feet tall, was designed as the focal point for ship launchings.

MISCELLANEOUS MEASUREMENTS

BARREL: A container usually holding 228 liters of wine—the equivalent of twenty cases.

BARRICA: An oak barrel with a 225-liter capacity; associated with Rioja.

BARRIQUE: The standard oak cask in Bordeaux, holding 225 liters.

BUTT: A sherry cask holding 490.68 liters.

CARAFE: An open-necked bottle used in serving; it varies in capacity from $1/2$ to a full liter.

CARATELLE: An Italian oak cask holding 50 liters.

CASE: A box made of wood or cardboard, usually holding twelve standard bottles. A case of 1.5-liter bottles holds six, a case of 3-liter bottles holds three, and a case of 6-liter bottles holds one.

CONTAINER: A receptacle used in shipping wine; it holds 700 cases.

DEMI-JOHN: A squat, round, oversized, small-necked bottle, often covered with straw or wicker and set in a wooden supporting frame. It can range from 1 to 14 gallons in capacity but most commonly holds 4.9 gallons.

FUDER: A German cask holding 100 liters.

HALBSTÜCK: A German cask holding 600 liters; the preferred size in the Rheingau.

HECTARE: A parcel of land approximately $2^1/2$ acres.

HOGSHEAD: A cask holding 225 liters (somewhat larger for ports and sherries). In Bordeaux, it's called a *barrique;* in Rioja, a *barrica,* in Burgundy, a *pièce.*

PICHET: A small French earthenware pitcher, used for serving wine at home and in restaurants.

PIÈCE: A Burgundy cask holding about 225 liters.

PIPE: A cask holding anywhere from 100 to about 125 gallons. (For port, 550-liter pipes are used.)

POT: A small, heavy-bottomed bottle with a capacity of about $^1/2$ liter, used in serving Beaujolais from the cask.

QUART: A French carafe whose capacity is about $^1/4$ liter, enough for a single serving. In Italy, it's called a quartino.

TONNEAU: About a hundred cases or twelve hundred bottles; the equivalent of four barriques.

SUMMARIES

VINEYARD SUMMARY

In the spring, the soil is cultivated; the trellis wires are tightened and new canes are tied to them. The vines blossom in April or May.

Cultivation continues through June; the flowering shoots are thinned and the young vines are suckered. In June or July, the grape set occurs.

By late summer, the wine maker has trimmed his vines and is monitoring the shifting balance of the sugars and acids in his grapes to determine their ripeness.

In September, the harvest begins. By October or November, most of the fruit has been gathered and wine making gets under way.

In winter, the dormant vines are pruned and cuttings are taken. The wine maker samples his new wines.

In March, the vine emerges from hibernation. The vineyards are cleared and the weeds and brush chopped up. The wine maker anxiously monitors his new crop, assessing its prospects for the coming year.

NOTE: In the Southern Hemisphere, grapes are cultivated in autumn and gathered in late winter or early spring.

RED AND WHITE WINEMAKING

Red wines are generally more complicated and costly to produce than white wines, with more intricate results. White wines, which aren't usually fermented on their skins, tend to be less complex as a group, although their exceptional examples can be quite extraordinary.

RED WINES	WHITE WINES
The grapes are gathered and crushed.	The grapes are gathered and crushed.
The must, including the skins and seeds, goes to a vat or tank.	The crushed grapes go to the press; the must is run off into a vat or tank, leaving the skins and seeds behind.
Primary fermentation begins.	Primary fermentation begins.
The skins and solids form a dense floating cap, which must be dispersed.	
Secondary fermentation begins.	Secondary fermentation begins.
The cap goes to the press.	
Racking and other forms of clarification follow.	Racking and other forms of clarification follow.

RED WINES	WHITE WINES
The wine is aged in wood.	The wine may be briefly aged in wood.
The wine is blended.	The wine is blended.
The wine may be aged in glass.	The wine is rarely aged in glass.

NOTE: Blending can precede and/or follow aging, and may even precede the fermentation process itself.

Red Wines

Light, Fruity Reds include French, Burgundies such as Beaujolais and Savigny-les-Beaune; Bordeaux's Graves and Juliénas; Côte de Provence reds such as Corbieres, Bandol, Roussillon, Minervois, and Fronsac; Loire reds such as Chinon and Bourgueil; Italian Corvos, Valpolicellas, Barberas, Bardolinos, Grignolinos, Lambruscos, Amarones, lighter Chiantis, Lagreins del Alto-Adige, Gattinaras, Merlots and Dolcettos; Spain's lighter Riojas and red Penedés; California's Gamays, Merlots, Petite Sirahs, and some Pinot Noirs, Cabernet Sauvignons and Zinfandels.

    Medium- to Full-bodied Reds include Bordeaux's Médoc and Graves, St-Émilion and Pomerol; Burgundies from the Côte de Beaune and the Côte de Nuits, and southern Burgundies such as Mercurey, Rully, Santenay, and Cahors, along with the more substantial Beaujolais; Côte de Beaune wines such as Volnay; Rhône wines such as Gigondas, Châteauneuf-du-Pape, Hermitage and Cornas; Italian Barolos, Brunellos di Montalcino, Chiantis, Amarones, Nebbiolos, Corvos, Barberas, Rossos di Montalcino, Rossos Piceno, Sassellas, Ghemmes, Infernos, Dolcettos d'Alba, Valtellinas, Spannas, Taurasis, Barbarescos and Sangioveses; heavier Spanish Riojas and Penedés reds; American varietals such as the Pinot Noir, Cabernet Sauvignon, Merlot, Ruby Cabernet, Carignane, Petite Sirah, heavier Zinfandels and eastern Baco Noirs.

    Robust, Assertive Reds include big Burgundies and big Rhône wines; Italy's Amarones della Valpolicella and heavier

Brunellos di Montalcino, Barolos, Barbarescos, and Vinos Nobile di Montepulciano; Australia's Cabernet Sauvignons; and certain California Cabernets and Zinfandels.

White Wines

Light or Crisp Dry Whites include Burgundies such as Chablis; Bordeaux wines from Graves; also Pouilly-Fumé, Muscadet, Sancerre, Pouilly-Fuissé, St-Véran, Chenin Blancs, Sauvignon Blancs, light Muscats and Pinot Gris; Alsatian Pinot Blancs and Sylvaners; Italian Soaves, Orvietos, Frascatis, Albariños, Verdicchios, Vernaccias di San Gimignano, Trebbianos, Est! Est! Est!, Corteses di Gavi, Lacryma Christis and Pinot Grigios; Germany's light Rhine Rieslings and Mosels; Swiss Fendants, Neuchatels, and Dezaleys; Chilean Rieslings; Portuguese vinho verdes and Hungarian Furmint and Szamorodni wines.

Medium Dry Whites include French Meursaults, Vouvrays, Sancerres, Blanc Fumé de Pouilly, Chenin Blancs, Sauvignon Blancs; Graves from Bordeaux; most Loire wines, including Muscadets and Gros Plants; Alsatian Gewürztraminers and Rieslings; Germany's Rhine and Mosel wines; Italian Corvos, Pinot Grigios, Frascatis, Cinqueterres; Greek retsinas; American Chardonnays, Chenin Blancs, Fumé Blancs, Johannisberg Rieslings, and the northeastern Seyval Blancs.

Fullish Whites include French Burgundies such as Montrachets, Meursaults, and the better Chablis; Pouilly-Fumés; Hermitages from the Rhône; Monbazillacs, Muscadets; Alsatian Gewürztraminers, Pinot Gris, Sylvaners, and Rieslings; Germany's Rhine and Mosel Rieslings up to and including Spätleses, and also those from the Saar and Franconia; Spanish white wines from Rioja; American Chardonnays and Pouilly-Fumés.

Luscious Whites include the sweeter Beaumes-de-Venise, Monbazillacs, Vouvrays and Anjous from the Loire; Sauternes and Barsacs; rich German Rieslings: Beerenausleses and Trockenbeerenausleses; Italy's richer Asti Spumantes and vin santos; certain Riojas; some American Chardonnays, Chenin Blancs, and sparkling Blancs de Noirs.

The Classic Champagne Method

Épluchage: After the harvest, the grapes are carefully inspected by specially trained workers, who discard the overripe, underripe and blemished berries.

Blending and Bottling: The wine is fermented, aged briefly in wood and blended into cuvées. A precisely measured solution of sugar and yeast (*liqueur de tirage*) restimulates secondary fermentation in the bottle. A temporary cork (*bouchon de tirage*) seals the bottle. A sturdy metal clamp (*agrafe*) anchors the cork firmly in place.

Tierage (Tirage): The bottles are stacked horizontally in cool underground vaults. Secondary fermentation proceeds at a very slow pace and the wines gradually mature on their rich, yeasty deposits.

Riddling (Remuage): The bottles are placed in slotted racks, known as pulpits (*pupitres*), and over a period of several months are rotated, rapped and tilted daily by bottle-turning workmen (*remueurs*) until they're positioned neck-down (*sur pointe*) with the sediment lodged compactly against the corks.

Disgorging (Dégorgement): The bottle necks are dipped into a brine solution, which congeals the sediment. Then the metal clamp (*agrafe*) is released, ejecting the cork with its icy clump of sediment, along with a bit of wine.

Adding the Dosage: The bottles are topped off with a dosage syrup (*liqueur d'expédition*) consisting of wine, sugar and brandy. The dosage establishes the Champagne's final style or classification.

Recorking: A mushroom-shaped shipping cork (*bouchon d'expédition*) is anchored firmly in place with a wire hood or muzzle. The wine is then binned away briefly to rest.

Port Wine Making

The crushed grapes ferment on their skins. Fermentation is then halted to retain the desired amount of grape sugar by transferring the still-active must to casks containing a predetermined amount of brandy.

During the winter months, the wine settles down and precipitates out its gross lees.

Racked into fresh casks in the spring, the wine is transported downriver to the shippers' lodges at Vila Nova de Gaia, where it is tasted, classified and blended.

After further fortification, the wine is aged in wood and glass for varying lengths of time—depending on the style of port desired.

SHERRY WINE MAKING

After the harvest, the high-sugar grapes are heaped on mats to raisin in the sun.

Their rich must, fermenting out completely, leaves the wine bone-dry.

Kept outdoors in loosely stoppered casks, the wine oxidizes and may or may not develop flor.

After its classification as flor or nonflor, the wine receives its preliminary fortification. (The finos get the least fortification, the olorosos the most.)

Passing through a solera system, the wine emerges after a number of years fully blended and aged. It may then be fortified further, and sweetened and colored—according to the type and style of sherry desired.

MADEIRA WINE MAKING

After fermentation, the wine is fortified early or late, depending on the desired sweetness or dryness.

It is then baked in an estufa to accelerate its oxidation and to caramelize its residual sugar. (This creates in the wine a richness of color, a smoothness of texture and a bittersweet taste.)

After a period of blending and aging in a solera, the wine is bottled and released.

INDEX